Entrepreneur
MAGAZINE'S

ULTIMATE

BOOK OF

LOW-COST

FRANCHISES

2005/2006

. . . .

RIEVA LESONSKY
and MARIA ANTON-CONLEY

EP
Entrepreneur
Press

Entrepreneur Press
Editorial Director: Jere L. Calmes
Cover Design: Beth Hansen-Winter

Entrepreneur Magazine
Articles Editor: Janean Chun
Projects Editor: Maggie Iskander
Listings Assistant: Tracy Stapp
Production Designer: Stephanie Thomas

This publication is designed to provide accurate and authoritative information in regard to the subject matter covered. It is sold with the understanding that the publisher is not engaged in rendering legal, accounting or other professional services. If legal advice or other expert assistance is required, the services of a competent professional person should be sought.

Library of Congress Cataloging-in-Publication Data

Lesonsky, Rieva.
  Ultimate book of low-cost franchises 2005/2006/Rieva Lesonsky and Maria Anton-Conley.
    p.   cm.
  ISBN 1-932531-39-4 (alk. paper)
  1. Franchises (Retail trade) 2. Franchises (Retail trade)—Law and legislation. 3. New business enterprises. I. Anton-Conley, Maria. II. Title.
  HF5429.23.L474 2005
  658.8'708—dc22

                                                        2005005995

Printed in Canada

11 10 09 08 07 06 05   10 9 8 7 6 5 4 3 2 1

Table of Contents

SECTION ONE
How To Buy a Low-Cost Franchise

SECTION TWO

Ultimate Low-Cost Franchise Directory

Acknowledgments

I T TAKES A TALENTED, DEDICATED GROUP OF people to create a work of this magnitude, so we are grateful to all who have contributed. Several *Entrepreneur* magazine staffers went well above and beyond their job duties to make this book possible. There aren't enough words to properly thank projects editor Maggie Iskander; designer Stephanie Thomas; articles editor Janean Chun, who edited this book with her usual flair; and listings assistant Tracy Stapp. Also, a special thank you to Matt Samarin, art director, and Marla Markman, managing editor of business guides and products, who provided additional guidance.

Every aspiring or current business owner needs a good accountant, someone he or she can trust without hesitation. And we have one. Many thanks to CPA David R. Juedes, who, as the former CFO of a franchise company, is especially qualified to review and rate the financials of the franchises in the listing section.

Many years ago, when *Entrepreneur's* Franchise 500® was still young, we were lucky enough to meet Andrew A. Caffey, who, at the time, was an attorney for the International Franchise Association. Today, from his law practice in Washington, DC, Andy is a frequent contributor to *Entrepreneur*, using his years of experience as a franchise and business opportunity attorney to demystify the franchise buying process. Most of the first section of the *Ultimate Book of Low-Cost Franchises* is adapted from Andy's book, *Franchise & Business Opportunities*. Jeff Elgin, CEO of FranChoice Inc., a U.S. network of franchise referral consultants, wrote Chapter 5—*Entrepreneur* staff writer Nichole L. Torres also contributed. Without these authors, this book would not be worthy of the word "ultimate."

Rieva Lesonsky
Maria Anton-Conley

Introduction

IF YOU ARE LIKE MOST AMERICANS, CHANCES are you or some member of your family spends time—and money—in a franchise nearly every week. Doubt it? Well, do you ever get gas? Stay in a hotel or motel? Get a cup of coffee at a place other than Starbucks? Pick up a fast meal at the drive-thru? Go to a staffing service in search of a job? Have your house (or office) cleaned? Grab a sandwich or ice cream cone on the run? Think about buying or selling a house? Well, you get our point—franchising is a central part of our everyday lives. In fact, as an industry it generates more than $200 billion in annual revenue.

But though the industry might generate a lot, it doesn't always cost a lot to be a part of it. Since you purchased the *Ultimate Book of Low-Cost Franchises*, you must have at least considered buying a franchise. That's a good start, but to be a successful franchisee, you need to do more than just think about it—

you need to actually get started. We can guess what you're thinking: "There are so many franchises to choose from, where do I even begin?" The obvious answer: right here. You can't start a business without doing your homework. Consider this book your cheat sheet—we've done a lot of the work for you.

First, a word about franchising. A type of business opportunity, franchises are essentially business packages that enable you to, as the franchisors say, be in business for yourself, but not by yourself. All franchises are offered with the same premise: "We (the franchisor) have already developed a successful business program. For your investment, we will provide you with all the tools you need to own and operate a successful business." All business startups entail some risk. But franchises generally are less risky to start: After all, you are buying a proven system. That's not to say there is no risk in franchising; obviously, there is. But you can mitigate that risk by knowing what to expect from franchisors, by understanding the rules and regulations that govern franchising and by getting the inside scoop on the hundreds of franchise opportunities available. And that's where we come in.

We are the folks who publish *Entrepreneur* magazine, and for more than 25 years we've been telling people how to start and grow their own businesses. Since 1980, we've produced *Entrepreneur's Franchise 500*®, the most authoritative and comprehensive ranking of franchise opportunities in the world. And we've taken the many months of research that go into the Franchise 500 and applied it to this book.

Ultimate Book of Low-Cost Franchises is divided into two sections. In the first section, "How to Buy a Low-Cost Franchise," Andrew A. Caffey—a franchise attorney, internationally recognized specialist in franchise and business opportunity law and former general counsel of the International Franchise Association—provides you with an overall look at the world of franchising. Here you'll find information on everything from researching a franchise on the Internet to negotiating your franchise agreements.

The rest of the book is made up of franchise listings with minimum total investments of under $50,000. Organized by Maria Anton-Conley, Maggie Iskander and Tracy Stapp, here you'll find the 411 on opportunities ranging from the tried and true, like Jackson Hewitt Tax Service and Merry Maids, to newer franchises, like Abrakadoodle.

While it's likely there is an opportunity just right for you, not all opportunities are suited for everyone. And chances are, you're going to invest a lot of your savings into your venture, so you need to invest wisely. As Chinese philosopher Laotzu said, "Every journey begins with a single step." So turn the page, and put your best foot forward.

How to Buy a Low-Cost Franchise

CHAPTER 1

So You Want to Own a Business?

A T THE AGE OF 30, SUCCESS WAS ELUDING Jon, and he knew something was wrong. After a promising high school athletic career and a fair academic showing at his state's university, he bounced from one job to the next with no sense of purpose and without achieving the success he knew was in him. People liked him, and he was presentable, but his 30th birthday stopped him in his tracks. How and when was he going to realize his potential? He hungered for success but didn't quite know how to go about it. Somehow that part was not taught in school.

BUSINESS OWNERSHIP

The Advantages

Owning your own business—a sparkling, elusive goal of the American dream. It wasn't until Jon began considering starting his own business that he felt some optimism about his life's goals.

Business ownership seems out of reach to many would-be entrepreneurs because it appears expensive, complicated and intimidating. Yet business ownership is the most common route taken by Americans to substantial wealth.

There are a number of advantages to owning a business:

- Small-business ownership can bring *independence*—no more punching a time clock and worrying whether your job will be there tomorrow.
- It can mean *flexibility* so that you are free to take time off and spend time with the ones you love.
- It can bring a *healthy variety* of daily tasks instead of the repetitive routines of so many workplace specialties.
- Business ownership can bring immense *pride in accomplishment.*
- Business owners make a *difference* in the lives of everyone involved, especially employees who depend on the owner's business savvy to keep their jobs.

- Owning your own business gives you the chance to do it *your way*. It gives you the chance to bring your pride, your style, your gifts to a business operation.
- Business ownership can bring *wealth*. You don't need to be Bill Gates to realize the rewards of starting your own business. Ownership gives you the opportunity to build equity value over time, so that once your business is up and running, it will have acquired a substantial value. It puts to shame the apparent value of a week-to-week paycheck after those taxes are taken out.

The Challenges

Given these benefits, why don't even more people own their own businesses? It takes an enormous amount of work, perseverance and drive to overcome the challenges of getting started. To many people, those challenges can seem insurmountable. Just take a look at what it was like for Jon:

Jon had a fevered panic dream: Look at this checklist of things I have to do! I can't do this! It's a mess. Borrow $50,000? Who is going to lend me that kind of dough? Quit my job and launch out on my own? What if I fail? The national failure rates for small businesses are staggering. Am I nuts?! Even if I find the money, I will have to learn the traps of the business. Sure, there are lots of other businesses in my line I could talk to, but they are all competitors! No way are they going to

tell me how to run one of these operations. I have to hire people, buy advertising, buy inventory ... I don't know how to do that. I'll probably get ripped off at every turn and lose my shirt.

In some ways, Jon is right. It is difficult to find the information you need to set up and operate a business, create the trademark and graphics, and amass the cash and borrowed funds necessary to get going. As they say, if it were easy, everyone would do it.

But owning a successful business is possible, and one way to make it a reality is to buy a franchise. The franchise concept is designed to help the average person overcome the challenges of small-business ownership and get into a proven business, while providing the type of training and continued coaching that is not available anywhere else.

There are lots of ways to skin the business cat, of course. Whether you choose a franchise or something else entirely, it must be a program that fits your needs and gets you on the road to building wealth through small-business ownership.

SUMMARY NOTES

- ✓ Avenues to success are often not taught in our schools.
- ✓ Business ownership is a proven pathway to success and wealth.
- ✓ You can overcome the intimidating challenges of business ownership.
- ✓ A popular way to get into business is owning a franchise.

Action **PLAN**

Write down on a single sheet of paper three goals of a business you would start. How do you imagine it would change your life? Then write down three aspects of business that appeal to you. If you have any general ideas of the type of business that would appeal to you, note them on the same sheet. Keep this paper in a folder labeled "Business Planning"; you will want to refer to it again.

CHAPTER 2

Organizing for Business

*O*NCE MERRY DECIDED TO GET INTO *business for herself, she realized that she didn't know much about business organization. She had heard the horror stories: A friend's dad had lost everything in a stupid business concept, and because of the liabilities of the business failure, the friend and her family had to move out of their house and into an apartment when she was in high school. Merry was determined to be smart about her own business, protect herself as best she could and build an organization that could stand on its own feet. However, despite her firm resolve, she didn't even know what questions to ask to get started.*

ADVANTAGES AND DISADVANTAGES OF DIFFERENT BUSINESS ORGANIZATIONS

One of the early decisions all businesspeople have to make is how best to organize legally to be in business. Do you form a corporation? Do you have to? Are there other choices? This can be confusing if you are new to business ownership. There are lots of choices and a number of concerns to consider as you sift through the options.

You can operate as a sole proprietor, a corporation, a partnership or a limited liability company. Even if you buy a franchise, you need to select a form of business organization. Take a look at each one.

The Sole Proprietorship

A sole proprietorship is a business owned directly by one person. This is the simplest type of business organization, and some may even find it hard to think of it as an "organization." However, some sole proprietorships may be large and complex with many employees. For now think of a sole proprietorship as one person running the business as both owner and manager.

The greatest advantage to running the sole proprietorship is the ease with which it is formed. There are no papers to file or meetings to hold in order to keep it in existence. From an organizational point of view, you may simply start doing business as a sole proprietor with no further legal maintenance required. Of course there may be licenses or permits required for the type of business you are starting, but the "organization" of your business is done.

The greatest disadvantage of the sole proprietorship is personal liability. The owner is required to repay any amount borrowed personally no matter what happens to the business. This means they could lose more than their initial investment. There is no distinction between business and personal assets. A bank or other creditor may try to collect any money owed from the sole proprietor's personal assets if the business fails. You may obtain liability insurance, but it will not cover you if your business fails.

Another serious limitation for a sole proprietor is the inability to take on investors or partners. This may be unimportant for many businesses but could make all the difference in financing others.

A lot of businesses start out as sole proprietorships and then morph into corporations or limited liability companies (LLCs). If you are buying a franchise, however, it may be important to consider forming a separate legal entity before you sign on to the franchised business, because it can be difficult to transfer the franchise rights to your new entity after you sign the franchise agreement.

Partnership

A partnership exists when two or more people agree to run a business together and share control and profits. Creating a partnership does not require any formal steps. The agreement to form a partnership may be either expressed or implied, oral or written. However, it is highly recommended that a written partnership agreement be prepared and signed by the partners.

The partnership agreement should cover such issues as the amount of each partner's contribution, how profits will be shared, what authority each partner has, and how interests may be transferred. If a partnership is formed without a written agreement, the law will impose a series of standard terms that may not be intended by the partners. If you wish to have a partnership agreement, it is recommended that you consult with an attorney licensed in your state with some experience in the area.

Business partners should understand the significance the law places on sharing control. They may act on behalf of one another and the partnership in making agreements, incurring debt, and taking any other action in the course of running the business. The obligations of the business become personal to all. State law will impose equally shared liability on each general partner, unless the partnership agreement states otherwise. For example, if your partner takes out a loan on behalf of the business and the business fails, the bank will seek repayment from both your partner *and* you. If your partner or the partnership has no assets to satisfy the debt, the creditor may look to you personally.

So far we have been discussing a general partnership; however, there is another form of partnership known as a limited partnership. A limited partnership has at least one general partner and one limited partner. The main difference between these two types of partners is that a limited partner has no liability for the debts of the partnership. Nor do they have rights to management or control of the business. The general partner controls the business and has unlimited liability. To form a limited partnership, you must carefully consult the laws of the state in which you do business and seek the assistance of a competent attorney. For accountability purposes, the partnership is required to report its income on IRS Form 1065.

Corporation

The corporation is radically different from the other forms of business organization. It is controlled by statute, and each state's laws vary to some extent. You should therefore contact the secretary of state's office in the state in which you incorporate for more information.

In the eyes of the law, a corporation is a legal entity separate and apart from its shareholders. It may buy, sell or inherit property; enter into contracts; and sue or be sued in court. It is also responsible for its own debts. If the corporation fails, creditors may not seek payment from investors in the company. The shareholder's liability is therefore limited to his or her initial investment.

Shareholders in a corporation are ultimately responsible for all corporate actions, somewhat like citizens in a democracy. Shareholders elect representatives to the board of directors and the board of directors appoints the officers of the corporation to handle its everyday affairs. This three-tier structure applies to nearly all corporations, from General Motors to the smallest one-owner, home-based corporation.

If you form a legal entity like a corporation or an LLC, make sure that whenever you enter a business contract or other important obligation, you bind the entity to the obligation and not to yourself. To do this, make sure you sign in your official capacity showing your title, such as "President" or "Member." Make sure your title appears under your name and that you are committing the entity to the obligation.

Subchapter S Corporation

Most smaller businesses will benefit from selecting the tax treatment of a subchapter S corporation. A subchapter S corporation receives special tax treatment under the Internal Revenue Code and has some distinct advantages. These include:

- *No Double Taxation.* A subchapter S corporation sidesteps the principal disadvantage of the corporate form of doing business by receiving tax treatment that is similar to a partnership. It is not taxed at the corporate level, but the income of the entity is passed through to the shareholders and reported on each individual's personal tax return.
- *Ease of Election.* A new corporation or an existing corporation may elect subchapter S corporation treatment simply by filing IRS Form 2553.

In order to qualify for subchapter S corporation treatment, the corporation must be a domestic (U.S.) entity with one class of stock and no more than 35 shareholders. Its shareholders must be individuals, estates or certain trusts and not other corporations. Finally, it may not have a nonresident alien among its shareholders. Most personally owned and family-owned businesses qualify for subchapter S corporation treatment and should seriously consider electing it.

The drawback to a subchapter S corporation is that many of the corporate perks of a regular corporation may not be realized. For instance, a regular corporation can pay for the health plan of its shareholders, but a subchapter S corporation may not. There may be other drawbacks, as well, which you should review with your attorney.

Limited Liability Company

The limited liability company is a recently developed concept in business organization that has a number of advantages for small-business owners. Like a subchapter S corporation, a limited liability company (LLC) offers the liability protection of a corporation and the tax benefits of a partnership but does not require compliance with the legal formalities that characterize a corporation.

Wyoming first adopted an LLC statute in 1977, but the concept really caught on in the 1980s. In

1988, the IRS ruled that an LLC under Wyoming law would receive tax treatment like a partnership (on a pass-through basis to individual managers), and its popularity has since soared.

An LLC has an enormous advantage over the corporation: flexibility in its management. Depending on the particular requirements of your state's law, an LLC is operated by either members or by appointed or elected managers. It may be structured for governance and economics by agreement of its owner-members, and there are few limitations on the way it is organized and operated. Most new business owners are well-advised to take a close look at the LLC concept.

For most small-business owners, the answer will be to stay a sole proprietor (and run whatever liability risks there may be), create a corporation and elect subchapter S treatment under the Tax Code, or form a limited liability company. Buying a franchise will accelerate your decision-making because the franchisor may demand you have your organization in place at the beginning of the franchise term.

CONCERNS UNDERLYING BUSINESS ORGANIZATIONS

In order to make the right choice of business organization, it is important to consider the following:

Personal Liability

If you do not form any legal entity to hold your business, you will be operating under your own name, as yourself, and putting your personal assets on the line. Your form of business ownership will be known as a "sole proprietor," and you will have no protection from claims anyone may have against your business.

Here's a quick example. You start a home business of buying and selling used video games. It takes off like a jack rabbit, and soon you are dealing in large wholesale lots of games. You enter into a contract with a new local games store to buy all of its used games for a year at a negotiated price, a contract that you estimate is worth $25,000. You

do this because you have a buyer lined up who tells you he will buy as many games as you can produce for him.

One bleak day your buyer goes out of business and disappears. The games store expects you to continue buying from them, but you don't have the cash or the buyers to move the merchandise. When you don't buy the used games as required in your contract, the seller files a lawsuit on the contract, seeking $25,000 in damages. Your lawyer tells you that because you operate as a sole proprietor, all your personal assets are exposed to this claim, and you could lose your car and/or your house if you lose the case. If you operated as a corporation, he tells you, then it would be liable, and your personal assets would be out of your creditors' reach.

When someone talks about the disadvantages of operating under your own name, you need to weigh the potential liability that you could incur in the business. In large measure your decision depends on the type of business (will you be entering into contracts for substantial obligations?) and the state of your personal assets (can you absorb all potential losses of the business?).

Taxation

This is a biggie. There are dramatically different tax consequences depending on the form of business organization you use. Taxation concerns drive a lot of the business organization decisions, and some of the legal forms available strike a balance between liability and taxation.

If you operate as an individual sole proprietor, then your tax picture is straightforward. You simply add a Schedule C to your annual personal return.

Corporations have another story to tell. The law (and the IRS) recognize that a corporation is a separate entity and must pay its own taxes on its own net income. Then, when the corporation pays out a dividend to its owners, the owners must pay taxes on that income when they file their personal returns. In an important sense, a corporation is taxed twice:

once on its own revenue, and again when the owners take money out of the corporation.

A traditional answer to this double whammy is an IRS tax treatment as a "subchapter S corporation." This is a corporation that has met a series of qualifications (mostly as to size and the number of shareholders) and has elected to receive special tax treatment. As a result, the subchapter S corporation has the liability protection of a standard corporation but is not taxed twice. The IRS allows the corporation to pass through its revenues to its owners and the taxation on that revenue at the owners' level. The subchapter S corporation does not pay taxes separately. The result: one-time taxation. Problem solved.

A partnership has always been taxed directly to the individual partners; it is not considered a separate entity for liability or taxation purposes. Limited liability companies have also solved the taxation problem by receiving single tax treatment.

Flexibility

This concern becomes evident when you are told what directors and officers you must have and what annual meetings you must conduct in order to maintain a corporation. The law imposes rather extensive rules on the owners of a corporation, and if the rules are not followed, the liability shield effectiveness is lost. Partnerships are quite flexible. So are limited liability companies. Sole proprietorships are the most flexible of all, of course, because there is no organization to nurture along the way.

Flexibility has another dimension. Say you want to take in other owners and give them different shares of ownership. You cannot do that if you are a sole proprietor, but the other legal structures are designed for multiple owners.

SUMMARY NOTES

✓ Business organizations will change depending on the needs of the business itself and the organizers.

✓ Limiting personal liability, maximizing tax benefits and flexibility are principal concerns.

✓ Understand the major forms of business organization before consulting with an attorney; it will save you time and money.

✓ One of the most attractive new forms of business organization is the limited liability company. It is fast becoming the leading choice of small-business owners.

Action PLAN

Make a checklist of goals for your business as well as concerns you may have about things like ownership and liability. Take the list to a good attorney, and ask what you need to do to form a solid business entity for your business plan.

CHAPTER 3

Buying a Low-Cost Franchise

AIDAN DECIDED TO START A CHILDREN'S learning business, but needed some guidance to help him break into the market. Buying a franchise would be perfect, but he always thought of franchises as investments for people with multimillion-dollar budgets. Could Aidan find something in his industry ... and price range?

Low-cost franchises have become hot commodities. Prospective franchisees know if they can start a business without the heavy front-end investment of a retail location and choose wisely, they can increase the potential return on their money.

It's a well-known numbers game—the typical new restaurant build-out, including franchise fees, can run you $400,000 or more. That means some serious lender-financing for most people, as in signing a 30-year personal note and putting your house

on the line. You'll find similarly sobering numbers when building out a franchised muffler shop or convenience store. These businesses ratchet-up the franchise investment to a level that puts it out of reach for mere mortal entrepreneurs trying to make the jump into business ownership.

What is a low-investment franchise? The category includes perfectly robust businesses that can be run from an inexpensive office space or executive suite arrangement, or even from your home office. Cleaning services, in-home care services, magazine publishing, trademarked product distribution, interior decorating, and a variety of mobile van-based repair services are just a few of the categories. If you can get into the business for a total investment in five figures, consider it a lower end franchise investment.

As with all franchises, however, it pays to assess the stability of the program and the financial risks you're undertaking. Just because the level of the investment is manageable doesn't make it low risk; being able to swing a $45,000 investment doesn't mean you can afford to lose it all. So here is a nugget of franchise advice that's worth its weight in pink slips: in a word, research.

With a modest amount of diligent research, you can lower many of the risks inherent in a franchise business investment. Don't let the idea discourage you—this is rather enjoyable research, gathering information that will make you better at running your franchise. It's asking people the right questions; it's an organized way to investigate a serious investment.

EGO HAS NO PLACE HERE

When you're working with a small (or in some cases, miniscule) budget, you have to check your ego at the door. Putting emphasis on the prettiest office views, the best location or the coolest, newfangled office equipment is not on the agenda of a shoestring business. Instead, you'll have to start getting used to the words makeshift, secondhand and donated.

Though we're talking about a secondhand, saw-dust-on-the-floor mentality, that doesn't mean your business is in any way substandard—far from it. It just means you're being wise with your money and practical with all your decisions. Investors and advisors want to know you're spending your money on the important things clients will see—not on stellar office furnishings.

You can even be frugal with your low-cost marketing materials. Just don't skimp too much. Low-cost marketing strategies include printing out your letterhead from your printer when you need it, instead of buying an expensive order of paper all at once. Make a cool flier on your computer and post it on local bulletin boards, slip it under doors—anywhere you can think of. Get press attention with e-mailed press releases, which require no mailing cost, or be a guest on a local talk show . . . anything to get your name out there.

Check out local colleges and universities for low-cost or even free marketing help. Some marketing classes, for example, do real-life marketing campaigns for local businesses as part of their curriculum. Make yourself known to marketing or PR professors to see if your business can be one of the classroom case studies. It's a win-win situation—the students get real-world experience, and you get fresh marketing ideas from young minds.

LOW COST, HIGH POTENTIAL

The action at the lower investment levels of franchising is white-hot, no question about it. For several years now, since the mid-1990s, the power of the PC has allowed many businesses to become homebased, dramatically lowering overhead and opening up a remarkable array of business franchise concepts that don't require the investment expense of a built-out retail location.

Just because it is a relatively low investment, you need to take the time and spend the effort necessary to thoroughly research the opportunity. Read the UFOC, talk to current franchisees, call a few former franchisees and ask tough questions. You'll very quickly form a clear picture of the company and its franchise program, and be able to make the franchise investment with confidence.

SUMMARY NOTES ————————————

✓ Low-cost franchises are available in many different categories, and are usually defined as a franchise with a total investment in the five-figure range.

✓ The key to successfully buying a low-cost franchise is to research—don't skimp when it comes to investigating a franchise.

✓ Don't let your ego get in the way of starting a low-cost business. Look for secondhand or donated equipment, and seek out low-cost or free marketing help.

Action **PLAN**

Decide what business categories you're interested in, and research the range in investment costs. Request UFOCs and other literature from the lower-cost franchises in the category, so you can compare what they offer.

CHAPTER 4

Exploring the Franchise Concept

PAUL HAD ALWAYS WANTED TO OWN HIS own business, but the opportunity had just never presented itself. On a fishing trip to Minnesota, he came across a business concept that he could not get out of his mind. It was new and fresh, and he thought it had a huge market potential. He wanted to get in on the business somehow and learned it was being offered as a new franchise program. This might mean he could bring the concept to his hometown and open a sensational business. He had never considered a franchise. Where should he start?

INDEPENDENT OWNERSHIP

Start at the beginning. A business format franchise is a long-term business relationship in which the purchaser (the "franchisee") is granted the right to operate a business under the trademark of an established business owner (the "franchisor") and use its business techniques. This franchise relationship gives the franchisee the right to start up a business concept that the franchisor has already invented and perfected, using an established trademark and a comprehensive set of operating techniques.

Once licensed to use the franchisor's trademark and business system, the franchisee has the right to set up a business—usually under the franchisor's close scrutiny—that looks and operates *exactly* like other franchises in the franchise network. The magic in this formula—the simple fact that drives the success of the entire concept of business franchising—is that *the franchise owner remains an independent businessperson*. A franchisee is never an employee and is subject only to the limited control exercised by the franchisor under the franchise agreement. Independence means that if the franchisee is very successful in operating the business, he or she will reap the financial rewards. And the rewards can be substantial: Franchising has created an untold number of millionaires (think McDonald's and Holiday Inn). Of course, the converse also remains true: If the franchised business is not successful, the franchisee absorbs the loss.

THE BUSINESS OF FRANCHISING

Contrary to the impression conveyed nightly by the business press, it is small-business ownership, not big business, that is the bedrock strength of the American economy. Franchising gives the individual investor the opportunity to own their own small business without having to go it alone or invent and perfect a profitable retail concept that is, statistically at least, doomed to failure.

The franchise relationship we describe here has been adopted by hundreds of successful business programs, many of which are familiar cultural icons: Burger King, Dairy Queen, Holiday Inn, Jani-King, Jiffy Lube, McDonald's, Midas, Quality Inn, 7-Eleven and Subway stores. Many American towns have strip malls and mile-long commercial streets that are dominated by such franchised businesses.

While quick-service restaurants may be some of the best known franchises, the franchise concept has actually been applied in more than 50 different industry categories. These include everything from children's fitness programs and dollar stores to automobile dent removal and management training businesses.

Are gas station dealers and automobile dealers part of business franchising? Yes and no. Most systems are made up of independent dealers licensed to operate under a particular company's trademark and are said to own "product franchises," but they generally do not pay the franchise fees described here. The traditional practice in these industries is for dealers to buy product from the manufacturer at wholesale and sell it through their dealerships at retail. In contrast, the McDonald's restaurant franchisee does not buy any product from the franchisor—not even one sesame seed. Supplies are bought exclusively from third-party suppliers approved by the company. Ray Kroc, the legendary founder of the McDonald's system, did not want any buyer/seller tension to creep into his relationship with franchise owners.

Franchising by itself is not an "industry," but a form of distribution. The franchisor is distributing products and services through licensed franchisees. This is important because two businesses may be franchised, say a convenience store and a hotel, but have absolutely nothing else in common.

In recent years, there has also been an explosive growth in international franchising. The McDonald's trademark has become nothing short of a symbol of American culture, the restaurant's golden arches established now in more than 120 countries.

THE FRANCHISEE VIEW

Consider three important measures of a franchise system from the franchisee point of view: independence, training and money dynamics.

Independent Ownership

This concept energizes franchising because of the motivation, commitment and drive of an on-site owner. An employee manager working on an hourly wage is usually not motivated to work as hard or as long as an owner. It's that simple: An employee is involved; an owner is committed. It is the lesson taught when a pig and a chicken form a partnership to produce a ham and egg sandwich. The chicken is "involved," but the pig is *committed*.

Training Says It All

Training and support are keys to a strong business franchise. A well-established franchisor has something valuable to impart to the franchisee: know-how. It's one thing to perfect a business concept; it is quite another to transfer the essence of that concept to someone who knows nothing about the business and enable them to find success.

The strongest and best franchise programs are those able to convey know-how through rigorous training. Fresh-baked whole wheat bread franchisor Great Harvest Bread Co. requires that new franchisees spend one week in classroom training at its Montana headquarters and another two weeks doing hands-on training in an existing franchised bakery in their system. Additional in-store training takes place when the franchisee opens for business.

INsight

Among franchisors, the phrase "fast food" is discouraged. As commonly used, it has become a pejorative comment on the quality of the food. Preferred, more politically correct expressions in franchise circles include "quick service" food and "quality service" restaurants.

How the Money Works

How does the money work in a franchise relationship? While there are no hard and fast rules, the franchisee generally pays the franchisor in three ways: the initial franchise fee, royalties and advertising contributions.

The *initial franchise fee* is a lump sum paid when the contract is signed. This payment can range from a few thousand dollars to as high as $50,000 or more. A typical initial franchise fee for a restaurant franchise is in the $20,000 to $30,000 range. This fee generally covers the franchisor's cost of recruiting franchisees and of initial services, like site location and training.

The franchisee also pays the franchisor a continuing *royalty fee*. This is usually calculated as a percentage of the business's gross sales, somewhere in the range of 3 to 8 percent. It is important to understand the significance of the royalty fee being calculated on gross sales rather than on a net figure

or a flat-fee basis, such as $500 per month. Calculating the royalty on gross sales means that the percentage is measured on every dollar that comes in the door. Gross sales are those that are made by the business before any expenses, salaries, rent or other overhead is paid. They have nothing to do with the profitability of the business or with the net income that the owner might take home. Naturally, the franchisor wants to see the gross sales of the franchise maximized, since this increases the level of royalties paid. However, the franchisee, like any business owner, wants to maximize profitability. The franchisor does not have a direct interest in seeing that the business is run efficiently or profitably. The cold reality is that the franchisor will be paid the royalty whether or not the business is profitable for the franchisee.

The royalty fee is similar to a rent calculation. Your commercial landlord cares little whether your operation is profitable; however, if the rent is partly calculated on gross sales, he cares a lot that the gross sales figures are high. Both franchisor and landlord leave the task of making the business profitable entirely to the franchisee. A franchisee may have annual sales of $500,000 and pay the franchisor $25,000 in royalties (5 percent of gross sales) but still be losing money. Obviously, the franchisor wants to see every franchisee running a profitable business because healthy, profitable franchisees stay in business and keep paying royalties, but the franchisee is the only business player in this game with a direct interest in profitability.

Finally, most franchisees pay *advertising fund contributions*. Many franchisors organize franchise owners in a particular market or region and have them pool their advertising money for coordinated expenditures that benefit all stores operating under the system trademarks. This fee is usually within a range of 1 to 4 percent of gross sales.

If those are all the fees paid to the franchisor, the rest of the business expenses must be assumed by the franchise owner, as with any other form of business. At the same time, the revenues from the business belong to the franchisee.

In business terms, then, a franchise is a form of joint venture, with the neophyte paying the experienced company for the right to conduct a business using all the techniques that made the experienced company successful. The franchisor has its arm around the shoulders of the franchisee, training and assisting, and showing exactly how to run the business. A good franchisor is a patient mentor, a relentless teacher and a demanding partner.

With such a robust market of franchisors, you can expect to find brand-new sparkling programs, fading giants, troubled systems with rebellious franchise owners, systems on the way up, and systems crumbling under the weight of competition.

Be on the lookout for fad franchises that sound snazzy but probably won't be around long enough for you to get any return on your investment. My all-time favorite is the freestanding bungee-jump tower franchise of a few years ago; a close second is the corrugated cardboard coffins dealerships spotted at a franchise trade show in the late 1980s. Other fads might include laser tag games and low-carb stores. Also look out for businesses that may be eclipsed by fundamental changes in equipment or the marketplace. How would you like to have a franchise for the best typewriter repair shop in town? The Internet is profoundly changing lots of businesses, such as travel agencies. Don't get stuck with a buggy-whip franchise. So before you invest in such a company, you owe it to yourself to do the research, just as you would before buying stock in a publicly traded corporation.

The underlying message here should be clear: You can get hurt financially if you invest in the wrong franchise.

THE ALL-AMERICAN HARD SELL

One feature of a robust franchise marketplace is that franchisors are under extreme pressure to make the franchise sale. They have invested heavily in their program (it takes a chunk of change to pull together the business organization and meet the legal requirements), and the sales process itself is difficult and time-consuming. The cost of the sale (representative's salary, trade show costs, advertising, promotional materials, etc.) can also be substantial. The result is often the all-American hard sell: sales representatives pressing too hard to move a vaguely interested prospect to make a commitment, selling a franchise to anyone with a heartbeat, and making untenable promises or inappropriate representations about the financial potential of the business. Many franchisor sales specialists will employ crude closing techniques that would make a used car salesman proud.

Never allow yourself to be stampeded into making a franchise investment decision because of urgencies created by the sales representative. "Buy today before the price increase"; "Territories are going fast. Get in on this or the prime markets will be taken"; and "We only have a couple territories left" are just some of the claims you might hear. In all likelihood, these statements are entirely false. If you could see behind the curtain, you would understand that the salesman is scrambling to make his sales numbers, probably paid on straight commission, and having a devil of a time closing on his leads. He wants to close you on his schedule, not yours.

Your best defense is to anticipate this hard sell and use it to your advantage. Learn to hear and

INsight

Many franchise sales representatives are paid a large portion of their salary on commission, and will sometimes bring an overenthusiasm to their work that gets them in trouble with their employers, and sometimes with consumer protection agencies or franchise regulators.

appreciate a closing technique for what it is—a salesperson working hard to move you to commitment. Know that many franchise organizations would love to have you buy into their business concept, but in front of the curtain, they're cool about their eagerness. The better companies want to make sure that there is a great match between their concept and their franchisees and want to spend time exploring that match with a prospective investor. Ask them what qualifications they look for in a franchisee and what strengths among franchisees have led to success in their business. By listening closely during the sales process, you will learn a lot about the business of franchising.

Here is a little-known secret in franchising: The buyer has an enormous amount of control and power in the sales process. Many franchisors make buyers feel unworthy or poorly qualified to own and operate the franchise. They portray themselves as powerful trademark owners who control all aspects of their business, and they require detailed information in order for prospects to qualify for the right to buy a franchise. However, the prospective franchisee actually has the greater power since they can choose to invest or move on to the next opportunity. Experienced franchisors are aware of

this; but you wouldn't know it from the noise surrounding most franchise sales.

The business of franchising is not slow, sedate and welcoming. It is fast, exciting, a hard sell and sometimes intimidating to the uninitiated. But read on. By the time you finish this book, you won't qualify as uninitiated anymore.

SUMMARY NOTES

✓ A business format franchise is a continuing relationship in which the franchisee is granted rights to operate under the trademark, business format and techniques owned by the franchisor.

✓ As a franchisee you are an independent business owner, never an employee. That includes risk and reward, success and failure.

✓ Franchisors like to say that in a franchise you are in business for yourself, not by yourself.

✓ Training is one key to a successful franchise program.

✓ Initial franchise fees, royalties and advertising fees define your money relationship with the franchisor.

✓ Franchising represents a huge marketplace, so it takes some research to find a solid program.

Action PLAN

Identify as many franchises in your immediate market as you can, and list them. Ask the managers if the business is a franchise and where you can learn more about the program. Look up the businesses on the Internet, and send away for franchise information of those business concepts you like.

CHAPTER 5

The Four "Cs" of Franchise Financing

*M*ELISSA FOUND THE FRANCHISE SHE *wanted, but didn't have enough cash to completely fund the startup of the business. In search of a loan, she started talking to banks, which requested things she didn't have, such as a complete business plan with projections for the business. They also expected her to personally guarantee the loan even though the business is a corporation. Wondering whether her best option was to use the SBA in order to avoid these hassles, Melissa needed clear advice on how to finance her franchise.*

The best source of information about your financing options is the franchisor. They should be able to tell you, from experience, how likely it is for you to obtain financing from any particular source.

It may also be helpful to understand the principles that underlie your ability to get financing, regardless of the lending source. There are "Cs" involved in any decision to loan money to someone: Cash, Credit, Collateral and Character.

The fact is that it doesn't matter whether you go to a bank, use the SBA guarantee service or go to a friend or relative for the loan. The same basic rules apply to any successful attempt to get credit. Here's how the four Cs work:

1. ***Cash.*** One of the most common misconceptions people have is that they can borrow all the money they need to open a business. Unless your personal net worth is far larger than what you need to borrow, this is almost certainly not true. For SBA loans, you'll most likely have to come up with funds—either from your own assets or other sources—probably equal to at least 25 to 30 percent of the total investment needed to start the business, before the SBA will consider

lending to you. Lenders like to make sure you personally have "skin in the game."

2. *Credit.* Another thing lenders insist on is a strong credit history. This means they want to see a track record of you borrowing money and making your payments on time. Though your home mortgage might be the best example of a large loan you have serviced well, you'll find you get almost no credit for that type of loan. Everyone realizes most people will take care of their mortgage before their other bills, so what they really want to see is a pattern involving timely payments on other types of loans. While a good credit history doesn't mean you'll get a loan, a bad one almost guarantees that you won't.

3. *Collateral.* Most lenders require you to completely secure any loan you want with personal assets sufficient to provide for 100 percent recovery if you default on the loan. It doesn't matter one bit whether your business is a corporation or any other type of entity, or whether you go through the SBA process—they are going to look to you for collateral.

4. *Character.* The final condition you must meet relates to your character or reputation. Frankly, this is like your credit history—having great character won't ensure you'll receive a loan, but having a bad reputation will almost guarantee that you won't. Having strong enough character and a great reputation used to be enough to offset a lack in some of the other Cs, but those days went out the window with the S&L crisis 15 years ago, at least as far as any regulated lender is concerned.

You should have a complete business plan before embarking on any new business startup for a host of other reasons besides just financing. If you don't have one, stop everything else and put it together. The franchisor you're working with should have a lot of helpful information or even a template already developed for this purpose.

Many franchisors have also set up programs with selected financial sources to facilitate rapid funding of their franchisees. In this case, they should be able to walk you through the process with a minimum of hassle for you. The first thing you should do, once you're fairly certain you've found the franchise you want to buy, is to request this information from the franchisor and start looking into your options.

SUMMARY NOTES

✓ Your best source for information on your financing options is your franchisor.

✓ Four "Cs" affect your ability to get financing: Cash, Credit, Collateral and Character. Assess your strength on each of these levels, so you can be better prepared when seeking financing.

✓ Make sure you have a complete business plan before applying for any type of loan.

Action PLAN

Approach franchisors to discuss your financing options, to find out what programs they offer and to see whether they provide assistance or a template for a business plan you can use when seeking outside financing.

CHAPTER 6

Buying Multiple Franchise Rights

*G*EORGE HAS THE HIGHEST CAREER *ambitions of anyone in his family. He longs for a life of wealth and is determined to get there. Business ownership appeals to him, and he understands that most millionaires in the United States own their own businesses. He is interested in buying a franchised business but is already looking down the road to his second, fifth and 10th businesses. George never has done anything on a small scale.*

Most investors like George and many franchise owners understand the real path to substantial personal wealth is ownership of multiple businesses. Many ultrasuccessful franchisees establish a profitable franchised operation and then go on to develop or buy a dozen other franchised businesses. Before they know it, they have built an empire.

Multiple franchise development is a challenging part of the franchising business and varies from one company to the next. Is it possible to purchase the right to develop an entire state or region of the country? Do you need to be a subfranchisor or master franchisee for a region, or is there another way? What legal rights are granted for multiple franchise ownership? What if the franchise owner wants to purchase only two or three additional units?

TYPES OF MULTI-UNIT FRANCHISE PROGRAMS

Start with a look at some of the basic concepts of multiple franchising.

Multiple Unit Ownership

This is when the same individual is granted franchise rights at more than one location. Most franchisors encourage multiple unit ownership once a franchisee shows they are capable of operating a successful business. Everybody wins under this arrangement. The franchisee expands their business one step at a time, as their resources grow. The franchisor enhances its relationship with successful franchise owners, rewarding those who prove themselves successful. The franchisor does not have the costs and risks associated with recruiting a new franchisee into the system. No special legal rights are created for multiple unit ownership. The franchisor simply grants standard unit franchise rights for newly identified locations or markets. Some companies will grant a right of first refusal, which says essentially, "We will give you the first shot at another franchise in this market if we want to grant one." Once George has established one territory, he requests the rights to another across town, and the franchisor decides to grant him a unit franchise agreement exactly like his first franchise. A year later he may want to go for a third.

Ask the sales representative what kind of multiple unit franchising the company has done in the past and what it offers now. You may find that a development agreement is included in the company's unit offering Uniform Franchise Offering Circular (UFOC). Other companies may have a separate UFOC for their multiple unit offering.

Area Franchise

Here the franchisor grants the franchisee, through a contract usually referred to as a development agreement, the right to develop a specified number of franchised units in a given territory. The development agreement details the time frame in which the units must be developed and opened for business, development quotas, geographic area in which the franchisee has rights, and fee obligations. This type of development agreement is essentially an option agreement with a development schedule; it grants the developer option rights to enter into contracts in the future.

Master Franchise

While not typically a low-cost option, a master franchise agreement involves the franchisor granting to a franchisee the limited right to recruit new fran-

chisees and to provide specified field support services to franchisees in a given area. In exchange, the master franchisee receives a commission on franchise sales made and a percentage of the royalty revenues generated among the franchisees it serves. George's franchisor appoints him to serve as a master franchisee in Texas. He runs advertising to generate interested investors in Texas and meets with all prospects who respond. Serious, qualified investors are sent to the franchisor's headquarters, where the sale is closed. George has a regular schedule for visiting all 19 Texas franchises twice a year and runs three regional meetings each year. In return, George receives 35 percent of the initial franchise fees of sales made through his efforts and 25 percent of all royalties paid by Texas franchisees.

Subfranchising

Under a subfranchising arrangement, the franchisor grants to another entity (a subfranchisor) the right to enter into unit franchise agreements with subfranchisees in a specified area. The franchisor usually dictates the terms on which unit franchises are granted. As a subfranchisor, George has near complete autonomy in the franchise sales process. He grants franchises, provides training and field support, and has the right to collect royalties and advertising contributions. George pays the franchisor 45 percent of all franchise revenue.

The most common of these types of multiple-unit programs is the area franchise. If an investor wants to secure the right to develop a large number of franchises in a favorite market, they should consider negotiating for a development agreement. A development agreement has the advantage of being relatively straightforward conceptually. It balances the aggression of the large developer with the franchisor's need to make sure that a designated market is fully developed in a timely manner.

The least common type of multiple-unit program is subfranchising. True subfranchising is relatively rare in the world of franchising.

PROTECTING YOUR DEVELOPMENT INVESTMENT

In order to balance these interests and risks financially, the developer usually pays upfront a substantial portion of the initial franchise fees of the units to be developed. Look at a quick example. Our ambitious George signs a development agreement and receives the right to develop six territories in Salt Lake City over 10 years. He pays a nonrefundable, upfront development fee of $60,000, which represents half of the $20,000 per-store initial franchise fee for the six units. The development agreement promises that George will have exclusive rights to develop Salt Lake City for the next decade. He signs six standard unit franchise agreements within his development period and achieves his financial ambition. If George defaults under the development agreement and slips off the development schedule agreed upon, he may forfeit the unallocated portion of the upfront $60,000.

Clearly, multiple franchise development occurs at the higher financial end of franchising. It can be extremely expensive to secure the rights to multiple franchises, and the legal rights granted can be quite complicated.

If you are presented with an opportunity to purchase the rights to multiple franchises, be sure to take the program to your attorney for a detailed review of your rights and obligations. Developers, especially those who are inexperienced in the business being franchised or who are not well capitalized, can put a significant investment at risk by signing onto an aggressive development schedule. When negotiating the terms of development, it is vital that the build-out schedule is reasonable and that the exchange of fees is properly weighted for the risks being taken by both sides.

SUMMARY NOTES

✓ There are several ways that multiple-franchise rights are granted.

✓ Development fees may be paid upfront, so it is important to protect the investment by carefully negotiating your legal rights.

Action **PLAN**

Read a development contract for a complete understanding of its dynamics. Sketch out a business plan and projection of the money that might be required to develop an entire market.

CHAPTER 7

How the Government Protects You

*J*IM THOUGHT HE WAS BEING HUSTLED. *THE franchisor had not delivered any information about its program, and he was being pressured to sign a 40-page contract by the end of the week before it was offered to "the next person in line for the territory." It didn't feel right. Jim wondered "Isn't there a body of franchise law that protects the little guy?"*

Given the early franchise success of companies like Holiday Inn and McDonald's and the sizzle that became associated with anything franchised ("Get in now—this is the next McDonald's!"), problems in the marketplace were perhaps inevitable.

In the 1970s, a number of fraudulent operators sold empty franchise opportunities that were all sizzle and no steak. Many people lost money investing in "can't lose" franchise propositions, and their shocking stories were told in

the press. It wasn't long before state and federal regulators moved in. A dozen states and the FTC defined the franchise business concept in statutes and imposed a strict set of rules for franchising, based in large part on state and federal securities regulation. The rules are designed to counter the tendency in franchising to overhype the opportunity and to provide the prospective franchisee investor with key information on which to base a purchase decision. A number of states have also adopted regulations designed to protect franchise owners from the arbitrary termination of their rights.

The franchise laws require that the seller register the offering with state authorities and provide presale disclosure of material information to prospective investors.

Franchise regulation has a huge influence on how franchising is practiced. The following is a discussion of these rules of the franchise road.

HOW THE LAW DEFINES A FRANCHISE

How is a franchise defined under franchise laws? Ready for a little law school action? The law regulates a franchise transaction when three distinct elements are present:

1. The franchisor licenses the right to use its trademark in the operation of the business;
2. The franchisor prescribes in substantial part a marketing plan or provides significant assistance or control over the franchisee's business (some state definitions look for a "community of interest" between the franchisor and the franchisee); and
3. The franchisee is required to pay, directly or indirectly, a fee for the right to participate in the franchise program.

 **IN**sight

As a prospective franchisee, you should have little concern about complying with the franchise investment laws. They impose no obligations on you. But recognizing a franchise when you see one could be an important asset in protecting yourself. If you see a franchise but someone tells you it is not one, ask why not, and listen carefully! You may want to share your notes with your attorney or the enforcement authorities in your state.

If one of these elements is missing, whatever the business transaction is, it is not regulated as a business franchise. In many circumstances the investment is then regulated as that close cousin, the "business opportunity."

It is quite possible to invest in a business program that enables you to start a business that is not a franchise. There are dozens and dozens of such programs available. You can spend a couple thousand dollars and receive a package of materials designed to teach you how to make money with a new business application of your computer. You are not granted the right to use a trademark, and you are expected to operate under your own name. It may be a business opportunity, but it is not a franchise.

THE CONSEQUENCES OF BEING A FRANCHISE

What if a transaction meets the franchise definition? Then there are three consequences:

1. ***Presale disclosure must be delivered.*** Under the FTC's Trade Regulation Rule on Franchising, if a franchise is offered anywhere in the United States, a franchisor must deliver a disclosure document to a prospective franchisee, using either the FTC's format or the Uniform Franchise Offering Circular (UFOC) format. The franchisor does not have to register or file anything with the FTC; complying with the disclosure requirements satisfies the requirements of the federal rule.

   The UFOC is a gold mine of information for the franchise investor. Ask for one early; it will help you evaluate the offering.

   When must the UFOC be delivered to the prospective franchisee? Either 1) at the first face-to-face personal meeting for the purpose of discussing the franchise sale, or 2) at least 10 business days (14 calendar days in Illinois) before money is paid for the franchise or a binding franchise agreement is signed by the franchisee, whichever comes first. That means that the franchisor is not required by law to deliver a UFOC until fairly far along in the sales process. Talking to a franchisor representative at a trade show exhibitor's booth is not considered to be a "first personal meeting" that would trigger disclosure obligations, even though it is "face to face." The disclosure obligation will trigger if the meeting is a detailed, extended discussion about the franchise opportunity.

2. ***The offering must comply with state law.*** Fourteen states (California, Hawaii, Illinois, Indiana, Maryland, Michigan, Minnesota, New York, North Dakota, Rhode Island, South Dakota, Virginia, Washington, Wisconsin) require franchisors to file or register with the state officials prior to any offering activity taking place. The franchisor will submit its UFOC, adapted to meet the particular requirements of each state, along with an application form and the appropriate fees. State franchise examiners review the disclosure document to assure that it is complete. They do not determine if the offer is reasonable or exercise any judgment regarding whether it is a good deal, or fair. They only make sure that the franchisor has complied with the UFOC guidelines.

When approved, the franchisor is authorized to sell franchises and must renew the registration at the end of the registration period. Some states will grant a registration period of a full calendar year; others such as California and Hawaii will automatically end the registration period a certain number of days after the end of the franchisor's fiscal year. That means a company with a fiscal year ending on December 31 remains registered in Hawaii until March 31 and in California until April 20.

3. ***Relationship laws may apply.*** A transaction meeting the franchise definition may also fall under the protections of the various state franchise relationship laws. These generally prohibit termination and nonrenewal of a franchise in the absence of "good cause."

So what does this mean for investors? Franchise investors receive a generous amount of valuable information in the disclosure document. If the franchisee is in one of the 14 registration states, it means that the franchisor has gone through the process of document review by state examiners and achieved registration, clearing an important hurdle in the life of a franchisor. It is not easy to become registered in these states, although some are tougher than others.

Registration is no guarantee for the investor, of course. It does not tell you anything about the company, and it is not a qualifier in any sense. It simply means that the company has taken an important step to comply with the law. It has filed its offering on the public record in that state and will remain under the annual scrutiny of the state officials.

If you live in one of the registration states, you should plan to call the appropriate agency (see Appendix A) and confirm that the company is currently registered to offer and sell franchises.

SUMMARY NOTES

✓ If a business meets the legal definition of a franchise, it will be regulated as a franchise.

✓ The consequences of meeting the franchise definition include disclosure, registration in a number of states, and possible application of relationship laws.

✓ Registration under a state law is no guarantee of anything.

Action **PLAN**

Call the appropriate agencies to find out how franchising is regulated in your state. Keep addresses and phone numbers for key state officials on file so you can contact them later with specific questions.

CHAPTER 8

Are You Suited to Be a Franchisee?

*B*ILL WAS EAGER TO GET INTO A GOOD BUSI-
*ness and jumped at the chance to buy
an established one in his home town
when he heard it was up for sale. It
was a holiday ham and sandwich shop, and Bill
soon learned it was also franchised. This meant
every aspect of the operation—from the cases
used to display product to the uniforms worn by
the counter staff—was dictated by the terms of
an operating manual. He had always wanted to
own a business in which he could express his
own creativity and offbeat sense of humor.
Looking at the detailed operational requirements, he now wondered whether he was cut
out to be a franchisee.*

IS A FRANCHISE FOR EVERYONE?

Clearly, owning a franchise is not for everyone. A capable person in the wrong program
is not likely to stay happy for very long.
Buying into a franchise is especially risky

since the investment can involve your life's
savings and a long-term legal commitment.

Fiercely independent entrepreneurs are
rarely happy in the franchise harness. If you
are interested in running and designing every
aspect of the operation, think twice before
you buy that franchise. You might actually be
better off with your own independent business. Most franchising programs impose a
strict regimen on franchise owners, dictating
everything from how to greet customers to
how to prepare and present the product or
service, and many people find the restrictions
far too confining. They might be better off
choosing a business opportunity program
that offers more independence.

If you have been a secure employee of a
large corporation for a long time, the jolt of
small-business ownership can be difficult.
Franchise owners have to put themselves
completely into the daily operation of the

business; small-business owners do not delegate. They do whatever needs to be done. Remember the old line: You can always identify the owner of a small business—he or she is the one sweeping up after 6 o'clock.

Nevertheless, there are many downsized middle managers bringing a wealth of business savvy to the franchise market. They are at that stage in their careers where they have some capital to invest, are not interested in inventing a new (and risky) business concept, and yet are attracted to the dream of self-employment. For them, franchising may be the ticket.

QUESTIONS TO CONSIDER

A careful approach to deciding whether or not owning a franchise is for you starts with a self-examination and a brief planning exercise. Consider the following key questions:

- *Are you motivated to invest the time and energy—not to mention money—necessary for small-business ownership?* The first year of business can be especially trying; the time required to get a business up and running— even a sophisticated franchise—is intimidating. Your days of punching and watching the clock will be long gone. Small-business ownership requires a sea change in your mental attitudes toward work, and a new level of dedication and perseverance.

- *Is your family behind you?* Many businesses are designed for total family involvement. Even if you invest in one that is not, you cannot commit the time and energy needed without the full support of every member of your family. Have you discussed it in detail with them? Your spouse may be supportive but skeptical (which is healthy). Involve them in the decision-making process, and listen to all their doubts or concerns. Try to help your kids understand that they are part of the whole family effort. You may also want to seek

out experienced businesspeople you know who can help make sure you are thinking straight and not just daydreaming. Ask them to serve on your informal board of advisors so you can turn to them with questions.

- *Have you evaluated your resources?* Take out a pad of paper and jot down all possible sources of investment capital. Include not only cash, securities and other liquid assets, but also insurance policies, the equity in your home and retirement funds. Don't forget what the bankers refer to as NAR and NAF ("nail a relative" and "nail a friend"): your well-heeled friends and relatives could make all the difference, especially if you need a cosignature or additional equity pledged as security when applying for financing. If your dear Aunt Edna once said she would back you in a business venture, now is the time to go see her.

  Consider that you may need to maintain a revenue stream while the new business is being established. Your spouse may want to land a job to make ends meet until your franchise is kicking out a salary, which may take a while. Talk to a banker and an accountant. Discuss what you are planning, and ask about sources of capital, loans, investors and angels.

- *Have you evaluated your dreams?* Dreams provide the courage and drive that new entrepreneurs need to make the leap of faith into business ownership. But you must transform your dreams into an action plan. If you dream of being wealthy and living in a million-dollar home, turn your attention to the steps it will take to get there. If you start with owning a service business, research how much money such a business is likely to put in your pocket, and then determine how many of those businesses and how much time you will need to achieve your dream of a million-dollar house. Use dollars in your calculations, and add time frames. Anticipate milestones along the path, and work back to where you are today. Make notes about what you need to accomplish to make it successfully to the next milestone, and before you know it you will have created what looks to others like a business plan, but to you is nothing more than your dream path.

- *Are you ready for the physical challenge?* This question surprises a lot of people. Depending, of course, on the type of business you get involved in, business ownership can be physically demanding. Your sleep patterns may change, and you may be on your feet for 12 hours or more a day. Daily frustrations and the heightened stress of responding to unfamiliar challenges will draw on your deepest energy resources. You will need physical stamina and a healthy, positive mental outlook. We strongly recommend that as part of your preparation for owning a business, you step up your exercise and stick to to a healthy diet. You will need every ounce of energy your personal fitness can deliver.

SUMMARY NOTES

✓ Owning a franchise is not for everyone. Strong-willed entrepreneurs who want to do things their own way may be unhappy owning a franchise.

✓ Before buying a franchise, consider the level of your motivation, how your family feels about the idea, your resources, how realistic your plans are, and whether you are ready for the physical challenge.

Action PLAN

Write out complete responses to the questions in this chapter (be honest here; no one else will see your answers), and file them in your business planning folder.

CHAPTER 9

Attending a Franchise Trade Show

*J*ENNIFER HAD NEVER BEEN TO A FRANCHISE
*trade show before, but she was told it is a
great place to get started in business and
learn a bit about franchising and other
packaged business programs. She had no plan
or goals for the show, but she wanted to cruise
through. However, she was overwhelmed by the
atmosphere. "I got so wrapped up in the games
and cookies offered at one booth, I never saw
most of the exhibitors. Maybe I'll go again when
it comes through town next year."*

Attending a franchise trade show is the
quickest, most enlightening way to search for
the franchise program that best suits your
needs. It can also be fun.

However, it helps to understand what you
can expect at the show and to go with a plan.
As many as 300 companies may be standing at
their booths ready to talk to investors about
their programs. Up to 10,000 people could
pass through the convention center, each
exploring the idea of buying a franchise as the
ticket to business success. The effect can be
dazzling: so many concepts to evaluate and
hardly enough time to see them all!

Of course, many of the investors attending
the show, like Jennifer, are there out of curios-
ity and will have no focused plan. They may
be lost in the crowd and have no clue as to
how to get the most out of the show. We recommend that you be different.

PREPARE FOR THE SHOW

The first step in setting yourself apart from the
crowd is to prepare and set goals for the session.
Decide what types of businesses interest you.
Are you fascinated by automobiles and interested in a business that is part of that industry? Do
you want a high-end consumer products business that brings you into direct contact with

your customers? What are your financial resources? Do you have the money and credit to establish a retail location, or would a business you can operate from home be better? Giving some thought to these questions will allow you to focus your time at the show on programs that fit your needs.

It's a good idea to leave your usual funky weekend attire at home and dress conservatively. Your goal is to show franchisor representatives that you are there for business. A casual business look is fine; a suit is optional, but be sure you look sharp. If possible, leave the kids at home and take personal business cards if you have them. If you don't, consider having some printed up. They are inexpensive, project a business-like impression, and relieve you of having to dictate your name, address and telephone number over and over. Don't forget your briefcase for the papers you collect, and take paper and pen for taking notes. You are not there just to pass a few idle hours and eat the free cookies. Show the representatives you meet that you are a serious prospect and there to consider their business program.

HOW TO DEVELOP AN EFFECTIVE METHOD OF ATTENDING

Plan to arrive early in the morning on one of the first days of the show. The typical franchise show lasts for three days, from Friday to Sunday. By Sunday, everyone is tired and spent, so try to be there on Friday (typically the least crowded day) or early Saturday (the most crowded day). This is when everyone involved should be fresh, with anticipation running high.

When you arrive at the convention center to register, take a few minutes with the show brochure to understand the floor layout, and review the list of companies that are exhibiting. Find a quiet corner with a cup of coffee and read what the show offers. Mark those companies whose offerings appeal to you and seem to fit your

needs and financial resources. As you stop by their booths during the day, you can check them off and make sure you are covering all the promising companies on your list.

It is important to understand why the exhibitors are there. They consider the show a success if they collect the names of several serious, qualified candidates and come away with a list of leads for follow-up calls. We are told by franchisors that if they sell one or two franchises as the result of a trade show, they can cover all their exhibiting costs and make a profit. To get that list of hot leads, they have to make about 1,000 contacts a day.

Many franchise shows schedule seminars for investors on subjects like "How to Buy a Franchise" and "Financing Your Franchise Purchase." Mark the ones that look interesting, and schedule time to attend them. This may be the most valuable part of your day at the trade show, especially if you actually purchase a business package.

Try to approach the exhibit floor methodically. The franchise investment possibilities are virtually endless, and you may feel overwhelmed if you do not remember the interests you identified before attending the show. Stick to your plan, and find as many of the exhibitors you marked off earlier in the day as you can.

It is easy to underestimate the time needed to meet with all the interesting exhibitors on your list. You might spend as much as five or 10 minutes with each exhibitor and discover in a couple of hours that you have met with only 10 or 15 companies, a mere fraction of those on your list.

THE RIGHT QUESTIONS

The secret is not to spend time with exhibitors whose programs are inappropriate for you or out of your financial reach. Prepare three "knock-out" questions that will allow you to eliminate those companies quickly and move on to more promising conversations. What are those questions? That depends on you and your circumstances. If you have limited resources (and who doesn't?), try "What are the minimum financial qualifications for your applicants?" or "What kind of business experience do you require?" and "Are you looking for franchisees in my town?" The franchisor's answers will tell you quickly whether their program is within your reach. If it seems to be, stay and find out more. If there is no fit, move on.

If you want to find out more about a particular franchisor, here are a few more good queries to generate useful conversation:

- **How would you describe the culture in your franchise/business opportunity system?** This wonderfully open-ended probe should draw a variety of responses. Every franchise system has a cultural character. Is it clubby, friendly, chilly, all business or distant? Listen carefully to the answer. You will pick up some good information that does not appear in any glossy brochures.

- **What are your plans for growth in this region over the next three years?** The answer to this question will give you an idea of the effort and energy that the organization has committed to your market. If you get a vague answer or a grandiose statement suggesting that the company expects to take over the retail world in that modest time period, well, you've been forewarned.

- **May I take a complete set of promotional materials?** Many exhibitors will have a limited supply of full brochures behind the table and less expensive fliers out front for the hundreds of casual visitors who stop by. Express serious interest in the investment, and ask if there are other materials you can study at home. Request a copy of the company's Uniform Franchise Offering Circular. If it is not readily available, ask if the company can send you one, along with a set of promotional materials and an application package.

- **Tell me about your training program.** Find out how long it is (i.e., two weeks at the company headquarters and 10 days in the field), where it takes place and the general subjects covered. Look for a well-organized plan that combines classroom time with field orientation. A solid training program is the mark of a careful franchisor who is interested in the business success of its franchise owners.

- **Tell me about your franchisee support program.** Good support from a franchisor can spell the difference between failure and success. Look for support from the very beginning, as soon as you start to write a business plan. Will the company help you find financing? Will people be available when you are opening for business? Will someone be at the other end of the phone when things get crazy?

A question you might expect to be on this list, but that isn't, is "How much money can I expect to make with one of your businesses?" This is a difficult question for a franchisor to answer. Most would like to boast about the potential of their franchise, but it is a subject that is closely regulated under the franchise laws. In addition, no franchisor knows how much you can expect to make in a franchised business. The variables—including your business acumen and industry—make such estimates impossible.

Slinging numbers at a trade show would be a misleading and unfair inducement by the seller to get you to purchase the franchise. Franchisors generally do know how their existing franchise owners have performed, and some companies will make this information available in the disclosure document. Our best advice: check it out for yourself. Go visit as many franchise owners as time and distances allow. Ask them how they have performed and whether, knowing what they now know, they would make the investment again. Their answers will be invaluable in your assessment of the franchise.

It is also important to understand that a franchise trade show event is designed to make an initial contact only. It is a meeting place that operates merely to introduce sellers to potential investors. The conversation on the floor of the trade show is preliminary and rarely delves deeply into the investment itself. The more in-depth discussion usually takes place in a follow-up meeting or sometimes in a nearby hospitality suite the seller has reserved. Leave behind one of your business cards so sellers may send you additional information. And make sure that you have contact information, either a contact listing in the program or the business card of the sales representative.

TRADE SHOW RED FLAGS

Risks abound in the search for a franchise. While at the trade show, keep alert to red flags that should tell you to avoid one company or another. Here are a few:

Shouting Performance Numbers

Dollar signs have no place at a franchise trade show. They can be the source of any number of legal problems for franchisors and should be avoided by well-disciplined companies. If performance information is discussed, check out item 19 in the company's UFOC, which you will see sometime after the show. Any big talk about what you will earn should be a warning sign that this is not an experienced or well-disciplined representative. The talk may also be totally misleading.

The Hard Sell

A solid franchise investment should sell itself. If you find yourself at the receiving end of a hard sell, back slowly away.

The Start-Up Rookie

A franchising company with no track record presents risks that you should carefully evaluate. You may determine that the program is new enough and exciting enough that the potential for success outweighs the risks, but protect yourself as best you can. A new franchisor cannot offer the most attractive features of the franchise concept: a business that has been proven in the marketplace and experience that can help you handle the challenges of the business.

The Franchise Fad

Fads come and go in the franchise community. Remember that your investment needs to survive for the long term. Look out for concepts that are the flavor of the month but may have little staying power.

Limited Regional Hits

Do not assume that because a shop can sell truckloads of fresh-baked whole wheat bread in Cincinnati, the same product will move as well in Palm Beach. It may not be true, and you can't afford to prove it with your life's savings.

The Poorly Financed Franchisor

Most franchise financial advisors will tell you that one of the most common business mistakes made in this field is for the franchisor not to have enough capital to finance its rapid growth. The resulting under-financed company is weak and may not be in a position to deliver on its promises to new franchisees. The best measure of the franchisor's financial standing is its audited financial statements, which you will find as part of the UFOC.

THE FOLLOW-UP

Expect a follow-up call or visit after the show from any company where you showed serious interest. Remember, the companies that prepared and

INsight

Your follow-up call may not come from the person you met at the show, but from a staff representative at the company's headquarters or a regional office. Find out who you are talking to, and get a good idea of where they fit into the company's organization.

A franchise trade show may be your first step toward an exciting new business future. Increase the odds of your personal success by preparing carefully for the show and evaluating the opportunities presented with a detailed—and realistic—eye.

SUMMARY NOTES

✓ A franchise trade show can be overwhelming if you are not prepared for it.

✓ Prepare for the show with a battle plan.

✓ Ask the right questions on the floor. If there is no fit with your plan, quickly move on down the aisle.

✓ Look for the red flags.

✓ Follow up with your show contacts to confirm you are serious about finding the right franchise program.

staffed a booth invested heavily in finding you—a qualified and interested investor. The follow-up is your opportunity to dig into the investment and explore every question that might occur to you. Be diligent and skeptical in your evaluation of the information you collect from the franchisor.

Action PLAN

Find out when a good franchise trade show is coming to a city near you. Try searching the Internet for trade show cities and dates. (See the next chapter for ideas on using the Internet.)

CHAPTER 10

Research on the Internet

*M*ARCIE WAS DETERMINED TO FIND A *franchise that would allow her to work part-time at home around her young children and bring in more money for the family. Getting out of the house was difficult with the kids. She heard that a franchise show was coming to the downtown arena in a few weeks, and she wanted to find out a lot more about the whole concept of a home business. Marcie was a new Internet user but thought it would be a good place to start.*

Enter the word "franchise" into any of the competent search engines on the Internet, and you may feel a bit like Alice falling down the rabbit hole.

A Google search kicks up 16.7 million franchise listings; on Yahoo! 12.4 million. Head down any of these pathways, and you will quickly find yourself browsing through dozens of sites extolling the virtues of various franchises, touting association membership benefits and describing individual franchise investment benefits.

WHAT TO LOOK FOR

The Internet is an essential tool in the search for the right franchise. It has its strengths and weaknesses, of course, but you cannot afford to overlook it. Its greatest strength is that it gives you the ability to browse for ideas and prospects. If you have leads you want to check out or if you are curious about a particular franchise, a quick search will provide at least brochure-level information about the program.

The law has been slow to catch up to the franchise regulation implications of electronic commerce on the Internet. The FTC has promised to address the rules surrounding electronic distribution of the UFOC and the posting of disclosure information on a Web site, but the rules are not yet final. Under current law, with rare exception, a franchisor may not comply with disclosure requirements by delivering a document in electronic form. This may change as early as 2005. Some states have issued regulations telling franchisors what disclaimers they must put on their sites, and you will find them in the small print of well-managed sites. In essence, the disclaimer says that the information on the site does not constitute an offer in franchise registration states. Seeing this disclaimer conveys to the experienced eye a subtle but important message: The company is receiving, and paying attention to, informed legal advice. You should wonder about franchise company sites that do not have this legal disclaimer.

 INsight

The hype level tells you something about franchising sales. This is a market that enjoys a robust level of aggressive selling.

HANDLING THE HIGH HYPE-TO-FACT RATIO

The Internet's weakness is the low quality and reliability of the information at its busy commercial locations. Lists of available "franchises" are littered with nonfranchised business opportunity offerings, and much of the information you see is essentially sponsored advertising. If you understand this inescapable feature of the Internet and make allowances for it, you will not be misled.

THE IMPORTANCE OF FOCUS

The FTC has assembled a surprisingly useful site for franchise investors (www.ftc.gov). Here you will find general information about franchising, the federal laws that apply to a franchise sale, and current and recent investigations and legal actions taken by the FTC against offending franchisors.

Also, www.entrepreneur.com/franchise offers a site specifically for franchise seekers—it includes franchise listings and in-depth articles. Another information-packed site is www.franchise.org, the site of the International Franchise Association.

These are just a start. The problem with the Internet, of course, is the sensation of trying to take a sip from a fire hose of information. The sites dedicated to franchising go on and on and may cause even an experienced Internet researcher to suffer from MEGO (my eyes glaze over) in no time.

The secret to effective use of the Internet for your franchise search is the same as with other kinds of franchise research: focus, focus, focus. Know your targets and general interest areas. Don't be distracted by the glitter, the pop-up ads, the eager virtual experts. Plan to use your computer connection for first-level contact and brochure-level information. Then roll up your sleeves and plan for person-to-person meetings and in-depth discussions about the franchise opportunity.

SUMMARY NOTES

- ✓ Use the Internet judiciously. There is a high hype-to-fact ratio at most information sites.
- ✓ The Internet is great for brochure-level information.
- ✓ Focus your search to your areas of interest.

 *Action* **PLAN**

Spend some time on the Net and bookmark the sites that seem most helpful.

CHAPTER 11

Organizing the Information You Gather

*A*L WAS NOT WELL-ORGANIZED IN HIS JOB *life, but then he never had a job that required him to be. He was determined to find a good franchise. He had the money to buy one, and he had been in contact with a couple dozen companies. The amount of paper generated in his search surprised him, and it had formed a few messy piles on the floor of his bedroom. Now he was going to a trade show and dreaded the prospect of taking more paper home to his piles. Maybe this wasn't for him.*

The franchise search process can generate a lot of paper, and you will quickly become discouraged if you do not prepare to receive and keep it in an organized fashion. This is particularly true if you attend franchise trade shows, which are notorious for generating piles of promotional pieces of paper. (And you wondered why they handed you that big plastic bag with handles when you walked in!)

You may also receive a stack of promotional materials when you write to franchisors for information.

 IN*sight*

From the company's point of view, distributing glossy brochures is a cost of being a franchisor, and it can be quite expensive. More and more franchisors are putting their brochure money into Web site presentations. You may find that the quality of the brochures you receive will be modest, but the Web sites will be eye-popping.

SETTING UP A FILING SYSTEM

So get prepared before you go. Set up a few files, one for each seller with internal tabs or manila folders for different subjects. Take a quick trip to an office supply store, and buy a few packets of file folders, pocket files and tab labels.

Divide each seller's file into subsections, such as:

- **Promotional pieces.** Drop into this folder all the glossy brochures, fliers, handouts and form letters you pick up.
- **Letters, notes, contact information.** Take notes on each of the companies you visit at the trade show or elsewhere, and keep all the personalized letters they send you as well as copies of any letters you write. Staple into the file—or slide into a plastic sleeve—all the sales representatives' business cards you are handed.
- **UFOC.** After you read and mark up the UFOC with any questions or comments, drop it in the file for future use. If the franchisor is a serious prospect, you will want to take this document to your attorney and accountant. It is amazing how many people buy a franchise yet never read the UFOC. You must take the time to look through this important document. If you get serious about a program, take the documents to your attorney and your CPA for review.

- **Contracts.** Form contracts will be included in the UFOC, but other versions will be provided to you as you approach closing.
- **Site information, lease forms.** As you meet with landlords to review available sites for the business you have in mind, keep the information in its own section of your file.

With these files prepared ahead of time, you will be able to quickly file all the paperwork you bring home and have it easily accessible for follow-up reading.

Retain all your files until you have actually made a choice and invested in a franchise. Only then should you sort through them, keeping in your permanent records all of the documents relating to the business you purchase or remain interested in, and discarding the rest.

SUMMARY NOTES

✓ Prepare to organize informational materials before the franchise search begins.
✓ Set up labeled file folders so that you can file your papers when you get home from a trade show or other franchise or business opportunity meeting.

Action **PLAN**

Head to the supply store for the materials you will need to organize your franchise search files.

CHAPTER 12

Understanding the UFOC

R OBIN INQUIRED ABOUT A FRANCHISE PRO-
*gram and received a heavy spiral-
bound book in the mail. It was at
least an inch and a half thick! She did
not know what it was or why they sent it. She
flipped through it but did not expect to spend
the time it would take to read it all.*

WHAT IS A UFOC?

Robin didn't know it yet, but what she had
was the franchisee's bible: the Uniform
Franchise Offering Circular, or UFOC.

Like Robin, all prospective franchisees
receive detailed and extensive information
about the franchisor, the franchise being
offered and the franchise system. This gives
you a distinct advantage over other investors.
It contains sample forms of every contract
you will be asked to sign as well as a set of
audited financial statements for the franchisor. In franchise circles, the UFOC is also

referred to as a "franchise disclosure document" or an "offering prospectus."

The UFOC format and presentation is prescribed by state and federal law and is
designed to deliver key information about the
franchise investment. In it you will find 23
different items of information that are all
important to your investment decision. If
there is one piece of advice you take, it should
be to read the UFOC carefully. Sure, it may
read like an insurance policy in places, but it
is a treasure trove of details for the alert
investor. The good news is, all UFOC documents must be written in "plain English"—no
Latin phrases, no "hereinafters," no "wherein-
befores," and no run-on sentences that only a
lawyer could love. At least, that's the theory.

Does everyone get a UFOC? As a practical
matter, franchisors do not deliver a UFOC to
everyone who applies for a franchise. The typical UFOC runs from 75 to 350 pages in
length and can be expensive to reproduce in

INsight

Put yourself in the franchisor's shoes. You want to deliver a UFOC only to candidates who have been qualified and appear serious about the investment because each copy costs several dollars to reproduce. Let them know you are serious about their program and are genuinely interested in the information contained in their UFOC, and you increase your chances of receiving one early in the process.

large numbers. Expect to receive a copy as you progress through the evaluation process or if you visit the company's headquarters for a "first personal meeting," which will trigger the legal requirement that you receive a UFOC.

The best approach is to request a UFOC early in your discussions. If you are at all serious about a particular franchise, it makes no sense to spend time on it until you have a chance to read the UFOC.

THE SECTIONS OF THE UFOC

How do you read and comprehend a UFOC? Some sections are more important than others, but all are worth your attention.

Here is a short rundown of what to look for, section by section.

The Cover Page

This page shows the franchise logo. It also has a summary of the initial franchise fees and the total investment, followed by "Risk Factors" in all capitals. Most of the risk factors are boilerplate and address whether the franchise agreement requires the franchisee to litigate or arbitrate outside of the franchisee's home state. They also caution if the franchisor has little or no experience in business or in franchising. Make a note to discuss any such risk factor with your attorney.

Item 1: The Franchisor, Its Predecessors and Affiliates

This is a concise overview of the franchisor, its formal corporate name and state of incorporation, and its background, business experience, predecessors and affiliates. It tells you how long the company has been offering franchises and gives a general description of the franchisee's potential competition. Read the franchisor's business record carefully.

Item 2: Business Experience

This section gives you a bare-bones five-year outline of the business experience of the franchisor's key executives. It's just the facts: title, employer, dates of employment and city. Note if there are any gaps in the employment history (such as might be created by some time out of work).

Item 3: Litigation

This section requires the franchisor to reveal details about specific types of litigation that may be "material" (important) to prospective franchisees. If in the past 10 years the company itself or any of its directors or officers listed in item 2 have been defendants in cases involving claims of franchise law, securities law, fraud, unfair or deceptive trade practices or comparable allegations, you will see it described here. You will also see arbitration actions listed in this section.

Don't be alarmed if there are one or two cases disclosed here. It is a rare franchisor, or one that has not been in the franchising business long, that has no litigation to disclose in item 3. In this great country anyone can file a lawsuit alleging anything, so the cases disclosed may not convey the right impression of the company or its dispute resolution style. On the other hand, an item 3 that discloses many cases may tell you a lot about the company. The best approach is to make a note to discuss with your own attorney and your franchisor representative any questions you have about disclosures in this item. You may also want to ask any existing franchisees you interview about the company's litigation history. They can probably shed light on what the company's litigation style means to franchisees.

Item 4: Bankruptcy

If there is a bankruptcy in the 10-year background of the franchisor, its predecessors, affiliates, partners or officers, you will see it briefly described in item 4.

Item 5: Initial Franchise Fee

This section details all moneys paid to the franchisor prior to the time the franchisee opens for business. Typically, the franchisor imposes an initial franchise fee that is a lump sum payment—as much as $20,000, $30,000 or more—to be made at the time the franchise agreement is signed. Look for other fees, such as training fees, that may be included, and the circumstances in which they might be refundable.

Item 6: Other Fees

The chart in item 6 summarizes all the recurring or isolated fees that the franchisee must pay to the franchisor or its affiliates during the course of the franchise relationship. The royalty is listed, of course. The chart also includes any continuing advertising contributions to an advertising fund or otherwise, cooperative advertising organizations that charge advertising fees, transfer fees and audit costs.

Item 7: Initial Investment

This section of the UFOC is one of the most important for your planning purposes. In chart form, it summarizes the total initial expenses you can expect when opening the franchised business. It tells you what categories of expenses are typical, to whom payments are to be made, and when they are due. It also tells you whether payments are refundable under any circumstances. Use these figures when preparing your own business plan, but check

with a good accountant and existing franchisees in the system to see if there are other expenses you should anticipate that are not included in item 7. For instance, if you borrow a substantial portion of the investment, you will have debt service to anticipate that will not appear in this disclosure document. Consider this item as the starting point in your financial planning.

Item 8: Restrictions on Sources of Products and Services

The area of product sourcing is one of the most important aspects of franchise operations, but it is often well-hidden. Imagine that you are considering a franchise for an ice cream shop that sells a premium ice cream that is manufactured especially for the franchise system. There is only one source of the product, the franchisor. You are required by the franchise agreement to purchase only from the designated source. Would you know whether $11.35 per tub is a reasonable price for ice cream inventory? What will you do if the franchisor raises its prices and cuts down your (already razor-thin) margins? Some franchisees feel trapped by a confining supply arrangement where they have no opportunity to seek out a competitive price. Supply arrangements are described in this item but may not paint the entire picture for you.

Item 9: Franchisee's Obligations

This item is nothing more than a cross-reference chart showing you where certain subjects are addressed in the franchise agreement.

Item 10: Financing

If the franchisor offers financing, either directly or indirectly, you will find it detailed here. It should lay out the terms of the financing in chart form and specify which portion of the purchase qualifies for the financing. Copies of any loan documents will be included as exhibits.

Item 11: Franchisor's Obligations

This provides a lengthy recital of the promises made by the franchisor, the services they will supply to you in the course of the franchise relationship, and details about some of the training and other programs offered. This is the longest section of the UFOC and it contains a wealth of information. Among the topics addressed are the pre-opening and post-opening services to be provided by the franchisor, the time that typically elapses between the date of signing the franchise agreement and opening the business, the specifications for any computerized cash registers or computers necessary in the business, and a detailed description of the training program.

Item 12: Territory

This is a description of any territorial rights granted as a part of the franchise agreement. It is fair to say that most, but not all, franchise systems include some form of territorial protection for the franchisee. The key point for the prospective franchisee is to read this section carefully and without the natural assumptions you may have of these intangible concepts. For instance, it may include a promise by the franchisor that says something like, "We will not develop ourselves or grant franchises to others to develop another franchise in your territory." Does this mean that you have absolute exclusivity in the territory? No. In fact, it is a rather narrow promise that prevents the establishment of competing units in your area but does not prevent the franchisor from selling product to customers in your territory. Ask your attorney to review the promises in this section so that you are clear on the nature of the rights you are receiving. They are important.

Item 13: Trademarks

It has been said that the trademark is the cornerstone of the franchise relationship. Item 13 provides some key details about the primary trademarks associated with the franchise package. First it tells you whether the trademark has been registered with the U.S. Patent and Trademark Office. While that registration is not necessary for a protectable trademark, it is an important step for the franchisor, and if it has not been done, it tells you and your attorney a lot. Having an unregistered mark may increase your risks that someone else with the same mark can claim superior legal rights and force you and the franchisor to find another trade name. If the franchisor has any litigation pending that pertains to the marks, it is described here, as are promises made by the franchisor to protect franchisees from claims of trademark infringement by third parties. Make sure that your attorney reviews item 13 and advises you of any apparent problems.

Item 14: Patents, Copyrights and Proprietary Information

The majority of UFOCs contain boilerplate language in this section because so few franchise programs have patent rights that pertain to the franchise. What is usually protected by copyright are the operations manual and other printed advertising and operating materials. There is also language in this section protecting the "trade secrets" and other "proprietary rights" of the franchisor in various aspects of the franchised business.

Item 15: Obligation to Participate in the Actual Operation of the Franchise Business

If the contract requires you to be present at the business for a certain number of hours each week, or that a trained manager supervise the operation at all times, it should be disclosed here.

Item 16: Restrictions on What the Franchisee May Sell

If you will be required to sell only approved products, or only those supplied to you by approved suppliers, it will say so here.

Item 17: Renewal, Termination, Transfer and Dispute Resolution

This multipage chart provides the reader with a full cross-reference to the franchise agreement along with a summary of the key legal provisions relating to renewal (what happens at the end of the contract term), termination (the circumstances under which you and the franchisor may choose to end the contract before its expiration), transfer (the restrictions on your right to sell all or part of your franchised business), and dispute resolution (where and how legal disputes will be resolved). These topics are the most legally intense sections of the franchise agreement and deserve careful review by your attorney.

Item 18: Public Figures

This section describes the terms of any endorsement or other involvement by a well-known figure who is promoting the franchise.

Item 19: Earnings Claims

This item may provide some of your most important clues to answering the question, "How much money does one of these babies make?" Franchisors are not required to supply any performance information about their program, but if they do, it must be disclosed here. Only about 20 percent of all UFOCs contain performance information. There could be a number of reasons for a company leaving this disclosure blank. It may be that they are concerned about potential misrepresentations and legal liability if they list performance figures for their existing franchisees. It may also be that the performance statistics do not tell a compelling story, and the company does not want to focus your attention on the low performance of its franchised businesses. If you do find performance information, be sure to use it when you prepare your business plan. Then supplement the bare statistics with franchisee interviews. If the company does not disclose anything, find out why, and press for per-formance information from other sources. Again, existing franchisees are the best place to start.

Item 20: List of Outlets

This section includes a series of charts about the growth or contraction of the franchise system for the prior three years as well as information about existing company-owned units and projected growth of the system during the coming year. There is an attached list of the names, addresses and telephone numbers of current franchisees, as well as a list of the names and the last-known addresses and telephone numbers of all franchisees who have left the system during the prior year or have not been in contact with the franchisor for at least 10 weeks. These lists are often attached as exhibits to the UFOC. Find out from these former franchise owners why they left and whether it was related to shortcomings in the program itself.

Item 21: Financial Statements

The law requires that a franchisor attach to the body of the UFOC as an exhibit a copy of its financial balance sheet and operating statements for the prior three years, all of which must be audited (or "certified") by a certified public accountant. If the franchisor has been in existence for less than three years or has only recently begun franchising, you may find fewer than three years of financial statements. However, the company is required to provide at least one certified statement, even if it is only an opening balance sheet. Make sure your accountant sees this information. You want to make sure the franchisor is on solid financial footing and in business for the long haul.

Item 22: Contracts

You will find a description of all the contracts you need to sign in order to purchase the franchise in this item. Copies of the contracts will also be attached to the UFOC as an exhibit. If the franchisor provides loan documents, equipment or real estate leases, they are also included in an exhibit, along with a sample franchise agreement form. Before you close on the transaction, make sure your attorney has a chance to review all these contracts.

Item 23: Receipt

The UFOC requires that two receipts be attached to it, one for the franchisee and the other for the franchisor. This is important for the franchisor in case they have to prove they delivered a disclosure document to you and that you received it. (Was it at least 10 business days before you signed the franchise agreement?) You must sign and date the receipt.

That's a lot of investment information in one document—and well worth reading through it.

SUMMARY NOTES

- ✓ The UFOC is a key document in your search for a franchise.
- ✓ READ the UFOC!
- ✓ Have professionals help you with parts of this document.
- ✓ Review the various sections of the UFOC. Some are more important than others.
- ✓ The UFOC does not contain *all* of the information you need to evaluate the franchise.

Action **PLAN**

Get a UFOC—any UFOC—and flip through it to see how it is organized and where to find key information.

CHAPTER 13

Five Great Questions *Not* Answered in the UFOC

*E*LLEN SLOGGED THROUGH THE *UFOC* FOR *the franchise she was interested in and was proud of herself. She had every reason to be impressed by the program and wondered if there was anything else she needed to dig into. Surely, she thought, this huge tome told her everything she needed to know. Right?*

THE UFOC DOES NOT DELIVER EVERYTHING

Ellen makes a mistake if she assumes that the UFOC will tell her everything she needs to know about the franchise investment. It is designed by regulators to deliver information that they consider "material" to the investment—that is, information that should be important to the investor. However, there are some gaping holes in the UFOC, key pieces of information it does not convey that are material to your purchase

decision. Take a look at five of the most important areas. There may be more, depending on the type of business you are buying.

- *Pricing/product distribution.* Item 8 of the UFOC delivers some of the product and pricing information you need, but the guidelines for franchisors to follow in preparing this section are complex and cumbersome, resulting in confusing disclosures that are not particularly helpful. After all, smooth product sourcing, the savings on prices available to franchisees based on large group purchases, and carefully considered product specifications are all fundamental business reasons for buying a franchise. If this part of the business is not working well, there may be little reason to go into the franchise.

  Make a point of exploring product dynamics with the franchisees you meet.

51

IN*sight*

We talked to a franchisee of an ice cream concept who was beside himself. He has an MBA and thought his business looked great on paper. He liked the taste of the product, the well-designed brand name, the modern look of the stores, the sales figures he had seen, and the location in an enclosed mall without a food court. What he didn't count on was the price of the premium ice cream, which, under the terms of the franchise agreement, could be purchased only from the franchisor. The price was way too high, but he didn't realize it until he got into the business and learned about wholesale ice cream prices. The president of the company told him that there was no UFOC because, they were "not a public company." "How was I to know about that?" he says. Now he is saddled with an expensive business that is breaking even but not making much of a profit, and he is embarrassed to admit this could happen to an MBA.

Press the franchisor representatives about purchasing arrangements, any buying cooperatives in your area and pricing strategies. Check the franchise agreement and any other paperwork from the franchisor describing product matters. In many franchises, this is the economic engine of the business. It never hurts to look under the hood and make sure it is running well.

- **Franchisee associations.** Nowhere in the UFOC is a franchisor required to disclose the existence of a franchisee association or advisory council. Yet this is an important aspect of the franchise program for a new investor. The presence of a strong association that is well-attended and governed by franchisees is an attractive asset of any franchise program.

I have long suspected that omitting any mention of a franchisee association in the UFOC is due to the swift internal political waters surrounding franchisee associations. Some associations are created by the franchisor and promoted by the company; others are "renegade associations" created by the franchisees and resented by the franchisor. Ask current franchisees about the role they play through an association or a franchisee council.

- **Training.** One of the keys to franchisee success is solid training. The UFOC will give you some of the basic facts, including a chart outlining the sections of the training, who teaches the sections, the experience of the trainers, how much time is devoted to each topic, and where the training takes place. However, you need assurances about the program that cannot be delivered in a disclosure document. Is the training effective? Do franchisees feel that they are well-prepared to run a successful business upon completing it? Is the training

IN*sight*

A franchisee association or council organizes and provides to the franchisor and all franchisees a valuable franchisee viewpoint of the business. Franchisee associations generally meet on a regular basis, and the prudent franchisor listens carefully to the advice and recommendations offered. They can provide new investors with a knowledgeable perspective independent of the franchisor and an in-depth evaluation of the whole franchise organization.

based on current thinking, and is it the best available in the field? Is it complete, and how much of it is hands-on, under supervision? Be sure you explore these ideas with franchisees and your franchisor representatives.

- **Market for product/service.** This is a basic but intangible question that is difficult to address in a disclosure document: Is the market for the product or service a strong one? Is the growth of the market for the business on the rise or decline?

- **Franchisor support.** The language in a franchise agreement that describes the level of the franchisor's continuing support may be surprising. You are likely to find something like: "The franchisor will provide such continuing advice and support as it deems appropriate in its absolute discretion."

How's that for reassurance?! Attorneys for franchisors learned decades ago that specific promises of support in the franchise agreement, such as quarterly meetings, monthly newsletters and regular telephone calls, would lead to legal trouble when the franchisor's business practices changed. And they always change. The result is the smallest, most flexible promise of support imaginable.

Even though the promises might be modest, the practice is important. Find out exactly—from franchisees and the franchisor's representatives—what the company does for its new franchisees when they are planning to locate the business, when they are hiring staff, and during the opening and start-up phase. Is help available? Is it responsive? Will the franchisor be there to help if and when things go wrong?

SUMMARY NOTES

- ✓ As lengthy as it is, the UFOC will not deliver all the information you need to know about a franchise program.
- ✓ Look to some key topics for more information: product distribution, franchisee associations, training, the market for the product and/or service, and franchisee support by the franchisor.

Action PLAN

Write a single-page list of questions and topics you want to discuss with any franchisor representative you meet. Ask your attorney and accountant if you should add other questions to your list.

CHAPTER 14

Key Sections of the Franchise Agreement

*B*ILL RECEIVED HIS FRANCHISE AGREEMENT *and figured he'd just look it over himself. Why hire an attorney? He knew attorneys could be expensive. After all, the contract was in English and looked straightforward to him. Sure it was long and the language was a little dense, but it was registered under Bill's state franchise law and seemed to be fully described in the UFOC. What could go wrong?*

UNDERSTANDING THE BASIC DYNAMIC OF THE FRANCHISE AGREEMENT

Bill is setting himself up for an expensive lesson. The agreement that grants a franchisee the right to operate a business in the franchisor's system is a complex commercial contract. It is designed to create a continuing business relationship that could span 20 years or more. It grants a panoply of intangible "intellectual property" rights, describes product and service standards, and sets the ground rules for the transfer, renewal and termination of the relationship.

This agreement is not an easy document to read or understand, and it makes sense to take it to an attorney who can help you understand it in detail. While the size, shape and style of franchise agreements are tailored to each system, many of their basic features are universal. You will be well ahead of the franchise game if you comprehend the basic legal dynamics of this complex contract.

KEY PROVISIONS CONSIDERED
Intellectual Property Rights

A franchise agreement has been described as a trademark license with overdrive. It grants to the franchisee the limited right to use the trademarks, techniques, procedures, trade dress and know-how that comprise the franchise system. These rights are "limited" so that the franchisor can preserve its

IN*sight*

A franchise is, at its essence, the licensing of intellectual property. All the valuable information delivered to the franchisee, from the trademark, to the operating manuals, to the techniques taught in training, to the color designs of a retail franchise, is a form of intangible intellectual property.

ownership rights of trademarks, copyrights and trade secrets.

Look closely at these terms:

- **Trademark.** This a word, name, phrase, symbol, logo, or in some cases a design that traditionally represents the source of a product or service. A leading example is McDonald's® brand sandwiches, including the famous Big Mac® sandwich. A trademark owner has the legal right to license other people to use the trademark, and those licenses generally require correct display of the mark. If the colors of red and yellow in the McDonald's golden arches brand name are a bit off—if they turn out maroon and gold—you can expect the trademark owner to object. A "service mark" is the same thing as a trademark, but it specifically identifies a service, not a product.

- **Franchise system techniques and procedures.** In a franchise system, these terms denote the specifications, equipment and routines that are part of the franchise rights and obligations. They are usually found in an operating manual provided by the franchisor. In a restaurant franchise, for instance, the operating manual details the preparation of all menu items and their components, as well as things such as the timing of cooking and the temperature of cooking oil. Equipment specifications

are included, as well as the uniform attire of employees. Many of these techniques that are not obvious to the public may be claimed by the franchisor as trade secrets, which are confidential and not to be disclosed. All franchisees need to be aware of claimed trade secrets and take steps to keep them confidential.

- **Trade dress.** This is a legal term that describes the appearance of a product, product packaging, or the distinctive style of a building or restaurant. Trade dress may be protected under the law in the same fashion as a trademark. What does this mean to a franchisee? If you operate a restaurant franchise in a building with a distinctive color design or roof line, those features may have to be changed if you leave the system because they are owned by the franchisor.

- **Know-how.** This is often used to describe the knowledge and entire set of techniques that go into a franchise system. It includes the franchisor's experience in business and its knowledge of the bumps and bruises of the marketplace and how to avoid them, and it is imparted to the franchisee in a healthy franchise system.

- **Copyright.** This is the legal protection of an original work that is fixed in a tangible form, including books, songs, plays, software and all printed material. The legal copyright protects the author's exclusive right to use and exploit the value of the work. It cannot be published, copied or used without the author's permission. An author—and this is important—cannot protect an idea but can claim a copyright for the original expression of an idea (like a novel or a franchise operations manual). The franchise system's operations manual, advertising and other printed material may be copyright-protected by the franchisor. As a franchisee, you may be restricted in the ways you can use and exploit these materials for your own purposes.

- **Patent.** A patent is a property right, secured in the U.S. Constitution, protecting the rights to an invention, new device or innovation. As with a trademark, the owner has the right to license the use of his or her patented device to other people.
- **License rights.** The franchisee receives the right to use and display the trademark, or a family of trademarks, only as the franchisor authorizes, and only during the term of the franchise agreement. This means that all signs displaying the mark, and all printed materials, vehicles and even Web locations used by the franchisee, must be approved in form, color and design by the franchisor.

Although this is a point of some contention in the franchise community, the "goodwill" of the franchised business represented by the trademark—which is to say much of the goodwill of the business itself—remains in the ownership of the franchisor, not the franchisee. In that sense, a franchise agreement is similar to a commercial lease: At the end of the lease term, the property that is granted reverts completely to the owner, not the tenant.

The same may be said of any of the other intellectual property of the franchise system. Its use is licensed only in the manner prescribed and only for the term of the franchise agreement. When the franchise agreement is expired or terminated, all rights to use the trademarks, copyrighted material, patents and/or trade secrets will also cease.

Contract Flexibility Over Time

How does the franchise relationship handle the marketplace changes that occur in the franchise system over a number of years? The changed appearance of American business establishments in the past 20 years, or even 10 years, is dramatic. Look at a picture of a McDonald's restaurant or a Holiday Inn from the 1980s. They've definitely changed!

Franchise relationships must allow for change over time, and they do it by incorporating a reference in the contract to a living, changing set of policies, standards, guidance and know-how contained in a confidential set of documents, usually called operating manuals. The manuals are typically updated as changes in the system occur or new policies are adopted.

The franchise agreement also usually describes a dynamic franchise system that changes over time. The parties stipulate that many aspects of the franchise will require alteration as the years go by.

Franchise agreements accommodate changes over time by expressly anticipating them, while assuring the franchisee that the fundamental rights of the contract will not change. While franchisees clearly want to receive their full contract rights and the undiluted benefit of their bargain, they also want the franchisor to take the lead in keeping their business concept fresh and competitive in the marketplace. Obviously, this creates something of a dynamic legal tension for the franchisee and franchisor. What is fundamental and what is allowed to change over time?

While there is no easy answer, the courts and franchise systems ask whether a particular change is "material" to the franchisee's business. Is a proposed change so important (or fundamental) that it would have affected the franchisee's decision to purchase the franchise if they had known that such a change would be made to the program? If it is material or fundamental to the franchise, it may be in violation of the contract's promises to the franchisee.

Product Standards

The essential genius of franchising is the delivery of consistent products or services through independent businesses licensed to operate under a universal display mark. Isn't it remarkable that a Big Mac® sandwich purchased at a McDonald's in Bangor, Maine, tastes the same as one bought in Hawaii or Australia? What is more remarkable is that all the ingredients and sandwich components are provided by unaffiliated, third-party suppliers to the McDonald's system.

The franchise agreement addresses the requirements of product and service supply in one of several different ways, reflecting varying degrees of control that the company needs to exercise over the delivery of the products or services of the franchised business. In some systems, of course, the franchisor is the manufacturer of the product line carried by the franchisee, and the franchise is itself a "product franchise" through which independent franchisees distribute the line.

In most business format franchise programs, franchisees are required to purchase only from suppliers who have received the company's prior written approval. If the franchisee wants to buy product from a supplier who has not received approval, the franchise agreement requires that an application must be made to the franchisor. This way the franchisor can assure that all suppliers to the system are capable of delivering specialized product and that system standards are not eroded through poor supply selections (which are often driven by price considerations) made by franchisees.

An even-handed supplier approval process also allows the franchisor to control quality without unreasonably restricting supplier access to its system of franchise buyers, which could have serious antitrust implications for the franchisor. An unreasonably restrictive supply arrangement might injure competition among suppliers to franchisees. Injury to competition is what antitrust laws were designed to combat.

Transfer

Can the franchisee build up the business and then sell it to another person? In most systems the franchisee can sell the business only if the franchisor issues written permission, and permission is generally granted by a franchisor only after reviewing the qualifications of the prospective buyer. Most franchisors apply the same standards of qualification on the proposed transferee (the buyer) as they apply to new applicants.

If the transferee does not measure up, the franchisor has every right to deny consent to the transfer. The courts have made it clear that a franchisor has a legitimate interest in preventing its franchised businesses from being owned by businesspeople who are undercapitalized, lack necessary levels of business experience or fail to meet the company's objective qualifications.

The transfer, or assignment, sections of the typical franchise agreement are the most lengthy and dense legalese of the entire contract but are also the most important to the value of the franchisee's business. Your ability to sell your business and pull out your sweat equity is essential to the original decision to purchase the franchise.

It surprises many franchisees to learn that the transfer language of the contract may cover events that do not amount to the sale of the business, such as taking in a new partner, granting stock in an existing corporation that is the franchisee, the death of a minority owner of a franchise, and shifting ownership of the unit's assets to a newly formed corporation or limited liability company. All these events require the prior written consent of the franchisor, if the contract's transfer provisions are typical.

CORPORATE OWNERSHIP

Private Corporations, Limited Liability Companies (LLCs) and Personal Guarantees

Most franchisors allow an individual investor to create these legal entities to serve as the formal franchisee under the franchise agreement. It often makes sense: Create an LLC to hold the franchise rights, sign the franchise agreement, hold the assets of the operation, and accommodate multiple ownership and various positions and roles. However, there is usually one catch, and it's a significant one: Under the franchise agreement, you will be asked to personally guarantee to the franchisor the obligations of your new legal entity.

"Wait a minute," you say. "My lawyer told me that the main reason for creating an LLC was to shield my personal assets from the liabilities of the business!" That's right. The personal guarantee, if required by the franchisor, defeats that objective, at least insofar as you wanted to be shielded from the claims of the franchisor. If it is narrowly drafted, the guarantee should not defeat your objective relating to other aspects of the business.

What does this personal guarantee mean as a practical matter? Suppose your business falls on difficult times and you are unable to pay the royalties, and perhaps the franchisor terminates your franchise or you close the business. The franchisor will have legal claim for royalties and other damages against the LLC *and* you personally, as well as others who have guaranteed the obligations of your legal entity.

Right of First Refusal

Many franchise agreements reserve to the franchisor a "right of first refusal." This means that if you receive a formal offer to purchase your business, you must present the offer to the franchisor and allow them the opportunity to purchase your business on the same terms. This allows the franchisor to maintain control over the buying and selling of its franchises, but also draws criticism from

INsight

Most franchisors include a right of first refusal in their franchise agreements in order to control ownership of the franchised businesses and to buy out a franchisee if it fits with the company's business plans for that area. However, it is a right rarely exercised by a franchisor.

franchisees who believe that it hampers their ability to attract a serious buyer. What buyer wants to go through the effort of putting together a detailed purchase offer, only to have the franchisor take it out from under them?

Termination

Oh, the dreaded termination section! It seems to rattle on ad nauseam, listing dozens of situations in which the franchisor may terminate the relationship, while rarely including even one circumstance in which the franchisee may terminate the relationship. Franchisors generally have only one enforcement tool, the threat of termination. They describe it at length, but use it gingerly.

Here are some of the typical termination grounds you will see in a franchise agreement, with notes on what to look out for:

- **Business abandonment.** Make sure you understand how abandonment is defined. You don't want a spring vacation to amount to abandonment of your business.
- **Criminal conviction.** How is a crime defined here? Is it a felony or any crime? The franchisor wants to protect its reputation if the franchisee commits a crime.
- **Lying on the application.** If you mislead the company during the application process, it wants to reserve the right to terminate the relationship.
- **Bankruptcy.** If your business does declare bankruptcy, the franchisor wants to be able to terminate the contractual relationship. This termination provision is often set to occur "automatically" if bankruptcy is declared, but in fact a whole body of federal bankruptcy law will take effect immediately. Bankruptcy legal specialists caution that the law may not allow the franchisor to terminate after a bankruptcy, regardless of what the contract says.
- **Termination after notice.** Most franchise agreements allow the franchisor to terminate

IN*sight*

Many franchise agreements also include the broader termination grounds of the franchisee committing an act that injures the goodwill of the trademark. Plan to discuss this provision with your attorney.

the relationship if the franchisee receives notice of any default and does not correct the problem within a reasonable amount of time. The typical time to cure is 30 days, but it certainly could be a longer or shorter period, depending on the nature of the default.

Termination after notice is how most franchise terminations occur. If you receive a default notice that warns of the possible termination of your franchise rights, do not file it away. Respond to it immediately.

The franchise agreement, drafted by lawyers in the interests of franchisors, allows them to protect their trademarks, systems and other intellectual property if a franchisee abuses, misuses or misappropriates any portion of the franchised business. At the same time, exacting termination language allows the franchisor to protect other franchisees.

Look at it this way: If a franchisee on the other side of your small town is running a slovenly or dirty operation, your *own* business will suffer. That is the other sharp blade of the two-edged sword of franchising: You operate under the same trademark as many other operators; their businesses are indistinguishable from yours in the eye of the customer.

Most franchisees dislike the seemingly overbearing language of their own franchise agreement but are the first to insist that the franchisor use those rights to enforce system standards against another owner who is not doing the job.

The franchise laws of about 19 jurisdictions impose standards of termination that preempt conflicting language of a franchise agreement, allowing for termination or failure to renew only when the franchisor has good cause, as that term is defined in the statute. These statutes come into play if you get into a tangle with the franchisor and they notify you that your franchise is or will be canceled.

DISPUTE RESOLUTION PROVISIONS

The truth is, franchising tends to generate disputes. The interests of franchisor and franchisee are fundamentally at odds in a number of ways. Remember, the franchisor receives royalties based on a percentage of the gross sales of the business, *before* expenses are paid; franchisees take money home at the end of the day if they maximize profits, *after* expenses are paid. Franchisors therefore push for higher sales; franchisees for better profits.

One measure of excellence in franchising is the ability of the franchisor to avoid the courtroom when they must enforce the terms of its franchise agreements. The contract may contain a provision that requires the parties to submit all disputes to an arbitration process before any lawsuit may be filed. Where must that arbitration take place? Many franchise agreements specify that the process take place at the American Arbitration Association office closest

IN*sight*

Franchisors have additional motivation to avoid a courtroom or an arbitration procedure: disclosure. The UFOC requires that a franchisor disclose in item 3 certain lawsuits and arbitration procedures during the prior 10 years as well as the terms of any settlement of those actions.

to the franchisor headquarters. That means you have to travel to the franchisor's backyard in order to resolve a dispute.

Even if there is no arbitration language in place, the franchise agreement may specify where a lawsuit must be filed if either party makes a legal claim under the contract. Franchisee attorneys generally resist accepting language mandating that legal actions must be filed in the home jurisdiction of the franchisor.

Remember, no prospective franchisee should attempt to fully comprehend a franchise agreement without the benefit of legal counsel. Your attorney is far more familiar with the complexities and limitations of contract law and can advise you about the obligations and rights it stipulates.

For all the attention the contract receives at the start of the relationship, it should not loom large in your daily business. When everything is going well,

the franchised business is succeeding, and your relationship with the franchisor is on solid footing, that carefully evaluated franchise agreement—the foundation of your business investment—will not even come out of the drawer. All solid foundations are supposed to work that way.

SUMMARY NOTES

- ✓ Take the proposed franchise agreement to an attorney. It's important.
- ✓ It is also important to understand some of the basic dynamics of a franchise agreement, such as intellectual property, license rights, product standards, transfer and termination.
- ✓ If the business works out well, the contract will not come out of the drawer. If problems arise, it is the key to resolving any disputes.

Action PLAN

Look immediately for a good attorney. Ask current franchisees or friends in business who they use, or contact your state bar association.

CHAPTER 15

Franchisor Financial Information in the UFOC

(and How Do I Read This Gobbledegook?)

*E*RIC NEVER HAD A HEAD FOR NUMBERS BUT *thought he was pretty good at judging the financial status of a company by its balance sheets. Now the UFOC gave him an opportunity to do just that for the home health-care franchise he was evaluating. But he had never seen a franchisor balance sheet and operating statement before and was not sure what to make of them. So he decided to take them to his accountant. Something told him this was too important to be left to his amateur accounting skills.*

FRANCHISOR FINANCIAL DISCLOSURES

Eric's instincts are serving him well. Item 21 of the UFOC requires franchisors to supply two years of audited balance sheets and three years of audited operational statements. This is extremely important information for a prospective franchisee and should not be left

to an amateur evaluation. It shows whether the franchisor is well-capitalized, how well they are managing their cash flow, and whether the company is healthy and profitable. In short, it is a snapshot of the franchisor's finances, and it is invaluable to you.

You are considering entering into a five-, 10- or even 20-year relationship when you execute a franchise agreement. You want to know whether the franchisor has staying power and will be there for the duration.

AUDITS ACCORDING TO GAAP

What does it mean that a financial statement is "audited"? It means that a certified public accounting firm has independently reviewed the company's books and expressed its professional opinion in writing that the financial statements accurately reflect the company's financial position and have been prepared in accordance with

INsight

The auditors must consent to the inclusion of their report in the UFOC. They go through a rigorous process of inspecting the company's records for the period they are auditing, as required by the standards of the accounting profession. A Compilation Report or Review Report does not involve that level of accounting scrutiny.

Generally Accepted Accounting Principles (GAAP)—the standard financial statement rules.

This audit opinion is a big deal in the world of accountants. It is the highest level of review that a CPA conducts (the other two are a Compilation Report and a Review Report), and it is as close as you're going to get to an independent third party approving the accuracy of a set of financials. You can usually rely on the accuracy of an audited statement.

So you peek at the exhibits in the back of your UFOC and there they are, the franchisor's financials. They are a sea of numbers. Now what do you do? Well, it goes without saying that most people have not made a study of how to read a financial statement. Now is not the time to start. Take the UFOC to an accountant, preferably a CPA, and have them conduct a review. You are going to need the services of a good accountant anyway when it comes time to plan the business, make some projections and create a business road map, so asking for a quick review of a set of financials is a good first step. Talk to the accountant about what it is you need and how much it will cost. Can't afford the full Cadillac review? Then ask how much half an hour of time costs. Present the financials, and ask the accountant to go over them slowly and explain what they mean to an experienced eye.

ACCOUNTANT'S ANALYSIS TIPS

We asked Roger Heymann of small-business accounting firm Heymann, Suissa and Stone P.C. in Rockville, Maryland, to summarize some of the lingo you may encounter in this session and to recommend what to listen for and what to ask. Here is what Heymann says:

"For a prospective franchisee, there are three major points to keep in mind when looking at financial statements. These are: Look at the relevant ratio analyses, pay close attention to footnotes, and conduct an industry analysis.

"Qualitative information from financial statements can be gathered by performing a ratio analysis, which expresses the relationship among selected financial statement data. As a franchisee, you want to pay close attention to relevant ratios, which may include the current ratio, quick ratio, inventory turnover, and return on assets ratio. Current ratio and quick ratio measure short-term debt-paying ability. Inventory turnover presents the liquidity of inventory. Return on assets ratio measures the overall profitability of assets.

"The second major point is to pay close attention to the footnotes to the financial statement. These provide the additional key information that supplements the principal financial statement. There are two types of footnotes. First, the major accounting policies of the business have to be identified and explained. They tell an investor what method the company chooses to present its accounts in the financial statement. For example, the cost of goods sold expense method will be included in this type of footnote. The second kind of footnote provides additional information that cannot be placed in the main body of the financial statement. For example, the maturity date or interest rate of a particular loan will be stated in the footnotes.

"The last major point is to conduct an industry analysis. A company's financial statements can tell you how well the business ran in the past, but not how well it has been doing in the context of a specific industry. Therefore, an industry analysis is needed to put the figures in perspective."

EVALUATING THE FRANCHISOR'S FINANCIAL STANDING

Now that an accountant has advised you about the franchisor's financial standing, how do you evaluate it in your investment decisions? Take a look at a common example. Say the franchisor is a subsidiary of a well-known corporation but is showing only a small net worth on an opening balance sheet with no operating history. What do you make of that?

First, understand why you are looking at a franchisor with a small net worth. When a well-established corporation considers franchising for the first time, the attorneys explain that it will need to provide a set of audited financial statements for the UFOC. If the company has never prepared an audited statement in the past, this can pose an extremely expensive problem. Auditors have to go over the corporation's old books in painful detail, and probably charge the corporation an arm and a leg. On top of that, the company is concerned about litigation arising out of the franchise program and figures that a subsidiary corporation will add an additional level of protection for the corporation. So the company decides it will be cheaper and smarter to create a new corporation to serve as the franchisor. A newly formed franchisor must provide only an audited opening balance sheet, which is a relatively simple matter for the auditor to complete. If the franchise program results in litigation, the assets of the established corporation are shielded.

This is perfectly legal, and quite common in franchising. When a thinly capitalized franchisor files in one of the registration states, however, it will probably be required to provide a surety bond to the state or make some other protective financial arrangement for investors as a condition of registration.

What does a surety bond do for franchisees? Imagine you have paid a $30,000 initial franchise fee, and the franchisor tells you that it cannot provide the promised training because it is low on funds and the training managers have quit. You request your money back, and the franchisor says it does not have that amount of cash in its accounts. In that situation, you would probably qualify to apply to be reimbursed under the surety bond on file with state authorities. It makes it relatively easy to be reimbursed for the investment of an initial fee if the franchisor goes out of business or is otherwise unable to perform basic obligations because it has no substantial assets. Without a protection like a surety bond, you may have no recourse at all, except filing a lawsuit against the franchisor and its principals.

Whether or not you are in a registration state, a low franchisor net worth increases the risks you are taking when you invest in a franchised business. If you are looking at a young program that has not been in operation very long, it may have an extremely low net worth. The profit potential of buying a franchise from a new concept may be high, but the concomitant risks should be part of your calculation when you evaluate any franchise investment.

The regulation of franchise sales is not designed to make all franchise investments safe. In order not to interfere unnecessarily in the marketplace, franchise regulation is designed to deliver all pertinent information into the hands of the investor, and then step back so that the investor can make an informed decision. That leaves a substantial burden on the prospective franchisee to consider all the relevant information.

SUMMARY NOTES ——————

✓ The UFOC requires the inclusion of the franchisor's audited financial statements.

✓ Audits are generally presented by independent accountants, and they confirm that the numbers are prepared and presented according to the standards adopted in the business accounting industry known as Generally Accepted Accounting Principles (GAAP).

✓ Accountants conduct a ratio analysis and industry analysis and review the footnotes to the statements.

✓ A low net worth or otherwise shaky financial statement increases the risk that the company may not be there for the long term.

Action PLAN

Find a good accountant by asking current franchisees and friends or contacts already in business who they use. Check the Yellow Pages, or search for a local CPA at the American Institute of Certified Public Accountants Web site (www.aicpa.org).

CHAPTER 16

Top 10 Warning Signs in Franchise Investments

*C*HRIS WAS HAVING TROUBLE EVALUATING *a restaurant franchise. The company would not give her a UFOC, its answers to her questions were confusing, and franchisees were giving a mixed review on some key issues. At what point, she wondered, should she back away from the program?*

DON'T GET SNAGGED

As exciting as it may be to purchase a franchise, this business requires all buyers to exercise caution. Regulations require franchisors to give you a UFOC, that's all. Once you have this document in hand, it is your responsibility to review it carefully and to ask more questions of the franchisor and as many franchisees as you can.

KEY WARNING SIGNS

Even if you follow this advice, how do you know if there are problems with a franchise

you have your eye on? Although there is no way to be absolutely certain about a given investment, you can improve your odds of success if you keep an eye out for some of these key warning signs:

10. **Weak financial statements.** The UFOC contains three years of the franchisor's audited financial statements. Review them carefully, and take them to a knowledgeable CPA. If the franchisor is in a weak financial condition, it will raise the risk levels for your investment. You may find some terrific programs being offered by thinly capitalized franchisors or start-up companies, but understand that your risks as a franchisee are magnified by the company's weak financial standing.

9. *No answers.* If you do not get all your questions answered by the franchisor,

or if you start getting the feeling that the company is being evasive, move on.

8. *The hustle.* Buying a franchise is a substantial investment. It might wipe out your life savings and put you on a financial bubble. If the seller is hurrying you along, telling you that the window of opportunity is closing, or using any other tried and true closing techniques, be prepared to walk away from the deal. This is too important to rush.

7. *Product price squeeze.* Product supply is the ticklish underbelly of franchise relationships. If you are buying a business that is designed to distribute the franchisor's product line, then you had better make sure the pricing of the product will allow you to be competitive in the marketplace. Ask other franchise owners how the pricing structure works for them. If you are going into a "business format" program where product is supplied by third parties, or some is supplied by the franchisor, make sure that it runs well. Have the franchisees established a buying cooperative? Do franchisees have input on the supply arrangements? Make sure this key aspect of your business will not frustrate you.

6. *High turnover rates.* Check item 20 of the UFOC and confirm how many franchisees have left the system in the past three years. There is no rule of thumb to determine when the number is too high; this depends largely on the type of business. Lower-investment franchises generally have a higher turnover rate than more expensive businesses. If anything looks out of line, ask the franchisor what's going on.

5. *Attorney avoidance.* The franchisor discourages you from getting a lawyer involved, telling you it will unnecessarily complicate and slow the process.

4. *Too many lawsuits.* Ours has become a litigious society, of course, and most franchisors reflect that fact. Item 3 of the UFOC will reveal the 10-year history of "material" lawsuits and/or arbitration cases filed against the company. If you see a heavy litigation history, find out what has been going on. Ask your attorney's opinion. It could mean that franchisees are fundamentally unhappy in the business.

3. *Earnings claims mumbo jumbo.* Ask the seller's representative: "How much money can I make with this franchise?" If it is not in the UFOC, the company must decline to answer the question. If they say, "We are prohibited by federal law from answering the question," realize that although that may be true, it may also be because the earnings picture is not a pretty one.

2. *No UFOC.* All franchisors are required by federal law and many state laws to deliver a UFOC before you pay any money for the franchise or sign a franchise agreement. If you do not receive one, don't even think about buying the franchised business.

And the number-one warning sign in franchise investments:

1. *Consistently bad reports from current franchisees.* If you make the effort to visit with some current franchisees of the company, and each one tells you they are unhappy or would not make the investment in this franchise again, think long and hard about your own decision. There is no stronger or more trustworthy source of information about the company than those independents who are in the trenches. If they feel that the franchisor has let them down or has a flawed program, it will tell you to look more carefully before you take the plunge.

These warning signs should prompt you to ask more questions. If you don't like the answers you receive, and your gut (or your professional advisor) tells you to head for the door, this is probably not the program for you. Take the time to look around at other programs. For a decision as important as this one, you owe it to yourself and your family to be confident that it is the right business investment for you.

SUMMARY NOTES

✓ Look for red flags indicating problems in the franchise program.

✓ The decision about whether to invest in a particular franchise is yours, and no one knows better than you what will fit with your needs. Carefully consider anything else that appears to be a red flag in your own judgment.

Action PLAN

Move on if you encounter any serious problems regarding a franchise that are not cleared up to your satisfaction.

CHAPTER 17

Closing on Your Franchise Purchase

*N*ow IT WAS GETTING EXCITING FOR *Kevin. He had gone through all the steps with the franchisor, lined up the financing he needed to develop the new business, and was ready to close the transaction. In just a few days he would launch a new chapter of personal success in his life. What did he need to know going into the closing meeting?*

Once the franchisor has thoroughly checked out the applicant's qualifications, and the applicant has reviewed all documents, seen an accountant and an attorney, scraped together the money necessary to buy the franchise, and completed all necessary discussions, it is time to close on the transaction.

Purchasing the franchise rights for a business that has not yet been built is not a complicated transaction, and the closing involves nothing more than signing a few contracts and sliding a check across the table for the initial

franchise fee. Most "closings" for franchise sales do not take place in a room face to face with the franchisor. They take place through the mail. The company sends you a final package with tabs showing where your signature is needed and a cover letter stating the amount of the initial franchise fee. You sign and return, and it is done.

A CHECKLIST FOR CLOSING

However, you should pay attention to the following before you sign on the dotted line:

The Franchise Agreement

This contract should have been in your hands with all blanks filled in for at least five business days before you sign and date it. That is a requirement imposed on the franchisor by state and federal law; it is not the franchisee's responsibility to see that this is met. Make sure your attorney has reviewed the contract and signed off on it. If you have requested any changes to be made to accommodate you, make sure they appear in the final form of the contract.

Many companies ask you to sign two originals and return them to the company. The franchisor then executes them and returns one original to you for your records.

Always Date Your Signature

Begin the habit of adding a date to any legal document that contains your signature. If the signature form does not have a space to show the date, simply jot it immediately after your signature. Dates are important in the regulation of franchise sales, and you may be called upon to swear as to a series of dated events. The date of delivery of the UFOC, the date you first had a face-to-face meeting with the franchisor, the date on which you received a completed franchise agreement, and the date on which you signed the franchise agreement are all important.

Never backdate a document, even if asked to do so by the franchisor; it will only confuse your recollection of events. Make sure your document record is clear on the dates.

Other Contracts

You may be presented with other contracts to sign that are ancillary to the franchise agreement. All such documents should be included in the UFOC and should not come as a surprise at closing. If you do receive a surprise contract, check it with your attorney. Ancillary contracts may include a site selection agreement (if you do not have a site selected yet), an agreement regarding necessary lease terms, and an acknowledgment of the training schedule.

UFOC

If you have not received the franchisor's UFOC at least 10 business days before you are asked to sign the franchise agreement, stop. Don't sign the contract, and don't send any money. This could indicate a mere oversight, or it could mean that you have a more serious problem. Contact your franchisor representative.

Lease Paperwork

If you have selected a location for the franchised business, you probably have received a proposed lease from the landlord. Make sure that your attorney sees this lease form and that you understand what requirements the franchisor might impose on the lease terms. It probably will not hold up the closing if this is not resolved, but you want to give all parties—and their attorneys—as much notice as possible regarding the potential terms of any lease.

Bank Paperwork

If you have arranged a loan from a bank or other lending institution, it will want to receive a copy of the franchise agreement (and every other piece of paper related to the franchise) as soon as possible. Talk to your banker about the steps necessary to provide the money you are borrowing and when it will be available. Make sure all is in order before you close.

SUMMARY NOTES

✓ Prepare paperwork as you approach the closing.

✓ Prepare a checklist for the closing so that nothing is dropped. Confirm the list with your attorney.

✓ You should have checklist items for the contracts, the UFOC, your lease paperwork and financing paperwork.

Action **PLAN**

Plan ahead so that you are sure of your costs and obligations before the closing. Meet with your attorney to consider all contingencies.

CHAPTER 18

Resolving Legal Disputes

*A*CCORDING TO *JEFF*, *"*IT SEEMED LIKE A *good idea at the time." Jeff had carefully selected a franchise—a restaurant—and it would be the first and the best in his town. He found a strip mall location and threw his heart into it. He borrowed $50,000 and worked at the business 12 hours a day, seven days a week. He mopped floors after closing and managed the buying, hiring and money. He personally welcomed his customers and spent a fortune on build-out and grand-opening advertising. Six months after the opening, the restaurant just wasn't cutting it, and Jeff was nearly out of operating cash. He stopped paying his royalties, telling the company that the program was not working in his town, and that he would pay the royalties as soon as the business made some money. Rather than come in to help, the franchisor sent a letter on lawyer's letterhead threatening termination*

for failure to pay royalties if the account was not brought up-to-date in 30 days.

"Now what do I do?" a bewildered Jeff asked.

The termination of a franchise agreement has been a legal flash point since the earliest days of franchising. Nowhere are the divergent interests of franchisors and franchisees brought into sharper focus, and no other feature of the franchise relationship has generated more disputes, arbitration and litigation. When you combine the complexities of the typical franchise agreement, the regulation of franchise sales, the perception that big corporations (franchisors) are against the little guy (franchisees), and the substantial amounts of money invested, it presents a ready-made formula for legal disputes.

Attorneys are building lucrative careers helping franchisors and franchisees resolve these disputes. There are almost 2,000 members of the Forum on Franchising of the American Bar Association, and the number is growing.

LINES OF DEFENSE: CONTRACT TERMS AND PROTECTIVE LAWS

Franchisees do have some tools, however. The first is the franchise agreement.

The Contract

The first line of defense for the franchisee, and the fundamental legal guideline for any termination for the franchisor, is the franchise agreement. The contract spells out the conditions under which either party may terminate the relationship. Typically the franchisor will reserve the right to terminate on a series of grounds, some based on the franchisee's failure to cure a default after a written notice is delivered, and others based on incurable violations that lead to immediate or automatic termination.

If a termination occurs in violation of the terms of the franchise agreement, the franchisee has the right to bring a lawsuit against the franchisor under state law, seeking either a court order that the termination be stopped, or damages, or both.

State Relationship Laws

The franchise relationship laws are state laws that regulate terminations, nonrenewals and some franchising practices. There are 19 U.S. jurisdictions that have adopted some form of franchise relationship law. The typical relationship law requires that a franchisor have "good cause" before it moves to terminate a franchisee. This protects a franchisee from arbitrary or baseless terminations and creates a right to sue the franchisor for damages if the standard is violated.

These laws were adopted in response to perceived widespread abuses in franchising. Unjust terminations and the absence of renewal rights seemed to be depriving franchisees of the value of the businesses they had built. Other abuses, such as

no right of assignment, restricted right of association, unreasonable performance standards and encroachment (placing another unit too close to a franchised unit), also led to the legislative attempt to level the playing field.

If the franchisee has an argument that a state relationship law supersedes the contract, there may be an opportunity to seek court relief under that law. The state relationship laws allow termination where the franchisor has "good cause" to terminate the franchise. What is "good cause"?

GENERAL STANDARD. Where the state law does define the concept, "good cause" means "failure of the franchisee to comply substantially with the requirements imposed by the franchisor." In other words, it means a breach of the franchise agreement.

STATUTORY GROUNDS. Here are some of the additional statutory grounds where termination is lawful:

- Voluntary abandonment
- Criminal conviction of the franchisee on a charge related to the franchised business
- The franchisee's insolvency or declaration of bankruptcy
- Failure to pay the franchisor sums due
- Loss of the right to occupy the franchisee's business premises
- A material misrepresentation by the franchisee relating to the business
- Franchisee conduct that materially impairs the goodwill of the franchised business or the franchisor's trademark
- The franchisee's repeated noncompliance with the requirements of the franchise
- Imminent danger to public health or safety
- Failure to act in good faith and in a commercially reasonable manner
- A written agreement to terminate
- The franchisee's failure to comply with any law applicable to the operation of the franchise

- Government seizure of the franchised business or foreclosure by a creditor

DISPUTE RESOLUTION TOOLBOX

Obviously, there are lots of land mines on the path to franchise success. Given the strong interests and even stronger feelings among franchisors and franchisees over termination issues, resolving the inevitable disputes is something of an art form. As a franchisee, you need to understand the tools in your dispute resolution toolbox.

There are four distinct types of dispute resolution tools, and each of them can be used in the franchise context.

1. **Negotiation.** It has been said that negotiation and compromise are the oils that smooth the gears of business. Negotiation is the process of give and take that results in an acceptable solution for the parties involved. It takes a willingness to explore the possibilities with the other side and benefits from face-to-face discussions.

What could our franchisee, Jeff, negotiate for in his situation? Perhaps he could seek a royalty concession until his business is on its feet, or propose to sign a promissory note for the amount of royalty owing with an installment repayment schedule. Or he could begin negotiations to either sell the business to a more aggressive owner or to the franchisor, or close the business with both parties working to minimize the financial impact on Jeff. The principal advantage of an effective negotiation is that it quickly embraces creative, business-oriented resolutions. With clever businesspeople working in good faith, a negotiated resolution of a difficult situation offers the greatest hope for a solution that is fair to all involved.

2. **Mediation.** Mediation is professionally assisted negotiation. Where franchisor and franchisee are unable to negotiate a satisfactory solution, they may choose to bring into the discussion a professional mediator. This is someone trained in the mediation process and possibly experienced in the franchised business, who can use their skills to help the parties fashion a creative resolution. Often the most effective mediators are retired civil court judges. Mediation is nonbinding unless and until the parties find an agreeable solution; then they may commit to binding terms. Disputing parties can turn to the American Arbitration Association or national private organizations like JAMS for mediation services. Of particular interest to franchisors is the fact that a franchisor/franchisee dispute that is taken through a mediation process need not be disclosed in item 3 of the UFOC.

3. **Arbitration.** Arbitration is a more formal dispute resolution process that results in a final, nonappealable decision made by an arbitrator or a panel of three arbitrators. Think of arbitration as litigation without the courtroom. The result is just as binding on the parties as a court decision, and it must be disclosed in item 3 of the UFOC, just as with court cases.

 INsight

Franchise disputes can often be resolved if they are recognized and handled at an early moment in the dispute. Many franchisors express frustration that their contracts give them only one response to a serious problem—termination—and it is an atomic bomb. Mediation has become popular among franchisors and their lawyers as an effective technique for resolving business disputes without resorting to nuclear weaponry.

If your franchise agreement contains a provision that commits all disputes to binding arbitration, then you will not have the right to sue in a court of law. Except in rather extreme cases of fraud in the formation of the contract, the arbitration provision is almost always enforced by a court if challenged by one of the parties. The Federal Arbitration Act and court decisions of the past 50 years have created an extremely strong policy in favor of enforcing arbitration agreements. The policy reduces the crushing case load in our public courts and allows private parties to resolve their disputes privately. It is not entirely private, however, because disputes submitted to arbitration must be disclosed in item 3 of the franchisor's UFOC.

4. *Litigation.* A franchisee can always sue a franchisor in court to enforce the terms of the franchise agreement and try to stop a threatened termination. Of course, the franchisor can also sue to enforce the payment requirements or other terms of the franchise agreement. Of all the dispute resolution tools available to franchisors and franchisees, litigation is by far the most expensive and time-consuming.

One of your most important objectives in business is to avoid litigation, and to a lesser degree arbitration. Use these tools only as a last resort. It is a rare business owner who finds litigation satisfactory as a dispute resolution process.

SUMMARY NOTES

✓ In franchising, disputes happen.

✓ Your first line of defense as a franchisee is the franchise agreement. Look to the terms and conditions articulated in the contract, and ask your attorney for assistance.

✓ The second line of defense are specific standards adopted in the various franchise relationship laws.

✓ Dispute resolution techniques are important tools in your franchise business life. Familiarize yourself with the basic advantages and disadvantages of negotiation, mediation, arbitration and litigation.

Action PLAN

Talk to your attorney about alternate forms of dispute resolution, and ask how dispute resolution is addressed in the contract. Discuss with the franchisor how you both will handle a dispute if and when it arises.

CHAPTER 19

Renewing Your Franchise Rights

*S*AM REALIZED WITH A START ONE DAY THAT *his franchise agreement was due to expire in a year. "Where has the time gone?" he thought. The foreseeable arrival of the expiration date means that Sam has some decisions to make. "Do I want to sign on for another five years? If I don't re-up, what will happen to my business? If I have a buyer for my business walk in tomorrow, what do I have to sell? What hoops do I have to jump through to renew the franchise rights? Will the renewal contract be on the same terms as my current contract?"*

CONTRACT TERMS AND RENEWAL RIGHTS

The franchise agreement is a long-term arrangement that can last more than 20 years. Many of the earliest McDonald's franchise agreements from the 1960s and 1970s have completed their initial 20-year terms

and have been renewed for another 20 years. We suspect some of those may even be coming around again.

Think of a franchise agreement as you would a lease for real estate. The lease/franchise agreement grants the tenant/franchisee the right to use the company's property (the building/franchise system) for a period of years and then, when the time is up, the relationship ends. The tenant/franchisee moves out and both parties go their separate ways.

As with many commercial leases, the franchise agreement often grants the franchisee the conditional right to renew the relationship for another term of years, and the renewal right usually depends on meeting a short list of preconditions.

Before looking at those preconditions, it is necessary to understand the overall structure of the franchise agreement term. Current practice and conventional wisdom among fran-

79

chisors suggest that you are not likely to find a full 20-year term granted at the outset of the relationship. Why? Because things change too much over such a long period of time. When circumstances change, or when the franchise system itself changes, the franchisor does not want to be locked into contracts that cannot keep up with these changes.

For instance, say that in its first 15 franchise agreements, a franchisor designated that the franchisee had an exclusive territory covering a radius of 30 miles from the store location. But then things change: The franchise system expands at an astonishing rate so there are lots of new locations; the company develops smaller, mobile locations, for the service that can be flexible and nimble in following the market for the franchise product; the company develops a catalog to offer products directly to the customer; the company increases its standard royalty rate from 4 to 5 percent; the Internet is invented; and so on. The franchisor wants to be able to respond to such changes, so it structures the franchise agreement to be for a five-year initial term with the option to renew for three additional terms of five years each.

The effect of such a multiterm structure is to allow the franchisor to present the franchisee with a new form of franchise agreement every five years, and each form can adapt the system to the current market circumstances. The franchisor wants to reduce the size of the exclusive territory and modify the concept of exclusivity. The franchisor can make those changes only if the terms of renewal allow the changes. The renewal also gives the franchisee a chance to evaluate the continuing value of participating in the franchise program. The franchisee can always walk away at the date of expiration. Today terms are shorter, and there are more renewals than in the past. That's why contract renewal is an important topic for any franchisee looking at a new franchise agreement.

RENEWAL CONDITIONS

Renewal by the franchisee is typically articulated as a "right" or "option," but it always comes with conditions to be met. As with any legal contract, read the fine print to understand the steps necessary to satisfy the conditions and enjoy the full rights under the agreement.

What sorts of conditions will you encounter at renewal time? Here are the most common:

Give Written Notice to the Franchisor

This provision usually requires a written notice no less than x months and no more than y months prior to the date of expiration. It is designed this way so that renewal paperwork can be prepared and the franchisor can comply with state laws that may require a franchisor to give a certain amount of notice before failing to renew a franchise.

No Defaults and In Full Compliance

Look for a provision that says something like "You must not currently be in default under the franchise agreement and must have remained in compliance during its term." What if you cured a minor default in your first year—are you in full compliance?

Sign a New Form of Franchise Agreement

This is the most sensitive of the renewal conditions. Does the contract allow the substitution of a new form of agreement and advise you that the terms of the renewal agreement may be substantially different from the current agreement? That allows the franchisor to increase your royalty rates, alter your grant of territorial protections, and change other features that might directly affect the value of your business. Some franchise agreements specify that royalty rates and territories will not be changed but that other provisions may be changed on renewal. This is a step in the right direction. Be sure to go over this provision with your attorney.

Sign a Release of Claims

Why does the franchisor require you to release legal claims as a condition of renewal? It has everything to do with the company's opportunity to cut off problems that might have occurred during the expiring term. This way, the franchisor can begin the new term on a new slate without concern that it will renew the contract and then get hit with a lawsuit over something that occurred in the earlier term. One idea that is usually acceptable to the franchisor: Make the release mutual, so that the franchisor also releases any claims it may have against the franchisee under the expiring contract. Discuss this provision and any claims you may have under the current contract with your legal counsel.

Pay a Renewal Fee

A minority of franchise agreements require a renewal fee. Most don't, because franchisors generally want to impose no impediment to renewal. They want the franchisee to re-up. The franchisee represents an exceedingly valuable revenue stream for the franchisor, which would be expensive to replace if the franchisee did not renew.

Renewal is the strongest vote for the value of the franchise program that a franchisee can make. You will find that most franchisors generally want you to renew and will make renewal as easy and favorable as possible. A renewed franchise is far less expensive than finding, training and establishing a new franchisee.

The answers to most of the questions Sam was pondering at the beginning of this chapter should be answered in his franchise agreement and by the renewal policies of the particular franchise system. Many of the franchise relationship laws discussed in Chapter 16 apply the "good cause" standard to a franchisor's failure to renew a franchise agreement and may therefore preempt the renewal terms laid out in your franchise agreement. Check with your attorney to consider any applicable statutory renewal standards.

SUMMARY NOTES

✓ Like a commercial lease, a franchise agreement typically grants a term of years with conditional renewal rights.

✓ The duration of franchise agreement terms is getting shorter. This offers flexibility to franchisor and franchisee alike.

✓ The conditions imposed on renewal may include notice, contract compliance, a new form of franchise agreement, a release of claims and payment of a renewal fee.

Action PLAN

Keep these renewal concerns in mind when analyzing the initial franchise agreement. Ask the franchisor representative about renewal rights. Make sure your attorney is comfortable with the contract renewal language.

CHAPTER 20

International Franchising

ENRIQUE LIVES IN MEXICO CITY, BUT HE has traveled to the United States many times. He is excited about bringing an American restaurant concept to Mexico because his cosmopolitan city has never seen anything like it. Enrique contacted the franchisor in Minneapolis, thinking it was a long shot, and was surprised to find that the company has an active international franchising department with a Spanish-speaking specialist in Latin America. Things are looking up for Enrique.

THE GLOBALIZATION OF FRANCHISING

The global expansion of U.S. franchisors is one of the most interesting business success stories of the past 30 years. The American franchise concept has dispersed its various familiar brand names in large and small countries around the world at an astonishing rate.

 INsight

The history of international franchise expansion has not been—as they say in the United Kingdom—all beer and skittles. In the 1980s, McDonald's restaurants reported enormous difficulties in establishing their foods supply organization in foreign locations like Russia and Asia. Other franchisors have had their international expansion plans frustrated at huge expense by national laws restricting money transfer, trademark pirates and poorly enforced intellectual property laws, poor reception of their products because of cultural concerns, and communications problems.

McDonald's has been a global franchise expansion leader. It has established over 30,000 restaurants in almost 120 countries. The company says that 70 percent of its restaurants worldwide are franchised. The InterContinental Hotels Group, a franchisor of Holiday Inn hotels and other brands, has opened hotels in nearly 100 countries and territories.

Franchise regulation has been growing as well. The countries with a form of presale disclosure requirements for franchisors include Australia, Brazil, Canada (Ontario and Alberta), China, France, Indonesia, Italy, Japan, Malaysia, Mexico, South Africa, South Korea, Spain and the United States. Buy a franchise in one of these countries, and you will likely receive a presale disclosure statement presenting some of the key information you will need to evaluate the proposed franchise investment.

KEYS TO FOREIGN-BASED FRANCHISES

The international expansion of franchising has now come full circle as franchisors from other lands expand into the U.S. market. If you are interested in purchasing an international franchise, located in the U.S. market or another country, make sure you consider the following:

Find out if the company has taken steps to comply with all the laws on franchising in this country. Does the company have a UFOC or other disclosure statement? Is it complete? Has the company registered its offering in the U.S. registration states? If it has complied with these laws, that tells you the company has made a substantial investment in seeking successful franchisees in the U.S. market. If it has sidestepped these requirements, it is trying to cut some important corners, and you should be careful. You could be the next corner.

Is the program a regional offering or limited to one market? Will you receive rights for several markets or multiple states? Many companies new to the U.S. market divide up the country into separate, multistate regions so that penetrating such a huge commercial country is manageable.

How is the U.S. expansion going to be managed? Is there a regional manager or a master franchisee? Make sure you understand how the relationships are set up so that you know who will provide things like training and services. This may not be clear after you review the UFOC, so plan to discuss it with the sales representatives you meet.

One of the largest challenges of international franchising is effective communication. Will the company be communicating directly with the U.S. franchisees, or will it go through its regional managers/master franchisees? Find out if regular meetings will be held, and where. If they are overseas, be sure that you include these costs in your budgeting. Ask if the franchisor will assist with any meeting expenses.

Trademark protection can be a challenge for a franchisor from outside the United States. Be sure to check item 13 of the UFOC describing the U.S. registration status of the principal trademark. If it is not registered with the U.S. Patent and Trademark Office, exercise extreme caution and have your attorney check it out.

Is the cultural fit of the business a good one? Has the product/service been tested in the U.S. market, or are you the test? If you are the pioneer for this program, make sure you will not be too badly hurt if the product/service flops. It does happen. And it will happen regardless of the level of your enthusiasm and industry. Make sure your lawyer takes steps to protect you in the event the project goes south.

Don't shy away from an opportunity just because it is a franchisor from another country. The UFOC will tell you a lot about the company and how it is organized to service the U.S. market. Ask for the UFOC early on. If it does not exist, always proceed with extreme caution.

SUMMARY NOTES ────────────

✓ An international franchise can make an exciting investment, and more and more foreign-based franchisors tackle the U.S. market.

✓ Protect yourself by looking into the three key areas of an international relationship: control, communication and commitment.

✓ Find out how the market will be managed. Is there a regional manager or a U.S. master franchisee, or will the company manage its franchisees directly?

✓ Make sure that the program will be successful in the U.S. market. Foreign success does not always translate to the U.S. market.

Action PLAN

Contact and meet with managers responsible for franchising an international brand in your area. Locate other franchisees of the system in your area.

CHAPTER 21

Negotiating Franchise Agreements

*M**ARIA DISLIKES BUYING CARS FOR one reason: She hates having to negotiate aggressively on the price to get a fair deal. Now that she is buying a franchise, she has the same feeling as she gets closer to closing the transaction. Is it supposed to be like buying a car? Is she expected to negotiate? Maria wonders if she has enough information to negotiate on this purchase but remembers her dad always saying, "Everything is negotiable."*

The purchase of a franchise can be an intimidating process. Most Americans have never seen, let alone signed, a contract of such length and complexity as a typical business format franchise agreement. Signing one under any circumstances takes an act of courage and a leap of faith.

The lesson that Maria's dad taught her is always true in business, and it applies with equal force to franchises. Don't miss the opportunity to negotiate your purchase.

NEGOTIATING A FRANCHISE AGREEMENT

Signing a franchise agreement comes at the end of a lengthy process, highlighted by the delivery of a UFOC, promotional brochures, other system literature and personal interviews. Pressing for favorable contract terms may be the last thought on your mind. However, with some planning and understanding of the franchisor's position, you can cut a far better legal and financial deal.

WHY IS THE FRANCHISE AGREEMENT SO ONE-SIDED?

Franchise agreements have always been weighted in the franchisor's favor for one simple reason: The franchisor is not only your partner in this venture; it is the system-wide enforcer. It is in everyone's interests—the franchisor's, yours, and other franchisees'—that all franchisees operate in a manner that meets the highest system standards. In a retail system, all stores must be clean and well-run. If the store closest to you is dirty, slow or run-down, it affects your business directly and dramatically. Both units operate under the same trademark; if your neighbor is injuring the local reputation of the mark, you pay the price. Customers who have visited the dirty store will naturally assume that your store is in the same condition and stay away in droves. To paraphrase the great Yogi Berra, "If people don't want to come to your store, how are you going to stop them?"

As the system standards enforcer, the franchisor must reserve draconian enforcement rights in the franchise agreement. These may strike you as overbearing, but they are designed to allow the franchisor to take action if a franchisee's operation is subpar. In a sense, the enforcement provisions are there to protect you as well. When your neighbor's careless operation starts to hurt your business, you will be the first one to request that the franchisor do something to correct the situation. The franchisor had better have tough enforcement provisions in the franchise agreement, or it will be powerless to do anything. Negotiating some of these provisions will be tough.

UNDERSTANDING THE SELLER'S POSITION

Powerful financial forces drive the franchisor to complete the franchise transaction. It is difficult, time-consuming and expensive for a franchisor to locate a qualified franchisee. Selling a franchise is the ultimate hard sell; the sales cycle is measured in months, not days. Most franchisors devote tens of thousands of dollars a year to recruiting franchisees, and once a qualified applicant shows an interest, the franchisor is highly motivated to complete the sale. A new franchisee in the system means a stream of revenue that will last for years and continued growth for the system.

INsight

The power of your position is expressed in your attitude: You are interested in buying but not overeager. You let the seller know that you are interested, but there are lots of other investments you are evaluating (even if in your heart you know this is the one). Negotiation expert Herb Cohen says the best negotiating attitude says to the other side: "I care about making this commitment, but not that much."

Franchise sales representatives are often paid in whole or in part on commission. They are extremely motivated to see the transaction close; if you walk away, they lose money.

The point is that you are in a position of considerable power when it comes to negotiating a franchise agreement. Use that power to your advantage.

TAKE IT OR LEAVE IT?

How easy is it to negotiate the terms of a franchise agreement? While it complicates the life of franchisors, it is a well-known secret in the franchisor community that these contracts are negotiated all the time. You may hear from a franchisor that franchise law prohibits negotiation (it doesn't), or the company does not want to negotiate the terms that are offered to you, but you should not understand that to mean that the company *cannot* change its contract for you.

In fact, even the law of California—the toughest jurisdiction on negotiated changes in a franchise offering—allows franchisors to negotiate the terms of a franchise, but imposes a series of disclosure and registration obligations on a franchisor who changes the terms of its standard, registered offer. At the other end of the legal spectrum, the franchise law in the

Commonwealth of Virginia states that a franchise agreement may be voided by the franchisee within a short time if it is not negotiated by the franchisor.

A franchisor can change the standard contract terms for you if it chooses to make the changes.

NEGOTIATING RULES

Steven B. Wiley, a motivator and instructor of top corporate executives in matters of building partnerships and negotiating techniques, has some key suggestions for your negotiation. "First, there is no substitute for doing your homework," says Wiley. "Talk to other franchisees and find out where the company has shown flexibility in the past; talk to an experienced franchise lawyer; ask the franchisor for as much background information as you can. When you meet with the company to talk about the terms of the franchise agreement, you want to know as much as you can about that contract. You will be prepared, and you will not be thrown off balance when the give and take starts."

Keep in mind that you are about to commence a long-term business relationship with the franchisor. It is in your and the franchisor's best interests that both parties are happy with the deal struck and comfortable with any changes you agree to make. If you are not happy with any aspect of the contract, or there is a provision that you do not understand, you need to make your position known to the franchisor representatives.

According to Steve Wiley, the number-one negotiating principle to keep in mind is to "start high." "I teach corporate managers at the largest companies in the world that they need to start with an aggressive opening position," says Wiley. "Not because they should be greedy—rather, it is so that they can make concessions along the way of the discussion and work toward their target position. If you open at what you consider a fair position, you will have no room to maneuver when the other side asks you for something."

IN*sight*

Check item 5 of the UFOC ("Initial Franchise Fee"). If the initial franchise fee is not uniform, the company is required to disclose a formula or actual initial fees paid in the prior fiscal year. If the company cut some deals on the initial franchise fee, they will be at least mentioned here.

A prospective franchisee negotiating the franchise agreement should always be prepared to walk away from the deal. "This is the real strength of any negotiator," says Wiley. "Your neutral attitude says to the other side that you are not overeager to conclude the deal, that you want the deal but only if it is on reasonable terms. Even if you think this is the opportunity of a lifetime that will make you wealthy beyond your wildest dreams, never show it to the other side, or you will not conclude the deal on your terms."

FRANCHISORS' INFLEXIBLE POSITIONS

Many provisions of the franchise agreement can be negotiated, but there are a few areas where franchisors can be expected to dig in their heels:

Trademarks

As the owner of the trademarks, a franchisor will not be at all willing to water down their legal rights to control the display of the mark or protect the mark through enforcement actions. There is usually some wiggle room in the degree to which a franchisor is willing to stand behind the mark if the franchisee is attacked legally for its use of the mark. Look for language by which the company "indemnifies" (will pay) the franchisee for legal expenses incurred where the franchisee has properly used the marks and comes under legal attack by someone claiming infringement.

Royalty Rates

Conventional wisdom in the franchisor community suggests that all franchisees should pay the same rate of royalty whenever possible. This keeps everyone in the system on the same footing and avoids creating different classes of franchise citizens in the system. So if the standard royalty rate is set at 5 percent, don't expect the company to accept your suggestion that you pay a royalty rate of 4 percent.

There may be extenuating circumstances where you would be allowed to pay a lower rate for a period of time, but those are relatively rare. If you are taking over a store that has been poorly managed and the customer base is depleted, you may want to suggest a break in the royalty rate for your first year while you turn around the operation.

Assignment/Termination Controls

Franchisors will do their best to exercise control over the people who are allowed to own and operate their franchises. They have a direct interest; all those franchises are flying a flag owned by the company. If a weak operator is allowed to come in through a sale, or someone comes in who does not have the capital to run the business successfully, it creates a threat of business failure. That hurts the reputation of the system and indirectly all franchisees.

If an operator is not following the program or their operations are not clean or they are otherwise hurting the system's reputation, the company has little choice but to take corrective steps. For these reasons, franchisors are not likely to give on suggested changes to the assignment or termination provisions.

FRANCHISORS' FLEXIBLE POSITIONS

Franchisors tend to have more flexibility in other areas of the contract:

Initial Fee

The franchisor has great flexibility when it comes to the initial fee. If it is set at $30,000, you may be able to argue for a reduction of that amount or a plan by which you defer payment over time. Try suggesting that you pay $15,000 upfront and the balance over the first 18 months of your operation of the business.

There may be some resistance to this concept, of course. Perhaps the company needs the upfront fee to pay a commission to the broker or for its own operating expenses. Franchisors are also reluctant to make any changes that require additional disclosure. If there are variations in the initial fee, the company may have to disclose that fact in item 5 of its UFOC. If the company offers financing, it may be required to disclose those terms as well as in item 10. Ask anyway; it's your money, after all.

Territorial Rights

This is ticklish in some systems, but well worth exploring in negotiations. What are the dimensions of the territory you are granted? Can you request an expansion of that area or ask for an option right on an adjoining territory? Perhaps you could request additional time and territorial protection during the first few years of your franchise. It may take a bit of creativity on your part, but it is well worth exploring if there are ways that you can structure the territorial rights to your own needs.

Marketing Contributions

This topic, and the franchisor's flexibility on it, will be determined by the type and the circumstances of the business. You may suggest that a local marketing fee be waived because of the unusual location: If you are building a retail store on the grounds of a popular theme park, you should not be paying marketing fees to increase foot traffic to your location. Your rent rate may be higher precisely because you have a premium location where foot traffic is delivered by the park's own promotion.

Never forget the fundamental impulse of good negotiators: It never hurts to ask. Build a win-win franchise agreement going in, and your relationship will be that much stronger for the long term.

SUMMARY NOTES

✓ Get creative when buying a franchise or business opportunity. Propose price reductions and payment terms that fit your needs.

✓ When you first read a franchise agreement, it may strike you as one-sided. But there are reasons for that. There are other players here; this is not merely a two-party agreement.

✓ Position yourself for negotiation. Gather as much information as you can about deals the franchisor has granted to others.

✓ It's legal in all states to negotiate a franchise agreement.

✓ Remember some of the key rules of negotiation: do your homework, "start high," be willing to walk on the deal, and "it never hurts to ask."

✓ There are some areas (initial fees, territory, advertising contributions) where a franchisor is more likely to give than other areas (trademark, royalties and transfer rights).

Action PLAN

Become a good negotiator. Take a seminar on negotiation skills, or head to the library or the bookstore for a book on negotiation, such as the classic *You Can Negotiate Anything* by Herb Cohen (Bantam Books).

CHAPTER 22

Working with
Lawyers and Accountants

*B*OBBY IS A PRO AT COACHING HIGH *school kids but is lost when it comes to reading a balance sheet or understanding dense legal language in a contract. He had what he considered an excellent franchise investment opportunity but knew he needed some professional help. Could he afford it? Could he afford not to get help?*

USING LEGAL SERVICES

Anyone buying a franchise today is well-advised to retain the services of an experienced attorney to review the franchise agreement and any related contracts. Business opportunity buyers, depending on the size of the investment, may need an attorney's help as well. The objection is right on the tip of your tongue, isn't it? "How can I afford a lawyer? I am putting this business together on a shoestring as it is. A lawyer's going to cost me a fortune."

In the first place, using the services of an attorney need not cost a fortune, and you can work out in advance what fees are likely to be involved. Most lawyers still charge for their services by the hour, but many are willing to set a quoted fee or agree to a cap on the fee for a simple project like the review of a franchise agreement and UFOC. If it takes a lawyer two hours to review the document and another hour to meet with you to discuss

 IN*sight*

Attorneys know their clients are concerned about legal fees and generally encourage discussion of the subject at the first meeting. Gone are the days when attorneys thought it unprofessional to discuss money.

it, that suggests a legal fee—assuming a $150 hourly rate—that does not exceed $500. Hiring an attorney is like buying insurance. And as insurance goes, $500 is not expensive at all. You can expect to purchase casualty insurance, health coverage for your employees, and unemployment compensation insurance that will put the cost of your modest attorney fees to shame.

What can you expect to receive for your legal fees? At a minimum you want to hear from your learned counsel whether there are any provisions in the proposed contract that run distinctly against your interests. You also want to know about provisions that put your investment in a precarious position. For instance, what if the franchisor reserves the right to terminate the relationship with no advance notice if you fail to follow the standards in the operating manuals? Your lawyer should advise you that this is way too broad and threatens your business in an unacceptable manner. They may suggest that language be added that gives you the right to receive at least 30 days' written notice of the infraction and an opportunity to cure it without threatening your entire investment in the program.

You also want to hear from your lawyer if there are any other aspects of the franchise documents that cause concern or call for further investigation. If you live in one of the several states requiring a franchisor to register under a franchise law, your lawyer should make the phone call to check on the company's status. Ask your attorney to tell you if your state's law protects you from an arbitrary or groundless termination by the franchisor. They should be able to give you a copy of any such law.

DO YOU NEED A SPECIALIST?

In this age of professional specialization, how do you find a lawyer experienced enough to be of help reviewing a franchise agreement? Referrals are by far the most effective way to locate the right lawyer. As you meet franchise owners in the system you are investigating, ask them who they use. Every state has

a lawyer referral system you can look up in your phone book. Ask your friends and business acquaintances for referrals. You don't want the name of a cousin's brother-in-law who just graduated from law school in another state, but you do want to hear about lawyers a person has used and knows are experienced. Get familiar with the *Martindale-Hubbell Law Directory*, available in every law library and most public libraries, and online (www.martindale.com). This directory lists lawyers by state and town, and many entries include a short description of their professional background. It even offers a rating system of lawyers.

USING ACCOUNTING SERVICES

The other professional assistance you should consider hiring is a competent accountant. Accountants are worth their weight in Big Mac sandwiches if you are planning to go into business and are evaluating a franchise investment.

First and foremost, your accountant can put together a detailed projection for your business and help you consider how to finance the total investment. The projection will tell you a lot about the business. It should show where your break-even points will be, the number of customers you will need in order to generate your revenue, and the amount of your investment plus financing costs. It will also give you an idea of the return you can expect on your investment.

In short, your accountant can help you decide whether you would be better off financially buying the franchise or getting a job and putting your money in treasury bonds.

Your accountant can also look over the franchisor's three years of audited financial statements contained in the UFOC. These tell you a lot about the staying power of the company. Will it be there for the long haul? Do the statements show healthy growth or stagnating losses? Your accountant should be able to provide a professional opinion about the standing of the franchisor.

A full review by a CPA can be expensive, running into a few thousand dollars rather quickly. Talk to your accountant about what you need and what it's going to cost. Then figure out a way to do it.

WHAT TO ASK YOUR LEGAL AND ACCOUNTING ADVISORS

Some Great Questions for Your Attorney

Plan to explore these basic topics with your attorney, and add to the list whatever you think is appropriate for the franchise you are reviewing:

- How does this franchise agreement compare to others you have reviewed?
- Are there any provisions in this agreement that I should not agree to under any circumstances ("deal breakers")? Do you have any suggested changes for the agreement, and would they be accepted by the franchisor?
- Have you checked with state authorities to confirm that the company is registered to sell franchises or business opportunities in this state?
- How do the termination provisions stack up under this state's franchise laws or case law on termination? What exactly are my transfer rights under the agreement?
- Do any of the litigation or arbitration cases disclosed in item 3 concern you?
- What protections do I need when buying this business opportunity? Should I defer payments or otherwise structure the transaction? Are there any surety bonds, escrow arrangements or trust accounts in place in this state to protect buyers of this program?

Some Great Questions for Your Accountant/CPA

- What is the seller's net worth? How does this amount relate to the size of my total investment in the franchise? Should I be concerned about it?
- Can you tell from the financial statement whether the seller's business is profitable? How would you describe the seller's financial health?
- Does the financial statement show the average annual royalty payment received from a franchisee? Can we extrapolate any average sales figures from that?
- Is there a surety bond, escrow account or deferred payment in place in this state? Is there another entity that guarantees the obligations of the seller for this program?
- How do the item 7 figures strike you compared to other small businesses you have advised? Do they look reasonable?
- What is the break-even point for this business? What revenues will I need to cover my expenses and make the franchise or business opportunity profitable?

SUMMARY NOTES

✓ Ask franchisees you meet who they use for legal services. Do your research and find a good lawyer with experience representing small businesses.

✓ Think of legal and accounting expenses as part of your insurance costs.

✓ Get organized in your use of legal and accounting services. Know what questions you want answered in the preliminary review process.

Action PLAN

Interview a few attorneys and accountants to determine their individual styles, experience and capabilities. Be sure to confirm in advance that you will not be billed for the interview.

CHAPTER 23

Questions for Franchisees

NANCY KNEW SHE NEEDED TO TALK TO some franchisees in the ham store business she was investigating but was a bit intimidated. Was she imposing on them? Would she offend these experienced businesspeople with her intrusive call? What would she say?

THE KEY TO YOUR RESEARCH

Current franchisees are without a doubt the best source of information you will find on the benefits, drawbacks and strengths of the business you are investigating. They can also generally provide some great insights and advice. It takes a bit of gumption to approach a business owner, but you should not hesitate. Here are some thoughts on the approach.

First, check out the business as a customer. If it is a retail operation, go to the unit, sit for a while, and observe the operation. Return to do this again during different times of the day. Learn to be a keen observer on these visits: Count customers as they come in the door, observe how the employees handle their jobs (what do they say at the counter when they greet a customer?), note the amount of the purchases made by customers to get a rough estimate of the "average ticket" spent in the store, and observe what you can of the work going on out back.

The next step is to make arrangements to talk to the owner. Remember that retail business owners are extremely busy at certain times of the day. It's best to call ahead and find a good time to visit. When the owner does meet with you, be sensitive to the time you spend. If you requested a 20-minute interview, stick to it. If it is a busy lunch hour at a restaurant, you may want to find a better time of day.

FRANCHISE QUESTIONS

It also helps to have a set of questions prepared. Don't try to wing it. Here is a checklist of franchise questions to ask:

- Is the training program worthwhile? Did it leave you well-prepared to run this business?
- Has the franchisor's support been steady? Are they there when you need them?
- What is the culture of the franchise system? Are franchisees friendly with one another? Is it encouraging or discouraging to be with the franchisor?
- Is the business seasonal? What are the strongest and weakest times of the year?
- Does the franchisor provide continuing training?
- Is the market for this business a strong one? Is it growing or slowing?
- Is there a franchisee association or council? Do franchisees have a real role in the franchisor's decision-making process?
- Did you have a good year last year? Do you recall what your gross sales were? Will this year be stronger or weaker?
- How is product supply arranged for franchisees? Does it work well?
- What questions do you wish you had asked going into your franchise investment?
- Knowing what you now know, would you buy this franchise again?

 IN*sight*

Most franchise owners will discuss the performance of their business once you establish a rapport with them. They need to know you are not a competitor or a potential competitor but someone serious about making the same investment decision they made. Most want to help.

Don't hesitate to take notes during your conversations. It tells the franchisees you value their words and experience. And resist the urge to get too chatty or argumentative. Your objective is to gather information. If you hear comments that concern you, by all means follow up with the franchisor.

SUMMARY NOTES

✓ When approaching a franchisee, be respectful of time and business demands.
✓ Visit the business as a customer.
✓ Prepare a set of questions to discuss. Don't wing it.
✓ Take notes, and follow up with the franchisor if you hear answers that concern you.

Action PLAN

Create a list of owner questions for each franchise you investigate. Make full notes after each interview and drop them in your file.

CHAPTER 24

Skill Sets of the Successful Franchisee

*CAROLYN PLANS TO BUY A RETAIL BUSI-
ness because she has always dreamed
about having a stream of customers
whom she pleases with scrumptious
teas, cakes and other treats. She enjoys meeting her customers face to face and looks forward to owning her own shop. She wonders
what else she will need to know to be successful. Are there skills that she could learn that
will help in her business?*

Carolyn is asking the right questions,
because all successful small-business owners
develop a distinct skill set. At the heart of any
franchised business are some basic elements
of business operation and business development that must be mastered. Falter on these
basics, and your business may have some serious problems. The most successful business
owners develop these skill sets and drill them
into their employees.

THE ART OF THE SALE

Business is selling. All businesses boil down
quickly to this realization; franchises are no
exception. It does not matter whether you are
a junior manager in the world's largest organization or the owner of your own small business; the engine of both businesses is driven
by sales activity.

Remember this basic truth of business:
"Nothing happens in business until someone,
somewhere makes a sale."

It follows that your key to success is to
become a student of the sale; become an
expert in the process and the techniques used
by the best salespeople. Try to learn the basic
rules for presenting features and benefits,
overcoming objections and closing techniques. Park yourself in the business book
section of your local library, and crawl
through a few books on selling. There are
dozens of titles available. Drink them in.

COUNTER MAGIC

One of the most fascinating aspects of retail business is the study of what happens at the counter, that magic place where the front-line representatives of your business meet your customers. When I say the "counter" of your business, I mean it literally and metaphorically. All businesses meet customers, whether it is on the telephone, over the Internet, or at the customer's residence or place of business. In a traditional retail business, it will literally be a countertop at your location. Successful franchise organizations have pioneered and perfected the techniques at the counter that can have enormous payoffs in business.

No one has taught us more than the great Ray Kroc of McDonald's restaurants. He insisted that counter workers greet all customers with a smile and a cheery "Welcome to McDonald's!" The company reinforced the message with advertising showing the warm smiles of perky counter people welcoming you to McDonald's. "We love to see you smile."

Kroc also drove billions of dollars in sales, and propelled his organization to prominence, by teaching all counter people to say six simple words

to every customer: "Would you like fries with that?" The resulting sales figures changed the landscape of American business.

Whatever franchised business you manage, study what is happening at the counter. Put your training resources to work on the exchange. Make sure your employees follow your example and stick to your counter procedures. Study and watch their performance and try new ideas. Keep your counter fresh, enthusiastic and fun, and your customers will come back time and again for more.

YOUR PROFITS ARE IN THE DETAILS

One thundering lesson of business ownership is just how small is the portion of gross revenue that actually falls into your pocket as profit. These small "margins" can represent vast fortunes, of course, when a business is run on a modestly large scale. Even at a large scale, though, the details determine whether the business comes out on the profitable side of the small margins or on the loss side of the profit/loss measure.

You have no choice but to become a student of the details of your franchised business. A few cents break on the price of your wholesale inventory, the lower costs of office supplies when purchased in bulk, the small incremental costs of condiments, managing the costs of labor—these details make all the difference.

BECOME A BEAN COUNTER

Money is the language of business, and accountants are the interpreters of the language. As a business owner, you must master the language and become conversant in balance sheets and monthly operations statements. If problems are brewing in your business, they will show up first in the monthly numbers. You will get to know intimately your percentages of food costs, labor, administrative costs and gross profit. This takes some study, so cozy up to your favorite accountant and

IN*sight*

Pete and Laura Wakeman, founders of Great Harvest Bread Co., a whole-wheat bakery franchise, developed an entire marketing program based on their teachings of what should happen at the customer counter, which is vital to all Great Harvest bakeries today. Their counter techniques teach franchisees and their employees the value of smiling and generosity of spirit, and ways to personally connect with the customer.

tell them that you think this is the beginning of a beautiful friendship.

BE A SKILLED NEGOTIATOR

It often surprises people coming from a job into business ownership just how much of small-business dealings are subject to a fluid marketplace, where prices and terms are determined by the give and take of negotiation. It takes a spot of courage to ask for a better price or payment terms or faster delivery, but it gives you the edge you need in your business. Your suppliers and business customers expect many aspects of the sale to be negotiated, so be prepared to jump in.

INsight

In all negotiations, know beforehand how long you will go before you stop negotiating, and what you consider your target. When opening your discussion, "start high" and then be prepared to make concessions as the other side (starting low) pulls you down toward your target endpoint. Asking for more than you will settle for will not insult anyone. It will leave you some room to make concessions to the other side. That will put you in the give and take of business—right where you need to be.

PEOPLE MANAGEMENT

Small-business ownership is little more than the management of employees. Keep them happy, well-paid and motivated, and your business will be on solid ground. Give no personal attention, underpay, and discourage them with a punishing attitude, and you will experience high turnover and low productivity. Given typically

low margins in small businesses, this can make the difference between a profitable business and a troubled one.

BUILD AN ORGANIZATION

It's been said that the owner does not build a business; they build an organization of people and the organization builds the business. Think about building a team of talented people, look for the best you can find, and try to stay out of their way as they build your business.

BE AN A+ FRANCHISEE

If your business is a franchise, follow the rules of the system. Part of being a top-performing franchised business is full and careful compliance with all aspects of the franchise program. That means paying royalties on time, showing up for meetings and taking educational opportunities as they come along. Be a leader among franchise owners who do their best to promote the brand. Not only is this good business, but it will also add to the value of your business and may open opportunities down the road for expansion. The franchisor will naturally look to its A+ franchisees when new opportunities present themselves.

COLLECTING MONEY

The biggest challenge you face as a small-business owner is the collection of money owed to you. For all businesses, successful collection is a combination of smart routine business practice and persistence.

When do you know you have a collection problem? Here are the symptoms:

- An unacceptably high level of accounts receivable
- No office policy on collections
- Too many bad checks
- No information on the customer who pays on credit (including by check!)
- An inability to be decisive and move promptly

against the deadbeat

- No way to recover the expenses associated with debt collection, such as attorney's fees, interest and late charges

No one likes collection problems. If you are new to business, the reluctance of your customers to pay their bills can be a surprise. After all, you have always paid your mortgage, utility bills, credit card statements and household expenses on time. Why can't your customers do the same?

Often the reason they do not pay in a timely fashion is *you*. Your routine credit extension practices, the information you gather on your customers, and the way you respond to slow payment all dictate the success you have at getting paid.

The best advice is to create a written policy statement that details exactly how credit will be extended or how a new customer account will be set up. Give a copy of the policy to the customer. The policy should spell out all credit procedures and collection policies. For your internal use, develop form letters that you use when a customer is late, and prepare to respond immediately.

Use some form of credit application that gathers this basic information about the account: name, address, telephone number (work and residence), Social Security number (this is essential), place of employment, bank account information, and property ownership information (automobiles and homes). If you are extending credit to a corporation, be sure to obtain the formal corporate name, the date and state of incorporation and the employer identification number. Without this basic information, collections can be a nightmare. The following are some tips for smart collection practices:

Don't Accept Bad Checks

Examine all checks carefully. A quick way to spot a forged check is to look for the perforations. Most forged checks are produced on plain paper

stock with no perforated edges. Real check paper stock allows the check to be removed from a perforated edge. Bank tellers are trained to look for this distinctive feature.

Is the date correct? If the date is old (generally more than three or four weeks) or if it has been postdated, do not accept it.

Is the amount properly stated? Does the numerical figure agree with the written dollar amount? If the number, the written amount or the payee (you) is illegible, written over or hard to read in any way, do not take the check.

Be careful accepting a two-party check. A two-party check is made to one person, and that person offers to endorse the check to you. Unless you know both parties, you run a risk that the original maker will stop payment on the check.

Look out for checks that show a low sequence number. This indicates a recently opened account since most banks begin numbering a new checking account at #101. Just be more cautious when the number is low.

Do Not Put Off Collecting on the Debt

The longer you wait to take action, the more difficult it will be to collect on an overdue account. An account receivable that is more than 90 days old should be turned over for collection, either to a collection agency, which will handle the matter for a hefty percentage of the outstanding bill, or to your attorney.

Use a Credit Agreement

You cannot collect interest, late fees or attorney's fees without the written agreement of the customer. A credit agreement also spells out the terms of the credit being extended and shows you take this account, the credit and collections seriously.

SUMMARY NOTES
✓ Running your business is the ultimate chal-

lenge. Brush up on the skills that are essential to all business operations: master the art of the sale, manage details, count beans, negotiate, manage people effectively, build an organization, be an A+ franchisee, and collect the money you are owed.

Action PLAN

Take a course at a local college, university or business school to learn more about areas of business that are mystifying to you.

CHAPTER 25

Make it Happen

*S*EAN HAS TOYED WITH THE IDEA OF START-*ing his own business for more than five years. Since he was a boy, he has dreamed of building a successful business. He works up to a point of getting serious about an opportunity and then backs off and stays in the comfortable routine of his job. He is beginning to wonder if he will ever make the commitment.*

Starting a business, whether it is an independent one or a franchise, takes an enormous amount of initiative. If you have not done it before, it is easy not to start. That's Sean's problem. There are mental obstacles at every turn. You can fall into a trap of indecision, where you constantly search for the exact business of your dreams but never seem to find it. People you love and respect can talk you out of it. You can be discouraged by the doom and gloom of the popular press. You can decide that your route to wealth is working your way up to middle management. There are a thousand reasons not to start.

But you know in your heart that the world rewards courage and persistence.

So start! Make that call. Contact your support team. Start lining up your money resources. Go to that trade show. Ask those questions, and present yourself in the finest light possible to your new business contacts.

You will be pleasantly surprised at how your hard work and persistence pays off, and the interesting places your initiative can lead you. If the words in this book help you take that first step, then you have made my day.

Good luck in your new business!

Action **PLAN**

There is no substitute for taking action. No amount of dreaming, planning or talking takes its place. If you want to be in business for yourself, you must make it happen. Take action today.

Ultimate Low-Cost Franchise Directory

Understanding the Directory

SECTION TWO OF OUR BOOK DETAILS THE basic start-up information of 310 franchise opportunities with minimum total investments of less than $50,000. Use this information as a first step toward buying a franchise of your own.

This directory is not intended to endorse, advertise or recommend any particular franchise(s). It is solely a research tool you can use to compare franchise operations. You should always conduct your own independent investigation before you invest money in a franchise. If you haven't already, make sure you read Section One of this book.

KEY TO THE LISTINGS
Franchise 500® ranking

As an additional research tool, we've included the rankings of companies in *Entrepreneur* magazine's 2005 Franchise 500®.

Rankings are based on objective factors, including financial stability of the system, growth rate and size of the system, years in business, length of time franchising, start-up costs, litigation, percentage of terminations and whether the company provides financing. For more information regarding the methodology used in these rankings, go to www.entrepreneur.com/franchise500.

Financial rating

$$$$: Exceeded our standards

$$$: Met all our standards

$$: Met most of our standards

$: Met our minimal standards

0: Did not meet our minimal standards

An important step in researching a franchise opportunity is determining the financial strength of the company. If a franchise company is in a weak financial condition, it could raise the risk levels for your investment.

For our financial ratings, based on a financial analysis of the 2005 Franchise 500®, we examined, among other things, liquidity ratios, debt to net worth, revenue or sales volume, and profitability. This information was taken from the financial information provided in the companies' Uniform Franchise Offering Circulars (UFOCs).

We strongly suggest that, when researching a franchise, you have your accountant read the financial statements included in the UFOC and ask for a more detailed opinion of the financial condition of the company.

Franchise units

Besides providing data on the number of units in a system, we tell you where the company's current units are concentrated and where the company wants to expand this year. Here you'll also learn whether the franchise can be run from home or from a kiosk.

Exclusive territories

The majority of franchise companies offer exclusive territories to their franchisees. Territory size typically is based on population size or by geographic area.

Absentee ownership

Many franchise companies require their franchisees to be hands-on owners. Here you can see whether absentee ownership is allowed.

Costs

Total cost: the initial investment necessary to open the franchise. This amount includes costs for equipment, location, leasehold improvements, initial supplies, business licenses, signage, working capital as well as the initial franchise fee. We also indicate which franchises offer low-cost options to existing entrepreneurs only.

Franchise fee: a lump sum payment made at the time the franchise agreement is signed. This fee generally covers the franchisor's cost of recruiting franchisees and of initial services like site location and training.

Royalty fee: typically a monthly fee paid by the franchisee to the franchisor, which is either calculated as a percentage of the franchisee's gross sales or on a flat-fee basis.

Term of agreement: the length of time the franchisee is granted the right to operate under the franchise system. When the time is up, most franchise companies offer a right to renew either for a fee or for free.

Franchisees required to buy multiple units? While many franchise companies encourage franchisees to buy more than one unit at a time, there are franchisors that require multiple franchise ownership.

Financing

Types of financing provided by the franchisor are listed under the "in-house" heading.

When the franchisor has developed a relationship with an outside lender to provide financing to its franchisees, the types of financing are listed under the "3rd party" heading.

Qualifications, Training, Business support, Marketing support

We provide additional information on these factors to help you make an informed decision.

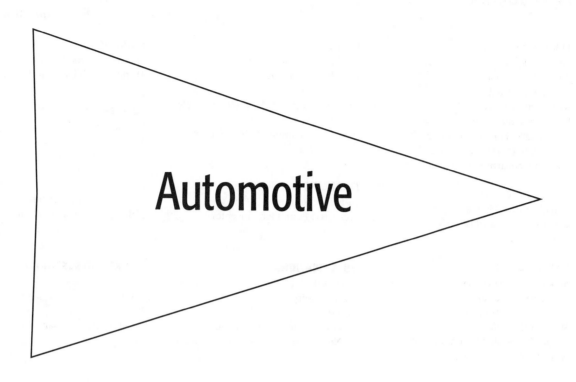

ALTRACOLOR SYSTEMS

Ranked #480 in Entrepreneur Magazine's 2005 Franchise 500   *Financial rating: $$$*

113 23rd St.
Kenner, LA 70062
Ph: (800)727-6567
Fax: (504)471-0144
www.altracolor.com
Mobile auto painting & plastic repair
Began: 1988, Franchising since: 1991
Headquarters size: 5 employees
Franchise department:
    Info not provided

U.S. franchises: 60
Canadian franchises: 0
Other foreign franchises: 0
Company-owned: 0
Units concentrated in all U.S.

Seeking: All U.S.
Seeking in Canada? No
Exclusive territories? Yes
Homebased option? Yes
Kiosk option? No
Employees needed to run franchise: 1
Absentee ownership? No

COSTS
Total cost: $37.5K-53.95K
Franchise fee: $8K-19.95K
Royalty fee: $95/wk.
Term of agreement: 15 years renewable
    at no charge
Franchisees required to buy multiple
    units? No

FINANCING
In-house: Equipment
3rd-party: None

QUALIFICATIONS
Cash liquidity: $11.7K

TRAINING
At headquarters: 1 week
At franchisee's location: 1 week
Additional training as needed

BUSINESS SUPPORT
Newsletter
Meetings
Toll-free phone line
Internet
Security/safety procedures
Field operations/evaluations

MARKETING SUPPORT
Marketing materials

DENT DOCTOR

Financial rating: $$$

11301 W. Markham
Little Rock, AR 72211
Ph: (501)224-0500
Fax: (501)224-0507
www.dentdoctor.com
Paint-free dent repair
Began: 1986, Franchising since: 1990
Headquarters size: 6 employees
Franchise department: 3 employees

U.S. franchises: 29
Canadian franchises: 1
Other foreign franchises: 1
Company-owned: 3

Seeking: All U.S.
Seeking in Canada? Yes
Exclusive territories? Yes
Homebased option? No
Kiosk option? No
Employees needed to run franchise: 3
Absentee ownership? Yes

COSTS
Total cost: $47.5K-84.9K
Franchise fee: $9.9K-19.9K+
Royalty fee: 6%
Term of agreement: 10 years renewable
   at no charge
Franchisees required to buy multiple
   units? No

FINANCING
In-house: None
3rd-party: Equipment, inventory,
   startup costs

QUALIFICATIONS
Net worth: $75K
Cash liquidity: $10K
Experience:
   General business experience
   No automotive experience required

TRAINING
At headquarters: 4 weeks
At franchisee's location: 4 weeks

BUSINESS SUPPORT
Newsletter
Meetings
Toll-free phone line
Grand opening
Internet
Security/safety procedures
Field operations/evaluations
Purchasing cooperatives

MARKETING SUPPORT
Co-op advertising
Ad slicks
Regional marketing
Local advertising plan

MARS INT'L. INC.

Financial rating: $$$

2001 E. Division, #101
Arlington, TX 76001
Ph: (800)909-6277
Fax: (800)230-2859
www.marsinternational.com
Cosmetic automotive reconditioning
Began: 1987, Franchising since: 1998
Headquarters size: 17 employees
Franchise department: 5 employees

U.S. franchises: 250
Canadian franchises: 0
Other foreign franchises: 0
Company-owned: 0
Units concentrated in all U.S.

Seeking: All U.S.
Seeking in Canada? No
Exclusive territories? No
Homebased option? Yes
Kiosk option? No
Employees needed to run franchise: 1
Absentee ownership? Yes

COSTS
Total cost: $49K
Franchise fee: $15K
Royalty fee: 10%
Term of agreement: 5 years renewable
   at 50% of franchise fee
Franchisees required to buy multiple
   units? No

FINANCING
In-house: None
3rd-party: Equipment, franchise fee,
   inventory, startup costs

QUALIFICATIONS
Experience:
   General business experience

TRAINING
At headquarters: 2 weeks
At franchisee's location: 2 weeks

BUSINESS SUPPORT
Newsletter
Meetings
Toll-free phone line
Internet
Security/safety procedures

MARKETING SUPPORT
Co-op advertising
Ad slicks
National media campaign
Online business development center

AFFILIATED CAR RENTAL LC

Ranked #119 in Entrepreneur Magazine's 2005 Franchise 500   *Financial rating: $$$$*

96 Freneau Ave., #2
Matawan, NJ 07747
Ph: (800)367-5159
Fax: (732)290-8305
www.sensiblecarrental.com
Car rentals
Began: 1987, Franchising since: 1987
Headquarters size: 7 employees
Franchise department: 7 employees

U.S. franchises: 245
Canadian franchises: 0
Other foreign franchises: 0
Company-owned: 0

Seeking: All U.S.
Seeking in Canada? No
Exclusive territories? Yes
Homebased option? No
Kiosk option? No
Employees needed to run franchise: 2-3
Absentee ownership? Yes

COSTS
Total cost: $46.5K-69.5K
Franchise fee: $6K-10.8K+
Royalty fee: Varies
Term of agreement: Perpetual
Franchisees required to buy multiple
    units? No

FINANCING
In-house: Franchise fee
3rd-party: Equipment, inventory

QUALIFICATIONS
Net worth: Varies
Cash liquidity: Varies
Experience:
    General business experience

TRAINING
At headquarters: 2 days
At franchisee's location: 2 days

BUSINESS SUPPORT
Newsletter
Meetings
Toll-free phone line
Internet
Security/safety procedures
Field operations/evaluations
Purchasing cooperatives

MARKETING SUPPORT
Co-op advertising
Ad slicks

BATES MOTOR HOME RENTAL NETWORK INC.

Current financial data not available

3690 S. Eastern Ave., #220
Las Vegas, NV 89109
Ph: (702)737-9050
Fax: (702)737-9149
www.batesintl.com
Motor home rentals
Began: 1973, Franchising since: 1995
Headquarters size: 5 employees
Franchise department: 3 employees

U.S. franchises: 16
Canadian franchises: 2
Other foreign franchises: 0
Company-owned: 0

Seeking: All U.S.
Seeking in Canada? No
Exclusive territories? Yes
Homebased option? Yes
Kiosk option? No
Employees needed to run franchise:
    Info not provided
Absentee ownership? Yes

COSTS
Total cost: $33.8K-250K
Franchise fee: $17K-35K
Royalty fee: 8%
Term of agreement: 10 years renewable
    at $1K
Franchisees required to buy multiple
    units? No

FINANCING
In-house: Accounts receivable,
    franchise fee
3rd-party: None
Other financing: Rent, phones, local
    advertising

QUALIFICATIONS
Net worth: $150K
Cash liquidity: $50K
Experience:
    General business experience
    Computer skills

TRAINING
At headquarters: 3 days

BUSINESS SUPPORT
Newsletter
Meetings
Internet
Security/safety procedures
Purchasing cooperatives

MARKETING SUPPORT
Co-op advertising

PRICELESS RENT-A-CAR

Ranked #485 in Entrepreneur Magazine's 2005 Franchise 500   *Financial rating: $$$$*

10324 S. Dolfield Rd.
Owings Mills, MD 21117
Ph: (800)662-8322
Fax: (410)581-1566
www.pricelesscar.com
Car rentals & leasing
Began: 1997, Franchising since: 1997
Headquarters size: 10 employees
Franchise department: 2 employees

U.S. franchises: 120
Canadian franchises: 0
Other foreign franchises: 0
Company-owned: 0

Seeking: All U.S.
Seeking in Canada? Yes
Exclusive territories? Yes
Homebased option? No
Kiosk option? No
Employees needed to run franchise: 2
Absentee ownership? Yes

COSTS
Total cost: $37.2K-216K
Franchise fee: $8K-26K
Royalty fee: $30/car/mo.
Term of agreement: 10 years renewable
    at no charge
Franchisees required to buy multiple
    units? Outside U.S. only

FINANCING
No financing available

QUALIFICATIONS
Experience:
    General business experience
    Marketing skills

TRAINING
At headquarters: 1 week
At franchisee's location: Varies

BUSINESS SUPPORT
Newsletter
Meetings
Toll-free phone line
Grand opening
Internet
Lease negotiations
Security/safety procedures
Field operations/evaluations
Purchasing cooperatives

MARKETING SUPPORT
Co-op advertising
Ad slicks
National media campaign
Regional marketing

RENT-A-WRECK

Ranked #370 in Entrepreneur Magazine's 2005 Franchise 500   *Financial rating: $$$$*

10324 S. Dolfield Rd.
Owings Mills, MD 21117
Ph: (410)581-5755
Fax: (410)581-1566
www.rentawreck.com
Auto rentals & leasing
Began: 1970, Franchising since: 1977
Headquarters size: 35 employees
Franchise department: 7 employees

U.S. franchises: 350
Canadian franchises: 0
Other foreign franchises: 26
Company-owned: 0

Seeking: All U.S.
Seeking in Canada? Yes
Exclusive territories? Yes
Homebased option? No
Kiosk option? No
Employees needed to run franchise: 2
Absentee ownership? Yes

COSTS
Total cost: $36.6K-211K
Franchise fee: $8K-26K
Royalty fee: $30/car/mo.
Term of agreement: 10 years renewable
    at no charge
Franchisees required to buy multiple
    units? No

FINANCING
No financing available

QUALIFICATIONS
Experience:
    General business experience
    Marketing skills

TRAINING
At headquarters: 1 week
At franchisee's location: Varies
Counter classes
Marketing seminars & newsletter

BUSINESS SUPPORT
Newsletter
Meetings
Toll-free phone line
Grand opening
Internet
Lease negotiations
Security/safety procedures
Field operations/evaluations
Purchasing cooperatives

MARKETING SUPPORT
Co-op advertising
Ad slicks
National media campaign
Regional marketing

WHEELCHAIR GETAWAYS INC.

Financial rating: $$$$

P.O. Box 605
Versailles, KY 40383
Ph: (800)536-5518/(859)873-4973
Fax: (859)873-8039
www.wheelchairgetaways.com
Wheelchair-accessible van rentals
Began: 1988, Franchising since: 1989
Headquarters size: 5 employees
Franchise department: 2 employees

U.S. franchises: 42
Canadian franchises: 0
Other foreign franchises: 0
Company-owned: 1
Units concentrated in all U.S.

Seeking: All U.S.
Focusing on: CT, FL, NY
Seeking in Canada? Yes
Exclusive territories? Yes
Homebased option? Yes
Kiosk option? No
Employees needed to run franchise: 3
Absentee ownership? Yes

COSTS
Total cost: $40K-112K
Franchise fee: $17.5K
Royalty fee: $550/van/yr.
Term of agreement: 10 years renewable
    at $5K
Franchisees required to buy multiple
    units? No

FINANCING
No financing available

QUALIFICATIONS
Experience:
    Industry experience
    General business experience
    Marketing skills

TRAINING
At existing location: 2 days

BUSINESS SUPPORT
Newsletter
Meetings
Toll-free phone line
Internet
Field operations/evaluations
Purchasing cooperatives

MARKETING SUPPORT
Co-op advertising
Ad slicks
National media campaign
Regional marketing

AUTOMOTIVE ▸ **REPAIR SERVICES**

OIL BUTLER INT'L. CORP.

Ranked #488 in Entrepreneur Magazine's 2005 Franchise 500

Financial rating: $$

1599 Rte. 22 W.
Union, NJ 07083
Ph: (908)687-3283
Fax: (908)687-7617
www.oilbutlerinternational.com
Mobile oil change/quick
    lube/windshield repair
Began: 1987, Franchising since: 1991
Headquarters size: 6 employees
Franchise department: 4 employees

U.S. franchises: 142
Canadian franchises: 3
Other foreign franchises: 19
Company-owned: 1

Seeking: All U.S.
Seeking in Canada? Yes
Exclusive territories? Yes
Homebased option? Yes
Kiosk option? No
Employees needed to run franchise: 0
Absentee ownership? Yes

COSTS
Total cost: $28K-40.7K
Franchise fee: $15K
Royalty fee: 7%
Term of agreement: 10 years renewable
    at $1K
Franchisees required to buy multiple
    units? No

FINANCING
In-house: None
3rd-party: Equipment, franchise fee,
    inventory, startup costs

QUALIFICATIONS
Cash liquidity: $15K

TRAINING
At headquarters: 4 days

BUSINESS SUPPORT
Newsletter
Toll-free phone line
Grand opening
Internet
Security/safety procedures
Field operations/evaluations

MARKETING SUPPORT
Co-op advertising
Ad slicks
National media campaign
Regional marketing
Weekly contact sheet evaluations

TECHZONE AIRBAG SERVICE

Financial rating: $$$

9675 S.E. 36th St., #100
Mercer Island, WA 98040
Ph: (800)224-7224/(206)275-4105
Fax: (206)275-4112
www.tzas.org
Auto interior repairs & airbag service
Began: 1992, Franchising since: 1994
Headquarters size: 9 employees
Franchise department: 1 employee

U.S. franchises: 32
Canadian franchises: 1
Other foreign franchises: 1
Company-owned: 1
Units concentrated in all U.S.

Seeking: All U.S.
Seeking in Canada? Yes
Exclusive territories? Yes
Homebased option? Yes
Kiosk option? No
Employees needed to run franchise: 1
Absentee ownership? Yes

COSTS
Total cost: $36.5K-108.9K
Franchise fee: $15K-35K
Royalty fee: 8.5%
Term of agreement: 10 years renewable
    at $5K
Franchisees required to buy multiple
    units? No

FINANCING
In-house: None
3rd-party: Accounts receivable,
    equipment, franchise fee,
    inventory, payroll, startup costs

QUALIFICATIONS
Net worth: $100K
Cash liquidity: $25K
Experience:
    Industry experience
    General business experience
    Marketing skills

TRAINING
At headquarters: 3 weeks

BUSINESS SUPPORT
Newsletter
Meetings
Toll-free phone line
Internet
Lease negotiations
Security/safety procedures
Field operations/evaluations
Purchasing cooperatives

MARKETING SUPPORT
Co-op advertising
Ad slicks
National media campaign
Regional marketing

AUTOMOTIVE **WINDSHIELD REPAIR**

ATLANTIC WINDSHIELD REPAIR

Current financial data not available

107 C David Green Rd.
Birmingham, AL 35244
Ph: (877)230-4487
Fax: (702)995-2724
www.atlanticwindshieldrepair.com
Windshield repair
Began: 1997, Franchising since: 2004
Headquarters size: 5 employees
Franchise department: 2 employees

U.S. franchises: 8
Canadian franchises: 0
Other foreign franchises: 0
Company-owned: 2

Seeking: All U.S.
Seeking in Canada? Yes
Exclusive territories? Yes
Homebased option? Yes
Kiosk option? Yes
Employees needed to run franchise: 1
Absentee ownership? Yes

COSTS
Total cost: $25K-45K
Kiosk cost: Varies
Franchise fee: $19K
Royalty fee: 6%
Term of agreement: 7 years renewable
    at no charge
Franchisees required to buy multiple
    units? No

FINANCING
In-house: None
3rd-party: Equipment, franchise fee,
    inventory

QUALIFICATIONS
Net worth: $25K
Cash liquidity: $15K
Experience:
    Customer service skills
    Must enjoy working outdoors

TRAINING
At headquarters: 3 days
Web-based training

BUSINESS SUPPORT
Newsletter
Toll-free phone line
Internet
Lease negotiations
Security/safety procedures
Purchasing cooperatives

MARKETING SUPPORT
Ad slicks
Regional marketing

NOVUS AUTO GLASS

Ranked #154 in Entrepreneur Magazine's 2005 Franchise 500   *Financial rating: $$$*

12800 Hwy. 13 S., #500
Savage, MN 55378
Ph: (800)944-6811
Fax: (952)946-0481
www.novusglass.com
Windshield repair/replacement
Began: 1972, Franchising since: 1985
Headquarters size: 40 employees
Franchise department: 13 employees

U.S. franchises: 344
Canadian franchises: 9
Other foreign franchises: 2,013
Company-owned: 5

Seeking: All U.S.
Seeking in Canada? No
Exclusive territories? Yes
Homebased option? Yes
Kiosk option? No
Employees needed to run franchise: 2-3
Absentee ownership? Yes

COSTS
Total cost: $38K-175K
Franchise fee: $7.5K
Royalty fee: 5-8%
Term of agreement: 10 years renewable
    at $2.5K
Franchisees required to buy multiple
    units? No

FINANCING
No financing available

QUALIFICATIONS
Net worth: $50K/100K
Cash liquidity: 25% of initial
    investment
Experience:
    General business experience
    Marketing skills

TRAINING
At headquarters: 8 days initial
At franchisee's location: 1 week follow up
Regional center: 2 weeks

BUSINESS SUPPORT
Newsletter
Meetings
Toll-free phone line
Internet
Security/safety procedures
Field operations/evaluations

MARKETING SUPPORT
Co-op advertising
Ad slicks
National media campaign
Regional marketing
PR support
Web locator
Brand awareness program
Insurance newsletter

SUPERGLASS WINDSHIELD REPAIR

Ranked #307 in Entrepreneur Magazine's 2005 Franchise 500   *Financial rating: $$$*

6101 Chancellor Dr., #200
Orlando, FL 32809
Ph: (407)240-1920
Fax: (407)240-3266
www.sgwr.com
Windshield repair
Began: 1992, Franchising since: 1993
Headquarters size: 5 employees
Franchise department: 2 employees

U.S. franchises: 213
Canadian franchises: 1
Other foreign franchises: 11
Company-owned: 0
Units concentrated in CA, FL, GA, NJ

Seeking: All U.S.
Seeking in Canada? No
Exclusive territories? Yes
Homebased option? Yes
Kiosk option? No
Employees needed to run franchise: 1
Absentee ownership? Yes

COSTS
Total cost: $9.9K-31K
Franchise fee: $9.5K+
Royalty fee: 4%
Term of agreement: 10 years renewable
    at $1K
Franchisees required to buy multiple
    units? Outside U.S. only

FINANCING
In-house: Equipment, franchise fee,
    inventory
3rd-party: None

QUALIFICATIONS
Net worth: $15K
Cash liquidity: $15K
Experience:
    Marketing skills
    Good people skills
    Must enjoy working outdoors

TRAINING
At headquarters: 5 days
At franchisee's location: 5 days
Ongoing seminars
CD-ROMS

BUSINESS SUPPORT
Newsletter
Meetings
Toll-free phone line
Grand opening
Internet
Security/safety procedures
Field operations/evaluations
Purchasing cooperatives

MARKETING SUPPORT
Co-op advertising
Ad slicks
National media campaign
Regional marketing
Phone marketing support with B2B
    accounts

AUTOMOTIVE ▸ OTHER FRANCHISES

ATLANTIC PINSTRIPING
5701 Chretien Point Dr.
Charlotte, NC 28270
(800)314-0244
www.atlanticpinstriping.com
Handpainted pinstriping for
automobiles
Financial rating: Current financial
info not available

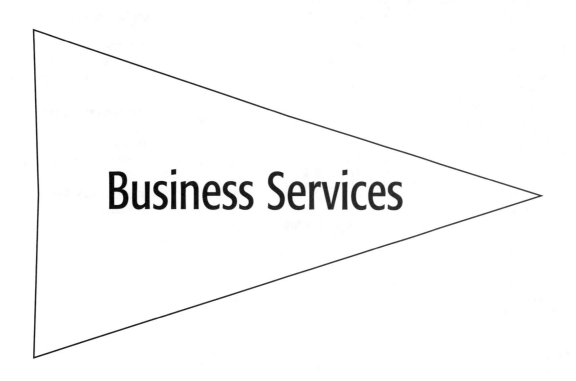

Business Services

BUSINESS **ADVERTISING**

AMERICAN TOWN MAILER

Current financial data not available

P.O. Box 31240
Mesa, AZ 85275
Ph: (480)649-0344
Fax: (480)641-9988
Co-op direct-mail advertising
Began: 1976, Franchising since: 2000
Headquarters size: 6 employees
Franchise department: 2 employees

U.S. franchises: 3
Canadian franchises: 0
Other foreign franchises: 0
Company-owned: 0

Seeking: All U.S.
Seeking in Canada? No
Exclusive territories? Yes
Homebased option? Yes
Kiosk option? No
Employees needed to run franchise: 1
Absentee ownership? Yes

COSTS
Total cost: $23.9K-37.2K
Franchise fee: $20K
Royalty fee: 0
Term of agreement: 10 years renewable
    at $1K
Franchisees required to buy multiple
    units? No

FINANCING
No financing available

QUALIFICATIONS
Net worth: $25K
Cash liquidity: $25K
Experience:
    General business experience
    Marketing skills

TRAINING
At headquarters: 1 week
At franchisee's location: 1 week

BUSINESS SUPPORT
Newsletter
Meetings
Toll-free phone line

MARKETING SUPPORT
Info not provided

AROUND TOWN COMMUNITY MAGAZINE INC.

Current financial data not available

1025 Rose Creek Dr., #340
Woodstock, GA 30189
Ph: (770)516-7105
Fax: (770)516-4809
www.aroundtowncm.com
Direct-mail community magazine
Began: 1996, Franchising since: 2003
Headquarters size: 6 employees
Franchise department: 6 employees

U.S. franchises: 2
Canadian franchises: 0
Other foreign franchises: 0
Company-owned: 2
Units concentrated in GA

Seeking: All U.S.
Focusing on: AL, FL, GA, NC, SC, TN
Seeking in Canada? No
Exclusive territories? Yes
Homebased option? Yes
Kiosk option? No
Employees needed to run franchise: 2
Absentee ownership? Yes

COSTS
Total cost: $32.5K-42.9K
Franchise fee: $25K
Royalty fee: 5%
Term of agreement: 5 years renewable
Franchisees required to buy multiple
   units? No

FINANCING
No financing available

QUALIFICATIONS
Net worth: $250K
Cash liquidity: $100K

TRAINING
At headquarters: 2 weeks
At franchisee's location: 1 week

BUSINESS SUPPORT
Meetings
Internet
Field operations/evaluations

MARKETING SUPPORT
Info not provided

BILLBOARD CONNECTION INC.

Financial rating: $$$

1801 Australian Ave. S.
West Palm Beach, FL 33409
Ph: (866)257-6025/(561)868-1497
Fax: (561)640-5580
www.billboardconnection.com
Ad agency specializing in outdoor
   media
Began: 1997, Franchising since: 2003
Headquarters size: 15 employees
Franchise department: 1 employee

U.S. franchises: 8
Canadian franchises: 0
Other foreign franchises: 0
Company-owned: 0
Units concentrated in all U.S.

Seeking: All U.S.
Seeking in Canada? No
Exclusive territories? Yes
Homebased option? Yes
Kiosk option? No
Employees needed to run franchise: 0
Absentee ownership? Yes

COSTS
Total cost: $34.7K
Franchise fee: $19.5K
Royalty fee: 3.5%
Term of agreement: 35 years renewable
   at $1.5K
Franchisees required to buy multiple
   units? No

FINANCING
No financing available

QUALIFICATIONS
Net worth: $35K+
Cash liquidity: $35K
Experience:
   General business experience
   Marketing skills

TRAINING
At headquarters: 1 week
At franchisee's location: 1 week

BUSINESS SUPPORT
Newsletter
Meetings
Toll-free phone line
Grand opening
Internet
Field operations/evaluations

MARKETING SUPPORT
Ad slicks
National media campaign
Regional marketing

BINGO BUGLE NEWSPAPER

Financial rating: $$$

P.O. Box 527
Vashon, WA 98070
Ph: (800)327-6437/(206)463-5656
Fax: (206)463-5630
www.bingobugle.com
Specialty newspaper
Began: 1981, Franchising since: 1983
Headquarters size: 3 employees
Franchise department: 2 employees

U.S. franchises: 59
Canadian franchises: 1
Other foreign franchises: 0
Company-owned: 0
Units concentrated in all U.S.

Seeking: All U.S.
Focusing on: FL, LA, MD, MS, NC,
    NE, PA, SC, WV
Seeking in Canada? Yes
Exclusive territories? Yes
Homebased option? Yes
Kiosk option? No
Employees needed to run franchise: 1
Absentee ownership? No

COSTS
Total cost: $5.1K-11.5K
Franchise fee: $1.5K
Royalty fee: 8%
Term of agreement: 5 years renewable
    at no charge
Franchisees required to buy multiple
    units? No

FINANCING
No financing available

QUALIFICATIONS
Cash liquidity: $5K
Experience:
    General business experience

TRAINING
At franchisee's location: 2 days
Training w/regional manager or at
    headquarters office

BUSINESS SUPPORT
Newsletter
Meetings
Toll-free phone line
Internet

MARKETING SUPPORT
Co-op advertising
Ad slicks

COFFEE NEWS

Ranked #236 in Entrepreneur Magazine's 2005 Franchise 500

Financial rating: $$

P.O. Box 8444
Bangor, ME 04402-8444
Ph: (207)941-0860
Fax: (207)941-1050
www.coffeenewsusa.com
Weekly newspaper distributed at
    restaurants
Began: 1988, Franchising since: 1994
Headquarters size: 7 employees
Franchise department: 2 employees

U.S. franchises: 215
Canadian franchises: 105
Other foreign franchises: 275
Company-owned: 0
Units concentrated in all U.S.

Seeking: All U.S.
Seeking in Canada? Yes
Exclusive territories? Yes
Homebased option? Yes
Kiosk option? No
Employees needed to run franchise: 1
Absentee ownership? Yes

COSTS
Total cost: $5K
Franchise fee: $4K/2.5K
Royalty fee: $20-75/wk.
Term of agreement: 4 years renewable
    at no charge
Franchisees required to buy multiple
    units? No

FINANCING
In-house: None
3rd-party: Franchise fee

QUALIFICATIONS
Experience:
    Industry experience
    General business experience
    Marketing skills
    Sales & advertising experience

TRAINING
At headquarters: 3 days
Mentor program

BUSINESS SUPPORT
Newsletter
Meetings
Internet
Purchasing cooperatives

MARKETING SUPPORT
Ad slicks

DISCOVERY MAP INT'L.

Financial rating: 0

918 4th St., #200
Anacortes, WA 98221
Ph: (877)820-7827/(360)588-0144
Fax: (360)588-8344
www.discoverymap.com
Specialty map advertising system
Began: 1987, Franchising since: 1999
Headquarters size: 9 employees
Franchise department: 2 employees

U.S. franchises: 23
Canadian franchises: 0
Other foreign franchises: 0
Company-owned: 3
Units concentrated in Western U.S.

Seeking: All U.S.
Seeking in Canada? No
Exclusive territories? Yes
Homebased option? Yes
Kiosk option? No
Employees needed to run franchise: 1
Absentee ownership? Yes

COSTS
Total cost: $40.3K-54.3K
Franchise fee: $20K-30K
Royalty fee: 0
Term of agreement: 10 years renewable
    at 1/3 of franchise fee
Franchisees required to buy multiple
    units? No

FINANCING
No financing available

QUALIFICATIONS
Net worth: $150K
Cash liquidity: $30K
Experience:
    General business experience
    Marketing skills

TRAINING
At headquarters: 5 days
At franchisee's location: 1 day

BUSINESS SUPPORT
Newsletter
Meetings
Toll-free phone line
Internet
Field operations/evaluations

MARKETING SUPPORT
Co-op advertising
Regional marketing
PR

EASYCHAIR MEDIA LLC

Current financial data not available

800 Third St.
Windsor, CO 80550-5424
Ph: (800)741-6308
Fax: (800)438-2150
www.easychairmedia.com
Regional/city publications
Began: 2000, Franchising since: 2002
Headquarters size: 10 employees
Franchise department: 3 employees

U.S. franchises: 1
Canadian franchises: 0
Other foreign franchises: 0
Company-owned: 5
Units concentrated in CO

Seeking: All U.S.
Focusing on: Midwest
Seeking in Canada? No
Exclusive territories? Yes
Homebased option? Yes
Kiosk option? No
Employees needed to run franchise: 1-2
Absentee ownership? Yes

COSTS
Total cost: $32.7K-36.7K
Franchise fee: $10K-20K
Royalty fee: 0
Term of agreement: 10 years renewable
    at 25% of franchise fee
Franchisees required to buy multiple
    units? No

FINANCING
No financing available

QUALIFICATIONS
Net worth: $100K
Cash liquidity: $30K
Experience:
    Industry experience

TRAINING
At headquarters: 2-3 days
At franchisee's location: 2-3 weeks

BUSINESS SUPPORT
Newsletter
Meetings
Toll-free phone line
Internet

MARKETING SUPPORT
Info not provided

INDUSTRY MAGAZINE

Financial rating: $$$

317 S. Northlake Blvd., #1020
Altamonte Springs, FL 32701
Ph: (407)767-0999
Fax: (407)532-9180
www.industrymagazine.com
Fashion publication
Began: 2001, Franchising since: 2004
Headquarters size: 15 employees
Franchise department: 3 employees

U.S. franchises: 20
Canadian franchises: 0
Other foreign franchises: 0
Company-owned: 1

Seeking: All U.S.
Seeking in Canada? Yes
Exclusive territories? Yes
Homebased option? No
Kiosk option? No
Employees needed to run franchise: 3-5
Absentee ownership? Yes

COSTS
Total cost: $34.3K-43.8K
Franchise fee: $25K
Royalty fee: 0
Term of agreement: 3 years renewable
    at $500
Franchisees required to buy multiple
    units? No

FINANCING
No financing available

QUALIFICATIONS
Net worth: $200K
Cash liquidity: $50K
Experience:
    General business experience
    Marketing skills

TRAINING
At headquarters: 5 days

BUSINESS SUPPORT
Newsletter
Meetings
Internet

MARKETING SUPPORT
National media campaign

MAGNETSIGNS ADVERTISING INC.

Ranked #459 in Entrepreneur Magazine's 2005 Franchise 500

Financial rating: 0

4802 50th Ave.
Camrose, AB T4V 0R9 Canada
Ph: (780)672-8720
Fax: (780)672-8716
www.magnetsigns.com
Permanent & portable sign rentals
Began: 1995, Franchising since: 1996
Headquarters size: 10 employees
Franchise department: 5 employees

U.S. franchises: 8
Canadian franchises: 82
Other foreign franchises: 0
Company-owned: 0
Units concentrated in AK, AL, IA, KS,
    MI, NV, OH, UT

Seeking: All U.S.
Seeking in Canada? No
Exclusive territories? No
Homebased option? Yes
Kiosk option? No
Employees needed to run franchise: 1-2
Absentee ownership? Yes

COSTS
Total cost: $24K-80K
Franchise fee: $5K
Royalty fee: 10%
Term of agreement: 10 years renewable
    at $3K
Franchisees required to buy multiple
    units? No

FINANCING
In-house: Equipment, inventory
3rd-party: None

QUALIFICATIONS
Net worth: $50K
Cash liquidity: $10K
Experience:
    General business experience

TRAINING
At headquarters: 3 days
Ongoing training materials
Visits, conventions & meetings

BUSINESS SUPPORT
Newsletter
Meetings
Toll-free phone line
Internet
Field operations/evaluations

MARKETING SUPPORT
Product brochures
Sales presentation binders

PROFIT-TELL INT'L.

Ranked #469 in Entrepreneur Magazine's 2005 Franchise 500　　　　*Financial rating: $$$*

15 Spinning Wheel Rd., #114
Hinsdale, IL 60521
Ph: (888)366-4653
Fax: (630)655-4542
www.profit-tell.com
Telephone "on hold" marketing system/audio marketing solutions
Began: 1993, Franchising since: 2001
Headquarters size: 7 employees
Franchise department: 7 employees

U.S. franchises: 12
Canadian franchises: 0
Other foreign franchises: 0
Company-owned: 1
Units concentrated in all U.S.

Seeking: All U.S.
Seeking in Canada? No
Exclusive territories? No
Homebased option? Yes
Kiosk option? No
Employees needed to run franchise: 1
Absentee ownership? No

COSTS
Total cost: $28.7K-48.3K
Franchise fee: $22.5K
Royalty fee: 0
Term of agreement: 20 years renewable at $1K
Franchisees required to buy multiple units? No

FINANCING
In-house: None
3rd-party: Equipment, franchise fee, inventory, startup costs

QUALIFICATIONS
Net worth: $125K
Cash liquidity: $25K
Experience:
　　General business experience
　　Sales experience
　　Interpersonal skills

TRAINING
At headquarters: 6 days
At franchisee's location: As needed
Initial training: 6 weeks
Ongoing coaching

BUSINESS SUPPORT
Newsletter
Meetings
Toll-free phone line
Internet
Field operations/evaluations

MARKETING SUPPORT
Ad slicks
National media campaign
Regional marketing
Ad support fund

REZCITY.COM PLUS

Ranked #269 in Entrepreneur Magazine's 2005 Franchise 500　　　　*Financial rating: $$$$*

560 Sylvan Ave.
Englewood Cliffs, NJ 07632
Ph: (800)669-9000/(201)567-8500
Fax: (201)567-3265
www.rezcity.biz
Online local city guides, travel store, eBay auction store
Began: 2002, Franchising since: 2002
Headquarters size: 18 employees
Franchise department: 8 employees

U.S. franchises: 238
Canadian franchises: 0
Other foreign franchises: 0
Company-owned: 2
Units concentrated in all U.S.

Seeking: All U.S.
Seeking in Canada? No
Exclusive territories? Yes
Homebased option? Yes
Kiosk option? No
Employees needed to run franchise: 1
Absentee ownership? Yes

COSTS
Total cost: $6.7K-61.2K
Franchise fee: $4.5K-50K
Royalty fee: 0
Term of agreement: 5 years renewable at $200
Franchisees required to buy multiple units? No

FINANCING
In-house: Franchise fee
3rd-party: None

QUALIFICATIONS
Cash liquidity: $5K-25K
Experience:
　　General business experience
　　Marketing skills

TRAINING
At headquarters: 2 days
Web conference training

BUSINESS SUPPORT
Newsletter
Meetings
Toll-free phone line
Grand opening
Internet

MARKETING SUPPORT
Co-op advertising
Ad slicks
National media campaign
Email clubs

RSVP PUBLICATIONS

Ranked #365 in Entrepreneur Magazine's 2005 Franchise 500   *Financial rating: $$$*

1156 N.E. Cleveland St.
Clearwater, FL 33755
Ph: (800)360-7787/(727)442-4000
Fax: (727)441-1315
www.rsvppublications.com
Direct-mail advertising
Began: 1985, Franchising since: 1998
Headquarters size: 10 employees
Franchise department: 2 employees

U.S. franchises: 77
Canadian franchises: 0
Other foreign franchises: 0
Company-owned: 0

Seeking: All U.S.
Seeking in Canada? Yes
Exclusive territories? Yes
Homebased option? Yes
Kiosk option? No
Employees needed to run franchise: 1
Absentee ownership? No

COSTS
Total cost: $29.3K-142.95K
Franchise fee: $15K-100K+
Royalty fee: 7%
Term of agreement: 10 years renewable
    at $5K
Franchisees required to buy multiple
    units? No

FINANCING
In-house: Franchise fee, inventory
3rd-party: Franchise fee, inventory

QUALIFICATIONS
Net worth: $50K
Experience:
    General business experience
    Marketing skills

TRAINING
At headquarters: 2 weeks

BUSINESS SUPPORT
Meetings
Toll-free phone line
Internet
Purchasing cooperatives

MARKETING SUPPORT
Info not provided

BUSINESS ▸ CONSULTING

ACCUTRAK INVENTORY SPECIALISTS

Financial rating: 0

1818C Hwy. 17 N., #320
Surfside Beach, SC 29575
Ph: (843)293-8274
Fax: (843)293-5075
www.accutrakinventory.com
Inventory consulting
Began: 1993, Franchising since: 2000
Headquarters size: 5 employees
Franchise department: 5 employees

U.S. franchises: 39
Canadian franchises: 0
Other foreign franchises: 1
Company-owned: 1

Seeking: All U.S.
Seeking in Canada? Yes
Exclusive territories? Yes
Homebased option? Yes
Kiosk option? No
Employees needed to run franchise: 1
Absentee ownership? Yes

COSTS
Total cost: $39K-48K
Franchise fee: $22.5K
Royalty fee: 7%
Term of agreement: 15 years renewable
    at $1K
Franchisees required to buy multiple
    units? No

FINANCING
In-house: Equipment
3rd-party: None

QUALIFICATIONS
Net worth: $120K
Cash liquidity: $30K
Experience:
    General business experience
    Marketing skills

TRAINING
At headquarters: 4 days
At franchisee's location: Varies
At training site: 4 days

BUSINESS SUPPORT
Newsletter
Meetings
Grand opening
Internet
Security/safety procedures
Field operations/evaluations
Purchasing cooperatives

MARKETING SUPPORT
Co-op advertising
Ad slicks
Regional marketing

THE ALTERNATIVE BOARD

Ranked #466 in Entrepreneur Magazine's 2005 Franchise 500　　　　*Financial rating: 0*

225 E. 16th Ave., #580
Denver, CO 80203-1622
Ph: (800)727-0126/(303)839-1200
Fax: (800)420-7055/(303)839-0012
www.tabboards.com
Peer advisory boards/business coaching
Began: 1990, Franchising since: 1996
Headquarters size: 25 employees
Franchise department: 5 employees

U.S. franchises: 89
Canadian franchises: 11
Other foreign franchises: 1
Company-owned: 6
Units concentrated in all U.S.

Seeking: All U.S.
Seeking in Canada? Yes
Exclusive territories? Yes
Homebased option? Yes
Kiosk option? No
Employees needed to run franchise: 1
Absentee ownership? No

COSTS
Total cost: $33.96K-98.7K
Franchise fee: $17K-47K
Royalty fee: Varies
Term of agreement: 10 years renewable
　　at $1.5K
Franchisees required to buy multiple
　　units? No

FINANCING
In-house: Franchise fee
3rd-party: Accounts receivable, equip-
　　ment, inventory, payroll, startup
　　costs

QUALIFICATIONS
Net worth: $75K+
Cash liquidity: $25K-50K
Experience:
　　Industry experience
　　Marketing skills
　　Ten years+ executive experience

TRAINING
At headquarters: 6 days initially
At franchisee's location: 4 weeks
Conference calls during first year

BUSINESS SUPPORT
Newsletter
Meetings
Toll-free phone line
Grand opening
Internet
Field operations/evaluations

MARKETING SUPPORT
Co-op advertising
Ad slicks
Regional marketing
Websites

BUSINESS ROUND TABLE

Current financial data not available

37 Chandler Crescent
Moncton, NB E1E 3W6 Canada
Ph: (506)857-8177
Fax: (506)858-5553
www.business-round-table.com
Mentoring groups for small businesses
Began: 1991, Franchising since: 1998
Headquarters size: Info not provided
Franchise department:
　　Info not provided

U.S. franchises: 0
Canadian franchises: 1
Other foreign franchises: 0
Company-owned: 1

Seeking: Not available in the U.S.
Seeking in Canada? No
Exclusive territories? Yes
Homebased option? Yes
Kiosk option? No
Employees needed to run franchise:
　　Info not provided
Absentee ownership? No

COSTS
Total cost: $20K
Franchise fee: $20K
Royalty fee: 5-10%
Term of agreement: 10 years renewable
　　at no charge
Franchisees required to buy multiple
　　units? Yes, within U.S.

FINANCING
In-house: Franchise fee
3rd-party: None

QUALIFICATIONS
Net worth: $100K
Cash liquidity: $25K

TRAINING
At franchisee's location: 2 weeks

BUSINESS SUPPORT
Newsletter
Toll-free phone line
Internet
Field operations/evaluations

MARKETING SUPPORT
Ad slicks

EWF INT'L.

Financial rating: 0

4900 Richmond Sq., #105
Oklahoma City, OK 73118
Ph: (405)843-3934
Fax: (405)843-3933
www.ewfinternational.com
Peer advisory groups for women in
    business
Began: 1998, Franchising since: 2002
Headquarters size: 3 employees
Franchise department: 1 employee

U.S. franchises: 2
Canadian franchises: 0
Other foreign franchises: 0
Company-owned: 1

Seeking: All U.S.
Seeking in Canada? Yes
Exclusive territories? Yes
Homebased option? Yes
Kiosk option? No
Employees needed to run franchise: 1
Absentee ownership? No

COSTS
Total cost: $30.5K-35K
Franchise fee: $25K
Royalty fee: 15%
Term of agreement: 5 years renewable
    at no charge
Franchisees required to buy multiple
    units? No

FINANCING
No financing available

QUALIFICATIONS
Experience:
    General business experience
    Marketing skills

TRAINING
At headquarters: 1 week
At franchisee's location: 4-6 days

BUSINESS SUPPORT
Meetings
Toll-free phone line
Internet

MARKETING SUPPORT
Ad slicks
Personalized electronic newsletter

THE GROWTH COACH

Financial rating: $$$

10700 Montgomery Rd., #300
Cincinnati, OH 45242
Ph: (888)292-7992
Fax: (513)563-2691
www.thegrowthcoach.com
Small-business coaching/mentoring
Began: 2002, Franchising since: 2003
Headquarters size: 10 employees
Franchise department: 10 employees

U.S. franchises: 45
Canadian franchises: 2
Other foreign franchises: 0
Company-owned: 0
Units concentrated in all U.S.

Seeking: All U.S.
Seeking in Canada? No
Exclusive territories? Yes
Homebased option? Yes
Kiosk option? No
Employees needed to run franchise: 0
Absentee ownership? No

COSTS
Total cost: $25.5K-39.9K
Franchise fee: $17.9K-23.9K
Royalty fee: 6%
Term of agreement: 10 years renewable
    at no charge
Franchisees required to buy multiple
    units? No

FINANCING
In-house: Franchise fee
3rd-party: None

QUALIFICATIONS
Cash liquidity: $10K
Experience:
    General business experience

TRAINING
At headquarters: 5 days
Ongoing phone training
Intranet membership

BUSINESS SUPPORT
Newsletter
Meetings
Toll-free phone line
Grand opening
Internet

MARKETING SUPPORT
Ad slicks
Marketing strategies & tools

PRO: PRESIDENT'S RESOURCE ORGANIZATION

Financial rating: $$$

100 E. Bellevue #4E
Chicago, IL 60611
Ph: (312)337-3658
Fax: (312)944-6815
www.propres.com
Peer advisory boards
Began: 1993, Franchising since: 1999
Headquarters size: 2 employees
Franchise department: 2 employees

U.S. franchises: 5
Canadian franchises: 0
Other foreign franchises: 0
Company-owned: 2

Seeking: All U.S.
Seeking in Canada? No
Exclusive territories? Yes
Homebased option? Yes
Kiosk option? No
Employees needed to run franchise:
    Info not provided
Absentee ownership? Yes

COSTS
Total cost: $18.9K-63K
Franchise fee: $8.5K-35K
Royalty fee: 20%
Term of agreement: Info not provided
Franchisees required to buy multiple
    units? No

FINANCING
In-house: Franchise fee
3rd-party: None

QUALIFICATIONS
Net worth: $100K
Cash liquidity: $20K
Experience:
    Industry experience
    General business experience
    Marketing skills

TRAINING
At headquarters: 1 week
At franchisee's location: 1 week

BUSINESS SUPPORT
Newsletter
Toll-free phone line
Grand opening
Internet
Field operations/evaluations

MARKETING SUPPORT
Direct mail
Telemarketing

BUSINESS ▶ SHIPPING

UNISHIPPERS

Current financial data not available

746 E. Winchester, #200
Salt Lake City, UT 84107
Ph: (800)999-8721/(801)487-0600
Fax: (801)487-0623
www.unishippers.com
Discounted express & freight
    shipments
Began: 1987, Franchising since: 1987
Headquarters size: 60 employees
Franchise department: 2 employees

U.S. franchises: 284
Canadian franchises: 0
Other foreign franchises: 0
Company-owned: 0

Seeking: Selling resales only in the U.S.
Seeking in Canada? Yes
Exclusive territories? Yes
Homebased option? Yes
Kiosk option? No
Employees needed to run franchise: 2
Absentee ownership? Yes

COSTS
Total cost: $31K+
Franchise fee: $10K
Royalty fee: 16.5%
Term of agreement: 5 years renewable
    at $5K
Franchisees required to buy multiple
    units? Outside U.S. only

FINANCING
No financing available

QUALIFICATIONS
Info not provided

TRAINING
At headquarters: 1 week
At franchisee's location: 2 days

BUSINESS SUPPORT
Newsletter
Meetings
Toll-free phone line
Internet
Security/safety procedures
Field operations/evaluations

MARKETING SUPPORT
Co-op advertising
Ad slicks
National media campaign

UNITED SHIPPING SOLUTIONS

Ranked #404 in Entrepreneur Magazine's 2005 Franchise 500   *Financial rating: $$$$*

6985 Union Park Ctr., #565
Midvale, UT 84047
Ph: (866)744-7486/(801)352-0012
Fax: (801)352-0339
www.usshipit.com
Transportation services
Began: 2002, Franchising since: 2002
Headquarters size: 8 employees
Franchise department: 4 employees

U.S. franchises: 120
Canadian franchises: 0
Other foreign franchises: 0
Company-owned: 0
Units concentrated in all U.S.

Seeking: All U.S.
Seeking in Canada? No
Exclusive territories? Yes
Homebased option? Yes
Kiosk option? No
Employees needed to run franchise: 1
Absentee ownership? Yes

COSTS
Total cost: $25K-86K
Franchise fee: $25K-30K
Royalty fee: 6%
Term of agreement: 5 years renewable
Franchisees required to buy multiple
    units? No

FINANCING
No financing available

QUALIFICATIONS
Experience:
    General business experience
    Marketing skills

TRAINING
At headquarters: 1 week
Ongoing

BUSINESS SUPPORT
Newsletter
Meetings
Toll-free phone line
Internet
Field operations/evaluations
Purchasing cooperatives

MARKETING SUPPORT
Regional marketing
Direct sales

WORLDWIDE EXPRESS

Ranked #256 in Entrepreneur Magazine's 2005 Franchise 500   *Financial rating: $$$*

2501 Cedar Springs Rd., #450
Dallas, TX 75201
Ph: (800)758-7447
Fax: (214)720-2446
www.wwex.com
Discounted air express services
Began: 1991, Franchising since: 1994
Headquarters size: 12 employees
Franchise department: 7 employees

U.S. franchises: 162
Canadian franchises: 0
Other foreign franchises: 0
Company-owned: 8

Seeking: All U.S.
Seeking in Canada? No
Exclusive territories? Yes
Homebased option? Yes
Kiosk option? No
Employees needed to run franchise: 1
Absentee ownership? Yes

COSTS
Total cost: $41.2K-295.7K
Franchise fee: $23.8K-266K
Royalty fee: 6%
Term of agreement: 5 years renewable
Franchisees required to buy multiple
    units? No

FINANCING
In-house: None
3rd-party: Equipment, franchise fee,
    startup costs

QUALIFICATIONS
Net worth: $50K
Cash liquidity: $50K
Experience:
    General business experience
    Marketing skills

TRAINING
At headquarters
At franchisee's location

BUSINESS SUPPORT
Newsletter
Meetings
Toll-free phone line

MARKETING SUPPORT
Info not provided

STAFFING

MEDTECH

Financial rating: $$$

777 Penn Center Blvd., #111
Pittsburgh, PA 15235
Ph: (412)829-8644
Fax: (412)829-8905
www.medtechfranchising.com
Medical staffing
Began: 1999, Franchising since: 2004
Headquarters size: 28 employees
Franchise department: 4 employees

U.S. franchises: 0
Canadian franchises: 0
Other foreign franchises: 0
Company-owned: 9

Seeking: All U.S.
Seeking in Canada? No
Exclusive territories? Yes
Homebased option? No
Kiosk option? No
Employees needed to run franchise: 3
Absentee ownership? Yes

COSTS
Total cost: $41.2K-65.8K
Franchise fee: $15K-25K
Royalty fee: 10-17%
Term of agreement: 10 years renewable
Franchisees required to buy multiple
  units? No

FINANCING
In-house: Accounts receivable, payroll
3rd-party: Equipment, franchise fee,
  inventory, startup costs

QUALIFICATIONS
Net worth: $100K
Cash liquidity: $15K-25K
Experience:
  General business experience

TRAINING
At headquarters: 1 week
At franchisee's location: 1 week

BUSINESS SUPPORT
Toll-free phone line
Grand opening
Internet
Field operations/evaluations
Purchasing cooperatives

MARKETING SUPPORT
Co-op advertising
Ad slicks
National media campaign
Regional marketing

PARTY PERSONNEL FRANCHISE SYSTEMS

Current financial data not available

11720 Hadley
Overland Park, KS 66210
Ph: (913)451-0218
Fax: (913)451-8941
www.partypersonnelkc.com
Hospitality & entertainment staffing
Began: 1993, Franchising since: 2003
Headquarters size: 5 employees
Franchise department: 5 employees

U.S. franchises: 0
Canadian franchises: 0
Other foreign franchises: 0
Company-owned: 1
Units concentrated in FL

Seeking: South, Southeast, Midwest,
  Southwest
Focusing on: AZ, FL, MO, NC
Seeking in Canada? No
Exclusive territories? Yes
Homebased option? Yes
Kiosk option? No
Employees needed to run franchise: 3
Absentee ownership? No

COSTS
Total cost: $22.5K-40K
Franchise fee: $15K
Royalty fee: 3%
Term of agreement: 5 years renewable
  at $7.5K
Franchisees required to buy multiple
  units? No

FINANCING
No financing available

QUALIFICATIONS
Experience:
  Industry experience
  General business experience
  Marketing skills

TRAINING
At headquarters: 2 weeks
At franchisee's location: 1 week/year

BUSINESS SUPPORT
Newsletter
Meetings
Toll-free phone line
Grand opening
Internet

MARKETING SUPPORT
Co-op advertising
Ad slicks
Regional marketing

PERSONET-THE PERSONNEL NETWORK

Financial rating: $$$

33907 U.S. 19 N.
Palm Harbor, FL 34684
Ph: (727)781-2983
Fax: (727)781-3023
www.personet.com
Staffing/payroll/PEO services
Began: 1994, Franchising since: 1994
Headquarters size: 8 employees
Franchise department: 8 employees

U.S. franchises: 6
Canadian franchises: 0
Other foreign franchises: 0
Company-owned: 0
Units concentrated in all U.S.

Seeking: All U.S.
Seeking in Canada? No
Exclusive territories? Yes
Homebased option? No
Kiosk option? No
Employees needed to run franchise: 2-3
Absentee ownership? No

COSTS
Total cost: $35.2K-100K+
Franchise fee: $15K-60K
Royalty fee: Varies
Term of agreement: 10 years renewable
    at no charge
Franchisees required to buy multiple
    units? No

FINANCING
In-house: Accounts receivable, payroll
3rd-party: Franchise fee, startup costs

QUALIFICATIONS
Net worth: $100K
Cash liquidity: $50K
Experience:
    General business experience

TRAINING
At headquarters: 1 week
At franchisee's location: 4 weeks/year
Ongoing

BUSINESS SUPPORT
Newsletter
Internet
Field operations/evaluations

MARKETING SUPPORT
Info not provided

PMA FRANCHISE SYSTEMS

Current financial data not available

1950 Spectrum Cir., #B-310
Marietta, GA 30067
Ph: (800)466-7822
Fax: (770)916-1429
www.pmafranchise.com
Management recruiting services
Began: 1985, Franchising since: 1998
Headquarters size: 5 employees
Franchise department: 4 employees

U.S. franchises: 9
Canadian franchises: 0
Other foreign franchises: 0
Company-owned: 1
Units concentrated in FL, GA, MA,
    OK, OR

Seeking: All U.S.
Seeking in Canada? No
Exclusive territories? Yes
Homebased option? No
Kiosk option? No
Employees needed to run franchise: 2
Absentee ownership? Yes

COSTS
Total cost: $43.3K-70K+
Franchise fee: $35K
Royalty fee: 10-8%
Term of agreement: 10 years renewable
    at $5K
Franchisees required to buy multiple
    units? No

FINANCING
In-house: Franchise fee
3rd-party: None

QUALIFICATIONS
Net worth: $100K
Cash liquidity: $60K
Experience:
    General business experience

TRAINING
At headquarters: 4 weeks

BUSINESS SUPPORT
Newsletter
Meetings
Toll-free phone line
Internet
Field operations/evaluations

MARKETING SUPPORT
Info not provided

BUSINESS TRAINING

LEADERSHIP MANAGEMENT INC.

Ranked #275 in Entrepreneur Magazine's 2005 Franchise 500

Financial rating: $$$$

4567 Lake Shore Dr.
Waco, TX 76710
Ph: (800)568-1241
Fax: (254)757-4600
www.lmi-bus.com
Executive/management training
Began: 1965, Franchising since: 1965
Headquarters size: 10 employees
Franchise department: 2 employees

U.S. franchises: 231
Canadian franchises: 0
Other foreign franchises: 0
Company-owned: 0
Units concentrated in all U.S.

Seeking: All U.S.
Seeking in Canada? No
Exclusive territories? No
Homebased option? Yes
Kiosk option? No
Employees needed to run franchise: 2-5
Absentee ownership? Yes

COSTS
Total cost: $33.5K-37.5K
Franchise fee: $30K
Royalty fee: 6%
Term of agreement: 10 years renewable
    at $5K
Franchisees required to buy multiple
    units? No

FINANCING
No financing available

QUALIFICATIONS
Experience:
    General business experience

TRAINING
At headquarters: Ongoing

BUSINESS SUPPORT
Meetings
Internet

MARKETING SUPPORT
Info not provided

TURBO LEADERSHIP SYSTEMS

Current financial data not available

36280 N.E. Wilsonville Rd.
Newberg, OR 97132
Ph: (503)625-1867
Fax: (503)625-2699
www.turboleadershipsystems.com
Leadership development/training
Began: 1985, Franchising since: 1995
Headquarters size: 6 employees
Franchise department: 6 employees

U.S. franchises: 0
Canadian franchises: 0
Other foreign franchises: 0
Company-owned: 1
Units concentrated in all U.S.

Seeking: All U.S.
Seeking in Canada? Yes
Exclusive territories? Yes
Homebased option? Yes
Kiosk option? No
Employees needed to run franchise: 2
Absentee ownership? No

COSTS
Total cost: $33.3K-56.8K
Franchise fee: $29K
Royalty fee: 10%
Term of agreement: 10 years renewable
    at no charge
Franchisees required to buy multiple
    units? Outside U.S. only

FINANCING
No financing available

QUALIFICATIONS
Net worth: $150K
Cash liquidity: $40K
Experience:
    Industry experience
    General business experience
    Marketing skills
    Public speaking skills

TRAINING
At headquarters: 30 days

BUSINESS SUPPORT
Newsletter
Meetings
Toll-free phone line
Grand opening
Internet
Field operations/evaluations

MARKETING SUPPORT
Co-op advertising
Ad slicks

BEVINCO BAR SYSTEMS LTD.

Current financial data not available

510-505 Consumers Rd.
Toronto, ON M2J 4V8 Canada
Ph: (888)238-4626/(416)490-6266
Fax: (416)490-6899
www.bevinco.com
Liquor inventory-control service
Began: 1987, Franchising since: 1990
Headquarters size: 14 employees
Franchise department: 5 employees

U.S. franchises: 185
Canadian franchises: 29
Other foreign franchises: 28
Company-owned: 1
Units concentrated in all U.S.

Seeking: All U.S.
Seeking in Canada? Yes
Exclusive territories? Yes
Homebased option? Yes
Kiosk option? No
Employees needed to run franchise: 2
Absentee ownership? No

COSTS
Total cost: $41.5K-45K
Franchise fee: $34.9K
Royalty fee: $12/audit
Term of agreement: 20 years renewable
at $1K every 5 years
Franchisees required to buy multiple
units?

FINANCING
No financing available

QUALIFICATIONS
Net worth: $50K
Cash liquidity: $30K
Experience:
Industry experience
General business experience
Marketing skills
Sales experience

TRAINING
At headquarters: 1 week
At franchisee's location: 2 weeks

BUSINESS SUPPORT
Newsletter
Meetings
Toll-free phone line
Grand opening
Internet
Field operations/evaluations

MARKETING SUPPORT
Co-op advertising
Ad slicks
National media campaign
Regional marketing

FOLIAGE DESIGN SYSTEMS

Financial rating: $$$

4496 35th St.
Orlando, FL 32811
Ph: (800)933-7351/(407)245-7776
Fax: (407)245-7533
www.foliagedesign.com
Interior foliage/plant maintenance
Began: 1971, Franchising since: 1980
Headquarters size: 7 employees
Franchise department: 7 employees

U.S. franchises: 32
Canadian franchises: 0
Other foreign franchises: 0
Company-owned: 4

Seeking: All U.S.
Seeking in Canada? No
Exclusive territories? Yes
Homebased option? Yes
Kiosk option? No
Employees needed to run franchise: 5
Absentee ownership? No

COSTS
Total cost: $44.4K-64.4K
Franchise fee: $20K+
Royalty fee: 6%
Term of agreement: 4-5 years
renewable
Franchisees required to buy multiple
units? No

FINANCING
No financing available

QUALIFICATIONS
Net worth: $250K
Cash liquidity: $33.95K-124.6K
Experience:
General business experience
Marketing skills
Sales experience

TRAINING
At headquarters: 8-10 days
At franchisee's location: 3 days

BUSINESS SUPPORT
Newsletter
Meetings
Toll-free phone line
Internet
Security/safety procedures
Field operations/evaluations

MARKETING SUPPORT
Ad slicks
National media campaign
Regional marketing
Leads

MR. PLANT

Current financial data not available

1106 2nd St.
Encinitas, CA 92024
Ph: (888)677-5268
Fax: (760)295-5629
www.mrplant.com
Interior plant maintenance
Began: 1980, Franchising since: 1990
Headquarters size: 6 employees
Franchise department: 3 employees

U.S. franchises: 40
Canadian franchises: 0
Other foreign franchises: 0
Company-owned: 1

Seeking: All U.S.
Seeking in Canada? Yes
Exclusive territories? Info not provided
Homebased option? Yes
Kiosk option? No
Employees needed to run franchise: 2
Absentee ownership? Yes

COSTS
Total cost: $18.5K-25K
Franchise fee: $14.95K
Royalty fee: Varies
Term of agreement: 5 years renewable
    at $1K
Franchisees required to buy multiple
    units? No

FINANCING
In-house: Franchise fee
3rd-party: None

QUALIFICATIONS
Net worth: $25K
Cash liquidity: $25K

TRAINING
At headquarters: 5 days
Home study course

BUSINESS SUPPORT
Newsletter
Toll-free phone line
Internet
Purchasing cooperatives

MARKETING SUPPORT
Co-op advertising
Ad slicks
Yellow Pages listing

PROFORMA

Ranked #76 in Entrepreneur Magazine's 2005 Franchise 500

Financial rating: $$$$

8800 E. Pleasant Valley Rd.
Cleveland, OH 44131
Ph: (800)825-1525/(216)520-8400
Fax: (216)520-8474
www.connectwithproforma.com
Printing/promotional products
Began: 1978, Franchising since: 1985
Headquarters size: 120 employees
Franchise department: 10 employees

U.S. franchises: 574
Canadian franchises: 41
Other foreign franchises: 0
Company-owned: 0

Seeking: All U.S.
Seeking in Canada? Yes
Exclusive territories? No
Homebased option? Yes
Kiosk option? No
Employees needed to run franchise: 1
Absentee ownership? No

COSTS
Total cost: $4.5K-34.1K
Franchise fee: to $14.9K
Royalty fee: 6-8%
Term of agreement: 10 years renewable
    at $1K
Franchisees required to buy multiple
    units? No

FINANCING
In-house: Accounts receivable
3rd-party: None

QUALIFICATIONS
Net worth: $50K-100K
Cash liquidity: $10K-20K
Experience:
    General business experience
    Marketing skills
    Sales background

TRAINING
At headquarters: 1 week
At franchisee's location: Quarterly
At regional/annual convention

BUSINESS SUPPORT
Newsletter
Meetings
Toll-free phone line
Internet
Field operations/evaluations
Purchasing cooperatives

MARKETING SUPPORT
National media campaign
Regional marketing
Collateral
Product promotions
Direct-mail campaigns

BUSINESS ▶ OTHER FRANCHISES

ALLIANCE OF PROFESSIONALS & CONSULTANTS INC.
9201 Leesville Rd., #201
Raleigh, NC 27613
Ph: (919)510-9696
www.apc-services.com
Professional tech staffing services
Financial rating: $$$$

BUSINESS AMERICA
2120 Greentree Rd.
Pittsburgh, PA 15220
Ph: (412)276-7701
www.pghbiznet.com
Business & franchise brokerage
Financial rating: Current financial
    data not available

GOTCHA MOBILE MEDIA
P.O. Box 555
Shafter, CA 93263
Ph: (661)746-0121
www.gotchamobilemedia.com
Mobile billboard advertising
Financial rating: Current financial
    data not available

NEXTAFF
11660 W. 75th St.
Shawnee, KS 66214
Ph: (913)562-5604
www.nextaff.com
Human capital services
Financial rating: Current financial
    data not available

PAID INC.
4800 W. Waco Dr., #100
Waco, TX 76710
Ph: (254)772-8131
Fax: (254)772-4642
www.paidinc.com
Electronic payments & e-commerce
    financial services
Financial rating: Current financial
    data not available

UNITED MARKETING SOLUTIONS INC.
7644 Dynatech Ct.
Springfield, VA 22153
Ph: (800)368-3501/(703)644-0200
www.unitedol.com
Direct-mail advertising/direct
    marketing/Internet marketing
Financial rating: Current financial
    data not available

WHEELS AMERICA ADVERTISING
545 Charles St.
Luzerne, PA 18709
Ph: (800)823-0044/(570)283-5000
www.wheelsamerica.com
Mobile billboard advertising
Financial rating: Current financial
    data not available

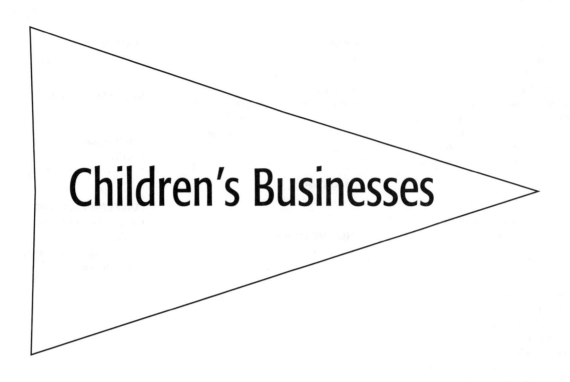

Children's Businesses

CHILDREN'S **FITNESS**

FUN BUS

Financial rating: $$$

32 Timothy Ln.
Tinton Falls, NJ 07724
Ph: (732)578-1287
Fax: (732)389-7824
www.funbuses.com
Mobile children's fitness program
Began: 2000, Franchising since: 2003
Headquarters size: 7 employees
Franchise department: 5 employees

U.S. franchises: 6
Canadian franchises: 0
Other foreign franchises: 0
Company-owned: 0
Units concentrated in NJ, NY

Seeking: All U.S.
Focusing on: CT, PA
Seeking in Canada? No
Exclusive territories? Yes
Homebased option? Yes
Kiosk option? No
Employees needed to run franchise: 2
Absentee ownership? Yes

COSTS
Total cost: $48.1K-70.3K
Franchise fee: $25K
Royalty fee: 7%
Term of agreement: 5 years renewable
    at 50% of current franchise fee
Franchisees required to buy multiple
    units? No

FINANCING
No financing available

QUALIFICATIONS
Net worth: $50K
Cash liquidity: $50K

TRAINING
At headquarters: 2 days
Bus driving school/on-the-road
    training: 2 days

BUSINESS SUPPORT
Toll-free phone line
Grand opening
Internet
Security/safety procedures
Field operations/evaluations
Purchasing cooperatives

MARKETING SUPPORT
Co-op advertising
Ad slicks
Ongoing support

JUMPBUNCH INC.

Financial rating: $$$

302 Annapolis St.
Annapolis, MD 21401
Ph: (410)703-2300
Fax: (928)441-7838
www.jumpbunch.com
Preschool sports & fitness programs
Began: 2002, Franchising since: 2002
Headquarters size: 3 employees
Franchise department: 3 employes

U.S. franchises: 8
Canadian franchises: 0
Other foreign franchises: 0
Company-owned: 1
Units concentrated in CA, CT, GA, IN,
    LA, MD, MO, TX

Seeking: All U.S.
Seeking in Canada? Yes
Exclusive territories? Yes
Homebased option? Yes
Kiosk option? No
Employees needed to run franchise: 2
Absentee ownership? No

COSTS
Total cost: $13.5K-41.2K
Franchise fee: $10K-20K
Royalty fee: 8%
Term of agreement: 5 years renewable
    at 25% of then-current fee
Franchisees required to buy multiple
    units? No

FINANCING
No financing available

QUALIFICATIONS
Net worth: $40K
Cash liquidity: $15K
Experience:
    General business experience

TRAINING
At headquarters: 2 days

BUSINESS SUPPORT
Newsletter
Meetings
Toll-free phone line
Internet
Security/safety procedures

MARKETING SUPPORT
Co-op advertising
Ad slicks
National media campaign
Regional marketing

KINDERDANCE INT'L. INC.

Ranked #268 in Entrepreneur Magazine's 2005 Franchise 500

Financial rating: $$$$

1333 Gateway Dr., #1003
Melbourne, FL 32901
Ph: (800)554-2334/(321)984-4448
Fax: (321)984-4490
www.kinderdance.com
Children's movement/educational
    programs
Began: 1979, Franchising since: 1985
Headquarters size: 7 employees
Franchise department: 3 employees

U.S. franchises: 108
Canadian franchises: 1
Other foreign franchises: 2
Company-owned: 1
Units concentrated in all U.S.

Seeking: All U.S.
Seeking in Canada? No
Exclusive territories? Yes
Homebased option? Yes
Kiosk option? No
Employees needed to run franchise: 1-2
Absentee ownership? No

COSTS
Total cost: $12.95K-27.1K
Franchise fee: $10K-21K
Royalty fee: 6-15%
Term of agreement: 10 years renewable
    at 10% of current fee
Franchisees required to buy multiple
    units? No

FINANCING
In-house: Franchise fee
3rd-party: None

QUALIFICATIONS
Net worth: $10K+
Cash liquidity: $9.3K+
Experience:
    Energetic
    Enjoy working with children

TRAINING
At headquarters: 6 days
At franchisee's location: As needed
Annual continuing education
    conferences

BUSINESS SUPPORT
Newsletter
Meetings
Toll-free phone line
Grand opening
Internet
Security/safety procedures
Field operations/evaluations
Purchasing cooperatives

MARKETING SUPPORT
Co-op advertising
Ad slicks
National media campaign
Regional marketing
PR releases

PEE WEE WORKOUT

Current financial data not available

34976 Aspenwood Ln.
Willoughby, OH 44094
Ph: (440)946-7888
Fax: (440)946-7888
www.peeweeworkout.com
Preschool fitness program
Began: 1986, Franchising since: 1988
Headquarters size: 3 employees
Franchise department: 1 employee

U.S. franchises: 8
Canadian franchises: 0
Other foreign franchises: 3
Company-owned: 1

Seeking: All U.S.
Seeking in Canada? Yes
Exclusive territories? No
Homebased option? Yes
Kiosk option? No
Employees needed to run franchise:
    Info not provided
Absentee ownership? Yes

COSTS
Total cost: $2.7K
Franchise fee: $2K
Royalty fee: 10%
Term of agreement: 5 years renewable
    at $250
Franchisees required to buy multiple
    units? No

FINANCING
No financing available

QUALIFICATIONS
Net worth: $2.2K
Cash liquidity: $2.2K
Experience:
    Industry experience
    General business experience
    Marketing skills

TRAINING
Video-based training program

BUSINESS SUPPORT
Newsletter
Toll-free phone line
Internet
Purchasing cooperatives

MARKETING SUPPORT
Ad slicks
Press releases

STRETCH-N-GROW INT'L. INC.

Ranked #239 in Entrepreneur Magazine's 2005 Franchise 500

Financial rating: $$$

P.O. Box 7599
Seminole, FL 33775
Ph: (727)596-7614
Fax: (727)596-7633
www.stretch-n-grow.com
On-site children's fitness program
Began: 1992, Franchising since: 1993
Headquarters size: 4 employees
Franchise department: 4 employees

U.S. franchises: 160
Canadian franchises: 6
Other foreign franchises: 41
Company-owned: 0

Seeking: All U.S.
Seeking in Canada? Yes
Exclusive territories? Yes
Homebased option? Yes
Kiosk option? No
Employees needed to run franchise: 1
Absentee ownership? No

COSTS
Total cost: $19.3K
Franchise fee: $18.6K
Royalty fee: $150/mo.
Term of agreement: Info not provided
Franchisees required to buy multiple
    units? No

FINANCING
No financing available

QUALIFICATIONS
Cash liquidity: $20K-25K
Experience:
    Enjoy working with children

TRAINING
At headquarters: 4 days
In Tampa, FL: As needed

BUSINESS SUPPORT
Newsletter
Meetings
Toll-free phone line
Internet

MARKETING SUPPORT
National media campaign
Ads in day-care center publication

STROLLERFIT INC.

Ranked #482 in Entrepreneur Magazine's 2005 Franchise 500   *Financial rating: $$$$*

100 E-Business Wy., #290
Cincinnati, OH 45241
Ph: (513)489-2920
Fax: (513)489-2964
www.strollerfit.com
Interactive fitness programs, classes &
    products for parents & babies
Began: 1997, Franchising since: 2001
Headquarters size: 4 employees
Franchise department: 4 employees

U.S. franchises: 12
Canadian franchises: 0
Other foreign franchises: 0
Company-owned: 0

Seeking: South, Southeast, Midwest
Seeking in Canada? No
Exclusive territories? Yes
Homebased option? Yes
Kiosk option? No
Employees needed to run franchise:
    Info not provided
Absentee ownership? Yes

COSTS
Total cost: $4.99K-12.4K
Franchise fee: $2.5K
Royalty fee: 15%
Term of agreement: 2 years renewable
    at no charge
Franchisees required to buy multiple
    units? No

FINANCING
No financing available

QUALIFICATIONS
Cash liquidity: $5K
Experience:
    General business experience
    Marketing skills

TRAINING
At headquarters

BUSINESS SUPPORT
Meetings
Toll-free phone line
Internet
Security/safety procedures
Field operations/evaluations
Purchasing cooperatives

MARKETING SUPPORT
Ad slicks

CHILDREN'S   ID SYSTEMS

IDENT-A-KID SERVICES OF AMERICA

Ranked #215 in Entrepreneur Magazine's 2005 Franchise 500   *Financial rating: $$$*

2810 Scherer Dr., #100
St. Petersburg, FL 33716
Ph: (727)577-4646
Fax: (727)576-8258
www.ident-a-kid.com
Children's identification products &
    services
Began: 1986, Franchising since: 2000
Headquarters size: 6 employees
Franchise department: 2 employees

U.S. franchises: 235
Canadian franchises: 0
Other foreign franchises: 0
Company-owned: 0
Units concentrated in all U.S.

Seeking: All U.S.
Seeking in Canada? Yes
Exclusive territories? Yes
Homebased option? Yes
Kiosk option? No

Employees needed to run franchise: 0-3
Absentee ownership? No

COSTS
Total cost: $29.5K-64.96K
Franchise fee: $29.5K
Royalty fee: 0
Term of agreement: 10 years renewable
    at no charge
Franchisees required to buy multiple
    units? No

FINANCING
No financing available

QUALIFICATIONS
Experience:
    General business experience
    Marketing skills

TRAINING
At franchisee's location: 3 days
By phone
Videos, operations manual, website

BUSINESS SUPPORT
Newsletter
Meetings
Toll-free phone line
Internet
Field operations/evaluations

MARKETING SUPPORT
National media campaign

MCGRUFF SAFE KIDS TOTAL IDENTIFICATION SYSTEM

Financial rating: $$

15500 Wayzata Blvd., #812
Wayzata, MN 55391
Ph: (888)209-4218
Fax: (727)781-9863
www.mcgruff-safe-kids.com
Computerized children's identification
   system
Began: 2001, Franchising since: 2002
Headquarters size: Info not provided
Franchise department:
   Info not provided

U.S. franchises: 35
Canadian franchises: 0
Other foreign franchises: 0
Company-owned: 0
Units concentrated in all U.S.

Seeking: All U.S.
Seeking in Canada? Yes
Exclusive territories? Yes
Homebased option? Yes
Kiosk option? Yes
Employees needed to run franchise: 1
Absentee ownership? No

COSTS
Total cost: $33.3K-38.5K
Kiosk cost: Varies
Franchise fee: $30K
Royalty fee: 0
Term of agreement: 3 years renewable
   at $3K
Franchisees required to buy multiple
   units? No

FINANCING
In-house: None
3rd-party: Accounts receivable, equip-
   ment, franchise fee, inventory, pay-
   roll, startup costs

QUALIFICATIONS
Net worth: $35K
Cash liquidity: $15K
Experience:
   General business experience

TRAINING
At franchisee's location: 24 hours

BUSINESS SUPPORT
Newsletter
Toll-free phone line
Grand opening
Internet
Field operations/evaluations

MARKETING SUPPORT
Ad slicks
National media campaign

SAFE KIDS CARD

Financial rating: $$$

17100-B Bear Valley Rd., PMB #238
Victorville, CA 92392
Ph: (909)496-9982
Fax: (760)249-5751
www.myfamilycd.com
Children's, adult & pet identification
   system
Began: 2002, Franchising since: 2003
Headquarters size: 2 employees
Franchise department: 1 employee

U.S. franchises: 30
Canadian franchises: 0
Other foreign franchises: 0
Company-owned: 0
Units concentrated in AZ, CA, CO, FL,
   GA, KY, MI, NC, NJ, PA, SC, TX,
   VA, WI

Seeking: All U.S.
Seeking in Canada? Yes
Exclusive territories? Yes
Homebased option? Yes
Kiosk option? Yes
Employees needed to run franchise: 2-3
Absentee ownership? Yes

COSTS
Total cost: $20.4K-48.4K
Kiosk cost: to $50K
Franchise fee: $18.9K
Royalty fee: $75/mo.
Term of agreement: 10 years renewable
   at $1K
Franchisees required to buy multiple
   units? No

FINANCING
No financing available

QUALIFICATIONS
Net worth: $20K
Cash liquidity: $7K+
Experience:
   General business experience
   Marketing skills
   Enjoy being with children

TRAINING
At headquarters: 2 days
At franchisee's location (optional)

BUSINESS SUPPORT
Newsletter
Internet
Security/safety procedures
Purchasing cooperatives

MARKETING SUPPORT
Co-op advertising

CHILDREN'S LEARNING

ABRAKADOODLE

Financial rating: $$$

1800 Robert Fulton Dr.
Reston, VA 22191
Ph: (703)871-7356
Fax: (703)766-3606
www.abrakadoodle.com
Art education classes
Began: 2002, Franchising since: 2004
Headquarters size: 9 employees
Franchise department: 2 employees

U.S. franchises: 13
Canadian franchises: 0
Other foreign franchises: 0
Company-owned: 1
Units concentrated in all U.S.

Seeking: All U.S.
Seeking in Canada? Yes
Exclusive territories? Yes
Homebased option? Yes
Kiosk option? No
Employees needed to run franchise: 5-10
Absentee ownership? No

COSTS
Total cost: $36.98K-44.7K
Franchise fee: $28.9K
Royalty fee: 8-6%
Term of agreement: 10 years renewable
     at 5% of current franchise fee
Franchisees required to buy multiple
     units? No

FINANCING
No financing available

QUALIFICATIONS
Net worth: $100K
Cash liquidity: $40K
Experience:
     Marketing skills

TRAINING
At headquarters: 5 days
At franchisee's location: 20-60 hours

BUSINESS SUPPORT
Newsletter
Meetings
Internet
Field operations/evaluations
Purchasing cooperatives

MARKETING SUPPORT
Co-op advertising
Ad slicks
National media campaign

COMPUCHILD

Financial rating: $

602 Main St., #2
Rochester, IN 46975
Ph: (800)619-5437
Fax: (574)223-4422
www.compuchild.com
Preschool computer education
Began: 1994, Franchising since: 2001
Headquarters size: 2 employees
Franchise department: 2 employees

U.S. franchises: 48
Canadian franchises: 0
Other foreign franchises: 0
Company-owned: 1
Units concentrated in CA, FL, NC,
     SC, TX

Seeking: All U.S.
Focusing on: All U.S. except ND, RI, SD
Seeking in Canada? Yes
Exclusive territories? Yes
Homebased option? Yes
Kiosk option? No
Employees needed to run franchise: 1
Absentee ownership? Yes

COSTS
Total cost: $13.9K-15K
Franchise fee: $12.5K
Royalty fee: Varies
Term of agreement: 5 years renewable
     at no charge
Franchisees required to buy multiple
     units? Outside U.S. only

FINANCING
No financing available

QUALIFICATIONS
Net worth: $50K
Cash liquidity: $13.9K-15K
Experience:
     General business experience
     Marketing skills

TRAINING
At headquarters: Varies
At franchisee's location: 3 days
At annual national meeting: 3 days

BUSINESS SUPPORT
Newsletter
Meetings
Toll-free phone line
Internet

MARKETING SUPPORT
National media campaign

COMPUTERTOTS/COMPUTER EXPLORERS

Ranked #414 in Entrepreneur Magazine's 2005 Franchise 500   *Financial rating: $$$$*

12715 Telge Rd.
Cypress, TX 77429
Ph: (888)638-8722/(281)256-4100
Fax: (281)256-4178
www.computertots.com
Tech training for schools, kids & adults
Began: 1983, Franchising since: 1988
Headquarters size: Info not provided
Franchise department:
   Info not provided

U.S. franchises: 89
Canadian franchises: 0
Other foreign franchises: 5
Company-owned: 0

Seeking: All U.S.
Seeking in Canada? Yes
Exclusive territories? Yes
Homebased option? Yes
Kiosk option? No
Employees needed to run franchise: 6
Absentee ownership? No

COSTS
Total cost: $47.7K-66.3K
Franchise fee: $30K
Royalty fee: 8%
Term of agreement: 15 years renewable
   at 5% of franchise fee
Franchisees required to buy multiple
   units? No

FINANCING
In-house: Franchise fee
3rd-party: None

QUALIFICATIONS
Cash liquidity: $25K
Experience:
   General business experience
   Marketing skills

TRAINING
At headquarters: 10 days
At franchisee's location: 2 days

BUSINESS SUPPORT
Newsletter
Meetings
Toll-free phone line
Internet
Security/safety procedures

MARKETING SUPPORT
National media campaign
Regional marketing
Direct-mail campaign

DRAMA KIDS INT'L. INC.

Ranked #388 in Entrepreneur Magazine's 2005 Franchise 500   *Financial rating: $$$$*

3225-B Corporate Ct.
Ellicott City, MD 21042
Ph: (410)480-2015
Fax: (410)480-2026
www.dramakids.com
After-school children's drama program
Began: 1979, Franchising since: 1989
Headquarters size: 8 employees
Franchise department: 3 employees

U.S. franchises: 26
Canadian franchises: 0
Other foreign franchises: 101
Company-owned: 2
Units concentrated in all U.S.

Seeking: All U.S.
Seeking in Canada? No
Exclusive territories? Yes
Homebased option? Yes
Kiosk option? No
Employees needed to run franchise: 3
Absentee ownership? No

COSTS
Total cost: $36.2K-43.2K
Franchise fee: $27.5K
Royalty fee: 10%
Term of agreement: 5 years renewable
   at $750
Franchisees required to buy multiple
   units? No

FINANCING
No financing available

QUALIFICATIONS
Net worth: $50K
Cash liquidity: $25K
Experience:
   General business experience

TRAINING
At headquarters: 5 days
At franchisee's location: 5 days
Regional training: 1 day
At annual conference

BUSINESS SUPPORT
Newsletter
Meetings
Toll-free phone line
Grand opening
Internet
Security/safety procedures
Field operations/evaluations

MARKETING SUPPORT
Co-op advertising
Ad slicks
National media campaign
Regional marketing
Direct mail
PR firm that works w/franchisees

ENOPI DAEKYO USA INC.

Ranked #225 in Entrepreneur Magazine's 2005 Franchise 500   *Financial rating: $$$$*

701 E. Palisades Ave., #201
Englewood Cliffs, NJ 07632
Ph: (888)835-1212/(201)894-1212
Fax: (201)894-8686
www.daekyo.com
Supplemental learning program
Began: 1976, Franchising since: 1976
Headquarters size: 30 employees
Franchise department: 10 employees

U.S. franchises: 47
Canadian franchises: 0
Other foreign franchises: 80
Company-owned: 420
Units concentrated in all U.S.

Seeking: All U.S.
Seeking in Canada? Yes
Exclusive territories? No
Homebased option? No
Kiosk option? No
Employees needed to run franchise: 3
Absentee ownership? No

COSTS
Total cost: $9.5K-17K
Franchise fee: $2K
Royalty fee: 28-40%
Term of agreement: 2 years renewable
    at no charge
Franchisees required to buy multiple
    units? No

FINANCING
No financing available

QUALIFICATIONS
Net worth: $30K
Cash liquidity: $10K
Experience:
    General business experience
    Marketing skills

TRAINING
At headquarters: 16 hours+
At franchisee's location: Ongoing
At regional office

BUSINESS SUPPORT
Newsletter
Meetings
Toll-free phone line
Grand opening
Internet
Security/safety procedures
Field operations/evaluations

MARKETING SUPPORT
Co-op advertising
National media campaign
Regional marketing
Statewide advertising

FASTRACKIDS INT'L. LTD.

Ranked #220 in Entrepreneur Magazine's 2005 Franchise 500   *Financial rating: $$$$*

6900 E. Belleview Ave., 1st Fl.
Greenwood Village, CO 80111
Ph: (303)224-0200
Fax: (303)224-0222
www.fastrackids.com
Enrichment education for young
    children
Began: 1998, Franchising since: 1998
Headquarters size: 12 employees
Franchise department: 10 employees

U.S. franchises: 76
Canadian franchises: 4
Other foreign franchises: 121
Company-owned: 0
Units concentrated in all U.S.

Seeking: All U.S.
Seeking in Canada? Yes
Exclusive territories? Yes
Homebased option? No
Kiosk option? No
Employees needed to run franchise: 1-2
Absentee ownership? Yes

COSTS
Total cost: $32.5K-87.5K
Franchise fee: $21.5K
Royalty fee: 1.5%
Term of agreement: 5 years renewable
    at $1K
Franchisees required to buy multiple
    units? No

FINANCING
In-house: Franchise fee
3rd-party: Franchise fee

QUALIFICATIONS
Experience:
    Industry experience
    General business experience
    Marketing skills

TRAINING
At headquarters: 5 days

BUSINESS SUPPORT
Newsletter
Meetings
Internet

MARKETING SUPPORT
Info not provided

HIGH TOUCH-HIGH TECH

Ranked #473 in Entrepreneur Magazine's 2005 Franchise 500　　　　　*Financial rating: $$$*

12352 Wiles Rd.
Coral Springs, FL 33076
Ph: (800)444-4968
Fax: (954)755-1242
www.hightouch-hightech.com
Science activities for schools/children's
　　parties
Began: 1990, Franchising since: 1993
Headquarters size: 9 employees
Franchise department: 3 employees

U.S. franchises: 70
Canadian franchises: 9
Other foreign franchises: 11
Company-owned: 2
Units concentrated in CT, FL, GA, IL,
　　MA, NJ, PA, SC, TX

Seeking: All U.S.
Seeking in Canada? Yes
Exclusive territories? Yes
Homebased option? Yes
Kiosk option? No
Employees needed to run franchise: 4
Absentee ownership? Yes

COSTS
Total cost: $20.1K
Franchise fee: $15K
Royalty fee: 7%
Term of agreement: 10 years renewable
　　at $2.5K
Franchisees required to buy multiple
　　units? No

FINANCING
In-house: Franchise fee
3rd-party: None

QUALIFICATIONS
Experience:
　　General business experience
　　Marketing skills
　　Education or teaching experience

TRAINING
At headquarters: 5 days

BUSINESS SUPPORT
Newsletter
Meetings
Toll-free phone line
Internet
Security/safety procedures
Field operations/evaluations

MARKETING SUPPORT
Ad slicks

KIDSTAGE

Current financial data not available

P.O. Box 1072
Appleton, WI 54912
Ph: (877)415-5115
Fax: (920)993-1193
www.kidstagefranchise.com
Children's theater program
Began: 1997, Franchising since: 2003
Headquarters size: 5 employees
Franchise department: 2 employees

U.S. franchises: 8
Canadian franchises: 0
Other foreign franchises: 0
Company-owned: 2
Units concentrated in AZ, CO, NV,
　　NY, TX, WI

Seeking: All U.S.
Focusing on: CA, MI, PA
Seeking in Canada? No
Exclusive territories? Yes
Homebased option? Yes
Kiosk option? No
Employees needed to run franchise: 0-5
Absentee ownership? Yes

COSTS
Total cost: $10K-18.5K
Franchise fee: $9.5K
Royalty fee: 6%
Term of agreement: 5 years renewable
　　at no charge
Franchisees required to buy multiple
　　units? No

FINANCING
In-house: Franchise fee
3rd-party: None

QUALIFICATIONS
Cash liquidity: $10K
Experience:
　　General business experience
　　Desire to work with children

TRAINING
At headquarters: 4 days
At franchisee's location: 4 days

BUSINESS SUPPORT
Newsletter
Meetings
Toll-free phone line
Internet

MARKETING SUPPORT
Co-op advertising
Ad slicks

KIDZART

Ranked #494 in Entrepreneur Magazine's 2005 Franchise 500　　　　*Financial rating: $$$*

1327 Dime Box Cir.
New Braunfels, TX 78130
Ph: (800)379-8302
Fax: (830)626-0260
www.kidzart.com
Drawing & art education for all ages
Began: 1997, Franchising since: 2002
Headquarters size: 4 employees
Franchise department: 4 employees

U.S. franchises: 43
Canadian franchises: 1
Other foreign franchises: 0
Company-owned: 1
Units concentrated in all U.S.

Seeking: All U.S.
Seeking in Canada? Yes
Exclusive territories? Yes
Homebased option? Yes
Kiosk option? No
Employees needed to run franchise: 1-5
Absentee ownership? No

COSTS

Total cost: $32.5K-42.5K
Franchise fee: $28.5K
Royalty fee: 7%
Term of agreement: 10 years renewable
　　at no charge
Franchisees required to buy multiple
　　units? No

FINANCING

No financing available

QUALIFICATIONS

Net worth: $100K
Cash liquidity: $30K
Experience:
　　General business experience
　　Marketing skills
　　Teaching skills
　　Creativity

TRAINING

At headquarters: 4-5 days
Ongoing

BUSINESS SUPPORT

Meetings
Toll-free phone line
Grand opening
Internet

MARKETING SUPPORT

Regional marketing
PR support

KUMON MATH & READING CENTERS

Ranked #17 in Entrepreneur Magazine's 2005 Franchise 500　　　　*Financial rating: $$$$*

300 Frank W. Burr Blvd., 5th Fl.
Teaneck, NJ 07666
Ph: (866)633-0740/(201)928-0444
Fax: (201)928-0044
www.kumon.com
Supplemental education
Began: 1958, Franchising since: 1958
Headquarters size: 400 employees
Franchise department: 12 employees

U.S. franchises: 1,190
Canadian franchises: 338
Other foreign franchises: 26,102
Company-owned: 22

Seeking: All U.S.
Seeking in Canada? Yes
Exclusive territories? No
Homebased option? No
Kiosk option? No
Employees needed to run franchise: 2-3
Absentee ownership? No

COSTS

Total cost: $9.3K-29.3K
Franchise fee: $1K
Royalty fee: $30+/student/mo.
Term of agreement: 2 years renewable
　　at no charge
Franchisees required to buy multiple
　　units? No

FINANCING

No financing available

QUALIFICATIONS

Experience:
　　General business experience
　　Marketing skills
　　Good math, reading &
　　communications skills

TRAINING

At headquarters: 3 months+
At franchisee's location: Ongoing
At regional offices

BUSINESS SUPPORT

Newsletter
Meetings
Toll-free phone line
Grand opening
Internet

MARKETING SUPPORT

Co-op advertising
Regional marketing

THE MAD SCIENCE GROUP

Ranked #230 in Entrepreneur Magazine's 2005 Franchise 500   *Financial rating: $$$$*

8360 Bougainville St., #201
Montreal, QC H4P 2G1 Canada
Ph: (800)586-5231
Fax: (514)344-6695
www.madscience.org
Science activities for children
Began: 1985, Franchising since: 1995
Headquarters size: 30 employees
Franchise department: 3 employees

U.S. franchises: 112
Canadian franchises: 21
Other foreign franchises: 32
Company-owned: 0
Units concentrated in all U.S.

Seeking: All U.S.
Seeking in Canada? Yes
Exclusive territories? Yes
Homebased option? Yes
Kiosk option? No
Employees needed to run franchise: 3-30
Absentee ownership? No

COSTS
Total cost: $37.3K-79K
Franchise fee: $10K-23.5K
Royalty fee: 8%
Term of agreement: 20 years renewable
    at no charge
Franchisees required to buy multiple
    units? No

FINANCING
In-house: None
3rd-party: Equipment, franchise fee,
    startup costs

QUALIFICATIONS
Net worth: $50K
Cash liquidity: $23.5K
Experience:
    General business experience

TRAINING
At headquarters: 5 days
At franchisee's location: 5 days

BUSINESS SUPPORT
Newsletter
Meetings
Toll-free phone line
Grand opening
Internet
Security/safety procedures
Field operations/evaluations

MARKETING SUPPORT
Co-op advertising
Regional marketing

MATHNASIUM LEARNING CENTERS

Financial rating: $$$

468 N. Camden Dr., #200
Beverly Hills, CA 90210
Ph: (877)531-6284
Fax: (310)943-6123
www.mathnasium.com
Math-only after-school learning centers
Began: 2002, Franchising since: 2003
Headquarters size: 7 employees
Franchise department: 4 employees

U.S. franchises: 15
Canadian franchises: 0
Other foreign franchises: 0
Company-owned: 2

Seeking: All U.S.
Seeking in Canada? Yes
Exclusive territories? No
Homebased option? No
Kiosk option? No
Employees needed to run franchise: 1
Absentee ownership? No

COSTS
Total cost: $33.5K-70K
Franchise fee: $5K
Royalty fee: Varies
Term of agreement: 3 years renewable
    at no charge
Franchisees required to buy multiple
    units? No

FINANCING
No financing available

QUALIFICATIONS
Cash liquidity: $27.1K
Experience:
    General business experience
    Marketing skills
    Must enjoy math
    Must enjoy teaching children

TRAINING
At headquarters: 10 days

BUSINESS SUPPORT
Meetings
Toll-free phone line
Internet
Field operations/evaluations

MARKETING SUPPORT
Ad slicks

ODYSSEY ART CENTERS

Current financial data not available

Box 512
Tarrytown, NY 10591
Ph: (914)631-7148
Fax: (914)631-8337
www.odysseyart.com
Art classes
Began: 1974, Franchising since: 1995
Headquarters size: Info not provided
Franchise department: 2 employees

U.S. franchises: 2
Canadian franchises: 0
Other foreign franchises: 0
Company-owned: 1
Units concentrated in Eastern U.S.

Seeking: All U.S.
Seeking in Canada? No
Exclusive territories? Yes
Homebased option? Yes
Kiosk option? No
Employees needed to run franchise: 1
Absentee ownership? No

COSTS
Total cost: $28.7K-56.2K
Franchise fee: $24K
Royalty fee: 6%
Term of agreement: 10 years renewable
    at no charge
Franchisees required to buy multiple
    units? No

FINANCING
No financing available

QUALIFICATIONS
Info not provided

TRAINING
At headquarters: 2 weeks
At franchisee's location: Periodic visits

BUSINESS SUPPORT
Newsletter
Meetings
Grand opening
Internet
Purchasing cooperatives

MARKETING SUPPORT
Info not provided

THE WHOLE CHILD LEARNING CO.

Current financial data not available

921 Belvin St.
San Marcos, TX 78666
Ph: (888)317-3535
Fax: (512)392-7820
www.wholechild.com
Children's enrichment programs
Began: 1996, Franchising since: 1999
Headquarters size: 3 employees
Franchise department: 1 employee

U.S. franchises: 12
Canadian franchises: 0
Other foreign franchises: 0
Company-owned: 7

Seeking: All U.S.
Seeking in Canada? Yes
Exclusive territories? Yes
Homebased option? Yes
Kiosk option? No
Employees needed to run franchise: 1
Absentee ownership? No

COSTS
Total cost: $17.5K
Franchise fee: $17.5K
Royalty fee: 6%
Term of agreement: 5 years renewable
    at no charge
Franchisees required to buy multiple
    units? No

FINANCING
In-house: Equipment, franchise fee,
    startup costs
3rd-party: None

QUALIFICATIONS
Net worth: $8K
Cash liquidity: $7.5K
Experience:
    Industry experience
    General business experience
    Marketing skills

TRAINING
At headquarters: 3 days
At franchisee's location: 5 days

BUSINESS SUPPORT
Newsletter
Meetings
Toll-free phone line
Grand opening
Internet
Field operations/evaluations

MARKETING SUPPORT
Co-op advertising
Regional marketing

YOUNG REMBRANDTS FRANCHISE INC.

Ranked #368 in Entrepreneur Magazine's 2005 Franchise 500　　　　*Financial rating: $$$*

23 N. Union St.
Elgin, IL 60123
Ph: (847)742-6966
Fax: (847)742-7197
www.youngrembrandts.com
Art classes for children ages 3 to 12
Began: 1988, Franchising since: 1997
Headquarters size: 15 employees
Franchise department: 8 employees

U.S. franchises: 41
Canadian franchises: 0
Other foreign franchises: 0
Company-owned: 1
Units concentrated in all U.S.

Seeking: All U.S.
Seeking in Canada? No
Exclusive territories? Yes
Homebased option? Yes
Kiosk option? No
Employees needed to run franchise: 2-20
Absentee ownership? No

COSTS
Total cost: $39.5K-48.8K
Franchise fee: $31.5K
Royalty fee: Varies
Term of agreement: 10 years renewable
　at $1.5K
Franchisees required to buy multiple
　units? No

FINANCING
No financing available

QUALIFICATIONS
Cash liquidity: $75K
Experience:
　Industry experience
　General business experience
　Marketing skills

TRAINING
At headquarters: 5 days

BUSINESS SUPPORT
Newsletter
Meetings
Toll-free phone line
Internet
Field operations/evaluations

MARKETING SUPPORT
Co-op advertising
Ad slicks
Complete marketing package

CHILDREN'S MISCELLANEOUS

BABIES 'N' BELLS INC.

Financial rating: 0

4489 Mira Vista Dr.
Frisco, TX 75034
Ph: (888)418-2229
Fax: (469)384-0138
www.babiesnbells.com
Invitations & announcements
Began: 1996, Franchising since: 1997
Headquarters size: 6 employees
Franchise department: 2 employees

U.S. franchises: 64
Canadian franchises: 0
Other foreign franchises: 0
Company-owned: 34
Units concentrated in all U.S.

Seeking: All U.S.
Seeking in Canada? No
Exclusive territories? Yes
Homebased option? Yes
Kiosk option? No
Employees needed to run franchise: 1
Absentee ownership? No

COSTS
Total cost: $16.7K-28.9K
Franchise fee: $9K
Royalty fee: 8%
Term of agreement: 5 years renewable
　at $2K
Franchisees required to buy multiple
　units? No

FINANCING
No financing available

QUALIFICATIONS
Cash liquidity: $15K
Experience:
　General business experience

TRAINING
At headquarters: 1 week

BUSINESS SUPPORT
Newsletter
Meetings
Toll-free phone line
Internet

MARKETING SUPPORT
Co-op advertising
National media campaign

INFANTHOUSE.COM

Current financial data not available

3119 W. 5th St.
Fort Worth, TX 76107
Ph: (866)463-2685/(817)810-0076
Fax: (817)810-0711
www.infanthouse.com
Childproofing services
Began: 2004, Franchising since: 2004
Headquarters size: 4 employees
Franchise department: 4 employees

U.S. franchises: 12
Canadian franchises: 0
Other foreign franchises: 0
Company-owned: 1

Seeking: All U.S.
Seeking in Canada? Yes
Exclusive territories? Yes
Homebased option? Yes
Kiosk option? No
Employees needed to run franchise:
    Info not provided
Absentee ownership? No

COSTS
Total cost: $5K-30K
Franchise fee: $5K
Royalty fee: 0
Term of agreement: 5 years renewable
    at $5K
Franchisees required to buy multiple
    units? No

FINANCING
In-house: Startup costs
3rd-party: None

QUALIFICATIONS
Net worth: $50K
Cash liquidity: $30K
Experience:
    General business experience
    General carpentry skills

TRAINING
At headquarters

BUSINESS SUPPORT
Newsletter
Meetings
Toll-free phone line
Grand opening
Internet
Security/safety procedures
Field operations/evaluations
Purchasing cooperatives

MARKETING SUPPORT
Co-op advertising
Ad slicks
Radio, print & TV ads

STORK NEWS OF AMERICA INC.

Current financial data not available

1305 Hope Mills Rd., #A
Fayetteville, NC 28304
Ph: (800)633-6395/(910)426-1357
Fax: (910)426-2473
www.storknews.com
Newborn announcement services &
    products
Began: 1983, Franchising since: 1984
Headquarters size: 10 employees
Franchise department: 5 employees

U.S. franchises: 117
Canadian franchises: 0
Other foreign franchises: 0
Company-owned: 1
Units concentrated in CA, CO, FL, IL,
    KY, MD, MN, NC, NY, PA, SC, TX

Seeking: All U.S.
Seeking in Canada? No
Exclusive territories? Yes
Homebased option? Yes
Kiosk option? No
Employees needed to run franchise: 1-2
Absentee ownership? Yes

COSTS
Total cost: $10K-18K
Franchise fee: $5K-10K
Royalty fee: $500-1.5K/yr.
Term of agreement: 1 year renewable
    at no charge
Franchisees required to buy multiple
    units? No

FINANCING
No financing available

QUALIFICATIONS
Cash liquidity: $3K
Experience:
    General business experience
    Marketing skills

TRAINING
At headquarters: As needed
At franchisee's location

BUSINESS SUPPORT
Newsletter
Toll-free phone line
Internet

MARKETING SUPPORT
Co-op advertising

CHILDREN'S OTHER FRANCHISES

CHIP - THE CHILD I.D. PROGRAM

*Ranked #402 in Entrepreneur
    Magazine's 2005 Franchise 500*
705 Lakefield Rd., Bldg. G
Westlake Village, CA 91361
Ph: (805)557-0577
www.4childid.com
Child identification & school safety
    program
Financial rating: $$$

CLUB Z IN-HOME TUTORING SERVICES

*Ranked #158 in Entrepreneur
    Magazine's 2005 Franchise 500*
15310 Amberly Dr., #185
Tampa, FL 33647
Ph: (800)434-2582
www.clubztutoring.com
In-home tutoring services
Financial rating: $$$$

HEAD OVER HEELS FRANCHISE SYSTEM INC.

500 Caldwell Trace
Birmingham, AL 35242
Ph: (800)850-3547/(205)940-3547
www.headoverheelsgyms.com
Children's gymnastics/motor skills
    development system
Financial rating: Current financial
    data not available

LANGUAGE LEADERS

3N503 Townhall Rd.
Elburn, IL 60119
Ph: (630)232-9150
www.language-leaders.com
Foreign language instruction for
    children & adults, translating,
    interpreting services
Financial rating: Current financial
    data not available

WEBBY DANCE COMPANY

6975B Dixie Hwy.
Fairfield, OH 45014
Ph: (513)942-0100
www.webbydancecompany.com
On-site children's dance program
Financial rating: Current financial
    data not available

Financial Services

FINANCIAL **TAX SERVICES**

BLACK AMERICAN INCOME TAX SERVICE

Current financial data not available

4650 S. Hampton, #122
Dallas, TX 75232
Ph: (888)289-2831
Fax: (214)333-1411
www.americantaxandfinancialgroup.com
Tax preparation & electronic-filing
    services
Began: 1997, Franchising since: 2003
Headquarters size: 3 employees
Franchise department: 3 employees

U.S. franchises: 1
Canadian franchises: 0
Other foreign franchises: 0
Company-owned: 1

Seeking: All U.S.
Seeking in Canada? No
Exclusive territories? Yes
Homebased option? No
Kiosk option? No
Employees needed to run franchise: 4
Absentee ownership? Yes

COSTS
Total cost: $33.6K-43K
Franchise fee: $15K
Royalty fee: 10%
Term of agreement: 5 years renewable
    at $2.5K
Franchisees required to buy multiple
    units? No

FINANCING
In-house: Franchise fee
3rd-party: None

QUALIFICATIONS
Net worth: $40K
Cash liquidity: $40K
Experience:
    Commitment to customer service

TRAINING
At headquarters: 5 days

BUSINESS SUPPORT
Toll-free phone line
Grand opening
Internet
Security/safety procedures
Field operations/evaluations

MARKETING SUPPORT
Ad slicks
Regional marketing

ECONOTAX

Ranked #354 in Entrepreneur Magazine's 2005 Franchise 500　　　*Financial rating: $$$*

5846 Ridgewood Rd., #B-101,
　　Box 13829
Jackson, MS 39236
Ph: (800)748-9106/(601)956-0500
Fax: (601)956-0583
www.econotax.com
Tax services
Began: 1965, Franchising since: 1968
Headquarters size: 6 employees
Franchise department: 6 employees

U.S. franchises: 66
Canadian franchises: 0
Other foreign franchises: 0
Company-owned: 0
Units concentrated in AL, FL, LA, MS

Seeking: All U.S.
Seeking in Canada? No
Exclusive territories? Yes
Homebased option? No
Kiosk option? No
Employees needed to run franchise: 3
Absentee ownership? No

COSTS
Total cost: $15.4K-33K
Franchise fee: $10K
Royalty fee: 12%
Term of agreement: 5 years renewable
　　at no charge
Franchisees required to buy multiple
　　units? No

FINANCING
In-house: Franchise fee
3rd-party: None

QUALIFICATIONS
Net worth: $50K
Cash liquidity: $10K
Experience:
　　General business experience
　　Customer service experience
　　Computer skills

TRAINING
At headquarters: 1 week
Continuing education seminars

BUSINESS SUPPORT
Meetings
Toll-free phone line
Internet

MARKETING SUPPORT
Co-op advertising
Ad slicks
Regional marketing

ELECTRONIC TAX FILERS

Current financial data not available

P.O. Box 2077
Cary, NC 27512-2077
Ph: (919)469-0651
Fax: (919)460-5935
www.electronictaxfilers.com
Electronic filing of financial data
Began: 1990, Franchising since: 1991
Headquarters size: Info not provided
Franchise department:
　　Info not provided

U.S. franchises: 44
Canadian franchises: 0
Other foreign franchises: 0
Company-owned: 2

Seeking: All U.S.
Seeking in Canada? No
Exclusive territories? Yes
Homebased option? No
Kiosk option? No
Employees needed to run franchise: 2-3
Absentee ownership? No

COSTS
Total cost: $22K
Franchise fee: $9K
Royalty fee: 8%
Term of agreement: 3 years renewable
　　at $15K
Franchisees required to buy multiple
　　units? No

FINANCING
In-house: Franchise fee
3rd-party: None

QUALIFICATIONS
Net worth: $25K
Cash liquidity: $20K
Experience:
　　General business experience

TRAINING
At headquarters: 1 week minimum
At franchisee's location: Varies

BUSINESS SUPPORT
Meetings
Toll-free phone line
Grand opening
Lease negotiations
Security/safety procedures
Field operations/evaluations
Purchasing cooperatives

MARKETING SUPPORT
Co-op advertising
Ad slicks
Regional marketing

EXPRESS TAX

Ranked #320 in Entrepreneur Magazine's 2005 Franchise 500   *Financial rating: $$$$*

3030 Hartley Rd., #320
Jacksonville, FL 32257
Ph: (888)417-4461
Fax: (904)262-2864
www.expresstaxservice.com
Tax preparation & electronic-filing
  services
Began: 1997, Franchising since: 2002
Headquarters size: 11 employees
Franchise department: 5 employees

U.S. franchises: 238
Canadian franchises: 0
Other foreign franchises: 0
Company-owned: 1
Units concentrated in all U.S.

Seeking: All U.S.
Seeking in Canada? No
Exclusive territories? Yes
Homebased option? No
Kiosk option? Yes
Employees needed to run franchise: 2
Absentee ownership? No

COSTS
Total cost: $9.9K-16.6K
Kiosk cost: Same as total cost
Franchise fee: $5K
Royalty fee: $12/return
Term of agreement: 10 years renewable
  at $1K
Franchisees required to buy multiple
  units? No

FINANCING
In-house: Franchise fee
3rd-party: None

QUALIFICATIONS
Cash liquidity: $9.9K-16.6K
Experience:
  General business experience
  Marketing skills

TRAINING
At headquarters: 3 days
At annual conference: 2 days

BUSINESS SUPPORT
Newsletter
Meetings
Toll-free phone line
Internet

MARKETING SUPPORT
Co-op advertising
Ad slicks
Regional marketing

JACKSON HEWITT TAX SERVICE

Ranked #4 in Entrepreneur Magazine's 2005 Franchise 500   *Financial rating: $$$$*

7 Sylvan Wy.
Parsippany, NJ 07054
Ph: (800)475-2904
Fax: (973)496-2760
www.jacksonhewitt.com
Tax preparation services
Began: 1960, Franchising since: 1986
Headquarters size: 322 employees
Franchise department: 19 employees

U.S. franchises: 4,330
Canadian franchises: 0
Other foreign franchises: 0
Company-owned: 605

Seeking: All U.S.
Seeking in Canada? No
Exclusive territories? Yes
Homebased option? No
Kiosk option? Yes
Employees needed to run franchise:
  Info not provided
Absentee ownership? Yes

COSTS
Total cost: $38.8K-85.4K
Kiosk cost: $38.8K-63.5K
Franchise fee: $25K
Royalty fee: 15%
Term of agreement: 10 years renewable
  at no charge
Franchisees required to buy multiple
  units? No

FINANCING
In-house: Franchise fee
3rd-party: Equipment, franchise fee,
  inventory, startup costs

QUALIFICATIONS
Net worth: $100K-200K
Cash liquidity: $50K

TRAINING
At headquarters: 5 days
Regional training: 2 days

BUSINESS SUPPORT
Newsletter
Meetings
Toll-free phone line
Grand opening
Internet
Security/safety procedures
Field operations/evaluations
Purchasing cooperatives

MARKETING SUPPORT
Co-op advertising
Ad slicks
National media campaign
Regional marketing
800 locator number
Website

LIBERTY TAX SERVICE
Ranked #15 in Entrepreneur Magazine's 2005 Franchise 500   *Financial rating: $$$$*

1716 Corporate Landing
Virginia Beach, VA 23454
Ph: (800)790-3863/(757)493-8855
Fax: (757)493-0694
www.libertytaxfranchise.com
Income-tax preparation services
Began: 1972, Franchising since: 1973
Headquarters size: 150 employees
Franchise department: 15 employees

U.S. franchises: 1,103
Canadian franchises: 291
Other foreign franchises: 0
Company-owned: 18

Seeking: All U.S.
Seeking in Canada? Yes
Exclusive territories? Yes
Homebased option? No
Kiosk option? Yes
Employees needed to run franchise: 5-10
Absentee ownership? Yes

COSTS
Total cost: $38.1K-49.1K
Kiosk cost: $30K-35K
Franchise fee: $25K
Royalty fee: Varies
Term of agreement: Perpetual
    renewable at no charge
Franchisees required to buy multiple
    units? No

FINANCING
In-house: Accounts receivable,
    equipment, franchise fee,
    inventory, payroll, startup costs
3rd-party: None

QUALIFICATIONS
Cash liquidity: $50K
Experience:
    General business experience
    Marketing skills
    Customer service experience

TRAINING
At headquarters: 1 week
At franchisee's location: 1 day
In various cities: 2 days

BUSINESS SUPPORT
Newsletter
Meetings
Toll-free phone line
Grand opening
Internet
Lease negotiations
Field operations/evaluations
Purchasing cooperatives

MARKETING SUPPORT
Co-op advertising
Ad slicks
Regional marketing
Local marketing plans

TAX CENTERS OF AMERICA
Current financial data not available

1611 E. Main
Russellville, AR 72801
Ph: (479)968-4796
Fax: (479)968-8012
www.tcoa.net
Tax preparation & electronic filing
    services
Began: 1994, Franchising since: 1997
Headquarters size: 15 employees
Franchise department: 3 employees

U.S. franchises: 123
Canadian franchises: 0
Other foreign franchises: 1
Company-owned: 2

Seeking: All U.S.
Seeking in Canada? No
Exclusive territories? Yes
Homebased option? No
Kiosk option? No
Employees needed to run franchise: 2
Absentee ownership? Yes

COSTS
Total cost: $28.9K
Franchise fee: $15.5K
Royalty fee: Varies
Term of agreement: 10 years renewable
    at $1K
Franchisees required to buy multiple
    units? No

FINANCING
No financing available

QUALIFICATIONS
Experience:
    General business experience

TRAINING
At headquarters: 4 days

BUSINESS SUPPORT
Newsletter
Meetings
Toll-free phone line
Internet

MARKETING SUPPORT
Ad slicks
Regional marketing

FINANCIAL ▸ **MISCELLANEOUS**

ACFN- THE ATM FRANCHISE BUSINESS

Financial rating: $$

96 N. 3rd St., #600
San Jose, CA 95112
Ph: (888)794-2236
Fax: (888)708-8600
www.acfnfranchised.com
ATM machines
Began: 1986, Franchising since: 2003
Headquarters size: 14 employees
Franchise department: 7 employees

U.S. franchises: 6
Canadian franchises: 0
Other foreign franchises: 0
Company-owned: 2
Units concentrated in CA, FL, MA,
    MD, NY, TX

Seeking: All U.S.
Seeking in Canada? No
Exclusive territories? Yes
Homebased option? Yes
Kiosk option? No
Employees needed to run franchise: 1
Absentee ownership? Yes

COSTS
Total cost: $36K-78K
Franchise fee: $29K
Royalty fee: 0
Term of agreement: 10 years renewable
    up to $5K
Franchisees required to buy multiple
    units? No

FINANCING
In-house: Franchise fee
3rd-party: None

QUALIFICATIONS
Cash liquidity: $29K

TRAINING
At headquarters: 3 days

BUSINESS SUPPORT
Newsletter
Meetings
Toll-free phone line
Internet
Lease negotiations
Purchasing cooperatives

MARKETING SUPPORT
Co-op advertising
Ad slicks
Location agreement negotiation
Market research

CFO TODAY

Current financial data not available

401 St. Francis St.
Tallahassee, FL 32301
Ph: (888)643-1348/(850)681-1941
www.cfotoday.com
Accounting, tax & financial services
Began: 1989, Franchising since: 1990
Headquarters size: 8 employees
Franchise department: 8 employees

U.S. franchises: 244
Canadian franchises: 2
Other foreign franchises: 0
Company-owned: 1

Seeking: All U.S.
Seeking in Canada? Yes
Exclusive territories? Yes
Homebased option? Yes
Kiosk option? No
Employees needed to run franchise: 1
Absentee ownership? Yes

COSTS
Total cost: $24.4K-40K
Franchise fee: $24K
Royalty fee: Varies
Term of agreement: 10 years renewable
    at $4.8K
Franchisees required to buy multiple
    units? No

FINANCING
In-house: Franchise fee
3rd-party: None

QUALIFICATIONS
Experience:
    General business experience

TRAINING
At headquarters: 5 days
At franchisee's location: 1 day

BUSINESS SUPPORT
Newsletter
Meetings
Toll-free phone line
Internet
Field operations/evaluations
Purchasing cooperatives

MARKETING SUPPORT
Co-op advertising
Ad slicks
National media campaign
Regional marketing

ELLIOTT & COMPANY APPRAISERS

Financial rating: $$$$

3316-A Battleground Ave.
Greensboro, NC 27410
Ph: (800)854-5889
Fax: (336)854-7734
www.appraisalsanywhere.com
Real estate appraisals
Began: 1980, Franchising since: 1993
Headquarters size: 18 employees
Franchise department: 1 employee

U.S. franchises: 5
Canadian franchises: 0
Other foreign franchises: 0
Company-owned: 2

Seeking: All U.S.
Seeking in Canada? No
Exclusive territories? Yes
Homebased option? Yes
Kiosk option? No
Employees needed to run franchise: 1-2
Absentee ownership? No

COSTS

Total cost: $3.7K-18.9K
Franchise fee: $900-9.9K
Royalty fee: 8-18%
Term of agreement: 5 years renewable at $500
Franchisees required to buy multiple units? No

FINANCING

No financing available

QUALIFICATIONS

Experience:
  Industry experience
  General business experience
  Marketing skills
  Real estate appraiser's license

TRAINING

At headquarters: 1 days
At franchisee's location: 1 day
Annual state-required continuing education

BUSINESS SUPPORT

Newsletter
Meetings
Toll-free phone line
Grand opening
Internet
Security/safety procedures
Field operations/evaluations

MARKETING SUPPORT

Co-op advertising
Ad slicks
National media campaign
Regional marketing
Specialty advertising

FED USA INSURANCE/FINANCIAL SERVICES

Ranked #400 in Entrepreneur Magazine's 2005 Franchise 500

Financial rating: $$$

3661 W. Oakland Park Blvd.
Lauderdale Lakes, FL 33311
Ph: (888)440-6875
Fax: (954)308-1256
www.fedusa.com
Insurance & financial services/tax preparation
Began: 2000, Franchising since: 2001
Headquarters size: 120 employees
Franchise department: 5 employees

U.S. franchises: 42
Canadian franchises: 0
Other foreign franchises: 0
Company-owned: 24
Units concentrated in FL

Seeking: Southeast
Focusing on: CA, IL, TX
Seeking in Canada? No
Exclusive territories? Yes
Homebased option? No
Kiosk option? No
Employees needed to run franchise: 1-4
Absentee ownership? No

COSTS

Total cost: $49.1K-71.1K
Franchise fee: $19.5K
Royalty fee: 7%
Term of agreement: 10 years renewable at $3K
Franchisees required to buy multiple units? No

FINANCING

In-house: None
3rd-party: Equipment

QUALIFICATIONS

Net worth: $75K
Cash liquidity: $20K
Experience:
  General business experience
  Ability to manage finances
  Must enjoy dealing with public

TRAINING

At headquarters: 1 week
At training facility: 3 weeks

BUSINESS SUPPORT

Newsletter
Meetings
Toll-free phone line
Grand opening
Internet
Lease negotiations
Security/safety procedures
Field operations/evaluations
Purchasing cooperatives

MARKETING SUPPORT

Co-op advertising
Ad slicks
Regional marketing
Local marketing

PROPERTY DAMAGE APPRAISERS
Ranked #233 in Entrepreneur Magazine's 2005 Franchise 500   *Financial rating: $$$$*

6100 Southwest Blvd., #200
Ft. Worth, TX 76109-3964
Ph: (817)731-5555
Fax: (817)731-5550
www.pdahomeoffice.com
Auto & property appraisals for
    insurance cos.
Began: 1963, Franchising since: 1963
Headquarters size: 35 employees
Franchise department: 3 employees

U.S. franchises: 282
Canadian franchises: 0
Other foreign franchises: 0
Company-owned: 0

Seeking: All U.S.
Seeking in Canada? No
Exclusive territories? No
Homebased option? No
Kiosk option? No
Employees needed to run franchise:
    Info not provided
Absentee ownership? No

COSTS
Total cost: $18.3K-35.95K
Franchise fee: $0
Royalty fee: 15%
Term of agreement: 3 years renewable
    at no charge
Franchisees required to buy multiple
    units? No

FINANCING
No financing available

QUALIFICATIONS
Experience:
    Industry experience

TRAINING
At headquarters: 4-1/2 days
At franchisee's location: 3 days
Ongoing

BUSINESS SUPPORT
Newsletter
Meetings
Toll-free phone line
Internet
Field operations/evaluations
Purchasing cooperatives

MARKETING SUPPORT
Regional marketing

FINANCIAL ▸ OTHER FRANCHISES

COLBERT/BALL TAX SERVICE
2616 S. Loop W., #110
Houston, TX 77054
Ph: (713)592-5555
www.colbertballtax.com
Tax preparation & electronic-filing
    services
Financial rating: Current financial
    data not available

COMMERCIAL UNION INC.
3127 E. Otero Cir.
Littleton, CO 80122
Ph: (303)689-0867
www.cuatm.com
ATM machines
Financial rating: Current financial
    data not available

EXPENSE REDUCTION CONSULTING
6920 Annapolis Ct.
Parkland, FL 33067
Ph: (954)255-2511
www.ercfranchise.com
Corporate cost reduction services
Financial rating: Current financial
    data not available

TAX SMART AMERICA
7520-1 El Cajon Blvd., #106
La Mesa, CA 91941
Ph: (619)465-7186
www.taxsmartamerica.biz
Accounting & tax services
Financial rating: Current financial
    data not available

Food Businesses

FOOD

CANDY BOUQUET

Ranked #111 in Entrepreneur Magazine's 2005 Franchise 500   *Financial rating: $$$$*

423 E. Third St.
Little Rock, AR 72201
Ph: (877)226-3901
Fax: (501)375-9998
www.candybouquet.com
Floral-like designer gifts & gourmet
    confections
Began: 1989, Franchising since: 1993
Headquarters size: 30 employees
Franchise department: 30 employees

U.S. franchises: 582
Canadian franchises: 39
Other foreign franchises: 42
Company-owned: 1
Units concentrated in all U.S.

Seeking: All U.S.
Seeking in Canada? Yes
Exclusive territories? Yes
Homebased option? Yes
Kiosk option? Yes
Employees needed to run franchise: 1
Absentee ownership? Yes

COSTS
Total cost: $7.5K-50K
Kiosk cost: $7.3K-44.1K
Franchise fee: $3.6K-29K
Royalty fee: 0
Term of agreement: 5 years renewable
    at 25% of original fee
Franchisees required to buy multiple
    units? No

FINANCING
No financing available

QUALIFICATIONS
Cash liquidity: $7.5K-50K
Experience:
    Industry experience
    General business experience
    Marketing skills

TRAINING
At headquarters: 5 days

BUSINESS SUPPORT
Newsletter
Meetings
Toll-free phone line
Internet

MARKETING SUPPORT
Co-op advertising
Ad slicks

CARVEL

Ranked #125 in Entrepreneur Magazine's 2005 Franchise 500   *Financial rating: $$$*

200 Glenridge Point Pkwy., #200
Atlanta, GA 30342
Ph: (404)255-3250
Fax: (404)255-4978
www.carvel.com
Ice cream & ice cream cakes
Began: 1934, Franchising since: 1947
Headquarters size: 316 employees
Franchise department: 50 employees

U.S. franchises: 500
Canadian franchises: 3
Other foreign franchises: 16
Company-owned: 0
Units concentrated in all U.S.

Seeking: Northeast, South, Southeast,
   Midwest, Southwest
Focusing on: All U.S.
Seeking in Canada? No
Exclusive territories? No
Homebased option? No
Kiosk option? Yes
Employees needed to run franchise: 6
Absentee ownership? Yes

COSTS
Total cost: $30K-241K
Kiosk cost: $30K-199.6K
Franchise fee: $30K
Royalty fee: $1.77/gal.
Term of agreement: 20 years renewable
   at then-current fee
Franchisees required to buy multiple
   units? No

FINANCING
In-house: None
3rd-party: Equipment, franchise fee,
   inventory, startup costs

QUALIFICATIONS
Net worth: $250K+
Cash liquidity: $75K
Experience:
   General business experience

TRAINING
At headquarters: 10 days
At franchisee's location: 5 days
Ongoing

BUSINESS SUPPORT
Newsletter
Meetings
Toll-free phone line
Grand opening
Internet
Security/safety procedures
Field operations/evaluations
Purchasing cooperatives

MARKETING SUPPORT
Co-op advertising
Ad slicks
Regional marketing
Broadcast media

GUMBALL GOURMET

Current financial data not available

11622 McBean Dr.
El Monte, CA 91732
Ph: (866)486-2255
Fax: (626)453-3892
www.gumballgourmet.com
Gumball machine kiosks
Began: 2001, Franchising since: 2001
Headquarters size: 6 employees
Franchise department: 2 employees

U.S. franchises: 186
Canadian franchises: 0
Other foreign franchises: 0
Company-owned: 15

Seeking: All U.S.
Seeking in Canada? Yes
Exclusive territories? Yes
Homebased option? Yes
Kiosk option? Yes
Employees needed to run franchise: 0
Absentee ownership? Yes

COSTS
Total cost: $24.6K-462.1K
Kiosk cost: $1K-500K
Franchise fee: $17.2K
Royalty fee: $100/mo.
Term of agreement: 5 years renewable
   at $2K
Franchisees required to buy multiple
   units? No

FINANCING
No financing available

QUALIFICATIONS
Net worth: $20K+
Cash liquidity: $20K+
Experience:
   General business experience

TRAINING
At headquarters: 1 day

BUSINESS SUPPORT
Newsletter
Meetings
Toll-free phone line
Lease negotiations
Field operations/evaluations

MARKETING SUPPORT
Internet & kiosk signs

HAPPY & HEALTHY PRODUCTS INC.

Ranked #471 in Entrepreneur Magazine's 2005 Franchise 500   *Financial rating: $$$$*

1600 S. Dixie Hwy., #200
Boca Raton, FL 33432
Ph: (800)764-6114
Fax: (561)368-5267
www.fruitfull.com
Frozen fruit bars & smoothies
Began: 1991, Franchising since: 1993
Headquarters size: 10 employees
Franchise department: 4 employees

U.S. franchises: 100
Canadian franchises: 0
Other foreign franchises: 0
Company-owned: 0
Units concentrated in all U.S.

Seeking: All U.S.
Focusing on: All U.S. except LA, ME, ND, SD
Seeking in Canada? No
Exclusive territories? No
Homebased option? Yes
Kiosk option? No
Employees needed to run franchise: 0
Absentee ownership? No

COSTS
Total cost: $27K-59K
Franchise fee: $21K
Royalty fee: 0
Term of agreement: 10 years renewable at $500
Franchisees required to buy multiple units? No

FINANCING
No financing available

QUALIFICATIONS
Net worth: $29K-65K
Cash liquidity: $29K-65K
Experience:
    General business experience
    Marketing skills

TRAINING
At franchisee's location: 1-2 weeks
Additional training after first year in business

BUSINESS SUPPORT
Newsletter
Meetings
Internet

MARKETING SUPPORT
Ad slicks
National media campaign

ORION FOOD SYSTEMS LLC

Ranked #42 in Entrepreneur Magazine's 2005 Franchise 500   *Financial rating: $$$$*

2930 W. Maple, P.O. Box 780
Sioux Falls, SD 57101
Ph: (605)336-6961
Fax: (605)336-0141
www.orionfoodsys.com
Fast-food systems for nontraditional markets
Began: 1982, Franchising since: 1993
Headquarters size: 300 employees
Franchise department: 40 employees

U.S. franchises: 1,110
Canadian franchises: 26
Other foreign franchises: 0
Company-owned: 0
Units concentrated in all U.S.

Seeking: All U.S.
Seeking in Canada? Yes
Exclusive territories? Yes
Homebased option? No
Kiosk option? Yes
Employees needed to run franchise:
    Info not provided
Absentee ownership? Yes

COSTS
Total cost: $49.99K-852.5K
Kiosk cost: $16K-680K
Franchise fee: $2.99K
Royalty fee: 0
Term of agreement: 10 years renewable at $1K
Franchisees required to buy multiple units? No

FINANCING
In-house: Equipment
3rd-party: Equipment

QUALIFICATIONS
Net worth: $100K
Experience:
    Industry experience
    General business experience
    Marketing skills

TRAINING
At franchisee's location: 5 days

BUSINESS SUPPORT
Newsletter
Meetings
Toll-free phone line
Grand opening
Internet
Security/safety procedures
Field operations/evaluations

MARKETING SUPPORT
Ad slicks
National media campaign
Regional marketing

PIZZA INN INC.

Ranked #334 in Entrepreneur Magazine's 2005 Franchise 500　　　*Financial rating: $$$$*

3551 Plano Pkwy.
The Colony, TX 75056
Ph: (469)384-5000
Fax: (469)384-5059
www.pizzainn.com
Pizza, pasta, salads
Began: 1960, Franchising since: 1963
Headquarters size: 75 employees
Franchise department: 5 employees

U.S. franchises: 337
Canadian franchises: 0
Other foreign franchises: 67
Company-owned: 2
Units concentrated in NC, TX

Seeking: South, Southeast, Southwest
Focusing on: Midwest, Southeast,
　　Southwest
Seeking in Canada? Yes
Exclusive territories? Yes
Homebased option? No
Kiosk option? Yes
Employees needed to run franchise:
　　Info not provided
Absentee ownership? Yes

COSTS
Total cost: $48.9K-284.2K
Kiosk cost: $48.9K-73.1K
Franchise fee: $5K-20K
Royalty fee: 4-6%
Term of agreement: 10 years renewable
Franchisees required to buy multiple
　　units? Outside U.S. only

FINANCING
No financing available

QUALIFICATIONS
Net worth: $100K-200K
Cash liquidity: $50K-125K
Experience:
　　General business experience

TRAINING
At headquarters: 24 days
At franchisee's location: 3-5 days

BUSINESS SUPPORT
Newsletter
Meetings
Toll-free phone line
Grand opening
Field operations/evaluations

MARKETING SUPPORT
Co-op advertising
Ad slicks
Regional marketing

T.J. CINNAMONS

Current financial data not available

1000 Corporate Dr.
Ft. Lauderdale, FL 33334
Ph: (800)592-6245/(954)351-5200
Fax: (954)351-5222
www.arbys.com
Cinnamon rolls & gourmet bakery
　　products
Began: 1985, Franchising since: 1985
Headquarters size: 120 employees
Franchise department: 59 employees

U.S. franchises: 292
Canadian franchises: 0
Other foreign franchises: 0
Company-owned: 3
Units concentrated in all U.S.

Seeking: All U.S.
Seeking in Canada? No
Exclusive territories? Yes
Homebased option? No
Kiosk option? Yes
Employees needed to run franchise:
　　Info not provided
Absentee ownership? Yes

COSTS
Total cost: $22.1K-39.2K
(Franchise sells add-ons only.)
Kiosk cost: Varies
Franchise fee: $5K
Royalty fee: 4%
Term of agreement: 10 years renewable
　　at then-current franchise fee
Franchisees required to buy multiple
　　units? No

FINANCING
In-house: None
3rd-party: Accounts receivable,
　　equipment, franchise fee,
　　inventory, payroll, startup costs

QUALIFICATIONS
Cash liquidity: $500K
Experience:
　　Industry experience
　　General business experience
　　Marketing skills

TRAINING
Manual

BUSINESS SUPPORT
Newsletter
Meetings
Toll-free phone line
Grand opening
Internet
Security/safety procedures
Field operations/evaluations
Purchasing cooperatives

MARKETING SUPPORT
Ad slicks

FOOD **OTHER FRANCHISES**

FOODNET FRANCHISING INC.
4101 Cox Rd., #120
Glen Allen, VA 23060-3320
Ph: (804)273-0600
www.foodnetbrands.com
Italian sausages, hot dogs & sandwiches
Financial rating: 0

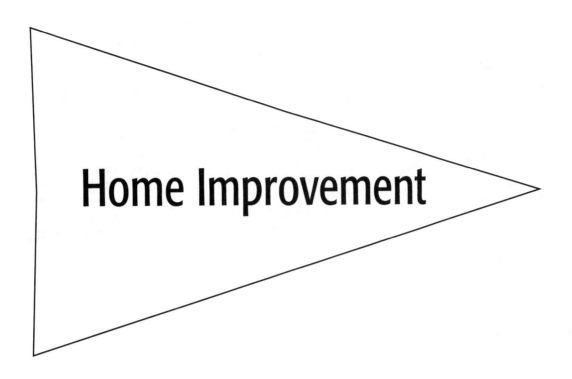

Home Improvement

HOME ▶ BUILDING & REMODELING

ARCHADECK

Ranked #289 in Entrepreneur Magazine's 2005 Franchise 500　　　　　*Financial rating: $$$$*

2112 W. Laburnum Ave., #100
Richmond, VA 23227
Ph: (800)789-3325/(804)353-6999
Fax: (804)358-1878
www.archadeck.com
Wooden decks/screened
　porches/gazebos
Began: 1980, Franchising since: 1984
Headquarters size: 25 employees
Franchise department: 2 employees

U.S. franchises: 81
Canadian franchises: 4
Other foreign franchises: 2
Company-owned: 1
Units concentrated in all U.S.

Seeking: All U.S.
Seeking in Canada? Yes
Exclusive territories? Yes
Homebased option? Yes
Kiosk option? No
Employees needed to run franchise: 2
Absentee ownership? No

COSTS
Total cost: $35K-95K
Franchise fee: $33.5K
Royalty fee: 3.5-5.5%+
Term of agreement: 10 years renewable
　at no charge
Franchisees required to buy multiple
　units? Outside U.S. only

FINANCING
In-house: Franchise fee
3rd-party: Franchise fee, startup costs

QUALIFICATIONS
Net worth: $150K
Cash liquidity: $40K-75K
Experience:
　General business experience

TRAINING
At headquarters: 20 days
At franchisee's location: 9 days

BUSINESS SUPPORT
Newsletter
Meetings
Toll-free phone line
Internet
Field operations/evaluations

MARKETING SUPPORT
Ad slicks
National media campaign

BORDER MAGIC

Financial rating: $$$

1503 CR 2700 N.
Rantoul, IL 61866
Ph: (217)892-2954
Fax: (217)893-3739
www.bordermagic.com
Concrete landscape edging
Began: 1987, Franchising since: 2003
Headquarters size: 10 employees
Franchise department: 3 employees

U.S. franchises: 76
Canadian franchises: 0
Other foreign franchises: 0
Company-owned: 0

Seeking: All U.S.
Seeking in Canada? Yes
Exclusive territories? Yes
Homebased option? Yes
Kiosk option? No
Employees needed to run franchise: 3
Absentee ownership? Yes

COSTS
Total cost: $38K-100K
Franchise fee: $5K
Royalty fee: $250/mo.
Term of agreement: 5 years renewable
   at $2.5K
Franchisees required to buy multiple
   units? No

FINANCING
In-house: None
3rd-party: Equipment, startup costs

QUALIFICATIONS
Experience:
   General business experience

TRAINING
At headquarters: 3 days

BUSINESS SUPPORT
Newsletter
Meetings
Toll-free phone line
Internet
Security/safety procedures
Field operations/evaluations
Purchasing cooperatives

MARKETING SUPPORT
Co-op advertising
Ad slicks
National media campaign

CONCRETE RAISING OF AMERICA INC.

Financial rating: $$$

2855 S. 166th St.
New Berlin, WI 53151
Ph: (800)270-0011/(262)827-5000
Fax: (262)827-5005
www.crc1.com
Concrete & foundation raising,
   stabilizing & repair
Began: 1947, Franchising since: 1993
Headquarters size: 14 employees
Franchise department: 4 employees

U.S. franchises: 12
Canadian franchises: 0
Other foreign franchises: 0
Company-owned: 3

Seeking: All U.S.
Seeking in Canada? Yes
Exclusive territories? Yes
Homebased option? Yes
Kiosk option? No
Employees needed to run franchise: 3-4
Absentee ownership? Yes

COSTS
Total cost: $16.9K-200K
Franchise fee: $16.9K-25K
Royalty fee: 4-8%
Term of agreement: 20 years renewable
   at no charge
Franchisees required to buy multiple
   units? No

FINANCING
In-house: Franchise fee
3rd-party: Equipment, franchise fee,
   startup costs

QUALIFICATIONS
Cash liquidity: $10K
Experience:
   Industry experience
   General business experience
   Marketing skills

TRAINING
At headquarters: 10 days
At franchisee's location: As needed
Biannual operator certification by
   franchisor

BUSINESS SUPPORT
Newsletter
Meetings
Toll-free phone line
Internet
Security/safety procedures
Field operations/evaluations
Purchasing cooperatives

MARKETING SUPPORT
Co-op advertising
Marketing planning & research

THE CRACK TEAM

Financial rating: 0

11694 Lackland Rd.
St. Louis, MO 63146
Ph: (866)272-2583/(314)426-0900
Fax: (314)426-0915
www.thecrackteam.com
Foundation crack repair
Began: 1985, Franchising since: 2000
Headquarters size: 20 employees
Franchise department: 5 employees

U.S. franchises: 11
Canadian franchises: 0
Other foreign franchises: 0
Company-owned: 6
Units concentrated in all U.S.

Seeking: All U.S.
Focusing on: All U.S. except AL, AZ,
    CA, FL, LA, MS, NM, NV, OK, TX
Seeking in Canada? Yes
Exclusive territories? Yes
Homebased option? Yes
Kiosk option? No
Employees needed to run franchise: 2-4
Absentee ownership? No

COSTS
Total cost: $44.6K-74.1K
Franchise fee: $15K
Royalty fee: 6%
Term of agreement: 20 years renewable
Franchisees required to buy multiple
    units? No

FINANCING
No financing available

QUALIFICATIONS
Cash liquidity: $60K
Experience:
    General business experience
    Marketing skills

TRAINING
At headquarters: 2 weeks
At franchisee's location: 1 week

BUSINESS SUPPORT
Newsletter
Meetings
Toll-free phone line
Internet
Security/safety procedures
Field operations/evaluations

MARKETING SUPPORT
Ad slicks
Regional marketing
Local publicity

HOMEPROS

Current financial data not available

2102 Kotter Ave., #A
Evansville, IN 47715
Ph: (812)473-1776
Fax: (812)473-1781
www.homepros.net
Home repair & renovation services
Began: 2001, Franchising since: 2002
Headquarters size: 12 employees
Franchise department: 4 employees

U.S. franchises: 8
Canadian franchises: 0
Other foreign franchises: 0
Company-owned: 2

Seeking: All U.S.
Seeking in Canada? No
Exclusive territories? Yes
Homebased option? Yes
Kiosk option? No
Employees needed to run franchise: 2
Absentee ownership? No

COSTS
Total cost: $39.8K-80.3K
Franchise fee: $26K
Royalty fee: 6%
Term of agreement: 5 years renewable
    at no charge
Franchisees required to buy multiple
    units? No

FINANCING
In-house: Franchise fee
3rd-party: None

QUALIFICATIONS
Net worth: $50K
Cash liquidity: $20K
Experience:
    Industry experience
    General business experience
    Basic home repair skills

TRAINING
At headquarters: 1 week
At franchisee's location: 1 day per
    quarter

BUSINESS SUPPORT
Newsletter
Meetings
Grand opening
Internet
Field operations/evaluations

MARKETING SUPPORT
Ad slicks
Ad campaigns
Ongoing

KITCHEN SOLVERS INC.

Ranked #290 in Entrepreneur Magazine's 2005 Franchise 500   *Financial rating: $$$*

401 Jay St.
LaCrosse, WI 54601
Ph: (800)845-6779/(608)791-5518
Fax: (608)784-2917
www.kitchensolvers.com
Kitchen/bath remodeling & cabinet
    refacing/flooring/closets
Began: 1982, Franchising since: 1984
Headquarters size: 9 employees
Franchise department: 9 employees

U.S. franchises: 123
Canadian franchises: 7
Other foreign franchises: 0
Company-owned: 0
Units concentrated in IA, IL, WI

Seeking: All U.S.
Focusing on: All U.S. except HI, RI
Seeking in Canada? Yes
Exclusive territories? Yes
Homebased option? Yes
Kiosk option? No
Employees needed to run franchise: 1-2
Absentee ownership? No

COSTS
Total cost: $40.3K-73K
Franchise fee: $25K-29.5K
Royalty fee: 4-6%
Term of agreement: 10 years renewable
    at no charge
Franchisees required to buy multiple
    units? No

FINANCING
In-house: Franchise fee
3rd-party: Equipment

QUALIFICATIONS
Net worth: $200K
Cash liquidity: $50K
Experience:
    General business experience
    Marketing skills

TRAINING
At headquarters: 5-10 days

BUSINESS SUPPORT
Newsletter
Meetings
Toll-free phone line
Internet
Field operations/evaluations

MARKETING SUPPORT
Co-op advertising
Ad slicks
National media campaign
Regional marketing

KITCHEN TUNE-UP

Ranked #169 in Entrepreneur Magazine's 2005 Franchise 500   *Financial rating: $$$*

813 Circle Dr.
Aberdeen, SD 57401
Ph: (800)333-6385/(605)225-4049
Fax: (605)225-1371
www.kitchentuneup.com
Custom cabinets, refacing &
    restoration
Began: 1986, Franchising since: 1988
Headquarters size: 13 employees
Franchise department: 12 employees

U.S. franchises: 308
Canadian franchises: 3
Other foreign franchises: 0
Company-owned: 0
Units concentrated in all U.S.

Seeking: All U.S.
Focusing on: All U.S. except HI
Seeking in Canada? Yes
Exclusive territories? Yes
Homebased option? Yes
Kiosk option? Yes
Employees needed to run franchise: 3
Absentee ownership? Yes

COSTS
Total cost: $18.6K-50.1K
Kiosk cost: $23.6K-55.1K
Franchise fee: $25K/10K
Royalty fee: 4.5-7%
Term of agreement: 10 years renewable
    at no charge
Franchisees required to buy multiple
    units? Outside U.S. only

FINANCING
In-house: Equipment
3rd-party: Franchise fee, inventory,
    startup costs

QUALIFICATIONS
Net worth: $75K
Cash liquidity: $15K-25K
Experience:
    General business experience

TRAINING
At headquarters: 8 days
At franchisee's location: Varies
At mentor location: 3-5 days

BUSINESS SUPPORT
Newsletter
Meetings
Toll-free phone line
Grand opening
Internet
Field operations/evaluations
Purchasing cooperatives

MARKETING SUPPORT
Co-op advertising
Ad slicks
National media campaign
Regional marketing
Internet advertising

RENOVATION PROFESSIONALS

Current financial data not available

1571 Hillview Dr.
Sarasota, FL 34239
Ph: (800)400-6455
Fax: (941)966-1526
www.renovationprofessionals.com
General contracting for renovation
   projects
Began: 1997, Franchising since: 2002
Headquarters size: 4 employees
Franchise department: 3 employees

U.S. franchises: 10
Canadian franchises: 0
Other foreign franchises: 0
Company-owned: 2

Seeking: South, Southeast, Midwest,
   Southwest
Seeking in Canada? No
Exclusive territories? Yes
Homebased option? Yes
Kiosk option? No
Employees needed to run franchise: 1
Absentee ownership? Yes

COSTS
Total cost: $28.5K-50.98K
Franchise fee: $24.5K
Royalty fee: 4%
Term of agreement: 5 years renewable
   at no charge
Franchisees required to buy multiple
   units? No

FINANCING
In-house: Franchise fee
3rd-party: None

QUALIFICATIONS
Net worth: $25K
Cash liquidity: $3K

TRAINING
At headquarters: 1 week
At franchisee's location: 1 week
Online training

BUSINESS SUPPORT
Newsletter
Meetings
Toll-free phone line
Grand opening
Internet
Field operations/evaluations
Purchasing cooperatives

MARKETING SUPPORT
Ad slicks
Regional marketing

UNITED STATES SEAMLESS INC.

Ranked #413 in Entrepreneur Magazine's 2005 Franchise 500　　　　*Financial rating: $$$$*

2001 1st Ave. N.
Fargo, ND 58102
Ph: (701)241-8888
Fax: (701)241-9999
www.usseamless.com
Seamless steel siding, gutters, windows
   & doors
Began: 1992, Franchising since: 1992
Headquarters size: 6 employees
Franchise department: 6 employees

U.S. franchises: 75
Canadian franchises: 0
Other foreign franchises: 0
Company-owned: 14

Seeking: South, Midwest, Southwest,
   West, Northwest
Focusing on: All U.S. except CA, FL,
   HI, MD, RI, VA
Seeking in Canada? No
Exclusive territories? Yes
Homebased option? Yes
Kiosk option? No
Employees needed to run franchise: 4
Absentee ownership? Yes

COSTS
Total cost: $49.5K-147K
Franchise fee: $8.5K
Royalty fee: Varies
Term of agreement: 15 years renewable
   at no charge
Franchisees required to buy multiple
   units? No

FINANCING
In-house: Equipment, franchise fee,
   inventory
3rd-party: Accounts receivable,
   payroll, startup costs

QUALIFICATIONS
Cash liquidity: $4.5K-18.5K
Experience:
   Industry experience
   General business experience

TRAINING
At headquarters: Unlimited
Annual training

BUSINESS SUPPORT
Newsletter
Meetings
Toll-free phone line
Internet
Lease negotiations
Security/safety procedures
Field operations/evaluations

MARKETING SUPPORT
Ad slicks
Pitch books
Marketing literature
Promotional clothing

HOME ▸ **DECORATING SERVICES**

CHRISTMAS DECOR INC.

Ranked #160 in Entrepreneur Magazine's 2005 Franchise 500   *Financial rating: $$$*

P.O. Box 5946
Lubbock, TX 79408-5946
Ph: (800)687-9551
Fax: (806)722-9627
www.christmasdecor.net
Holiday & event decorating services
Began: 1984, Franchising since: 1996
Headquarters size: 24 employees
Franchise department: 20 employees

U.S. franchises: 355
Canadian franchises: 17
Other foreign franchises: 1
Company-owned: 0
Units concentrated in all U.S.

Seeking: All U.S.
Seeking in Canada? Yes
Exclusive territories? Yes
Homebased option? Yes
Kiosk option? No
Employees needed to run franchise: 3-10
Absentee ownership? No

COSTS
Total cost: $19.2K-42.4K
Franchise fee: $10.9K-17.5K
Royalty fee: 2-4.5%
Term of agreement: 5 years renewable
    at $2K
Franchisees required to buy multiple
    units? No

FINANCING
In-house: Franchise fee
3rd-party: None

QUALIFICATIONS
Experience:
    General business experience

TRAINING
At headquarters: 4 days
At regional location: 4 days

BUSINESS SUPPORT
Newsletter
Meetings
Toll-free phone line
Internet
Security/safety procedures
Purchasing cooperatives

MARKETING SUPPORT
Co-op advertising
Ad slicks
National media campaign
Ronald McDonald House Charities
    Program

DECOR & YOU INC.

Ranked #379 in Entrepreneur Magazine's 2005 Franchise 500   *Financial rating: $$$*

900 Main St. S., Bldg. 2
Southbury, CT 06488
Ph: (203)264-3500
Fax: (203)264-5095
www.decorandyou.com
Interior decorating services &
    products
Began: 1994, Franchising since: 1998
Headquarters size: 5 employees
Franchise department: 3 employees

U.S. franchises: 51
Canadian franchises: 0
Other foreign franchises: 0
Company-owned: 0
Units concentrated in All except HI,
    ND, SD

Seeking: All U.S.
Focusing on: All except HI, ND, SD
Seeking in Canada? Yes
Exclusive territories? Yes
Homebased option? Yes
Kiosk option? No
Employees needed to run franchise: 0
Absentee ownership? No

COSTS
Total cost: $34.9K-123.6K
Franchise fee: $14.5K/75K+
Royalty fee: 10%
Term of agreement: 10 years renewable
    at 10% of franchise fee
Franchisees required to buy multiple
    units? Outside U.S. only

FINANCING
No financing available

QUALIFICATIONS
Net worth: $50K
Cash liquidity: $25K/50K
Experience:
    General business experience
    Marketing skills
    Interest in decorating

TRAINING
At headquarters: 13 days
At franchisee's location: As needed
Ongoing phone, seminars, conferences
    & web classes

BUSINESS SUPPORT
Meetings
Grand opening
Field operations/evaluations
Purchasing cooperatives

MARKETING SUPPORT
Ad slicks
National media campaign
Regional marketing
Local marketing events

INTERIORS BY DECORATING DEN
Ranked #121 in Entrepreneur Magazine's 2005 Franchise 500   *Financial rating: $$$$*

8659 Commerce Dr.
Easton, MD 21601
Ph: (410)822-9001
Fax: (410)820-5131
www.decoratingden.com
Interior decorating services &
    products
Began: 1969, Franchising since: 1970
Headquarters size: 38 employees
Franchise department: 6 employees

U.S. franchises: 404
Canadian franchises: 29
Other foreign franchises: 15
Company-owned: 0

Seeking: All U.S.
Seeking in Canada? Yes
Exclusive territories? Yes
Homebased option? Yes
Kiosk option? No
Employees needed to run franchise: 0
Absentee ownership? No

COSTS
Total cost: $39.9K
Franchise fee: $24.9K
Royalty fee: 7-9%
Term of agreement: 10 years renewable
    at no charge
Franchisees required to buy multiple
    units? No

FINANCING
In-house: Franchise fee, startup costs
3rd-party: None

QUALIFICATIONS
Net worth: $50K
Cash liquidity: $40K
Experience:
    Decorating skills
    People skills

TRAINING
At headquarters: 2 weeks
At franchisee's location: Ongoing

BUSINESS SUPPORT
Newsletter
Meetings
Toll-free phone line
Grand opening
Internet
Purchasing cooperatives

MARKETING SUPPORT
Co-op advertising
Ad slicks
National media campaign
Regional marketing

HOME SURFACE REFINISHING

GEMINI TUB REPAIR
Financial rating: $$

2592 River Rd.
Bainbridge, PA 17502
Ph: (717)367-7266
Fax: (717)361-2299
www.geminitubrepair.com
Bathtub repairs & refinishing
Began: 1984, Franchising since: 2003
Headquarters size: 7 employees
Franchise department:
    Info not provided

U.S. franchises: 2
Canadian franchises: 0
Other foreign franchises: 0
Company-owned: 1

Seeking: Northeast, South, Southeast,
    Midwest
Seeking in Canada? No
Exclusive territories? Yes
Homebased option? Yes
Kiosk option? No
Employees needed to run franchise: 0
Absentee ownership? Yes

COSTS
Total cost: $30.5K-34.8K
Franchise fee: $15K
Royalty fee: $49/wk.
Term of agreement: 10 years renewable
    at 10% of franchise fee
Franchisees required to buy multiple
    units? No

FINANCING
In-house: Franchise fee
3rd-party: None

QUALIFICATIONS
Experience:
    General business experience

TRAINING
At headquarters: 3 weeks
At franchisee's location: 1 week

BUSINESS SUPPORT
Newsletter
Toll-free phone line
Grand opening
Internet
Security/safety procedures
Field operations/evaluations

MARKETING SUPPORT
Info not provided

LUXURY BATH SYSTEMS

Current financial data not available

1958 Brandon Ct.
Glendale Heights, IL 60139
Ph: (800)354-2284
Fax: (630)295-9418
www.luxurybath.com
Bathtub liners
Began: 1989, Franchising since: 1994
Headquarters size: 40 employees
Franchise department: 4 employees

U.S. franchises: 95
Canadian franchises: 4
Other foreign franchises: 0
Company-owned: 0

Seeking: All U.S.
Seeking in Canada? Yes
Exclusive territories? Yes
Homebased option? No
Kiosk option? No
Employees needed to run franchise: 15
Absentee ownership? Yes

COSTS
Total cost: $20K-40K
Franchise fee: $16K
Royalty fee: 0
Term of agreement: 10 years renewable
  at $5K
Franchisees required to buy multiple
  units? No

FINANCING
In-house: Franchise fee, startup costs
3rd-party: None

QUALIFICATIONS
Cash liquidity: Varies
Experience:
  Industry experience
  General business experience
  Marketing skills
  Sales experience

TRAINING
At headquarters: 5 days
At franchisee's location: 3 days
Sales training
Marketing training

BUSINESS SUPPORT
Newsletter
Meetings
Toll-free phone line
Grand opening
Internet
Field operations/evaluations

MARKETING SUPPORT
Co-op advertising
Ad slicks
National media campaign

MIRACLE METHOD SURFACE RESTORATION

Ranked #332 in Entrepreneur Magazine's 2005 Franchise 500   *Financial rating: $$$*

4239 N. Nevada, #115
Colorado Springs, CO 80907
Ph: (800)444-8827/(719)594-9196
Fax: (719)594-9282
www.miraclemethod.com
Bathtub, sink, countertop & tile
  repair/refinishing
Began: 1977, Franchising since: 1980
Headquarters size: 3 employees
Franchise department: 3 employees

U.S. franchises: 86
Canadian franchises: 0
Other foreign franchises: 27
Company-owned: 0
Units concentrated in all U.S.

Seeking: All U.S.
Seeking in Canada? Yes
Exclusive territories? Yes
Homebased option? Yes
Kiosk option? No
Employees needed to run franchise: 1
Absentee ownership? Yes

COSTS
Total cost: $25K-45K
Franchise fee: $18.5K
Royalty fee: 5%
Term of agreement: 5 years renewable
Franchisees required to buy multiple
  units? Outside U.S. only

FINANCING
In-house: Franchise fee
3rd-party: None

QUALIFICATIONS
Net worth: $40K
Cash liquidity: $25K
Experience:
  Marketing skills

TRAINING
At headquarters: 2 weeks

BUSINESS SUPPORT
Newsletter
Meetings
Toll-free phone line
Internet
Security/safety procedures
Field operations/evaluations
Purchasing cooperatives

MARKETING SUPPORT
Co-op advertising
Ad slicks
National media campaign
Regional marketing

N-HANCE

Financial rating: $$$$

1530 N. 1000 West
Logan, UT 84321
Ph: (435)755-0099
Fax: (435)755-0021
www.nhancefranchise.com
Wood floor & cabinet renewal system
Began: 2001, Franchising since: 2003
Headquarters size: 60 employees
Franchise department: 6 employees

U.S. franchises: 57
Canadian franchises: 0
Other foreign franchises: 0
Company-owned: 0

Seeking: West, Northwest
Seeking in Canada? No
Exclusive territories? Yes
Homebased option? Yes
Kiosk option? No
Employees needed to run franchise: 2
Absentee ownership? Yes

COSTS
Total cost: $22.5K-37.5K
Franchise fee: Varies
Royalty fee: $220-660/mo.
Term of agreement: 5 years (not renewable)
Franchisees required to buy multiple units? No

FINANCING
In-house: Franchise fee
3rd-party: None

QUALIFICATIONS
Net worth: $27.5K-90.7K
Cash liquidity: $10K

TRAINING
At headquarters: 5 days

BUSINESS SUPPORT
Newsletter
Meetings
Toll-free phone line
Internet

MARKETING SUPPORT
Ad slicks

PERMA-GLAZE

Current financial data not available

1638 S. Research Loop Rd., #160
Tucson, AZ 85710
Ph: (520)722-9718
Fax: (520)296-4393
www.permaglaze.com
Bathroom/kitchen fixture restoration/refinishing
Began: 1978, Franchising since: 1981
Headquarters size: 10 employees
Franchise department: 3 employees

U.S. franchises: 130
Canadian franchises: 2
Other foreign franchises: 16
Company-owned: 2
Units concentrated in Eastern U.S.

Seeking: All U.S.
Seeking in Canada? Yes
Exclusive territories? Yes
Homebased option? Yes
Kiosk option? No
Employees needed to run franchise: 1
Absentee ownership? Yes

COSTS
Total cost: $26.5K-47.5K
Franchise fee: $21.5K+
Royalty fee: Varies
Term of agreement: 10 years renewable at no charge
Franchisees required to buy multiple units? Outside U.S. only

FINANCING
No financing available

QUALIFICATIONS
Cash liquidity: $26.5K-47.5K

TRAINING
At headquarters: 5-10 days

BUSINESS SUPPORT
Newsletter
Meetings
Toll-free phone line
Internet
Security/safety procedures

MARKETING SUPPORT
Ad slicks

RE-BATH LLC

Ranked #255 in Entrepreneur Magazine's 2005 Franchise 500   *Financial rating: $$$$*

1055 S. Country Club Dr., Bldg. 2
Mesa, AZ 85210-4613
Ph: (800)426-4573/(480)844-1575
Fax: (480)833-7199
www.re-bath.com
Acrylic liners for
    bathtubs/showers/walls
Began: 1979, Franchising since: 1991
Headquarters size: 13 employees
Franchise department: 3 employees

U.S. franchises: 149
Canadian franchises: 4
Other foreign franchises: 2
Company-owned: 0

Seeking: All U.S.
Seeking in Canada? Yes
Exclusive territories? Yes
Homebased option? No
Kiosk option? No
Employees needed to run franchise: 3-5
Absentee ownership? No

COSTS

Total cost: $33.9K-200K
Franchise fee: $3.5K-40K
Royalty fee: $25/liner
Term of agreement: 5 years renewable
    at $1K
Franchisees required to buy multiple
    units? No

FINANCING

In-house: Franchise fee
3rd-party: None

QUALIFICATIONS

Net worth: $250K
Cash liquidity: $100K
Experience:
    Industry experience
    General business experience
    Marketing skills

TRAINING

At headquarters: 9 days
At franchisee's location: As needed
Sales training: 3 days

BUSINESS SUPPORT

Newsletter
Meetings
Toll-free phone line
Internet

MARKETING SUPPORT

Co-op advertising
Ad slicks
National media campaign

SURFACE SPECIALISTS SYSTEMS INC.

Financial rating: $

621-B Stallings Rd.
Matthews, NC 28105
Ph: (866)239-8707
Fax: (704)821-2097
www.surfacespecialists.com
Kitchen & bath repair, refinishing &
    resurfacing
Began: 1981, Franchising since: 1982
Headquarters size: 3 employees
Franchise department: 1 employee

U.S. franchises: 39
Canadian franchises: 0
Other foreign franchises: 0
Company-owned: 0
Units concentrated in all U.S.

Seeking: All U.S.
Seeking in Canada? No
Exclusive territories? Yes
Homebased option? Yes
Kiosk option? No
Employees needed to run franchise: 2-3
Absentee ownership? No

COSTS

Total cost: $25.3K-34.9K
Franchise fee: $19.5K
Royalty fee: 5%
Term of agreement: 10 years renewable
    at no charge
Franchisees required to buy multiple
    units? No

FINANCING

In-house: Franchise fee
3rd-party: None

QUALIFICATIONS

Net worth: $75K
Cash liquidity: $25K
Experience:
    Industry experience
    General business experience
    Marketing skills

TRAINING

At headquarters: 3 weeks
Follow-up training available at
    franchisee's location

BUSINESS SUPPORT

Newsletter
Meetings
Toll-free phone line
Internet
Security/safety procedures
Purchasing cooperatives

MARKETING SUPPORT

Ad slicks
Library
Manual

HOME ◄ **WINDOWS & CARPETS**

BLIND MAN OF AMERICA

Current financial data not available

606 Freemont Cir.
Colorado Springs, CO 80919
Ph: (800)547-9889
Fax: (719)272-4105
www.blindmanofamerica.com
Mobile window coverings
Began: 1991, Franchising since: 1996
Headquarters size: 3 employees
Franchise department:
    Info not provided

U.S. franchises: 9
Canadian franchises: 0
Other foreign franchises: 0
Company-owned: 1
Units concentrated in CO

Seeking: All U.S.
Seeking in Canada? No
Exclusive territories? Yes
Homebased option? Yes

Kiosk option? No
Employees needed to run franchise:
    Info not provided
Absentee ownership? No

COSTS
Total cost: $45.5K-69.1K
Franchise fee: $15K
Royalty fee: 4.3%
Term of agreement: 5 years renewable
    at $1K
Franchisees required to buy multiple
    units? No

FINANCING
No financing available

QUALIFICATIONS
Experience:
    General business experience

TRAINING
At headquarters: 2 weeks

BUSINESS SUPPORT
Newsletter
Meetings
Toll-free phone line

MARKETING SUPPORT
Co-op advertising
Ad slicks

CARPET NETWORK

Financial rating: 0

109 Gaither Dr., #302
Mt. Laurel, NJ 08054
Ph: (800)428-1067/(856)273-9393
Fax: (856)273-0160
www.carpetnetwork.com
Mobile floor coverings/window
    treatments
Began: 1991, Franchising since: 1992
Headquarters size: 5 employees
Franchise department: 2 employees

U.S. franchises: 41
Canadian franchises: 0
Other foreign franchises: 0
Company-owned: 0
Units concentrated in all U.S.

Seeking: All U.S.
Seeking in Canada? No
Exclusive territories? Yes
Homebased option? Yes
Kiosk option? No
Employees needed to run franchise: 1
Absentee ownership? No

COSTS
Total cost: $29K-40.1K
Franchise fee: $17.5K
Royalty fee: 2-7%
Term of agreement: 15 years renewable
    at no charge
Franchisees required to buy multiple
    units? No

FINANCING
In-house: Franchise fee
3rd-party: None

QUALIFICATIONS
Net worth: $30K
Experience:
    People skills

TRAINING
At headquarters: 6 days
At franchisee's location: 14 days

BUSINESS SUPPORT
Newsletter
Meetings
Toll-free phone line
Internet
Purchasing cooperatives

MARKETING SUPPORT
Ad slicks
National media campaign

TODAY'S WINDOW FASHIONS

Financial rating: $$

1593 S. Mission Rd., #B
San Diego, CA 92028
Ph: (888)649-1600
Fax: (760)923-7234
www.todaysblinds.com
Custom blinds, shades & shutters
Began: 1993, Franchising since: 1997
Headquarters size: 3 employees
Franchise department: 3 employees

U.S. franchises: 28
Canadian franchises: 0
Other foreign franchises: 0
Company-owned: 2

Seeking: All U.S.
Seeking in Canada? No
Exclusive territories? Yes
Homebased option? Yes
Kiosk option? No
Employees needed to run franchise: 1-2
Absentee ownership? Yes

COSTS
Total cost: $33.4K-43.3K
Franchise fee: $29.5K
Royalty fee: 4%
Term of agreement: 5 years renewable
    at $750
Franchisees required to buy multiple
    units? No

FINANCING
No financing available

QUALIFICATIONS
Net worth: $25K
Cash liquidity: $15K
Experience:
    General business experience

TRAINING
At headquarters: 5 days
At franchisee's location: 3 days

BUSINESS SUPPORT
Newsletter
Meetings
Toll-free phone line
Internet
Purchasing cooperatives

MARKETING SUPPORT
Co-op advertising
Ad slicks
National media campaign
Regional marketing
Direct mail
Internet

HOME ▶ **MISCELLANEOUS**

GROUT DOCTOR GLOBAL FRANCHISE CORP.

Financial rating: 0

7293 E. Palm Ln.
Mesa, AZ 85207
Ph: (877)476-8800
Fax: (877)615-2173
www.groutdoctor.com
Ceramic tile grout repair &
    maintenance
Began: 1994, Franchising since: 2001
Headquarters size: 8 employees
Franchise department: 6 employees

U.S. franchises: 44
Canadian franchises: 0
Other foreign franchises: 0
Company-owned: 0
Units concentrated in AZ, CA, FL, IL,
    MN, MO, OH, TX, WA

Seeking: All U.S.
Seeking in Canada? Yes
Exclusive territories? Yes
Homebased option? Yes
Kiosk option? No
Employees needed to run franchise: 0
Absentee ownership? Yes

COSTS
Total cost: $15.7K-28.9K
Franchise fee: Varies
Royalty fee: Varies
Term of agreement: 7 years renewable
    at $1K
Franchisees required to buy multiple
    units? No

FINANCING
In-house: Franchise fee
3rd-party: None

QUALIFICATIONS
Cash liquidity: $10.4K

TRAINING
At headquarters: 5 days
At franchisee's location: 2 days
In Chicago or Charlotte, NC: 5 days

BUSINESS SUPPORT
Newsletter
Meetings
Toll-free phone line
Grand opening
Internet
Security/safety procedures
Field operations/evaluations
Purchasing cooperatives

MARKETING SUPPORT
Co-op advertising
Ad slicks
Regional marketing
TV & radio ads
Vehicle wraps

HUMITECH FRANCHISE CORP.

Ranked #486 in Entrepreneur Magazine's 2005 Franchise 500　　　*Financial rating: $$$$*

15851 Dallas Pkwy., #410
Addison, TX 75001
Ph: (972)490-9393
Fax: (972)490-9220
www.humitechgroup.com
Humidity control products
Began: 2001, Franchising since: 2002
Headquarters size: 14 employees
Franchise department: 4 employees

U.S. franchises: 56
Canadian franchises: 1
Other foreign franchises: 7
Company-owned: 1

Seeking: All U.S.
Seeking in Canada? Yes
Exclusive territories? Yes
Homebased option? Yes
Kiosk option? Yes
Employees needed to run franchise: 1-10
Absentee ownership? Yes

COSTS
Total cost: $18K-93K
Franchise fee: $12.5K-75K
Royalty fee: 0
Term of agreement: 10 years renewable
　　at $1K
Franchisees required to buy multiple
　　units? No

FINANCING
No financing available

QUALIFICATIONS
Net worth: $100K
Cash liquidity: $25K
Experience:
　　General business experience
　　Marketing skills
　　Sales experience

TRAINING
At franchisee's location: 1 week
Additional training as needed

BUSINESS SUPPORT
Newsletter
Meetings
Toll-free phone line
Internet
Security/safety procedures
Field operations/evaluations

MARKETING SUPPORT
Co-op advertising
Ad slicks
National media campaign
Regional marketing

TRULY FRAMELESS

Current financial data not available

7414 S.W. 48th St.
Miami, FL 33156
Ph: (305)284-8621
Fax: (305)667-3355
www.trulyframeless.com
Frameless shower enclosures
Began: 2002, Franchising since: 2004
Headquarters size: 2 employees
Franchise department: 1 employee

U.S. franchises: 2
Canadian franchises: 0
Other foreign franchises: 0
Company-owned: 0

Seeking: All U.S.
Seeking in Canada? No
Exclusive territories? Yes
Homebased option? Yes
Kiosk option? No
Employees needed to run franchise: 1
Absentee ownership? Yes

COSTS
Total cost: $40.8K
Franchise fee: $25K
Royalty fee: 7%
Term of agreement: 10 years renewable
Franchisees required to buy multiple
　　units? No

FINANCING
No financing available

QUALIFICATIONS
Experience:
　　Industry experience
　　General business experience
　　Marketing skills
　　Craftsman skills

TRAINING
At headquarters: 2-3 days
At franchisee's location: 2-4 days
At job site: 2 days

BUSINESS SUPPORT
Meetings
Lease negotiations
Security/safety procedures

MARKETING SUPPORT
Co-op advertising
Ad slicks
National media campaign

DECKARE SERVICES
P.O. Box 2483
Goose Creek, SC 29445
Ph: (800)711-3325
www.deckare.com
Exterior wood surface restoration &
    maintenance
Financial rating: Current financial
    data not available

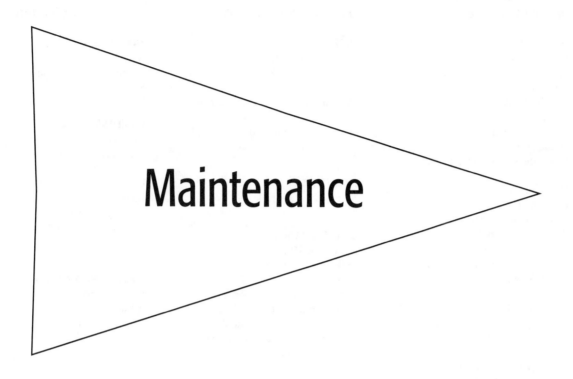

Maintenance

MAINTENANCE ASPHALT MAINTENANCE

AMERICAN ASPHALT SEALCOATING CO.
Ranked #496 in Entrepreneur Magazine's 2005 Franchise 500   *Financial rating: $$$*

P.O. Box 600
Chesterland, OH 44026
Ph: (888)603-7325/(440)729-8080
Fax: (440)729-2231
www.american-sealcoating.com
Asphalt maintenance
    services/protective coatings
Began: 1987, Franchising since: 1998
Headquarters size: 11 employees
Franchise department: 6 employees

U.S. franchises: 12
Canadian franchises: 0
Other foreign franchises: 0
Company-owned: 1
Units concentrated in IN, OH

Seeking: All U.S.
Seeking in Canada? Yes
Exclusive territories? Yes
Homebased option? Yes
Kiosk option? No
Employees needed to run franchise: 1-2
Absentee ownership? Yes

COSTS
Total cost: $35K-45K
Franchise fee: $15K
Royalty fee: 5-7%
Term of agreement: 15 years renewable
Franchisees required to buy multiple
    units? No

FINANCING
In-house: Equipment, inventory
3rd-party: Accounts receivable,
    franchise fee, payroll, startup costs

QUALIFICATIONS
Net worth: $50K
Cash liquidity: $50K

TRAINING
At headquarters: 7-10 days
At franchisee's location: 3 days
Additional training as needed

BUSINESS SUPPORT
Newsletter
Meetings
Toll-free phone line
Grand opening
Internet
Security/safety procedures
Field operations/evaluations
Purchasing cooperatives

MARKETING SUPPORT
Co-op advertising
Ad slicks
Ad designs
Rate negotiations

JET-BLACK INT'L. INC.

Ranked #347 in Entrepreneur Magazine's 2005 Franchise 500

Financial rating: $$$$

25 W. Cliff Rd., #103
Burnsville, MN 55337
Ph: (888)538-2525/(952)890-8343
Fax: (952)890-7022
www.jet-black.com
Asphalt maintenance services
Began: 1988, Franchising since: 1993
Headquarters size: 10 employees
Franchise department: 2 employees

U.S. franchises: 140
Canadian franchises: 0
Other foreign franchises: 0
Company-owned: 2
Units concentrated in CT, DE, MA,
    MD, ME, MN, NC, NH, NJ, NY,
    PA, RI, SC, VA, VT, WI, WV

Seeking: All U.S.
Focusing on: States where units are
    concentrated (see above)
Seeking in Canada? Yes
Exclusive territories? Yes
Homebased option? Yes
Kiosk option? No
Employees needed to run franchise: 3
Absentee ownership? Yes

COSTS

Total cost: $49K-150K
Franchise fee: $20K
Royalty fee: 8%
Term of agreement: 15 years renewable
    at no charge
Franchisees required to buy multiple
    units? No

FINANCING

No financing available

QUALIFICATIONS

Net worth: $75K
Cash liquidity: $49K
Experience:
    General business experience
    Marketing skills
    Management background
    Customer service background
    Retail experience

TRAINING

At headquarters: 1 week
At franchisee's location
Seminars

BUSINESS SUPPORT

Newsletter
Meetings
Toll-free phone line
Grand opening
Internet
Security/safety procedures
Field operations/evaluations
Purchasing cooperatives

MARKETING SUPPORT

Co-op advertising
Ad slicks
Regional marketing

KCS APPLICATIONS INC.

Financial rating: 0

4955 Creaser Rd.
Westmoreland, NY 13490
Ph: (315)853-4805
Fax: (315)853-4805
www.kcs1.com
Acrylic asphalt sealcoating
Began: 1992, Franchising since: 1994
Headquarters size: 2 employees
Franchise department: 2 employees

U.S. franchises: 27
Canadian franchises: 0
Other foreign franchises: 0
Company-owned: 0
Units concentrated in CT, ME, NY,
    OH, PA

Seeking: Northeast
Focusing on: CT, MA, ME, NH, NJ,
    NY, OH, PA, VT
Seeking in Canada? No
Exclusive territories? No
Homebased option? Yes

Kiosk option? No
Employees needed to run franchise: 0
Absentee ownership? No

COSTS

Total cost: $15.5K
Franchise fee: $15K
Royalty fee: $350/yr.
Term of agreement: 3 years renewable
    at no charge
Franchisees required to buy multiple
    units? No

FINANCING

No financing available

QUALIFICATIONS

Cash liquidity: $15K

TRAINING

At headquarters: 2 days
At franchisee's location: 1 day

BUSINESS SUPPORT

Meetings
Internet
Field operations/evaluations
Purchasing cooperatives

MARKETING SUPPORT

Local marketing support

MAINTENANCE ▶ **CARPET CLEANING**

CHEM-DRY CARPET DRAPERY & UPHOLSTERY CLEANING

Ranked #18 in Entrepreneur Magazine's 2005 Franchise 500   *Financial rating: $$$$*

1530 N. 1000 West
Logan, UT 84321
Ph: (877)307-8233
Fax: (435)755-0021
www.chemdry.com
Carpet, drapery & upholstery cleaning
Began: 1977, Franchising since: 1978
Headquarters size: 75 employees
Franchise department:
    Info not provided

U.S. franchises: 2,502
Canadian franchises: 117
Other foreign franchises: 1,296
Company-owned: 0

Seeking: Northeast, South, Southeast,
    Midwest, Southwest
Seeking in Canada? No
Exclusive territories? No
Homebased option? Yes
Kiosk option? No
Employees needed to run franchise:
    Info not provided
Absentee ownership? Yes

COSTS
Total cost: $24.95K-86.95K
Franchise fee: $11.95K
Royalty fee: $213/mo.
Term of agreement: 5 years renewable
    at $750
Franchisees required to buy multiple
    units? No

FINANCING
In-house: Accounts receivable,
    equipment, franchise fee, inventory
3rd-party: None

QUALIFICATIONS
Info not provided

TRAINING
At headquarters: 5 days
Video training

BUSINESS SUPPORT
Newsletter
Meetings
Toll-free phone line
Internet
Security/safety procedures
Field operations/evaluations

MARKETING SUPPORT
Co-op advertising
Ad slicks
National media campaign
Regional marketing
Video/radio ads

HEAVEN'S BEST CARPET & UPHOLSTERY CLEANING

Ranked #113 in Entrepreneur Magazine's 2005 Franchise 500   *Financial rating: $$*

247 N. First East, P.O. Box 607
Rexburg, ID 83440
Ph: (800)359-2095
Fax: (208)359-1236
www.heavensbest.com
Carpet & upholstery cleaning
Began: 1983, Franchising since: 1983
Headquarters size: 6 employees
Franchise department: 3 employees

U.S. franchises: 866
Canadian franchises: 5
Other foreign franchises: 11
Company-owned: 0

Seeking: All U.S.
Seeking in Canada? Yes
Exclusive territories? Yes
Homebased option? Yes
Kiosk option? No
Employees needed to run franchise: 0-1
Absentee ownership? Yes

COSTS
Total cost: $24.9K-47.4K
Franchise fee: $5.9K
Royalty fee: $80/mo.
Term of agreement: 5 years renewable
    at no charge
Franchisees required to buy multiple
    units? No

FINANCING
In-house: Franchise fee
3rd-party: None

QUALIFICATIONS
Net worth: $20K
Cash liquidity: $9K
Experience:
    Industry experience
    General business experience
    Marketing skills

TRAINING
At headquarters: 4 days

BUSINESS SUPPORT
Newsletter
Meetings
Toll-free phone line
Internet
Security/safety procedures
Field operations/evaluations

MARKETING SUPPORT
Ad slicks
Regional marketing

PROFESSIONAL CARPET SYSTEMS

Financial rating: 0

4211 Atlantic Ave.
Raleigh, NC 27604
Ph: (800)925-5055
Fax: (919)875-9855
www.procarpetsys.com
Carpet restoration & replacement
Began: 1978, Franchising since: 1981
Headquarters size: 18 employees
Franchise department: 4 employees

U.S. franchises: 55
Canadian franchises: 4
Other foreign franchises: 3
Company-owned: 0
Units concentrated in all U.S.

Seeking: All U.S.
Seeking in Canada? Yes
Exclusive territories? Yes
Homebased option? Yes
Kiosk option? No
Employees needed to run franchise: 1
Absentee ownership? Yes

COSTS
Total cost: $19.4K-52.5K
Franchise fee: $15K
Royalty fee: 2-6%
Term of agreement: 5 years renewable at $500
Franchisees required to buy multiple units? Outside U.S. only

FINANCING
In-house: Franchise fee
3rd-party: Equipment, inventory, startup costs

QUALIFICATIONS
Net worth: $20K
Cash liquidity: $20K
Experience:
    Computer skills helpful but not required

TRAINING
At headquarters: 2 weeks
At franchisee's location: 2 days
By mail: 1 week
Monthly certification programs

BUSINESS SUPPORT
Newsletter
Meetings
Toll-free phone line
Internet
Security/safety procedures

MARKETING SUPPORT
Ad slicks
Fax
Internet
Direct mail

SPARKLE CARPET CLEANING

Current financial data not available

1222 S. Main Ave.
Scranton, PA 18504
Ph: (570)344-4660
Fax: (570)344-7076
www.sparklecarpetcleaning.com
Carpet & upholstery cleaning
Began: 1981, Franchising since: 2004
Headquarters size: 4 employees
Franchise department: 4 employees

U.S. franchises: 4
Canadian franchises: 0
Other foreign franchises: 0
Company-owned: 5

Seeking: All U.S.
Seeking in Canada? No
Exclusive territories? Yes
Homebased option? Yes
Kiosk option? No
Employees needed to run franchise: 2
Absentee ownership? No

COSTS
Total cost: $10K-15K
Franchise fee: $5K-9K
Royalty fee: $75-150/mo.
Term of agreement: 10 years renewable at 1/3 of fee
Franchisees required to buy multiple units? No

FINANCING
In-house: Accounts receivable, equipment, franchise fee, inventory, payroll, startup costs
3rd-party: None

QUALIFICATIONS
Net worth: $25K
Cash liquidity: $3.95K
Experience:
    General business experience

TRAINING
At headquarters: 2 weeks

BUSINESS SUPPORT
Newsletter
Meetings
Toll-free phone line
Internet
Security/safety procedures
Field operations/evaluations
Purchasing cooperatives

MARKETING SUPPORT
Ad slicks
TV ads

STEAM BROTHERS INC.

Current financial data not available

2124 E. Sweet Ave.
Bismarck, ND 58504-6023
Ph: (800)767-5064
Fax: (701)222-1372
www.steambrothers.com
Carpet/upholstery/drapery/air-duct
    cleaning/restoration
Began: 1977, Franchising since: 1984
Headquarters size: 2 employees
Franchise department: 2 employees

U.S. franchises: 24
Canadian franchises: 0
Other foreign franchises: 0
Company-owned: 0
Units concentrated in Upper
    Midwestern states

Seeking: Midwest
Focusing on: CO, IA, MN, MT, NE,
    SD, WY
Seeking in Canada? No
Exclusive territories? Yes

Homebased option? Yes
Kiosk option? No
Employees needed to run franchise: 1-3
Absentee ownership? No

COSTS
Total cost: $22K-53.5K
Franchise fee: $16K
Royalty fee: 5-6.5%
Term of agreement: 10 years renewable
    at $1K
Franchisees required to buy multiple
    units? No

FINANCING
In-house: None
3rd-party: Equipment

QUALIFICATIONS
Net worth: $60K
Cash liquidity: $22K

TRAINING
At headquarters: 5 days
At franchisee's location: As needed

BUSINESS SUPPORT
Newsletter
Meetings
Toll-free phone line
Internet
Lease negotiations
Security/safety procedures
Field operations/evaluations

MARKETING SUPPORT
Ad slicks

MAINTENANCE ► **COMMERCIAL CLEANING**

ANAGO FRANCHISING INC.

Ranked #105 in Entrepreneur Magazine's 2005 Franchise 500

Financial rating: $$$

3111 N. University Dr., #625
Coral Springs, FL 33065
Ph: (800)213-5857
Fax: (954)752-1200
www.anagousa.com
Commercial cleaning
Began: 1989, Franchising since: 1991
Headquarters size: 10 employees
Franchise department: 10 employees

U.S. franchises: 564
Canadian franchises: 0
Other foreign franchises: 0
Company-owned: 0
Units concentrated in FL, GA, IL, NC,
    OH

Seeking: All U.S.
Seeking in Canada? Yes
Exclusive territories? Yes
Homebased option? Yes
Kiosk option? No
Employees needed to run franchise: 4-10
Absentee ownership? No

COSTS
Total cost: $8K-350K
Franchise fee: $2K-350K
Royalty fee: 5%
Term of agreement: 10 years renewable
    at no charge
Franchisees required to buy multiple
    units? No

FINANCING
In-house: Equipment, franchise fee
3rd-party: Equipment, franchise fee,
    startup costs

QUALIFICATIONS
Net worth: $10K-50K
Cash liquidity: $2K-50K
Experience:
    General business experience
    Marketing skills

TRAINING
At headquarters: 4 weeks
At franchisee's location: Ongoing

BUSINESS SUPPORT
Newsletter
Meetings
Toll-free phone line
Grand opening
Internet
Security/safety procedures
Field operations/evaluations

MARKETING SUPPORT
Regional marketing

BEARCOM BUILDING SERVICES

Financial rating: $

7022 S. 400 West
Midvale, UT 84047
Ph: (888)569-9533/(801)569-9500
Fax: (801)569-8400
www.bearcomservices.com
Commercial cleaning
Began: 1979, Franchising since: 1990
Headquarters size: 4 employees
Franchise department: 2 employees

U.S. franchises: 62
Canadian franchises: 0
Other foreign franchises: 0
Company-owned: 1
Units concentrated in UT

Seeking: All U.S.
Focusing on: UT
Seeking in Canada? No
Exclusive territories? No
Homebased option? Yes
Kiosk option? No
Employees needed to run franchise: 0-2
Absentee ownership? No

COSTS
Total cost: $12.8K-39.3K+
Franchise fee: $9.99K-14.99K+
Royalty fee: 6-8%
Term of agreement: 5 years renewable
    at no charge
Franchisees required to buy multiple
    units? No

FINANCING
In-house: Accounts receivable,
    franchise fee
3rd-party: None

QUALIFICATIONS
Info not provided

TRAINING
At headquarters: 24 hours

BUSINESS SUPPORT
Newsletter
Toll-free phone line
Internet
Field operations/evaluations

MARKETING SUPPORT
Marketing training

BONUS BUILDING CARE

Ranked #178 in Entrepreneur Magazine's 2005 Franchise 500

Financial rating: $

P.O. Box 300
Indianola, OK 74442
Ph: (918)823-4990
Fax: (918)823-4994
www.bonusbuildingcare.com
Commercial cleaning
Began: 1996, Franchising since: 1996
Headquarters size: 30 employees
Franchise department:
    Info not provided

U.S. franchises: 830
Canadian franchises: 0
Other foreign franchises: 0
Company-owned: 3
Units concentrated in all U.S.

Seeking: All U.S.
Seeking in Canada? Yes
Exclusive territories? Yes
Homebased option? Yes
Kiosk option? No
Employees needed to run franchise: 1-5
Absentee ownership? No

COSTS
Total cost: $7.6K-13.3K
Franchise fee: $6.5K
Royalty fee: 10%
Term of agreement: 20 years renewable
    at $2K
Franchisees required to buy multiple
    units? Outside U.S. only

FINANCING
In-house: Franchise fee
3rd-party: Accounts receivable,
    equipment, payroll, startup costs
Other: Growth financing available

QUALIFICATIONS
Info not provided

TRAINING
At headquarters: As needed
At franchisee's location: As needed
Ongoing

BUSINESS SUPPORT
Newsletter
Meetings
Toll-free phone line
Grand opening
Internet
Lease negotiations
Security/safety procedures
Field operations/evaluations
Purchasing cooperatives

MARKETING SUPPORT
Ad slicks
National media campaign
Regional marketing
Direct marketing in local areas
Newspaper ads
Trade shows
Referrals

BUILDINGSTARS INC.

Ranked #303 in Entrepreneur Magazine's 2005 Franchise 500   *Financial rating: $$$$*

11489 Page Service Dr.
St. Louis, MO 63146
Ph: (314)991-3356
Fax: (314)991-3198
www.buildingstars.com
Commercial cleaning
Began: 1994, Franchising since: 2000
Headquarters size: 18 employees
Franchise department: 3 employees

U.S. franchises: 145
Canadian franchises: 0
Other foreign franchises: 0
Company-owned: 0

Seeking: Midwest
Seeking in Canada? No
Exclusive territories? No
Homebased option? Yes
Kiosk option? No
Employees needed to run franchise: 5
Absentee ownership? No

COSTS
Total cost: $1.9K-42.2K
Franchise fee: $995-3.99K
Royalty fee: 10%
Term of agreement: 5 years renewable
   at no charge
Franchisees required to buy multiple
   units? No

FINANCING
In-house: Accounts receivable,
   equipment, franchise fee,
   inventory, startup costs
3rd-party: None

QUALIFICATIONS
Info not provided

TRAINING
At headquarters: 1 week

BUSINESS SUPPORT
Newsletter
Meetings
Internet

MARKETING SUPPORT
Info not provided

CHAMPION CLEAN

Current financial data not available

283 Cranes Roost Blvd., #111
Altamonte Springs, FL 32701
Ph: (407)379-0041
Fax: (407)379-0042
www.championclean.com
Commercial janitorial services
Began: 1997, Franchising since: 2003
Headquarters size: 6 employees
Franchise department: 4 employees

U.S. franchises: 28
Canadian franchises: 0
Other foreign franchises: 0
Company-owned: 1

Seeking: All U.S.
Seeking in Canada? Yes
Exclusive territories? Yes
Homebased option? Yes
Kiosk option? No
Employees needed to run franchise: 2-10
Absentee ownership? Yes

COSTS
Total cost: $3.3K-33K
Franchise fee: $2.5K-31K
Royalty fee: 4%
Term of agreement: 10 years renewable
   at no charge
Franchisees required to buy multiple
   units? No

FINANCING
In-house: Franchise fee
3rd-party: Accounts receivable,
   equipment, inventory, payroll,
   startup costs

QUALIFICATIONS
Net worth: $5K+
Cash liquidity: $1K+

TRAINING
At headquarters: 80 hours
At franchisee's location: 40 hours

BUSINESS SUPPORT
Toll-free phone line
Internet
Security/safety procedures

MARKETING SUPPORT
Co-op advertising

CLEANNET USA INC.

Ranked #29 in Entrepreneur Magazine's 2005 Franchise 500   *Financial rating: $$$$*

9861 Broken Land Pkwy., #208
Columbia, MD 21046
Ph: (800)735-8838/(410)720-6444
Fax: (410)720-5307
www.cleannetusa.com
Commercial office cleaning
Began: 1988, Franchising since: 1988
Headquarters size: 45 employees
Franchise department: 32 employees

U.S. franchises: 2,963
Canadian franchises: 0
Other foreign franchises: 0
Company-owned: 6

Seeking: All U.S.
Seeking in Canada? Yes
Exclusive territories? Yes
Homebased option? Yes
Kiosk option? No
Employees needed to run franchise: 3-10
Absentee ownership? Yes

COSTS
Total cost: $3.9K-35.5K
Franchise fee: $2.95K-32K
Royalty fee: 3%
Term of agreement: 20 years renewable
    at $5K
Franchisees required to buy multiple
    units? Yes, within U.S./outside U.S.

FINANCING
In-house: Accounts receivable,
    equipment, franchise fee,
    inventory, payroll, startup costs
3rd-party: None

QUALIFICATIONS
Net worth: $10K-300K
Cash liquidity: $5K-100K
Experience:
    General business experience

TRAINING
At headquarters: 1-4 weeks
At franchisee's location: 1-4 weeks

BUSINESS SUPPORT
Newsletter
Meetings
Toll-free phone line
Grand opening
Internet
Lease negotiations
Security/safety procedures
Field operations/evaluations
Purchasing cooperatives

MARKETING SUPPORT
Regional marketing

COVERALL CLEANING CONCEPTS

Ranked #46 in Entrepreneur Magazine's 2005 Franchise 500   *Financial rating: $*

500 W. Cypress Creek Rd., #580
Ft. Lauderdale, FL 33309
Ph: (800)537-3371/(954)351-1110
Fax: (954)492-5044
www.coverall.com
Commercial cleaning
Began: 1985, Franchising since: 1985
Headquarters size: 80 employees
Franchise department: 190 employees

U.S. franchises: 7,992
Canadian franchises: 201
Other foreign franchises: 258
Company-owned: 0
Units concentrated in all U.S.

Seeking: All U.S.
Seeking in Canada? Yes
Exclusive territories? Yes
Homebased option? Yes
Kiosk option? No
Employees needed to run franchise: 2
Absentee ownership? Yes

COSTS
Total cost: $6.3K-35.9K
Franchise fee: $6K-32.2K
Royalty fee: 5%
Term of agreement: 20 years renewable
    at no charge
Franchisees required to buy multiple
    units? No

FINANCING
In-house: Equipment, franchise fee,
    inventory, startup costs
3rd-party: None

QUALIFICATIONS
Net worth: $6K-32K
Cash liquidity: $1.5K

TRAINING
At headquarters: 80 hours
At franchisee's location: 40+ hours &
    ongoing
At international master office: 10
    weeks

BUSINESS SUPPORT
Newsletter
Meetings
Toll-free phone line
Grand opening
Internet
Field operations/evaluations

MARKETING SUPPORT
Co-op advertising
Ad slicks
National media campaign
Regional marketing

E.P.I.C. SYSTEMS INC.

Current financial data not available

402 E. Maryland St.
Evansville, IN 47711
Ph: (800)230-3742
Fax: (812)428-4162
Commercial cleaning
Began: 1994, Franchising since: 1994
Headquarters size: 3 employees
Franchise department: 2 employees

U.S. franchises: 7
Canadian franchises: 0
Other foreign franchises: 0
Company-owned: 0
Units concentrated in IN, KY, OH

Seeking: Southeast, Midwest
Focusing on: IN, KY, OH
Seeking in Canada? No
Exclusive territories? Info not provided
Homebased option? Yes
Kiosk option? No
Employees needed to run franchise: 4
Absentee ownership? Yes

COSTS
Total cost: $10.2K-28.5K
Franchise fee: $6.5K/25K
Royalty fee: 4-10%
Term of agreement: 10 years renewable
    at 10% of franchise fee
Franchisees required to buy multiple
    units? No

FINANCING
In-house: Franchise fee
3rd-party: Equipment, startup costs

QUALIFICATIONS
Net worth: $25K
Cash liquidity: $5K
Experience:
    General business experience

TRAINING
At headquarters: 2 weeks

BUSINESS SUPPORT
Toll-free phone line
Internet
Field operations/evaluations

MARKETING SUPPORT
Ad slicks

JAN-PRO FRANCHISING INT'L. INC.

Ranked #19 in Entrepreneur Magazine's 2005 Franchise 500

Financial rating: $$$$

383 Strand Industrial Dr.
Little River, SC 29566
Ph: (866)355-1064
Fax: (843)399-9890
www.jan-pro.com
Commercial cleaning
Began: 1991, Franchising since: 1992
Headquarters size: 10 employees
Franchise department: 6 employees

U.S. franchises: 3,737
Canadian franchises: 188
Other foreign franchises: 0
Company-owned: 0

Seeking: All U.S.
Seeking in Canada? Yes
Exclusive territories? Yes
Homebased option? Yes
Kiosk option? No
Employees needed to run franchise: 1
Absentee ownership? No

COSTS
Total cost: $5K-50K+
Franchise fee: $950-14K
Royalty fee: 8%
Term of agreement: 10 years renewable
    at no charge
Franchisees required to buy multiple
    units? No

FINANCING
In-house: Accounts receivable,
    equipment, franchise fee
3rd-party: None

QUALIFICATIONS
Net worth: $1K-14K+
Cash liquidity: $1K+
Experience:
    Management skills

TRAINING
At headquarters: 1 week
At franchisee's location: 4 weeks

BUSINESS SUPPORT
Newsletter
Meetings
Toll-free phone line
Grand opening
Internet
Security/safety procedures
Field operations/evaluations
Purchasing cooperatives

MARKETING SUPPORT
National media campaign
Regional marketing

JANI-KING

Ranked #7 in Entrepreneur Magazine's 2005 Franchise 500　　　　*Financial rating: $$$$*

16885 Dallas Pkwy.
Addison, TX 75001
Ph: (800)552-5264
Fax: (972)991-5723/(972)239-7706
www.janiking.com
Commercial cleaning
Began: 1969, Franchising since: 1974
Headquarters size: 100 employees
Franchise department: 100 employees

U.S. franchises: 9,023
Canadian franchises: 540
Other foreign franchises: 1,369
Company-owned: 22

Seeking: All U.S.
Seeking in Canada? Yes
Exclusive territories? Yes
Homebased option? Yes
Kiosk option? No
Employees needed to run franchise:
　　Info not provided
Absentee ownership? No

COSTS
Total cost: $11.3K-34.1K+
Franchise fee: $8.6K-16.3K+
Royalty fee: 10%
Term of agreement: 20 years renewable
　　at no charge
Franchisees required to buy multiple
　　units? No

FINANCING
In-house: Accounts receivable,
　　equipment
3rd-party: Equipment, franchise fee,
　　startup costs

QUALIFICATIONS
Net worth: Varies
Cash liquidity: Varies

TRAINING
At local office: 40-1/2+ hours

BUSINESS SUPPORT
Newsletter
Meetings
Toll-free phone line
Internet
Security/safety procedures
Field operations/evaluations
Purchasing cooperatives

MARKETING SUPPORT
Co-op advertising
Ad slicks
National media campaign
Regional marketing
Sponsorship of car racing program
PR support

JANTIZE AMERICA

Ranked #360 in Entrepreneur Magazine's 2005 Franchise 500　　　　*Financial rating: $$$*

15449 Middlebelt
Livonia, MI 48154
Ph: (800)968-9182
Fax: (734)421-4936
www.jantize.com
Commercial cleaning
Began: 1988, Franchising since: 1988
Headquarters size: 4 employees
Franchise department: 4 employees

U.S. franchises: 34
Canadian franchises: 0
Other foreign franchises: 0
Company-owned: 1
Units concentrated in MA, MI, NC

Seeking: All U.S.
Seeking in Canada? No
Exclusive territories? Yes
Homebased option? Yes
Kiosk option? No
Employees needed to run franchise: 4
Absentee ownership? No

COSTS
Total cost: $9.8K-16.8K
Franchise fee: $3.5K-8.5K
Royalty fee: 6-9%
Term of agreement: 10 years renewable
　　at no charge
Franchisees required to buy multiple
　　units? No

FINANCING
In-house: Franchise fee
3rd-party: Equipment

QUALIFICATIONS
Net worth: $50K
Cash liquidity: $25K
Experience:
　　General business experience
　　Marketing skills

TRAINING
At headquarters: 3 days
At franchisee's location: 2 days

BUSINESS SUPPORT
Toll-free phone line
Internet
Lease negotiations
Field operations/evaluations

MARKETING SUPPORT
National media campaign
Regional marketing

OPENWORKS
Ranked #141 in Entrepreneur Magazine's 2005 Franchise 500   *Financial rating: $$$$*

4742 N. 24th St., #300
Phoenix, AZ 85016
Ph: (800)777-6736
Fax: (602)468-3788
www.openworksweb.com
Office/commercial cleaning
Began: 1983, Franchising since: 1983
Headquarters size: 54 employees
Franchise department: 6 employees

U.S. franchises: 406
Canadian franchises: 0
Other foreign franchises: 0
Company-owned: 0
Units concentrated in AZ, CA, WA

Seeking: All U.S.
Focusing on: AZ, CA, WA
Seeking in Canada? No
Exclusive territories? Yes
Homebased option? Yes
Kiosk option? No
Employees needed to run franchise: 3
Absentee ownership? No

COSTS
Total cost: $15K-150K+
Franchise fee: $14K-67.5K
Royalty fee: 5-10%
Term of agreement: 10 years renewable
at no charge
Franchisees required to buy multiple
units? No

FINANCING
In-house: Accounts receivable,
equipment, franchise fee,
inventory, startup costs
3rd-party: None

QUALIFICATIONS
Cash liquidity: $7K-150K+
Experience:
General business experience

TRAINING
At headquarters: 2-4 weeks
At franchisee's location: Ongoing
At regional locations: 2 weeks+ &
ongoing

BUSINESS SUPPORT
Newsletter
Meetings
Toll-free phone line
Security/safety procedures
Field operations/evaluations
Purchasing cooperatives

MARKETING SUPPORT
Regional marketing
Bid preparation & presentation

SERVICEMASTER CLEAN
Ranked #12 in Entrepreneur Magazine's 2005 Franchise 500   *Financial rating: $$$$*

3839 Forest Hill Irene Rd.
Memphis, TN 38125
Ph: (800)255-9687/(901)597-7500
Fax: (901)597-7580
www.ownafranchise.com
Comm'l./residential cleaning &
disaster restoration
Began: 1947, Franchising since: 1952
Headquarters size: 134 employees
Franchise department: 10 employees

U.S. franchises: 2,839
Canadian franchises: 181
Other foreign franchises: 1,398
Company-owned: 0
Units concentrated in all U.S.

Seeking: All U.S.
Seeking in Canada? Yes
Exclusive territories? No
Homebased option? Yes
Kiosk option? No
Employees needed to run franchise: 3
Absentee ownership? No

COSTS
Total cost: $28.2K-99.9K
Franchise fee: $16.9K-43K
Royalty fee: 4-10%
Term of agreement: 5 years renewable
at no charge
Franchisees required to buy multiple
units? Outside U.S. only

FINANCING
In-house: Accounts receivable,
equipment, franchise fee,
inventory, payroll, startup
costs, vehicle
3rd-party: None

QUALIFICATIONS
Net worth: $50K
Cash liquidity: $15K-25K
Experience:
General business experience

TRAINING
At headquarters: 2 weeks
At franchisee's location: 1-2 days
At annual convention & regional
seminars

BUSINESS SUPPORT
Newsletter
Meetings
Toll-free phone line
Internet
Security/safety procedures
Field operations/evaluations

MARKETING SUPPORT
Co-op advertising
Ad slicks
National media campaign
Regional marketing
Intranet
Web design templates

SERVICE ONE JANITORIAL

Current financial data not available

5104 N. Orange Blossom Tr., #114
Orlando, FL 32810
Ph: (800)522-7111/(407)293-7645
Fax: (800)846-3992
Janitorial services
Began: 1967, Franchising since: 1985
Headquarters size: 6 employees
Franchise department: 4 employees

U.S. franchises: 185
Canadian franchises: 0
Other foreign franchises: 0
Company-owned: 0

Seeking: All U.S.
Seeking in Canada? No
Exclusive territories? No
Homebased option? Yes
Kiosk option? No
Employees needed to run franchise: 2
Absentee ownership? Yes

COSTS
Total cost: $6.8K-19.3K
Franchise fee: Incl. in start-up
Royalty fee: $175/mo.
Term of agreement: 10 years renewable
    at no charge
Franchisees required to buy multiple
    units? No

FINANCING
In-house: Franchise fee
3rd-party: None

QUALIFICATIONS
Net worth: $10K
Cash liquidity: $2K
Experience:
    General business experience

TRAINING
At headquarters: 3 days
At franchisee's location: 3 days

BUSINESS SUPPORT
Newsletter
Meetings
Toll-free phone line
Grand opening
Internet
Security/safety procedures

MARKETING SUPPORT
Ad slicks

TOWER CLEANING SYSTEMS

Ranked #363 in Entrepreneur Magazine's 2005 Franchise 500

Financial rating: $$$

P.O. Box 2468
Southeastern, PA 19399
Ph: (610)278-9000
Fax: (610)275-8025
www.toweronline.com
Office cleaning
Began: 1988, Franchising since: 1990
Headquarters size: 230 employees
Franchise department: 18 employees

U.S. franchises: 465
Canadian franchises: 0
Other foreign franchises: 0
Company-owned: 0
Units concentrated in CA, FL, GA, HI,
    MI, MN, NJ, OH, PA

Seeking: Northeast, Midwest, West
Focusing on: HI, MI, MN, NJ, PA
Seeking in Canada? No
Exclusive territories? No
Homebased option? Yes
Kiosk option? No
Employees needed to run franchise: 1
Absentee ownership? No

COSTS
Total cost: $1.9K-23.8K
Franchise fee: $1.5K-13.5K
Royalty fee: 3%
Term of agreement: 10 years renewable
    at no charge
Franchisees required to buy multiple
    units? No

FINANCING
In-house: Equipment, franchise fee
3rd-party: None

QUALIFICATIONS
Info not provided

TRAINING
At headquarters: 2 weeks

BUSINESS SUPPORT
Newsletter
Toll-free phone line
Security/safety procedures
Field operations/evaluations

MARKETING SUPPORT
Regional marketing

VANGUARD CLEANING SYSTEMS

Ranked #175 in Entrepreneur Magazine's 2005 Franchise 500　　　*Financial rating: $$$$*

655 Mariners Island Blvd., #303
San Mateo, CA 94404
Ph: (800)564-6422/(650)594-1500
Fax: (650)591-1545
www.vanguardcleaning.com
Commercial cleaning
Began: 1984, Franchising since: 1984
Headquarters size: 20 employees
Franchise department: 3 employees

U.S. franchises: 340
Canadian franchises: 0
Other foreign franchises: 0
Company-owned: 3
Units concentrated in CA, FL, GA,
　　NC, NJ, PA, UT, WA

Seeking: All U.S.
Focusing on: States where units are
　　concentrated (see above)
Seeking in Canada? Yes
Exclusive territories? No
Homebased option? Yes

Kiosk option? No
Employees needed to run franchise: 1-2
Absentee ownership? No

COSTS
Total cost: $2.2K-33.7K
Franchise fee: $1.9K-32.8K
Royalty fee: 5%
Term of agreement: 10 years renewable
　　at no charge
Franchisees required to buy multiple
　　units? No

FINANCING
In-house: Equipment, franchise fee
3rd-party: None

QUALIFICATIONS
Cash liquidity: $2.8K-9K
Experience:
　　General business experience

TRAINING
At headquarters: 2 weeks
At regional offices: 2 weeks

BUSINESS SUPPORT
Toll-free phone line
Field operations/evaluations

MARKETING SUPPORT
Regional marketing
Initial customer base

MAINTENANCE ▶ **HANDYMAN SERVICES/HOME REPAIRS**

AIRE SERV HEATING & AIR CONDITIONING INC.

Ranked #436 in Entrepreneur Magazine's 2005 Franchise 500　　　*Financial rating: $$$$*

1020 N. University Parks Dr.
Waco, TX 76707
Ph: (800)583-2662
Fax: (254)745-5098
www.aireserv.com
Heating & air conditioning services
Began: 1993, Franchising since: 1993
Headquarters size: 175 employees
Franchise department: 32 employees

U.S. franchises: 67
Canadian franchises: 0
Other foreign franchises: 12
Company-owned: 0
Units concentrated in all U.S.

Seeking: All U.S.
Seeking in Canada? Yes
Exclusive territories? Yes
Homebased option? Yes
Kiosk option? No
Employees needed to run franchise: 5-10
Absentee ownership? No

COSTS
Total cost: $31.6K-119.5K
Franchise fee: $17.5K
Royalty fee: 3-5%
Term of agreement: 10 years renewable
　　at $750
Franchisees required to buy multiple
　　units? Outside U.S. only

FINANCING
In-house: Franchise fee
3rd-party: Equipment, franchise fee,
　　inventory, startup costs

QUALIFICATIONS
Net worth: $150K+
Cash liquidity: $35K
Experience:
　　General business experience

TRAINING
At headquarters: 10 days
At franchisee's location: 3 days
Regional training meetings: 2 days
　　(4 per year)

BUSINESS SUPPORT
Newsletter
Meetings
Toll-free phone line
Grand opening
Internet
Field operations/evaluations
Purchasing cooperatives

MARKETING SUPPORT
Co-op advertising
Ad slicks
National media campaign

ANDY ONCALL
Ranked #283 in Entrepreneur Magazine's 2005 Franchise 500   *Financial rating: $$$$*

921 E. Main St.
Chattanooga, TN 37408
Ph: (423)242-0401
Fax: (423)622-0580
www.andyoncall.com
Handyman services
Began: 1993, Franchising since: 1999
Headquarters size: 12 employees
Franchise department: 3 employees

U.S. franchises: 37
Canadian franchises: 0
Other foreign franchises: 0
Company-owned: 0
Units concentrated in GA, IL, NC,
    OH, SC, TN

Seeking: All U.S.
Seeking in Canada? Yes
Exclusive territories? Yes
Homebased option? No
Kiosk option? No
Employees needed to run franchise: 2
Absentee ownership? No

COSTS
Total cost: $30.6K-49.2K
Franchise fee: $23K
Royalty fee: 5%
Term of agreement: 10 years renewable
    at no charge
Franchisees required to buy multiple
    units? No

FINANCING
In-house: Franchise fee
3rd-party: None

QUALIFICATIONS
Net worth: $150K
Cash liquidity: $50K
Experience:
    General business experience
    Sales & people skills

TRAINING
At headquarters: 8 days
At franchisee's location: 5 days

BUSINESS SUPPORT
Newsletter
Meetings
Toll-free phone line
Grand opening
Internet
Lease negotiations
Purchasing cooperatives

MARKETING SUPPORT
Ad slicks
Annual conference
Direct mail
Field operations/support

FURNITURE MEDIC
Ranked #150 in Entrepreneur Magazine's 2005 Franchise 500   *Financial rating: $$$$*

3839 Forest Hill Irene Rd.
Memphis, TN 38125
Ph: (800)255-9687/(901)597-8600
Fax: (901)597-8660
www.furnituremedicfranchise.com
Furniture restoration & repair services
Began: 1992, Franchising since: 1992
Headquarters size: 24 employees
Franchise department: 8 employees

U.S. franchises: 407
Canadian franchises: 70
Other foreign franchises: 103
Company-owned: 0
Units concentrated in all U.S.

Seeking: All U.S.
Seeking in Canada? Yes
Exclusive territories? No
Homebased option? Yes
Kiosk option? No
Employees needed to run franchise: 1
Absentee ownership? No

COSTS
Total cost: $35.5K-78.9K
Franchise fee: $22K
Royalty fee: 7%
Term of agreement: 5 years renewable
    at no charge
Franchisees required to buy multiple
    units? Outside U.S. only

FINANCING
In-house: Accounts receivable,
    equipment, franchise fee,
    inventory, payroll, startup
    costs, vehicle
3rd-party: None

QUALIFICATIONS
Net worth: $50K
Cash liquidity: $15K-25K
Experience:
    Industry experience
    General business experience
    Marketing skills

TRAINING
At headquarters: 2 weeks
Home study/mentor program:
    2 weeks+

BUSINESS SUPPORT
Newsletter
Meetings
Toll-free phone line
Internet
Security/safety procedures
Field operations/evaluations

MARKETING SUPPORT
Ad slicks
National media campaign
Website template

HANDYPRO HANDYMAN SERVICES INC.

Financial rating: $$$

995 S. Main
Plymouth, MI 48170
Ph: (800)942-6394
Fax: (734)254-9171
www.handypro.com
Professional handyman services
Began: 1996, Franchising since: 2000
Headquarters size: 13 employees
Franchise department: 3 employees

U.S. franchises: 5
Canadian franchises: 0
Other foreign franchises: 0
Company-owned: 1

Seeking: All U.S.
Seeking in Canada? No
Exclusive territories? Yes
Homebased option? Yes
Kiosk option? No
Employees needed to run franchise: 1-10
Absentee ownership? Yes

COSTS
Total cost: $36.4K-61.9K
Franchise fee: $25K
Royalty fee: $600-1.5K/mo.
Term of agreement: 7 years renewable
    at 25% of initial franchise fee
Franchisees required to buy multiple
    units? No

FINANCING
No financing available

QUALIFICATIONS
Net worth: $50K
Cash liquidity: $30K
Experience:
    General business experience
    Management experience

TRAINING
At headquarters: 1 week
At franchisee's location: 1 week
    quarterly

BUSINESS SUPPORT
Newsletter
Meetings
Toll-free phone line
Grand opening
Internet
Security/safety procedures
Field operations/evaluations
Purchasing cooperatives

MARKETING SUPPORT
Co-op advertising
Ad slicks

HOUSE DOCTORS

Ranked #209 in Entrepreneur Magazine's 2005 Franchise 500

Financial rating: $$$$

575 Chamber Dr.
Milford, OH 45150
Ph: (800)319-3359
Fax: (513)831-6010
www.housedoctors.com
Handyman services/home repairs
Began: 1994, Franchising since: 1995
Headquarters size: 23 employees
Franchise department: 12 employees

U.S. franchises: 204
Canadian franchises: 0
Other foreign franchises: 2
Company-owned: 0
Units concentrated in all U.S.

Seeking: All U.S.
Seeking in Canada? No
Exclusive territories? Yes
Homebased option? Yes
Kiosk option? No
Employees needed to run franchise:
    Info not provided
Absentee ownership? No

COSTS
Total cost: $25.5K-53.5K
Franchise fee: $13.9K-32.9K
Royalty fee: 6%
Term of agreement: 10 years renewable
    at no charge
Franchisees required to buy multiple
    units? No

FINANCING
In-house: Franchise fee
3rd-party: None

QUALIFICATIONS
Experience:
    General business experience

TRAINING
At headquarters: 1 week

BUSINESS SUPPORT
Newsletter
Meetings
Toll-free phone line
Internet
Field operations/evaluations

MARKETING SUPPORT
Ad slicks

MAINTENANCE MADE SIMPLE

Current financial data not available

7825 E. Redfield Rd., #C
Scottsdale, AZ 85260
Ph: (866)778-6283
www.m2simple.com
Handyman & home maintenance
    services
Began: 2003, Franchising since: 2003
Headquarters size: 11 employees
Franchise department:
    Info not provided

U.S. franchises: 36
Canadian franchises: 1
Other foreign franchises: 0
Company-owned: 0
Units concentrated in all U.S.

Seeking: All U.S.
Seeking in Canada? Yes
Exclusive territories? Yes
Homebased option? Yes
Kiosk option? No
Employees needed to run franchise: 1
Absentee ownership? Yes

COSTS
Total cost: $35.3K-64.8K
Franchise fee: $30K
Royalty fee: 7%
Term of agreement: 15 years renewable
    at no charge
Franchisees required to buy multiple
    units? No

FINANCING
In-house: None
3rd-party: Accounts receivable,
    equipment, franchise fee,
    inventory, payroll, startup costs

QUALIFICATIONS
Experience:
    General business experience

TRAINING
At headquarters: 7 days
At franchisee's location: 3 days

BUSINESS SUPPORT
Newsletter
Meetings
Toll-free phone line
Grand opening
Internet
Security/safety procedures
Field operations/evaluations
Purchasing cooperatives

MARKETING SUPPORT
Co-op advertising
Ad slicks
National media campaign
Regional marketing
Inbound & outbound call center
National accounts program
Catalog of marketing collateral

MR. APPLIANCE CORP.

Ranked #324 in Entrepreneur Magazine's 2005 Franchise 500

Financial rating: $$$$

1020 N. University Parks Dr.
Waco, TX 76707
Ph: (800)290-1422
Fax: (800)209-7621
www.mrappliance.com
Household appliance services &
    repairs
Began: 1996, Franchising since: 1996
Headquarters size: 110 employees
Franchise department: 30 employees

U.S. franchises: 62
Canadian franchises: 1
Other foreign franchises: 2
Company-owned: 0
Units concentrated in all U.S.

Seeking: All U.S.
Seeking in Canada? Yes
Exclusive territories? Yes
Homebased option? Yes
Kiosk option? No
Employees needed to run franchise: 1-3
Absentee ownership? No

COSTS
Total cost: $32.2K-68.9K
Franchise fee: $15.9K
Royalty fee: 3-7%
Term of agreement: 10 years renewable
    at $2.5K
Franchisees required to buy multiple
    units? Outside U.S. only

FINANCING
In-house: Franchise fee
3rd-party: None

QUALIFICATIONS
Net worth: $100K
Cash liquidity: $25K
Experience:
    Industry experience

TRAINING
At headquarters: 1 week
At franchisee's location: Varies
Regional meetings

BUSINESS SUPPORT
Newsletter
Meetings
Toll-free phone line
Internet
Field operations/evaluations

MARKETING SUPPORT
Co-op advertising
Ad slicks
National media campaign

ONE HOUR AIR CONDITIONING

Financial rating: $$$

2 N. Tamiami Trail, #506
Sarasota, FL 34236
Ph: (800)746-0458/(941)552-5100
Fax: (941)552-5130
www.onehourair.com
HVAC replacement & services
Began: 1999, Franchising since: 2003
Headquarters size: 12 employees
Franchise department: 8 employees

U.S. franchises: 83
Canadian franchises: 0
Other foreign franchises: 0
Company-owned: 7
Units concentrated in all U.S.

Seeking: All U.S.
Seeking in Canada? No
Exclusive territories? Yes
Homebased option? No
Kiosk option? No
Employees needed to run franchise: 5-16
Absentee ownership? No

COSTS
Total cost: $46K-400K
(Franchise sells conversions only.)
Franchise fee: $20K
Royalty fee: 4-5%
Term of agreement: 10 years renewable
at 50% of original franchise fee
Franchisees required to buy multiple
units? No

FINANCING
No financing available

QUALIFICATIONS
Experience:
Industry experience
General business experience
Marketing skills

TRAINING
At headquarters: 3 days
At franchisee's location: 3 days
per year
At model centers/training school

BUSINESS SUPPORT
Newsletter
Meetings
Toll-free phone line
Grand opening
Internet
Security/safety procedures
Field operations/evaluations
Purchasing cooperatives

MARKETING SUPPORT
Ad slicks

THE SCREEN MACHINE

Current financial data not available

4173 First St.
Livermore, CA 94557
Ph: (877)505-1985
Fax: (925)443-9983
www.screen-machine.com
Mobile window screen repair &
fabrication
Began: 1986, Franchising since: 1988
Headquarters size: 4 employees
Franchise department: 4 employees

U.S. franchises: 28
Canadian franchises: 0
Other foreign franchises: 0
Company-owned: 1

Seeking: All U.S., Northwest
Seeking in Canada? No
Exclusive territories? Yes
Homebased option? Yes
Kiosk option? No
Employees needed to run franchise: 1
Absentee ownership? No

COSTS
Total cost: $47K-72.1K
Franchise fee: $25K
Royalty fee: 5%
Term of agreement: 10 years renewable
at $2K
Franchisees required to buy multiple
units? No

FINANCING
In-house: None
3rd-party: Equipment, franchise fee,
startup costs

QUALIFICATIONS
Net worth: $50K
Cash liquidity: $25K
Experience:
General business experience
Marketing skills

TRAINING
At headquarters: 1 week
Annual meeting: 3 days

BUSINESS SUPPORT
Meetings
Toll-free phone line
Internet
Security/safety procedures
Field operations/evaluations
Purchasing cooperatives

MARKETING SUPPORT
Co-op advertising
Ad slicks

MAINTENANCE ▸ LAWN CARE

ENVIRO MASTERS LAWN CARE

Current financial data not available

Box 178
Caledon East, ON L0N 1E0 Canada
Ph: (905)584-9592
Fax: (905)584-0402
www.enviromasters.com
Organic lawn care
Began: 1987, Franchising since: 1991
Headquarters size: 4 employees
Franchise department: 4 employees

U.S. franchises: 0
Canadian franchises: 40
Other foreign franchises: 0
Company-owned: 3
Units concentrated in Canada

Seeking: All U.S.
Seeking in Canada? Yes
Exclusive territories? Yes
Homebased option? Yes
Kiosk option? No
Employees needed to run franchise:
    Info not provided
Absentee ownership? No

COSTS
Total cost: $30K-40K
Franchise fee: $25K
Royalty fee: 5%
Term of agreement: 10 years renewable
    at 25-50% of fee
Franchisees required to buy multiple
    units? No

FINANCING
No financing available

QUALIFICATIONS
Net worth: $40K
Cash liquidity: $25K
Experience:
    General business experience

TRAINING
At headquarters: Varies
At franchisee's location: 2 days
At existing location: Ongoing

BUSINESS SUPPORT
Newsletter
Meetings
Toll-free phone line
Grand opening
Internet
Security/safety procedures
Field operations/evaluations
Purchasing cooperatives

MARKETING SUPPORT
Co-op advertising
Ad slicks
Regional marketing

U.S. LAWNS

Ranked #208 in Entrepreneur Magazine's 2005 Franchise 500   *Financial rating: $$$$*

4407 Vineland Rd., #D-15
Orlando, FL 32811
Ph: (800)875-2967
Fax: (407)246-1623
www.uslawns.com
Landscape maintenance services
Began: 1986, Franchising since: 1987
Headquarters size: 9 employees
Franchise department: 3 employees

U.S. franchises: 124
Canadian franchises: 0
Other foreign franchises: 0
Company-owned: 0
Units concentrated in all U.S.

Seeking: All U.S.
Seeking in Canada? No
Exclusive territories? Yes
Homebased option? Yes
Kiosk option? No
Employees needed to run franchise:
    10-15
Absentee ownership? No

COSTS
Total cost: $48.5K-70K
Franchise fee: $29K
Royalty fee: 3-4%
Term of agreement: 10 years renewable
    at no charge
Franchisees required to buy multiple
    units? No

FINANCING
In-house: Franchise fee
3rd-party: Equipment, franchise fee,
    inventory, startup costs

QUALIFICATIONS
Cash liquidity: $15K+
Experience:
    General business experience
    Marketing skills

TRAINING
At headquarters: 1 week
At franchisee's location: Ongoing

BUSINESS SUPPORT
Newsletter
Meetings
Toll-free phone line
Internet
Security/safety procedures
Field operations/evaluations
Purchasing cooperatives

MARKETING SUPPORT
Co-op advertising
Ad slicks
National media campaign
Regional marketing
Internet support
National sales team

WEED MAN

Ranked #103 in Entrepreneur Magazine's 2005 Franchise 500   *Financial rating: $$$$*

11 Grand Marshall Dr.
Scarborough, ON M1B 5N6 Canada
Ph: (416)269-5754
Fax: (416)269-8233
www.weed-man.com
Lawn care
Began: 1970, Franchising since: 1976
Headquarters size: 8 employees
Franchise department: 4 employees

U.S. franchises: 166
Canadian franchises: 114
Other foreign franchises: 1
Company-owned: 0
Units concentrated in all U.S.

Seeking: All U.S.
Seeking in Canada? Yes
Exclusive territories? Yes
Homebased option? Yes
Kiosk option? No
Employees needed to run franchise: 4-6
Absentee ownership? Yes

COSTS
Total cost: $48.6K-70.3K
Franchise fee: $20K-33.8K
Royalty fee: 6%
Term of agreement: 10 years renewable
    at 50% of original fee
Franchisees required to buy multiple
    units? No

FINANCING
In-house: None
3rd-party: Equipment, franchise fee,
    startup costs

QUALIFICATIONS
Net worth: $60K
Cash liquidity: $30K
Experience:
    General business experience

TRAINING
At headquarters: 2 weeks
At franchisee's location: 2-4 days
At various locations: 3 days

BUSINESS SUPPORT
Newsletter
Meetings
Internet
Security/safety procedures
Field operations/evaluations
Purchasing cooperatives

MARKETING SUPPORT
National media campaign

MAINTENANCE ▸ PEST CONTROL

CRITTER CONTROL INC.

Ranked #323 in Entrepreneur Magazine's 2005 Franchise 500   *Financial rating: $$$$*

9435 E. Cherry Bend Rd.
Traverse City, MI 49684
Ph: (800)699-1953
Fax: (231)947-9440
www.crittercontrol.com
Urban/rural wildlife management
Began: 1983, Franchising since: 1987
Headquarters size: 10 employees
Franchise department: 4 employees

U.S. franchises: 94
Canadian franchises: 2
Other foreign franchises: 0
Company-owned: 5
Units concentrated in all U.S.

Seeking: All U.S.
Seeking in Canada? Yes
Exclusive territories? Yes
Homebased option? Yes
Kiosk option? No
Employees needed to run franchise: 1
Absentee ownership? No

COSTS
Total cost: $25.5K-69K
Franchise fee: $18-36K
Royalty fee: 6%
Term of agreement: 10 years renewable
    at no charge
Franchisees required to buy multiple
    units? No

FINANCING
In-house: Equipment, inventory
3rd-party: Accounts receivable,
    franchise fee, payroll, startup costs

QUALIFICATIONS
Experience:
    Marketing skills
    Customer service skills
    Interpersonal skills

TRAINING
In Columbus, OH or Fort Lauderdale,
    FL: 2 weeks
At annual conferences

BUSINESS SUPPORT
Newsletter
Meetings
Toll-free phone line
Internet
Security/safety procedures
Field operations/evaluations
Purchasing cooperatives

MARKETING SUPPORT
Co-op advertising
Ad slicks
National media campaign
Regional marketing
National call center
Sporting event sponsorship

ENVIRO-TECH PEST SERVICES

Current financial data not available

P.O. Box 567
Kearneysville, WV 25430
Ph: (304)728-5090
Fax: (304)724-5499
www.envirotechpestservices.com
Pest control
Began: 1985, Franchising since: 2004
Headquarters size: 35 employees
Franchise department: 4 employees

U.S. franchises: 0
Canadian franchises: 0
Other foreign franchises: 0
Company-owned: 3

Seeking: Northeast, South, Southeast
Seeking in Canada? No
Exclusive territories? Yes
Homebased option? Yes
Kiosk option? No
Employees needed to run franchise: 2
Absentee ownership? Yes

COSTS

Total cost: $34.6K-54.4K
Franchise fee: $19.5K-24.5K
Royalty fee: 7-5%
Term of agreement: 10 years renewable
    at 10% of initial franchise fee
Franchisees required to buy multiple
    units? No

FINANCING

No financing available

QUALIFICATIONS

Net worth: $25K
Cash liquidity: $25K
Experience:
    General business experience

TRAINING

At headquarters: 10 days
At existing office

BUSINESS SUPPORT

Newsletter
Meetings
Toll-free phone line
Grand opening
Internet
Lease negotiations
Security/safety procedures
Field operations/evaluations
Purchasing cooperatives

MARKETING SUPPORT

Ad slicks

NATURZONE PEST CONTROL INC.

Financial rating: $$$

1899 Porter Lake Dr., #103
Sarasota, FL 34240
Ph: (941)378-3334
Fax: (941)378-8584
www.naturzone.com
Pest control
Began: 1982, Franchising since: 1998
Headquarters size: 10 employees
Franchise department: 2 employees

U.S. franchises: 5
Canadian franchises: 0
Other foreign franchises: 5
Company-owned: 1
Units concentrated in FL

Seeking: All U.S.
Seeking in Canada? Yes
Exclusive territories? Yes
Homebased option? Yes
Kiosk option? No
Employees needed to run franchise: 2
Absentee ownership? No

COSTS

Total cost: $35K-44.3K
Franchise fee: $20K
Royalty fee: 5%
Term of agreement: Lifetime
Franchisees required to buy multiple
    units? No

FINANCING

No financing available

QUALIFICATIONS

Net worth: $50K
Cash liquidity: $10K
Experience:
    General business experience
    Marketing skills

TRAINING

At headquarters: 3 weeks

BUSINESS SUPPORT

Newsletter
Meetings
Internet
Security/safety procedures
Field operations/evaluations
Purchasing cooperatives

MARKETING SUPPORT

Co-op advertising
Ad slicks

PESTMASTER SERVICES

Current financial data not available

137 E. South St.
Bishop, CA 93514
Ph: (760)873-8100
Fax: (760)873-3268
www.pestmaster.com
Pest control services
Began: 1979, Franchising since: 1991
Headquarters size: 12 employees
Franchise department: 1 employee

U.S. franchises: 15
Canadian franchises: 0
Other foreign franchises: 0
Company-owned: 11

Seeking: All U.S.
Seeking in Canada? No
Exclusive territories? Yes
Homebased option? Yes
Kiosk option? No
Employees needed to run franchise: 2
Absentee ownership? No

COSTS
Total cost: $30K-79.3K
Franchise fee: $15K-30K
Royalty fee: 5-7%
Term of agreement: 10 years renewable
at no charge
Franchisees required to buy multiple
units? No

FINANCING
No financing available

QUALIFICATIONS
Net worth: $65K
Cash liquidity: $50K
Experience:
Industry experience
General business experience

TRAINING
At headquarters: 1 week
At franchisee's location: 2 weeks
At Pestmaster University: 1 week

BUSINESS SUPPORT
Newsletter
Meetings
Toll-free phone line
Grand opening
Internet
Field operations/evaluations
Purchasing cooperatives

MARKETING SUPPORT
Co-op advertising
Ad slicks

TERMINIX TERMITE & PEST CONTROL

Current financial data not available

860 Ridge Lake Blvd.
Memphis, TN 38120
Ph: (800)441-5390/(901)363-1132
Fax: (901)363-8541
www.terminix.com
Termite & pest control
Began: 1927, Franchising since: 1927
Headquarters size: 450 employees
Franchise department: 7 employees

U.S. franchises: 137
Canadian franchises: 0
Other foreign franchises: 0
Company-owned: 329

Seeking: All U.S.
Seeking in Canada? Yes
Exclusive territories? Yes
Homebased option? Yes
Kiosk option? No
Employees needed to run franchise:
Info not provided
Absentee ownership? Yes

COSTS
Total cost: $24.7K-85.3K
Franchise fee: $25K-50K
Royalty fee: 7-10%
Term of agreement: 5 years renewable
at no charge
Franchisees required to buy multiple
units? Outside U.S. only

FINANCING
In-house: Franchise fee
3rd-party: None

QUALIFICATIONS
Info not provided

TRAINING
In-field training
Ongoing self-tutorial

BUSINESS SUPPORT
Newsletter
Meetings
Toll-free phone line
Internet
Security/safety procedures
Field operations/evaluations
Purchasing cooperatives

MARKETING SUPPORT
Co-op advertising
National media campaign
Various marketing programs

TRULY NOLEN

Ranked #475 in Entrepreneur Magazine's 2005 Franchise 500　　　*Financial rating: $$$$*

3636 E. Speedway
Tucson, AZ 85716
Ph: (800)458-3664/(520)977-5817
Fax: (520)322-4010
www.trulynolen.com
Pest/termite control & lawn care
Began: 1938, Franchising since: 1996
Headquarters size: 35 employees
Franchise department: 2 employees

U.S. franchises: 9
Canadian franchises: 0
Other foreign franchises: 60
Company-owned: 65
Units concentrated in all U.S.

Seeking: All U.S.
Seeking in Canada? No
Exclusive territories? Yes
Homebased option? Yes
Kiosk option? Yes
Employees needed to run franchise: 2
Absentee ownership? Yes

COSTS
Total cost: $3.6K-300.5K
Kiosk cost: Same as total cost
Franchise fee: $1.5K-45K
Royalty fee: 7%
Term of agreement: 5 years renewable
　　at $1.5K
Franchisees required to buy multiple
　　units? No

FINANCING
In-house: None
3rd-party: Accounts receivable,
　　equipment, franchise fee,
　　inventory, payroll, startup costs

QUALIFICATIONS
Net worth: $50K
Cash liquidity: $10K
Experience:
　　Industry experience
　　General business experience
　　Marketing skills

TRAINING
At headquarters: 1 week
At franchisee's location: 1 week
At training centers

BUSINESS SUPPORT
Newsletter
Meetings
Toll-free phone line
Grand opening
Internet
Security/safety procedures
Field operations/evaluations
Purchasing cooperatives

MARKETING SUPPORT
Co-op advertising
Ad slicks
National media campaign
Regional marketing

MAINTENANCE　　▶　PET WASTE REMOVAL

DOODYCALLS

Current financial data not available

5 Burke Ct.
Palmyra, VA 22963
Ph: (434)589-3810
Fax: (703)995-0601
www.doodycalls.com
Pet waste removal service
Began: 2000, Franchising since: 2004
Headquarters size: 2 employees
Franchise department: 2 employees

U.S. franchises: 1
Canadian franchises: 0
Other foreign franchises: 0
Company-owned: 2

Seeking: All U.S.
Seeking in Canada? No
Exclusive territories? Yes
Homebased option? Yes
Kiosk option? No
Employees needed to run franchise: 2-4
Absentee ownership? No

COSTS
Total cost: $34.9K-59.2K
Franchise fee: $12.5K
Royalty fee: 6%
Term of agreement: 10 years renewable
　　at 25% of then-current fee
Franchisees required to buy multiple
　　units? No

FINANCING
No financing available

QUALIFICATIONS
Info not provided

TRAINING
At headquarters: 30 hours

BUSINESS SUPPORT
Newsletter
Meetings
Toll-free phone line
Grand opening
Internet
Purchasing cooperatives

MARKETING SUPPORT
Co-op advertising
Ad slicks
National media campaign
Regional marketing

WHOLLY CRAP

Current financial data not available

392 Seaburn St.
Brookfield, OH 44403
Ph: (330)448-1700
Fax: (330)448-0585
www.whollycrap.com
Pet waste removal service
Began: 2001, Franchising since: 2003
Headquarters size: 1 employee
Franchise department:
    Info not provided

U.S. franchises: 0
Canadian franchises: 0
Other foreign franchises: 0
Company-owned: 1

Seeking: Northeast, Midwest
Seeking in Canada? No
Exclusive territories? Yes
Homebased option? Yes
Kiosk option? No
Employees needed to run franchise: 1
Absentee ownership? No

COSTS
Total cost: $14.8K-16.8K
Franchise fee: $12.5K
Royalty fee: $100-150/mo.
Term of agreement: 5 years renewable
    at no charge
Franchisees required to buy multiple
    units? No

FINANCING
No financing available

QUALIFICATIONS
Net worth: to $100K
Experience:
    Marketing skills

TRAINING
At headquarters

BUSINESS SUPPORT
Newsletter
Internet

MARKETING SUPPORT
Co-op advertising

MAINTENANCE ▸ PLUMBING

BENJAMIN FRANKLIN PLUMBING

Ranked #383 in Entrepreneur Magazine's 2005 Franchise 500

Financial rating: $$$

One Sarasota Tower, #806
Sarasota, FL 34236
Ph: (800)695-3579/(941)552-5111
Fax: (941)552-5130
www.benfranklinplumbing.com
Plumbing services
Began: 2000, Franchising since: 2001
Headquarters size: 12 employees
Franchise department: 8 employees

U.S. franchises: 141
Canadian franchises: 0
Other foreign franchises: 0
Company-owned: 0
Units concentrated in all U.S.

Seeking: All U.S.
Seeking in Canada? Yes
Exclusive territories? Yes
Homebased option? No
Kiosk option? No
Employees needed to run franchise: 4-12
Absentee ownership? No

COSTS
Total cost: $34K-381.5K
(Franchise sells conversions only.)
Franchise fee: $15K
Royalty fee: 4-5%
Term of agreement: 10 years renewable
    at 50% of original franchise fee
Franchisees required to buy multiple
    units? No

FINANCING
No financing available

QUALIFICATIONS
Experience:
    Industry experience
    General business experience
    Marketing skills

TRAINING
At headquarters: 4 days
At franchisee's location: 3 days &
    as needed
Model centers/training schools:
    1-1/2 days

BUSINESS SUPPORT
Newsletter
Meetings
Toll-free phone line
Grand opening
Internet
Security/safety procedures
Field operations/evaluations
Purchasing cooperatives

MARKETING SUPPORT
Ad slicks

ROOTER-MAN

Ranked #187 in Entrepreneur Magazine's 2005 Franchise 500　　　*Financial rating: $$$*

268 Rangeway Rd.
North Billerica, MA 01862
Ph: (800)700-8062
Fax: (978)663-0061
www.rooterman.com
Plumbing, drain & sewer cleaning
Began: 1970, Franchising since: 1981
Headquarters size: 28 employees
Franchise department: 5 employees

U.S. franchises: 146
Canadian franchises: 4
Other foreign franchises: 1
Company-owned: 0

Seeking: All U.S.
Seeking in Canada? Yes
Exclusive territories? Yes
Homebased option? Yes
Kiosk option? No
Employees needed to run franchise: 3-5
Absentee ownership? Yes

COSTS
Total cost: $46.8K-137.6K
Franchise fee: $3.98K
Royalty fee: Varies
Term of agreement: 5 years renewable
  at $2.5K
Franchisees required to buy multiple
  units? No

FINANCING
In-house: Franchise fee
3rd-party: Equipment, inventory,
  startup costs

QUALIFICATIONS
Net worth: $25K
Cash liquidity: $10K
Experience:
  Mechanical ability

TRAINING
At headquarters: 6 weeks
At franchisee's location: 2 days
Training seminar: 2 days

BUSINESS SUPPORT
Newsletter
Meetings
Grand opening
Internet
Lease negotiations
Security/safety procedures
Field operations/evaluations
Purchasing cooperatives

MARKETING SUPPORT
Co-op advertising
Ad slicks
National media campaign
Regional marketing

MAINTENANCE　　RESIDENTIAL CLEANING

A SPECIAL TOUCH CLEANING SERVICE INC.

Financial rating: $$

705 Twin Ridge Ln., #10
Richmond, VA 23235
Ph: (804)272-0723
Fax: (804)272-0723
www.aspecialtouchcleaning.com
Maid service
Began: 1998, Franchising since: 2003
Headquarters size: 7 employees
Franchise department: 2 employees

U.S. franchises: 1
Canadian franchises: 0
Other foreign franchises: 0
Company-owned: 2

Seeking: All U.S.
Seeking in Canada? Yes
Exclusive territories? Yes
Homebased option? Yes
Kiosk option? No
Employees needed to run franchise: 5
Absentee ownership? No

COSTS
Total cost: $22.6K-53.5K
Franchise fee: $15K
Royalty fee: 7%
Term of agreement: 5 years renewable
  at no charge
Franchisees required to buy multiple
  units? No

FINANCING
No financing available

QUALIFICATIONS
Net worth: $100K
Cash liquidity: $25K
Experience:
  General business experience
  Customer service skills

TRAINING
At headquarters: 1 week
At franchisee's location: 1 week

BUSINESS SUPPORT
Meetings
Toll-free phone line
Grand opening
Internet
Field operations/evaluations

MARKETING SUPPORT
Ad slicks
Prepaid leads

COTTAGECARE INC.

Current financial data not available

6323 W. 110th St.
Overland Park, KS 66211
Ph: (913)469-8778
Fax: (913)469-0822
www.cottagecare.com
Residential cleaning
Began: 1988, Franchising since: 1989
Headquarters size: 13 employees
Franchise department: 3 employees

U.S. franchises: 51
Canadian franchises: 6
Other foreign franchises: 0
Company-owned: 3
Units concentrated in CO, KS, FL,
    MO, NC, NY, TX, VA

Seeking: All U.S.
Seeking in Canada? Yes
Exclusive territories? Yes
Homebased option? No
Kiosk option? No
Employees needed to run franchise: 10
Absentee ownership? Yes

COSTS
Total cost: $49.5K-75.5K
Franchise fee: $9.5K-17K
Royalty fee: 5.5%
Term of agreement: 10 years renewable
    at $3K
Franchisees required to buy multiple
    units? No

FINANCING
No financing available

QUALIFICATIONS
Cash liquidity: $46K-72.5K

TRAINING
At headquarters: 10 days

BUSINESS SUPPORT
Newsletter
Meetings
Internet
Field operations/evaluations

MARKETING SUPPORT
Ongoing direct-mail program

HOME CLEANING CENTERS OF AMERICA

Ranked #375 in Entrepreneur Magazine's 2005 Franchise 500   *Financial rating: $$$*

10851 Mastin Blvd., #130
Overland Park, KS 66210
Ph: (800)767-1118
Fax: (913)327-5272
www.homecleaningcenters.com
House, office, carpet & window cleaning
Began: 1981, Franchising since: 1984
Headquarters size: 2 employees
Franchise department: 2 employees

U.S. franchises: 39
Canadian franchises: 0
Other foreign franchises: 0
Company-owned: 0
Units concentrated in all U.S.

Seeking: All U.S.
Seeking in Canada? No
Exclusive territories? Yes
Homebased option? No
Kiosk option? No
Employees needed to run franchise: 12
Absentee ownership? No

COSTS
Total cost: $23.8K-25.8K
Franchise fee: $9.5K
Royalty fee: 3-5%
Term of agreement: 10 years renewable
    at no charge
Franchisees required to buy multiple
    units? No

FINANCING
No financing available

QUALIFICATIONS
Experience:
    Management skills

TRAINING
At franchisee's location: 1 week

BUSINESS SUPPORT
Newsletter
Meetings
Toll-free phone line
Grand opening
Internet
Lease negotiations
Security/safety procedures
Field operations/evaluations
Purchasing cooperatives

MARKETING SUPPORT
Ad slicks

MAIDPRO

Ranked #329 in Entrepreneur Magazine's 2005 Franchise 500　　　　*Financial rating: $$$*

180 Canal St.
Boston, MA 02114
Ph: (888)624-3776/(617)742-8787
Fax: (617)720-0700
www.maidpro.com
Professional home & office cleaning
Began: 1991, Franchising since: 1997
Headquarters size: 9 employees
Franchise department: 5 employees

U.S. franchises: 41
Canadian franchises: 0
Other foreign franchises: 0
Company-owned: 1

Seeking: All U.S.
Seeking in Canada? No
Exclusive territories? Yes
Homebased option? No
Kiosk option? No
Employees needed to run franchise: 6-25
Absentee ownership? No

COSTS
Total cost: $39.4K-75.9K
Franchise fee: $7.9K
Royalty fee: 3-6%
Term of agreement: 10 years renewable
　　at $500
Franchisees required to buy multiple
　　units? No

FINANCING
In-house: None
3rd-party: Accounts receivable,
　　equipment, franchise fee,
　　inventory, payroll, startup costs

QUALIFICATIONS
Net worth: $100K
Cash liquidity: $50K
Experience:
　　General business experience
　　Computer literate

TRAINING
At headquarters: 2 weeks
At franchisee's location: As needed

BUSINESS SUPPORT
Newsletter
Meetings
Toll-free phone line
Grand opening
Internet
Security/safety procedures
Field operations/evaluations
Purchasing cooperatives

MARKETING SUPPORT
Co-op advertising
Ad slicks
Regional marketing
Marketing designs
Direct-mail services

MAID TO PERFECTION

Ranked #183 in Entrepreneur Magazine's 2005 Franchise 500　　　　*Financial rating: $$$$*

1101 Opal Ct. 2nd Fl.
Hagerstown, MD 21740
Ph: (800)648-6243/(301)790-7900
Fax: (301)790-3949
www.maidtoperfectioncorp.com
Residential & light commercial cleaning
Began: 1980, Franchising since: 1990
Headquarters size: 8 employees
Franchise department: 8 employees

U.S. franchises: 232
Canadian franchises: 20
Other foreign franchises: 0
Company-owned: 0

Seeking: All U.S.
Seeking in Canada? Yes
Exclusive territories? Yes
Homebased option? No
Kiosk option? No
Employees needed to run franchise: 2
Absentee ownership? No

COSTS
Total cost: $38.2K-44K
Franchise fee: $9.95K
Royalty fee: 4-7%
Term of agreement: 5-10 years
　　renewable at no charge
Franchisees required to buy multiple
　　units? No

FINANCING
In-house: None
3rd-party: Equipment, franchise fee,
　　startup costs

QUALIFICATIONS
Net worth: $80K
Cash liquidity: $45K
Experience:
　　General business experience
　　Marketing skills

TRAINING
At headquarters: 5-7 days
At franchisee's location: 1-21 days
After startup: 5-7 days

BUSINESS SUPPORT
Newsletter
Meetings
Toll-free phone line
Grand opening
Internet
Field operations/evaluations
Purchasing cooperatives

MARKETING SUPPORT
Co-op advertising
Ad slicks
Regional marketing
Telephone routing

MAIDS TO ORDER

Ranked #319 in Entrepreneur Magazine's 2005 Franchise 500

Financial rating: $$$$

4000 Embassy Pkwy., #430
Akron, OH 44333
Ph: (800)701-6243/(330)666-9460
Fax: (330)666-9710
www.maidstoorder.com
Residential & commercial cleaning
Began: 1988, Franchising since: 1992
Headquarters size: 6 employees
Franchise department: 5 employees

U.S. franchises: 36
Canadian franchises: 0
Other foreign franchises: 4
Company-owned: 0

Seeking: All U.S.
Seeking in Canada? Yes
Exclusive territories? Yes
Homebased option? No
Kiosk option? No
Employees needed to run franchise:
    Info not provided
Absentee ownership? Yes

COSTS
Total cost: $35.1K-101.5K
Franchise fee: $12.5K-57.5K
Royalty fee: 5%
Term of agreement: 15 years renewable
    at no charge
Franchisees required to buy multiple
    units? Outside U.S. only

FINANCING
In-house: Franchise fee
3rd-party: None

QUALIFICATIONS
Cash liquidity: $5K-15K

TRAINING
At headquarters: 1 week
At franchisee's location: 1-2 days

BUSINESS SUPPORT
Newsletter
Meetings
Toll-free phone line
Grand opening
Internet

MARKETING SUPPORT
Co-op advertising
Ad slicks
All marketing materials

MERRY MAIDS

Ranked #45 in Entrepreneur Magazine's 2005 Franchise 500

Financial rating: $$$$

P.O. Box 751017
Memphis, TN 38175-1017
Ph: (800)798-8000
Fax: (901)597-8140
www.merrymaids.com
Residential cleaning
Began: 1979, Franchising since: 1980
Headquarters size: 60 employees
Franchise department: 25 employees

U.S. franchises: 772
Canadian franchises: 68
Other foreign franchises: 433
Company-owned: 149
Units concentrated in all U.S.

Seeking: All U.S.
Seeking in Canada? Yes
Exclusive territories? Yes
Homebased option? No
Kiosk option? No
Employees needed to run franchise: 12
Absentee ownership? Yes

COSTS
Total cost: $23.4K-54.5K
Franchise fee: $19K-27K
Royalty fee: 5-7%
Term of agreement: 5 years renewable
    at no charge
Franchisees required to buy multiple
    units? No

FINANCING
In-house: Equipment, franchise fee,
    inventory
3rd-party: None

QUALIFICATIONS
Cash liquidity: $23.4K-54.5K
Experience:
    General business experience
    Management experience

TRAINING
At headquarters: 8 days
At franchisee's location: As needed
At regional locations

BUSINESS SUPPORT
Newsletter
Meetings
Toll-free phone line
Internet
Security/safety procedures
Field operations/evaluations

MARKETING SUPPORT
Ad slicks
National media campaign
Yellow Pages ads and placement
    support
Internet ad composition site

MAINTENANCE ▸ RESTORATION

DISASTER KLEENUP INT'L.

Financial rating: $

P.O. Box 661368
Chicago, IL 60666-1368
Ph: (630)350-3000
Fax: (630)350-9354
www.disasterkleenup.com
Insurance restoration services
Began: 1974, Franchising since: 1994
Headquarters size: 10 employees
Franchise department: 10 employees

U.S. franchises: 101
Canadian franchises: 0
Other foreign franchises: 0
Company-owned: 0

Seeking: All U.S.
Seeking in Canada? No
Exclusive territories? Yes
Homebased option? No
Kiosk option? No
Employees needed to run franchise:
    10-100
Absentee ownership? No

COSTS
Total cost: $15.2K-40.2K
(Franchise sells conversions only.)
Franchise fee: $15K
Royalty fee: $600-1.95K/mo.
Term of agreement: 2 years renewable
    at $250
Franchisees required to buy multiple
    units? No

FINANCING
No financing available

QUALIFICATIONS
Experience:
    Industry experience
    Must own a restoration/remodeling
    construction company

TRAINING
At headquarters: 1 day & ongoing
National/regional conferences &
    meetings

BUSINESS SUPPORT
Newsletter
Meetings
Toll-free phone line
Internet
Purchasing cooperatives

MARKETING SUPPORT
Co-op advertising
National media campaign
Regional marketing

DURACLEAN INT'L.

Ranked #170 in Entrepreneur Magazine's 2005 Franchise 500

Financial rating: $$$$

220 Campus Dr.
Arlington Heights, IL 60004
Ph: (800)251-7070/(847)704-7100
Fax: (847)704-7101
www.duraclean.com
Disaster restoration, mold remediation
    & carpet cleaning
Began: 1930, Franchising since: 1945
Headquarters size: 20 employees
Franchise department: 3 employees

U.S. franchises: 245
Canadian franchises: 12
Other foreign franchises: 116
Company-owned: 2
Units concentrated in all U.S.

Seeking: All U.S.
Seeking in Canada? Yes
Exclusive territories? Yes
Homebased option? Yes
Kiosk option? No
Employees needed to run franchise:
    Info not provided
Absentee ownership? Yes

COSTS
Total cost: $38.99K-71.5K
Franchise fee: $10K
Royalty fee: 2-8%
Term of agreement: 5 years renewable
    at no charge
Franchisees required to buy multiple
    units? No

FINANCING
In-house: Franchise fee
3rd-party: None

QUALIFICATIONS
Net worth: $50K
Cash liquidity: $50K

TRAINING
At headquarters: 5 days
In-field training: 2 days

BUSINESS SUPPORT
Newsletter
Meetings
Toll-free phone line
Internet
Field operations/evaluations

MARKETING SUPPORT
Co-op advertising
Ad slicks

SERVICE TEAM OF PROFESSIONALS INC.

Financial rating: $$$$

10036 N.W. Ambassador Dr.
Kansas City, MO 64153-1362
Ph: (800)452-8326/(816)880-4746
Fax: (816)880-9395
www.stoprestoration.com
Disaster restoration, carpet cleaning,
  mold remediation
Began: 1971, Franchising since: 1996
Headquarters size: 3 employees
Franchise department: 3 employees

U.S. franchises: 35
Canadian franchises: 0
Other foreign franchises: 0
Company-owned: 0

Seeking: All U.S.
Seeking in Canada? No
Exclusive territories? Yes
Homebased option? Yes
Kiosk option? No
Employees needed to run franchise: 0-10
Absentee ownership? Yes

COSTS
Total cost: $3.5K-106.1K
Franchise fee: $3.4K-34K
Royalty fee: 5-9%
Term of agreement: 10 years renewable
  at no charge
Franchisees required to buy multiple
  units? No

FINANCING
No financing available

QUALIFICATIONS
Net worth: $10K
Cash liquidity: $10K+
Experience:
  Management skills

TRAINING
At headquarters: 1 week
Training conventions: 3 per year

BUSINESS SUPPORT
Meetings
Toll-free phone line
Internet
Purchasing cooperatives

MARKETING SUPPORT
Co-op advertising
Ad slicks
National marketing support
Corporate marketing plan

MAINTENANCE ◄ **RESTROOM MAINTENANCE**

AEROWEST/WESTAIR DEODORIZING SERVICES
Ranked #342 in Entrepreneur Magazine's 2005 Franchise 500

Financial rating: $$$$

3882 Del Amo Blvd., #3602
Torrance, CA 90503
Ph: (310)793-4242
Fax: (310)793-4250
www.westsanitation.com
Restroom deodorizing services
Began: 1943, Franchising since: 1978
Headquarters size: 20 employees
Franchise department: 10 employees

U.S. franchises: 55
Canadian franchises: 0
Other foreign franchises: 0
Company-owned: 17
Units concentrated in AL, CA, IL,
  NY, TX

Seeking: All U.S.
Seeking in Canada? No
Exclusive territories? No
Homebased option? Yes
Kiosk option? No
Employees needed to run franchise: 1
Absentee ownership? No

COSTS
Total cost: $10.3K-36.7K
Franchise fee: $4K
Royalty fee: 8%
Term of agreement: 5 years renewable
  at no charge
Franchisees required to buy multiple
  units? No

FINANCING
In-house: Accounts receivable,
  equipment, inventory, startup costs
3rd-party: None

QUALIFICATIONS
Net worth: $25K+
Cash liquidity: $10K
Experience:
  General business experience
  Marketing skills
  Sales & service skills

TRAINING
At franchisee's location: 2 weeks
Additional training as needed

BUSINESS SUPPORT
Newsletter
Toll-free phone line
Field operations/evaluations
Purchasing cooperatives

MARKETING SUPPORT
Regional marketing

AIRE-MASTER OF AMERICA INC.

Ranked #428 in Entrepreneur Magazine's 2005 Franchise 500   *Financial rating: $$$$*

1821 N. Hwy. CC, P.O. Box 2310
Nixa, MO 65714
Ph: (800)525-0957/(417)725-2691
Fax: (417)725-8227
www.airemaster.com
Restroom deodorizing & maintenance
    services
Began: 1958, Franchising since: 1976
Headquarters size: 66 employees
Franchise department: 2 employees

U.S. franchises: 57
Canadian franchises: 2
Other foreign franchises: 0
Company-owned: 5
Units concentrated in FL, IA, ID,
    MO, PA

Seeking: All U.S.
Seeking in Canada? Yes
Exclusive territories? Yes
Homebased option? Yes
Kiosk option? No
Employees needed to run franchise: 2
Absentee ownership? No

COSTS
Total cost: $40.6K-110.9K
Franchise fee: $23K-50.5K
Royalty fee: 5%
Term of agreement: 20 years renewable
    at no charge
Franchisees required to buy multiple
    units? No

FINANCING
In-house: Equipment
3rd-party: Franchise fee

QUALIFICATIONS
Net worth: Varies
Cash liquidity: Varies
Experience:
    Marketing skills

TRAINING
At headquarters: 5 days
At franchisee's location: 5 days
Quarterly training available at
    headquarters

BUSINESS SUPPORT
Newsletter
Meetings
Toll-free phone line
Internet
Field operations/evaluations

MARKETING SUPPORT
Customer analysis
Literature

SWISHER HYGIENE FRANCHISE CORP.

Ranked #412 in Entrepreneur Magazine's 2005 Franchise 500   *Financial rating: $$$$*

6849 Fairview Rd.
Charlotte, NC 28210
Ph: (800)444-4138/(704)364-7707
Fax: (800)444-4565
www.swisheronline.com
Restroom-hygiene/commercial
    pest-control services & products
Began: 1983, Franchising since: 1989
Headquarters size: 70 employees
Franchise department: 70 employees

U.S. franchises: 88
Canadian franchises: 8
Other foreign franchises: 37
Company-owned: 1

Seeking: All U.S.
Seeking in Canada? Yes
Exclusive territories? Yes
Homebased option? Yes
Kiosk option? No
Employees needed to run franchise:
    Info not provided
Absentee ownership? No

COSTS
Total cost: $44.2K-170.1K
Franchise fee: $35K-85K
Royalty fee: 6%
Term of agreement: 5 years renewable
Franchisees required to buy multiple
    units? Outside U.S. only

FINANCING
In-house: Franchise fee, inventory,
    startup costs
3rd-party: Franchise fee, inventory,
    startup costs

QUALIFICATIONS
Net worth: $50K-150K
Cash liquidity: $15K-50K
Experience:
    General business experience

TRAINING
At headquarters: 1 week
At franchisee's location: 1 week
Additional training as needed

BUSINESS SUPPORT
Newsletter
Meetings
Toll-free phone line
Grand opening
Internet

MARKETING SUPPORT
National media campaign

CARTEX LIMITED

Ranked #232 in Entrepreneur Magazine's 2005 Franchise 500

Financial rating: $$$

42816 Mound Rd.
Sterling Heights, MI 48314
Ph: (586)739-4330
Fax: (586)739-4331
www.fabrion.net
Leather, vinyl, plastic & cloth repair
Began: 1987, Franchising since: 1988
Headquarters size: 10 employees
Franchise department: 3 employees

U.S. franchises: 120
Canadian franchises: 1
Other foreign franchises: 0
Company-owned: 0
Units concentrated in CA, FL, IL, NY, OH, TX

Seeking: All U.S.
Focusing on: All U.S. except CA, CO, FL, ME, MA, MN, NH, NJ, NE, OK, RI, UT
Seeking in Canada? No
Exclusive territories? Yes
Homebased option? Yes

Kiosk option? No
Employees needed to run franchise: 1-3
Absentee ownership? No

COSTS
Total cost: $34.5K-95.2K
Franchise fee: $23.5K-36.5K
Royalty fee: 7%
Term of agreement: 5 years renewable at no charge
Franchisees required to buy multiple units? No

FINANCING
In-house: None
3rd-party: Equipment, franchise fee, inventory, startup costs

QUALIFICATIONS
Net worth: $50K
Cash liquidity: $35K

TRAINING
At franchisee's location: 1 week
In-field training: 2 weeks

BUSINESS SUPPORT
Newsletter
Meetings
Toll-free phone line
Internet
Field operations/evaluations

MARKETING SUPPORT
Info not provided

COLOR-GLO INT'L. INC.

Current financial data not available

7111 Ohms Ln.
Minneapolis, MN 55439
Ph: (800)328-6347/(952)835-1338
Fax: (952)835-1395
www.color-glo.com
Fabric dyeing & restoration
Began: 1979, Franchising since: 1983
Headquarters size: 15 employees
Franchise department: 3 employees

U.S. franchises: 108
Canadian franchises: 9
Other foreign franchises: 98
Company-owned: 1

Seeking: All U.S.
Seeking in Canada? Yes
Exclusive territories? Yes
Homebased option? Yes
Kiosk option? No
Employees needed to run franchise: 2
Absentee ownership? Yes

COSTS
Total cost: $29K-32K
Franchise fee: $27.5K
Royalty fee: 4%
Term of agreement: 10 years
Franchisees required to buy multiple units? Yes, within U.S.

FINANCING
In-house: Equipment, franchise fee, inventory, startup costs
3rd-party: None

QUALIFICATIONS
Net worth: $50K
Cash liquidity: $25K

TRAINING
At headquarters: 2 weeks
At franchisee's location: 1 week
Ongoing

BUSINESS SUPPORT
Newsletter
Meetings
Toll-free phone line
Grand opening
Internet
Lease negotiations
Security/safety procedures
Field operations/evaluations
Purchasing cooperatives

MARKETING SUPPORT
Co-op advertising
Ad slicks
National media campaign
Regional marketing

CREATIVE COLORS INT'L. INC.

Ranked #439 in Entrepreneur Magazine's 2005 Franchise 500

Financial rating: $$

5550 W. 175th St.
Tinley Park, IL 60477
Ph: (800)933-2656/(708)614-7786
Fax: (708)614-9685
www.creativecolorsintl.com
Mobile plastic/vinyl/leather restoration
   & repair
Began: 1980, Franchising since: 1991
Headquarters size: 10 employees
Franchise department: 10 employees

U.S. franchises: 48
Canadian franchises: 1
Other foreign franchises: 0
Company-owned: 10
Units concentrated in FL, Midwest

Seeking: All U.S.
Focusing on: Eastern U.S.
Seeking in Canada? No
Exclusive territories? Yes
Homebased option? Yes
Kiosk option? No
Employees needed to run franchise: 1-4
Absentee ownership? Yes

COSTS

Total cost: $37.5K-71.4K
Franchise fee: $19.5K+
Royalty fee: 6%
Term of agreement: 10 years renewable
   at up to 20% of current fee
Franchisees required to buy multiple
   units? No

FINANCING

In-house: Startup costs
3rd-party: Equipment, inventory

QUALIFICATIONS

Net worth: $50K+
Cash liquidity: $20K+
Experience:
   General business experience
   Marketing skills

TRAINING

At headquarters: 3 weeks
At franchisee's location: 1 week

BUSINESS SUPPORT

Newsletter
Meetings
Toll-free phone line
Grand opening
Internet
Security/safety procedures
Field operations/evaluations

MARKETING SUPPORT

Ad slicks
Regional marketing

DR. VINYL & ASSOCIATES LTD.

Ranked #385 in Entrepreneur Magazine's 2005 Franchise 500

Financial rating: $$$

821 N.W. Commerce
Lee's Summit, MO 64086
Ph: (800)531-6600
Fax: (816)525-6333
www.drvinyl.com
Mobile vinyl/leather repair/windshield
   repair
Began: 1972, Franchising since: 1981
Headquarters size: 14 employees
Franchise department: 11 employees

U.S. franchises: 183
Canadian franchises: 1
Other foreign franchises: 25
Company-owned: 0
Units concentrated in all U.S.

Seeking: All U.S.
Seeking in Canada? Yes
Exclusive territories? Yes
Homebased option? Yes
Kiosk option? No
Employees needed to run franchise: 1
Absentee ownership? No

COSTS

Total cost: $44K-69.5K
Franchise fee: $32.5K
Royalty fee: 7%
Term of agreement: 10 years renewable
   at no charge
Franchisees required to buy multiple
   units? Outside U.S. only

FINANCING

In-house: Franchise fee
3rd-party: Equipment, franchise fee,
   inventory, startup costs

QUALIFICATIONS

Net worth: $50K
Cash liquidity: $15K
Experience:
   General business experience
   Marketing skills

TRAINING

At headquarters: 2 weeks
At franchisee's location: 2 weeks
Corporate or in-field training: As
   needed

BUSINESS SUPPORT

Newsletter
Meetings
Toll-free phone line
Grand opening
Internet
Field operations/evaluations
Purchasing cooperatives

MARKETING SUPPORT

Co-op advertising
Ad slicks
National media campaign

FIBRENEW

Current financial data not available

Box 33, Site 16, RR8
Calgary, AB T2J 2T9 Canada
Ph: (403)278-7818
Fax: (403)278-1434
www.fibrenew.com
Leather, plastic & vinyl restoration
Began: 1985, Franchising since: 1987
Headquarters size: 5 employees
Franchise department: 2 employees

U.S. franchises: 24
Canadian franchises: 73
Other foreign franchises: 44
Company-owned: 2

Seeking: All U.S.
Seeking in Canada? Yes
Exclusive territories? Yes
Homebased option? Yes
Kiosk option? No
Employees needed to run franchise: 1
Absentee ownership? Yes

COSTS
Total cost: $30K-50K
Franchise fee: $30K-50K
Royalty fee: $300/mo.
Term of agreement: 5 years renewable
    at no charge
Franchisees required to buy multiple
    units? No

FINANCING
No financing available

QUALIFICATIONS
Net worth: $25K
Cash liquidity: $15K

TRAINING
At headquarters: 2 weeks

BUSINESS SUPPORT
Newsletter
Meetings
Toll-free phone line
Internet
Field operations/evaluations

MARKETING SUPPORT
Info not provided

MAINTENANCE ▶ **WINDOW CLEANING**

CLEAN & HAPPY WINDOWS

Current financial data not available

10019 Des Moines Memorial Dr.
Seattle, WA 98168
Ph: (866)762-7617
Fax: (206)762-7637
www.cleanhappy.com
Window & gutter cleaning/pressure
    washing/roof cleaning
Began: 1991, Franchising since: 2000
Headquarters size: 10 employees
Franchise department: 1 employee

U.S. franchises: 2
Canadian franchises: 0
Other foreign franchises: 0
Company-owned: 1

Seeking: All U.S.
Seeking in Canada? No
Exclusive territories? Yes
Homebased option? Yes
Kiosk option? No
Employees needed to run franchise: 1-2
Absentee ownership? No

COSTS
Total cost: $100-2K
Franchise fee: 0
Royalty fee: 7%
Term of agreement: 5 years renewable
    at no charge
Franchisees required to buy multiple
    units? No

FINANCING
No financing available

QUALIFICATIONS
Net worth: $4K
Cash liquidity: $4K
Experience:
    General business experience
    Marketing skills
    Able to work at heights up to
        3 stories

TRAINING
At headquarters: 7 days

BUSINESS SUPPORT
Toll-free phone line
Grand opening
Internet
Security/safety procedures
Field operations/evaluations

MARKETING SUPPORT
Ad slicks
Online scheduling service

DR. GLASS WINDOW WASHING

Financial rating: $$$

3573 Nyland Wy.
Lafayette, CO 80026
Ph: (888)282-0052
Fax: (303)499-0855
www.docglass.com
Window cleaning
Began: 1978, Franchising since: 2001
Headquarters size: 2 employees
Franchise department: 2 employees

U.S. franchises: 10
Canadian franchises: 0
Other foreign franchises: 0
Company-owned: 2

Seeking: Northeast
Seeking in Canada? Yes
Exclusive territories? Yes
Homebased option? Yes
Kiosk option? No
Employees needed to run franchise: 2
Absentee ownership? No

COSTS
Total cost: $4.6K
Franchise fee: $3K
Royalty fee: 10%
Term of agreement: Info not provided
Franchisees required to buy multiple
    units? No

FINANCING
No financing available

QUALIFICATIONS
Experience:
    General business experience

TRAINING
At headquarters: 1 week

BUSINESS SUPPORT
Newsletter
Toll-free phone line
Internet
Purchasing cooperatives

MARKETING SUPPORT
Info not provided

WINDOW GANG

Ranked #241 in Entrepreneur Magazine's 2005 Franchise 500

Financial rating: $$$$

1509 Ann St.
Beaufort, NC 28516
Ph: (877)946-4264
Fax: (252)726-2837
www.windowgang.com
Window/pressure cleaning
Began: 1986, Franchising since: 1996
Headquarters size: 6 employees
Franchise department: 3 employees

U.S. franchises: 135
Canadian franchises: 20
Other foreign franchises: 0
Company-owned: 0

Seeking: All U.S.
Seeking in Canada? Yes
Exclusive territories? Yes
Homebased option? Yes
Kiosk option? No
Employees needed to run franchise: 5
Absentee ownership? Yes

COSTS
Total cost: $14.4K-78.1K
Franchise fee: $5K-75K
Royalty fee: 6%
Term of agreement: 10 years renewable
    at $2.5K
Franchisees required to buy multiple
    units? No

FINANCING
In-house: Franchise fee
3rd-party: Accounts receivable,
    equipment, inventory, payroll,
    startup costs

QUALIFICATIONS
Net worth: $50K
Cash liquidity: $10K
Experience:
    Marketing skills

TRAINING
At headquarters: 7-14 days
At franchisee's location: 7 days

BUSINESS SUPPORT
Newsletter
Meetings
Toll-free phone line
Internet
Security/safety procedures
Field operations/evaluations
Purchasing cooperatives

MARKETING SUPPORT
Ad slicks

WINDOW GENIE

Ranked #351 in Entrepreneur Magazine's 2005 Franchise 500

Financial rating: $$$

350 Gest St.
Cincinnati, OH 45203
Ph: (800)700-0022
Fax: (513)412-7760
www.windowgenie.com
Resid. window clng./window
    tinting/pressure washing
Began: 1994, Franchising since: 1998
Headquarters size: 9 employees
Franchise department: 3 employees

U.S. franchises: 65
Canadian franchises: 0
Other foreign franchises: 0
Company-owned: 0
Units concentrated in all U.S.

Seeking: All U.S.
Seeking in Canada? Yes
Exclusive territories? Yes
Homebased option? Yes
Kiosk option? No
Employees needed to run franchise: 3
Absentee ownership? No

COSTS
Total cost: $44.7K-55.4K
Franchise fee: $19.5K
Royalty fee: 6%
Term of agreement: 10 years renewable
    at no charge
Franchisees required to buy multiple
    units? No

FINANCING
No financing available

QUALIFICATIONS
Net worth: $75K
Cash liquidity: $30K
Experience:
    General business experience

TRAINING
At headquarters: 5 days
At franchisee's location: 5 days

BUSINESS SUPPORT
Meetings
Toll-free phone line
Grand opening
Internet
Security/safety procedures
Field operations/evaluations
Purchasing cooperatives

MARKETING SUPPORT
Ad slicks
Regional marketing

MAINTENANCE ► **MISCELLANEOUS**

CLEAN FIRST TIME INC.

Current financial data not available

7353 W. Sandlake Rd., #201
Orlando, FL 32819
Ph: (866)390-2532
Fax: (407)352-1443
www.cleanfirsttime.com
New home construction cleaning
Began: 2003, Franchising since: 2004
Headquarters size: 7 employees
Franchise department: 2 employees

U.S. franchises: 3
Canadian franchises: 0
Other foreign franchises: 0
Company-owned: 1

Seeking: All U.S.
Seeking in Canada? Yes
Exclusive territories? Info not provided
Homebased option? Yes
Kiosk option? No
Employees needed to run franchise:
    Info not provided
Absentee ownership? Yes

COSTS
Total cost: $12K-150K
Franchise fee: $12K-150K
Royalty fee: 7%
Term of agreement: 10 years renewable
    at $1K
Franchisees required to buy multiple
    units? No

FINANCING
In-house: Accounts receivable,
    equipment, inventory, payroll
3rd-party: None

QUALIFICATIONS
Net worth: $12K
Cash liquidity: $12K
Experience:
    General business experience

TRAINING
At headquarters: 24 hours
At franchisee's location: 20 hours
Additional training as needed

BUSINESS SUPPORT
Newsletter
Meetings
Toll-free phone line
Grand opening
Internet
Lease negotiations
Security/safety procedures
Field operations/evaluations
Purchasing cooperatives

MARKETING SUPPORT
Co-op advertising
Ad slicks
National media campaign
Regional marketing
Printed marketing materials

DUCT DOCTOR USA INC.

Ranked #401 in Entrepreneur Magazine's 2005 Franchise 500   *Financial rating: $$$*

5555 Oakbrook Pkwy., #660
Atlanta, GA 30093
Ph: (770)446-1764
Fax: (770)447-4486
www.ductdoctorusa.com
Residential & commercial air duct
    cleaning
Began: 1985, Franchising since: 2000
Headquarters size: 12 employees
Franchise department: 2 employees

U.S. franchises: 10
Canadian franchises: 0
Other foreign franchises: 0
Company-owned: 8
Units concentrated in all U.S.

Seeking: All U.S.
Seeking in Canada? No
Exclusive territories? Yes
Homebased option? Yes
Kiosk option? No
Employees needed to run franchise: 2
Absentee ownership? No

COSTS
Total cost: $41K-64K
Franchise fee: $25K
Royalty fee: 5-8%
Term of agreement: 10 years renewable
    at 10% of initial franchise fee
Franchisees required to buy multiple
    units? No

FINANCING
In-house: None
3rd-party: Equipment

QUALIFICATIONS
Net worth: $100K
Cash liquidity: $50K
Experience:
    General business experience

TRAINING
At headquarters: 3 weeks
At franchisee's location: 1 week

BUSINESS SUPPORT
Newsletter
Meetings
Toll-free phone line
Grand opening
Internet
Security/safety procedures
Field operations/evaluations
Purchasing cooperatives

MARKETING SUPPORT
Ad slicks
Regional marketing
In-market business development

GROUT WIZARD

Current financial data not available

1056 El Capitan Dr.
Danville, CA 94526
Ph: (925)866-5000/(925)314-0369
Fax: (925)552-6358/(925)314-0579
www.groutwizard.com
Grout cleaning & restoration
Began: 1997, Franchising since: 2001
Headquarters size: 2 employees
Franchise department: 1 employee

U.S. franchises: 8
Canadian franchises: 0
Other foreign franchises: 0
Company-owned: 1
Units concentrated in CA

Seeking: All U.S.
Focusing on: West
Seeking in Canada? Yes
Exclusive territories? Yes
Homebased option? Yes
Kiosk option? No
Employees needed to run franchise: 2-4
Absentee ownership? No

COSTS
Total cost: $15.6K-25.2K
Franchise fee: $12.5K
Royalty fee: 5%
Term of agreement: 5 years renewable
    at no charge
Franchisees required to buy multiple
    units? No

FINANCING
In-house: Franchise fee
3rd-party: None

QUALIFICATIONS
Info not provided

TRAINING
At headquarters: 1 week minimum

BUSINESS SUPPORT
Meetings
Internet
Security/safety procedures
Field operations/evaluations

MARKETING SUPPORT
Ad slicks

RECEIL IT CEILING RESTORATION

Financial rating: $$$

175-B Liberty St.
Copiague, NY 11726
Ph: (800)234-5464
Fax: (631)980-7668
www.receilit.com
Ceiling restoration
Began: 1992, Franchising since: 2002
Headquarters size: 5 employees
Franchise department: 4 employees

U.S. franchises: 1
Canadian franchises: 0
Other foreign franchises: 0
Company-owned: 1
Units concentrated in NY

Seeking: Northeast, Southeast
Focusing on: CT, DE, IL, MA, NJ,
 NY, PA
Seeking in Canada? Yes
Exclusive territories? Yes
Homebased option? Yes
Kiosk option? No
Employees needed to run franchise: 2
Absentee ownership? No

COSTS
Total cost: $38.9K-55K
Franchise fee: $17.5K
Royalty fee: 7%
Term of agreement: 10 years renewable
 at $10K
Franchisees required to buy multiple
 units? No

FINANCING
No financing available

QUALIFICATIONS
Net worth: $100K
Cash liquidity: $53.9K
Experience:
 Sales background or aptitude

TRAINING
At headquarters: 6 days
At franchisee's location: 3 days

BUSINESS SUPPORT
Newsletter
Meetings
Toll-free phone line
Internet
Security/safety procedures
Field operations/evaluations

MARKETING SUPPORT
Regional marketing

MAINTENANCE — OTHER FRANCHISES

DUCTBUSTERS
*Ranked #393 in Entrepreneur
 Magazine's 2005 Franchise 500*
2054 Weaver Park Dr.
Clearwater, FL 33765-2130
Ph: (727)442-5530
www.ductbusters.com
Duct & HVAC-system cleaning
Financial rating: $$$$

LEATHER MEDIC
11532 Mahogany Run
Ft. Myers, FL 33913
Ph: (888)561-0423
www.leathermedic.com
Leather repair & refinishing
Financial rating: Current financial
 data not available

ROTO-STATIC INT'L.
90 Delta Park Blvd., #A
Brampton, ON L6T 5E7 Canada
Ph: (877)586-4469/(905)458-7002
www.rotostatic.com
Carpet/upholstery/floor mainte-
 nance/ceiling & wall cleaning
Financial rating: Current financial
 data not available

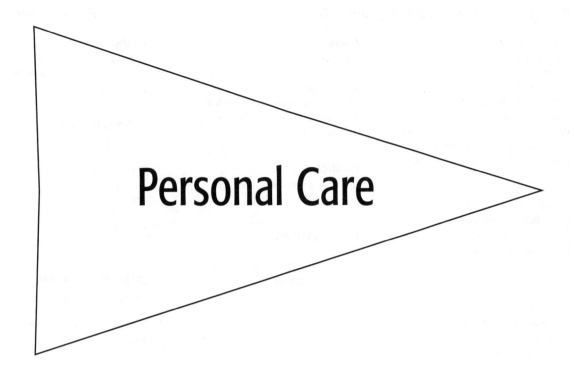

Personal Care

BONNE CHIMIE

Current financial data not available

3894 New Vision Dr.
Fort Wayne, IN 46845
Ph: (260)469-3258
Fax: (260)480-7813
www.bonnechimie.com
Custom skin-care, hair & cosmetic
  products
Began: 2002, Franchising since: 2003
Headquarters size: 4 employees
Franchise department: 4 employees

U.S. franchises: 0
Canadian franchises: 0
Other foreign franchises: 0
Company-owned: 1
Units concentrated in IN

Seeking: All U.S.
Focusing on: Midwest
Seeking in Canada? Yes
Exclusive territories? Yes
Homebased option? No

Kiosk option? No
Employees needed to run franchise: 3-6
Absentee ownership? Yes

COSTS
Total cost: $29.5K-109K
Franchise fee: $15K
Royalty fee: 9%
Term of agreement: 10 years renewable
Franchisees required to buy multiple
  units? Outside U.S. only

FINANCING
No financing available

QUALIFICATIONS
Net worth: $50K-150K
Cash liquidity: $50K

TRAINING
At headquarters: 4-5 days

BUSINESS SUPPORT
Grand opening
Internet

MARKETING SUPPORT
Info not provided

MERLE NORMAN COSMETICS

Ranked #23 in Entrepreneur Magazine's 2005 Franchise 500　　　*Financial rating: $$$$*

9130 Bellanca Ave.
Los Angeles, CA 90045
Ph: (800)421-6648/(310)641-3000
Fax: (310)337-2370
www.merlenorman.com
Cosmetics studios
Began: 1931, Franchising since: 1989
Headquarters size: 464 employees
Franchise department: 12 employees

U.S. franchises: 1,816
Canadian franchises: 91
Other foreign franchises: 0
Company-owned: 6
Units concentrated in all U.S.

Seeking: All U.S.
Seeking in Canada? Yes
Exclusive territories? No
Homebased option? No
Kiosk option? No
Employees needed to run franchise: 1-6
Absentee ownership? Yes

COSTS
Total cost: $33.1K-156K
Franchise fee: $0
Royalty fee: 0
Term of agreement: Open-ended
Franchisees required to buy multiple units? No

FINANCING
In-house: Equipment, inventory
3rd-party: None

QUALIFICATIONS
Experience:
　　General business experience
　　Retail background
　　Cosmetics experience
　　Customer service skills

TRAINING
At headquarters: 10 days
Field training classes & visits
Advanced training

BUSINESS SUPPORT
Newsletter
Meetings
Toll-free phone line
Grand opening
Internet
Lease negotiations
Security/safety procedures
Field operations/evaluations

MARKETING SUPPORT
Co-op advertising
Ad slicks
National media campaign
Regional marketing

SPRAY TAN OF AMERICA

Financial rating: 0

33505-B Pacific Hwy. S.
Federal Way, WA 98003
Ph: (888)777-2982/(253)835-9594
Fax: (253)835-9595
www.spraytanofamerica.com
Airbrush tanning salons/skin-care products
Began: 2002, Franchising since: 2002
Headquarters size: 4 employees
Franchise department: 3 employees

U.S. franchises: 5
Canadian franchises: 0
Other foreign franchises: 0
Company-owned: 1
Units concentrated in CA, MT, WA

Seeking: All U.S.
Focusing on: CA, FL, OH, PA, TX
Seeking in Canada? No
Exclusive territories? Yes
Homebased option? No
Kiosk option? No
Employees needed to run franchise: 2
Absentee ownership? Yes

COSTS
Total cost: $31K-52.3K
Franchise fee: $20K
Royalty fee: 8%
Term of agreement: 5 years renewable at no charge
Franchisees required to buy multiple units? No

FINANCING
No financing available

QUALIFICATIONS
Net worth: $100K
Cash liquidity: $30K

TRAINING
At headquarters: 1 week

BUSINESS SUPPORT
Grand opening
Lease negotiations
Field operations/evaluations

MARKETING SUPPORT
Co-op advertising

ANYTIME FITNESS

Current financial data not available

P.O. Box 18213
West St. Paul, MN 55118
Ph: (800)704-5004
Fax: (651)554-0311
www.anytimefitness.com
Fitness centers
Began: 2001, Franchising since: 2002
Headquarters size: 16 employees
Franchise department: 3 employees

U.S. franchises: 29
Canadian franchises: 0
Other foreign franchises: 0
Company-owned: 0
Units concentrated in all U.S.

Seeking: All U.S.
Seeking in Canada? No
Exclusive territories? Yes
Homebased option? No
Kiosk option? No
Employees needed to run franchise: 0
Absentee ownership? Yes

COSTS
Total cost: $22.1K-192.6K
Franchise fee: $1.99K
Royalty fee: $399
Term of agreement: 5 years renewable at $100
Franchisees required to buy multiple units? No

FINANCING
In-house: None
3rd-party: Equipment, franchise fee, inventory, startup costs

QUALIFICATIONS
Net worth: $80K
Cash liquidity: $13.5K
Experience:
   General business experience

TRAINING
At headquarters: 3 days minimum
At franchisee's location: 3 days minimum
Ongoing

BUSINESS SUPPORT
Newsletter
Meetings
Toll-free phone line
Grand opening
Internet
Lease negotiations
Security/safety procedures
Field operations/evaluations
Purchasing cooperatives

MARKETING SUPPORT
Co-op advertising
Ad slicks

THE BLITZ

Financial rating: $

980 E. Santa Fe
Gardner, KS 66030
Ph: (913)856-2424
Fax: (309)424-3558
www.timetoblitz.com
20-minute men's fitness program
Began: 2002, Franchising since: 2002
Headquarters size: 10 employees
Franchise department: 5 employees

U.S. franchises: 35
Canadian franchises: 18
Other foreign franchises: 0
Company-owned: 1
Units concentrated in all U.S.

Seeking: All U.S.
Seeking in Canada? Yes
Exclusive territories? Yes
Homebased option? No
Kiosk option? No
Employees needed to run franchise: 1-2
Absentee ownership? Yes

COSTS
Total cost: $36.5K-58.8K
Franchise fee: $26K
Royalty fee: $395
Term of agreement: 7 years renewable at no charge
Franchisees required to buy multiple units? No

FINANCING
In-house: None
3rd-party: Equipment, franchise fee, inventory, startup costs

QUALIFICATIONS
Net worth: $75K-100K
Cash liquidity: $26K

TRAINING
At headquarters: 4 days

BUSINESS SUPPORT
Newsletter
Toll-free phone line
Internet
Purchasing cooperatives

MARKETING SUPPORT
Ad slicks
TV & radio ads
Brochures
Websites

CONTOURS EXPRESS

Ranked #100 in Entrepreneur Magazine's 2005 Franchise 500   *Financial rating: $$$$*

156 Imperial Wy.
Nicholasville, KY 40356
Ph: (877)227-2282
Fax: (425)920-0534
www.contoursexpress.com
Women's fitness centers
Began: 1998, Franchising since: 1998
Headquarters size: 8 employees
Franchise department: 8 employees

U.S. franchises: 255
Canadian franchises: 19
Other foreign franchises: 3
Company-owned: 0
Units concentrated in all U.S.

Seeking: All U.S.
Seeking in Canada? No
Exclusive territories? Yes
Homebased option? No
Kiosk option? No
Employees needed to run franchise: 2
Absentee ownership? Yes

COSTS
Total cost: $33.7K-47.5K
Franchise fee: $10K
Royalty fee: $395/mo.
Term of agreement: 10 years renewable
   at no charge
Franchisees required to buy multiple
   units? No

FINANCING
In-house: None
3rd-party: Equipment

QUALIFICATIONS
Net worth: $50K
Cash liquidity: $15K

TRAINING
At headquarters: 4-5 days
At franchisee's location: 4-5 days

BUSINESS SUPPORT
Newsletter
Meetings
Toll-free phone line
Grand opening
Internet

MARKETING SUPPORT
Ad slicks

CURVES

Ranked #2 in Entrepreneur Magazine's 2005 Franchise 500   *Financial rating: $$$$*

100 Ritchie Rd.
Waco, TX 76712
Ph: (800)848-1096/(254)399-9285
Fax: (254)399-9731
www.buycurves.com
Women's fitness & weight-loss centers
Began: 1992, Franchising since: 1995
Headquarters size: 50 employees
Franchise department: 40 employees

U.S. franchises: 7,044
Canadian franchises: 641
Other foreign franchises: 324
Company-owned: 0

Seeking: All U.S.
Seeking in Canada? Yes
Exclusive territories? Yes
Homebased option? No
Kiosk option? No
Employees needed to run franchise: 2
Absentee ownership? Yes

COSTS
Total cost: $36.4K-42.9K
Franchise fee: $29.9K
Royalty fee: 5%
Term of agreement: 5 years renewable
   at no charge
Franchisees required to buy multiple
   units? No

FINANCING
In-house: Equipment, franchise fee
3rd-party: None

QUALIFICATIONS
Net worth: $75K
Cash liquidity: $50K

TRAINING
At headquarters: 1 week
At franchisee's location: 4 days
At regional meetings
At convention & local events

BUSINESS SUPPORT
Newsletter
Meetings
Toll-free phone line
Grand opening
Internet
Field operations/evaluations

MARKETING SUPPORT
Co-op advertising
Ad slicks
National media campaign
Regional marketing

CUTS FITNESS FOR MEN

Financial rating: $$$

109 Lefferts Ln.
Clark, NJ 07066
Ph: (732)574-0999
Fax: (732)574-1130
www.cutsfitness.com
Circuit training for men
Began: 2003, Franchising since: 2003
Headquarters size: 6 employees
Franchise department: 3 employees

U.S. franchises: 60
Canadian franchises: 0
Other foreign franchises: 1
Company-owned: 1

Seeking: All U.S.
Seeking in Canada? Yes
Exclusive territories? Yes
Homebased option? No
Kiosk option? No
Employees needed to run franchise: 1-2
Absentee ownership? No

COSTS
Total cost: $33.6K-77.9K
Franchise fee: $29.5K
Royalty fee: $400/mo.
Term of agreement: 10 years renewable
   at no charge
Franchisees required to buy multiple
   units? No

FINANCING
No financing available

QUALIFICATIONS
Experience:
   Industry experience
   General business experience
   Marketing skills

TRAINING
At headquarters: 2 days
At franchisee's location: As needed

BUSINESS SUPPORT
Newsletter
Meetings
Grand opening
Internet
Field operations/evaluations
Purchasing cooperatives

MARKETING SUPPORT
Co-op advertising
Regional marketing

IM=X PILATES STUDIO

Current financial data not available

265 Madison Ave., 2nd Fl.
New York, NY 10016
Ph: (800)469-1336/(212)997-5550
Fax: (212)997-7356
www.imxpilatesstudio.com
Pilates studio
Began: 1994, Franchising since: 2003
Headquarters size: Info not provided
Franchise department:
   Info not provided

U.S. franchises: 0
Canadian franchises: 0
Other foreign franchises: 0
Company-owned: 1

Seeking: All U.S.
Seeking in Canada? Yes
Exclusive territories? Info not provided
Homebased option? No
Kiosk option? No
Employees needed to run franchise: 2-8
Absentee ownership? Info not provided

COSTS
Total cost: $17.2K-30.8K
Franchise fee: $6K
Royalty fee: Varies
Term of agreement: 10 years renewable
Franchisees required to buy multiple
   units? Info not provided

FINANCING
No financing available

QUALIFICATIONS
Info not provided

TRAINING
At headquarters: 9 days
At franchisee's location: As needed

BUSINESS SUPPORT
Toll-free phone line
Internet
Field operations/evaluations
Purchasing cooperatives

MARKETING SUPPORT
Co-op advertising
Ad slicks
National media campaign
Marketing plans & materials

JAZZERCISE INC.

Ranked #26 in Entrepreneur Magazine's 2005 Franchise 500

Financial rating: $$$$

2460 Impala Dr.
Carlsbad, CA 92008
Ph: (760)476-1750
Fax: (760)602-7180
www.jazzercise.com
Dance/exercise classes
Began: 1977, Franchising since: 1983
Headquarters size: 125 employees
Franchise department: 4 employees

U.S. franchises: 4,912
Canadian franchises: 95
Other foreign franchises: 918
Company-owned: 1
Units concentrated in CA, FL, OH, TX

Seeking: All U.S.
Seeking in Canada? Yes
Exclusive territories? No
Homebased option? Yes
Kiosk option? No
Employees needed to run franchise:
  Info not provided
Absentee ownership? No

COSTS

Total cost: $3K-33.1K
Franchise fee: $500/$1K
Royalty fee: to 20%
Term of agreement: 5 years renewable
  at no charge
Franchisees required to buy multiple
  units? No

FINANCING

No financing available

QUALIFICATIONS

Experience:
  Movement skills
  Knowledge of health & fitness

TRAINING

At franchisee's location: 2-3 weeks
  home study
Seminars

BUSINESS SUPPORT

Newsletter
Meetings
Toll-free phone line
Internet
Security/safety procedures
Field operations/evaluations

MARKETING SUPPORT

Co-op advertising
Ad slicks
National media campaign
Regional marketing

SHAPE UP SISTERS INC.

Current financial data not available

425 W. Town Pl., #116
St. Augustine, FL 32092
Ph: (866)774-2738/(904)940-9331
Fax: (904)940-9336
www.shapeupsisters.com
Fitness boutique for women
Began: 2002, Franchising since: 2002
Headquarters size: 4 employees
Franchise department: 2 employees

U.S. franchises: 1
Canadian franchises: 0
Other foreign franchises: 0
Company-owned: 1

Seeking: All U.S.
Seeking in Canada? Yes
Exclusive territories? Yes
Homebased option? No
Kiosk option? No
Employees needed to run franchise: 2
Absentee ownership? No

COSTS

Total cost: $40K-51K
Franchise fee: $24.9K
Royalty fee: $375/mo.
Term of agreement: 10 years renewable
  at no charge
Franchisees required to buy multiple
  units? No

FINANCING

In-house: None
3rd-party: Equipment, franchise fee

QUALIFICATIONS

Net worth: $50K
Cash liquidity: $24.9K
Experience:
  Must enjoy working with &
  helping people

TRAINING

At headquarters: 4 days

BUSINESS SUPPORT

Newsletter
Toll-free phone line
Grand opening
Internet
Lease negotiations
Field operations/evaluations

MARKETING SUPPORT

Ad slicks
Regional marketing

SLIM AND TONE

Financial rating: 0

10 Penn Valley Dr.
Yardley, PA 19067
Ph: (215)321-6661
Fax: (215)321-5677
www.slimandtone.com
Fitness clubs for women
Began: 2002, Franchising since: 2002
Headquarters size: 7 employees
Franchise department: 7 employees

U.S. franchises: 107
Canadian franchises: 0
Other foreign franchises: 2
Company-owned: 0
Units concentrated in all U.S.

Seeking: All U.S.
Seeking in Canada? Yes
Exclusive territories? Yes
Homebased option? No
Kiosk option? No
Employees needed to run franchise: 2
Absentee ownership? Yes

COSTS
Total cost: $40.2K-84.7K
Franchise fee: $11.9K
Royalty fee: $395/mo.
Term of agreement: 5 years renewable
    at no charge
Franchisees required to buy multiple
    units? No

FINANCING
In-house: None
3rd-party: Equipment, franchise fee,
    startup costs

QUALIFICATIONS
Experience:
    Marketing skills

TRAINING
At headquarters: 4 days
At franchisee's location: 3 days

BUSINESS SUPPORT
Newsletter
Meetings
Toll-free phone line
Grand opening
Internet
Security/safety procedures
Field operations/evaluations
Purchasing cooperatives

MARKETING SUPPORT
Ad slicks
Marketing kit

STAR LADY FITNESS

Current financial data not available

608 Georgia Dr.
Bethel, OH 45106
Ph: (513)734-3338/(513)519-7664
Fax: (513)734-3378
www.starladyfitness.com
Women's-only circuit-training fitness
    center
Began: 2003, Franchising since: 2004
Headquarters size: 2 employees
Franchise department: 1 employee

U.S. franchises: 1
Canadian franchises: 0
Other foreign franchises: 0
Company-owned: 6

Seeking: All U.S.
Seeking in Canada? No
Exclusive territories? Yes
Homebased option? No
Kiosk option? No
Employees needed to run franchise: 2-3
Absentee ownership? No

COSTS
Total cost: to $40K
Franchise fee: $25K
Royalty fee: Varies
Term of agreement: 5 years renewable
    at $1K
Franchisees required to buy multiple
    units? No

FINANCING
No financing available

QUALIFICATIONS
Experience:
    General business experience
    Marketing skills

TRAINING
At franchisee's location: 2 weeks

BUSINESS SUPPORT
Grand opening

MARKETING SUPPORT
Co-op advertising

PERSONAL CARE ▶ **HAIR CARE**

THE LEMON TREE

Financial rating: $$

One Division Ave.
Levittown, NY 11756
Ph: (800)345-9156/(516)735-2828
Fax: (516)735-1851
www.lemontree.com
Family hair care
Began: 1974, Franchising since: 1976
Headquarters size: 5 employees
Franchise department: 3 employees

U.S. franchises: 58
Canadian franchises: 0
Other foreign franchises: 0
Company-owned: 0

Seeking: Northeast, Southeast
Seeking in Canada? No
Exclusive territories? Yes
Homebased option? No
Kiosk option? No
Employees needed to run franchise: 5-10
Absentee ownership? No

COSTS
Total cost: $44.9K-78K
Franchise fee: $15K
Royalty fee: 6%
Term of agreement: 15 years renewable
    at no charge
Franchisees required to buy multiple
    units? No

FINANCING
In-house: Equipment, franchise fee
3rd-party: None

QUALIFICATIONS
Net worth: $100K-200K
Cash liquidity: $50K-75K

TRAINING
At headquarters: 1 week
At franchisee's location: 1 week
Additional training as needed

BUSINESS SUPPORT
Meetings
Toll-free phone line
Grand opening
Field operations/evaluations
Purchasing cooperatives

MARKETING SUPPORT
Co-op advertising
Ad slicks
National media campaign
Regional marketing

N TIME FAMILY SALONS

Current financial data not available

P.O. Box 604
Daphne, AL 36526
Ph: (251)634-5173
Fax: (251)633-0772
www.ntimefamilysalons.com
Hair salon & hair-care products
Began: 2001, Franchising since: 2003
Headquarters size: 6 employees
Franchise department: 4 employees

U.S. franchises: 2
Canadian franchises: 0
Other foreign franchises: 0
Company-owned: 0

Seeking: All U.S.
Seeking in Canada? No
Exclusive territories? Yes
Homebased option? No
Kiosk option? No
Employees needed to run franchise: 10
Absentee ownership? Yes

COSTS
Total cost: $26.2K-43.5K
Franchise fee: $5K
Royalty fee: 5%
Term of agreement: 10 years renewable
    at no charge
Franchisees required to buy multiple
    units? No

FINANCING
No financing available

QUALIFICATIONS
Net worth: $250K
Cash liquidity: $15K
Experience:
    General business experience

TRAINING
At franchisee's location: 2 weeks

BUSINESS SUPPORT
Grand opening
Internet
Field operations/evaluations

MARKETING SUPPORT
Regional marketing

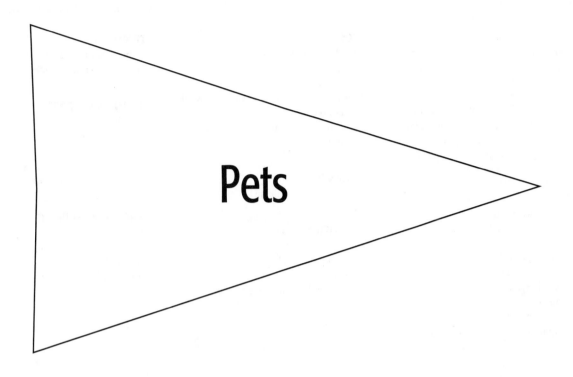

Pets

BARK BUSTERS
Ranked #278 in Entrepreneur Magazine's 2005 Franchise 500

Financial rating: $$$

5901 S. Vine St.
Greenwood Village, CO 80126
Ph: (877)280-7100
Fax: (303)703-1279
www.barkbusters.com
In-home dog training
Began: 1989, Franchising since: 1994
Headquarters size: 12 employees
Franchise department: 12 employees

U.S. franchises: 63
Canadian franchises: 2
Other foreign franchises: 73
Company-owned: 1
Units concentrated in CA, CO, FL, GA,
   MI, TX, VA

Seeking: All U.S.
Seeking in Canada? Yes
Exclusive territories? Yes
Homebased option? Yes
Kiosk option? No
Employees needed to run franchise: 0
Absentee ownership? No

COSTS
Total cost: $47.1K-74K
Franchise fee: $22.5K
Royalty fee: 8%
Term of agreement: 5 years renewable
   at $1.5K
Franchisees required to buy multiple
   units? No

FINANCING
In-house: None
3rd-party: Accounts receivable,
   equipment, franchise fee,
   inventory, payroll, startup costs

QUALIFICATIONS
Net worth: $100K
Cash liquidity: $10K-39K
Experience:
   General business experience
   Marketing skills
   Passion for dogs

TRAINING
At headquarters: 120 hours minimum

BUSINESS SUPPORT
Newsletter
Meetings
Toll-free phone line
Internet
Security/safety procedures
Field operations/evaluations

MARKETING SUPPORT
Co-op advertising
Ad slicks
National media campaign
PR support

FETCH! PET CARE INC.

Current financial data not available

2101 Los Angeles Ave.
Berkeley, CA 94707
Ph: (510)525-4054
Fax: (510)525-4054
www.fetchpetcare.com
Pet-sitting & dog walking services
Began: 2002, Franchising since: 2003
Headquarters size: 2 employees
Franchise department: 2 employees

U.S. franchises: 11
Canadian franchises: 0
Other foreign franchises: 0
Company-owned: 5

Seeking: All U.S.
Seeking in Canada? No
Exclusive territories? Yes
Homebased option? Yes
Kiosk option? No
Employees needed to run franchise: 1
Absentee ownership? Yes

COSTS
Total cost: $10K-20K
Franchise fee: $5K
Royalty fee: 5%
Term of agreement: 10 years renewable at no charge
Franchisees required to buy multiple units? No

FINANCING
No financing available

QUALIFICATIONS
Net worth: $25K
Cash liquidity: $15K
Experience:
    General business experience

TRAINING
At headquarters: 2 days (optional)
Training manual & video

BUSINESS SUPPORT
Newsletter
Toll-free phone line
Internet
Security/safety procedures
Purchasing cooperatives

MARKETING SUPPORT
Ad slicks
National media campaign
Regional marketing
Local marketing materials

HAWKEYE'S HOME SITTERS

Current financial data not available

Box 141
Edmonton, AB T5J 2G9 Canada
Ph: (888)247-2787/(780)473-4825
Fax: (780)988-8948
www.homesitter.com
In-home pet care/house-sitting services
Began: 1987, Franchising since: 1997
Headquarters size: 2 employees
Franchise department: 2 employees

U.S. franchises: 0
Canadian franchises: 10
Other foreign franchises: 0
Company-owned: 4

Seeking: Not available in the U.S.
Seeking in Canada? Yes
Exclusive territories? Yes
Homebased option? Yes
Kiosk option? No
Employees needed to run franchise: 1-2
Absentee ownership? No

COSTS
Total cost: $5K-10K
Franchise fee: $4K-8K
Royalty fee: 4%
Term of agreement: 5 years renewable at $125
Franchisees required to buy multiple units? No

FINANCING
No financing available

QUALIFICATIONS
Cash liquidity: $1K

TRAINING
At franchisee's location: Via training manual

BUSINESS SUPPORT
Newsletter
Toll-free phone line
Grand opening
Internet
Security/safety procedures
Purchasing cooperatives

MARKETING SUPPORT
Co-op advertising
National media campaign

PETS ARE INN

Financial rating: $$$

5100 Edina Industrial Blvd., #206
Minneapolis, MN 55439
Ph: (866)343-0086/(952)944-8298
Fax: (952)746-7648
www.petsareinn.com
Pet lodging service in private homes
Began: 1982, Franchising since: 1986
Headquarters size: 7 employees
Franchise department: 5 employees

U.S. franchises: 15
Canadian franchises: 0
Other foreign franchises: 0
Company-owned: 0
Units concentrated in CO, HI, MN,
    MO, PA, TX, VA, WA

Seeking: All U.S.
Seeking in Canada? No
Exclusive territories? Yes
Homebased option? Yes
Kiosk option? No
Employees needed to run franchise: 4
Absentee ownership? No

COSTS

Total cost: $20K-75K
Franchise fee: $15K
Royalty fee: 5-10%
Term of agreement: 10 years renewable
    at $1K
Franchisees required to buy multiple
    units? No

FINANCING

No financing available

QUALIFICATIONS

Net worth: $250K
Cash liquidity: $100K
Experience:
    General business experience
    Marketing skills
    Must love pets

TRAINING

At headquarters: 5 days
At franchisee's location: 1 day
Ongoing

BUSINESS SUPPORT

Newsletter
Meetings
Toll-free phone line
Grand opening
Internet
Security/safety procedures
Field operations/evaluations
Purchasing cooperatives

MARKETING SUPPORT

Co-op advertising
Ad slicks
Local PR efforts

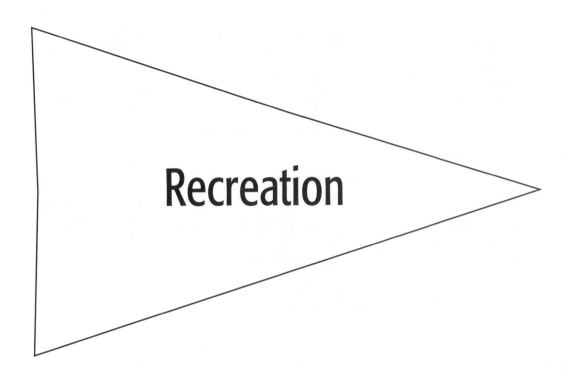

Recreation

AMERICAN POOLPLAYERS ASSOCIATION
Ranked #218 in Entrepreneur Magazine's 2005 Franchise 500

Financial rating: $$$$

1000 Lake St. Louis Blvd., #325
Lake St. Louis, MO 63367
Ph: (636)625-8611
Fax: (636)625-2975
www.poolplayers.com
Recreational billiard league
Began: 1981, Franchising since: 1982
Headquarters size: 50 employees
Franchise department: 3 employees

U.S. franchises: 252
Canadian franchises: 17
Other foreign franchises: 0
Company-owned: 0
Units concentrated in all U.S.

Seeking: All U.S.
Seeking in Canada? Yes
Exclusive territories? Yes
Homebased option? Yes
Kiosk option? No
Employees needed to run franchise: 1-3
Absentee ownership? No

COSTS
Total cost: $11.6K-14K
Franchise fee: $5K+
Royalty fee: 20%
Term of agreement: 2 years renewable
    at no charge
Franchisees required to buy multiple
    units? No

FINANCING
No financing available

QUALIFICATIONS
Experience:
    General business experience
    Marketing skills

TRAINING
At headquarters: 6 days

BUSINESS SUPPORT
Newsletter
Meetings
Toll-free phone line
Internet
Field operations/evaluations

MARKETING SUPPORT
Ad slicks

GLOBAL LEADERBOARD

Financial rating: 0

21043-2591 Panorama Dr.
Coquitlam, BC V3E 2Y0 Canada
Ph: (800)411-4448/(604)468-2211
Fax: (604)468-0101
www.ltsleaderboard.com
Golf tournament scoring, admin. &
    sponsorships
Began: 1995, Franchising since: 2001
Headquarters size: 7 employees
Franchise department: 3 employees

U.S. franchises: 20
Canadian franchises: 1
Other foreign franchises: 2
Company-owned: 1
Units concentrated in all U.S.

Seeking: All U.S.
Seeking in Canada? No
Exclusive territories? Yes
Homebased option? Yes
Kiosk option? No
Employees needed to run franchise: 2
Absentee ownership? No

COSTS
Total cost: $49K-173.1K
Franchise fee: $18K-71.1K
Royalty fee: Varies
Term of agreement: 5 years renewable
    at no charge
Franchisees required to buy multiple
    units? No

FINANCING
No financing available

QUALIFICATIONS
Net worth: $200K
Cash liquidity: $49K-102K
Experience:
    General business experience
    Marketing skills
    Golf knowledge

TRAINING
At headquarters: 2-1/2 weeks

BUSINESS SUPPORT
Newsletter
Meetings
Toll-free phone line
Internet
Field operations/evaluations

MARKETING SUPPORT
Co-op advertising
Regional marketing

I9 SPORTS

Financial rating: $$

1723 S. Kings Ave.
Brandon, FL 33511
Ph: (813)662-6773
Fax: (813)662-9114
www.i9sports.com
Amateur sports leagues, tournaments
    & events
Began: 2002, Franchising since: 2003
Headquarters size: 7 employees
Franchise department: 7 employees

U.S. franchises: 27
Canadian franchises: 0
Other foreign franchises: 0
Company-owned: 2
Units concentrated in all U.S.

Seeking: All U.S.
Seeking in Canada? No
Exclusive territories? Yes
Homebased option? Yes
Kiosk option? No
Employees needed to run franchise: 1-2
Absentee ownership? No

COSTS
Total cost: $23K-51K
Franchise fee: $12.5K-29.9K
Royalty fee: 7.5%
Term of agreement: 10 years renewable
    at no charge
Franchisees required to buy multiple
    units? No

FINANCING
In-house: Franchise fee
3rd-party: None

QUALIFICATIONS
Net worth: $100K
Cash liquidity: $25K
Experience:
    General business experience
    Marketing skills

TRAINING
At headquarters: 1 week
At franchisee's location: 4 days
Refresher training available

BUSINESS SUPPORT
Newsletter
Meetings
Toll-free phone line
Internet
Security/safety procedures
Field operations/evaluations
Purchasing cooperatives

MARKETING SUPPORT
Co-op advertising
Ad slicks
National media campaign
Regional marketing
Administrative, billing & commission
    payment support
Visits
Sales & PR guidance

OUTDOOR CONNECTION

Financial rating: 0

424 Neosho
Burlington, KS 66839
Ph: (620)364-5500
Fax: (620)364-5563
www.outdoor-connection.com
Fishing & hunting trips
Began: 1988, Franchising since: 1990
Headquarters size: 5 employees
Franchise department: 2 employees

U.S. franchises: 79
Canadian franchises: 0
Other foreign franchises: 0
Company-owned: 3
Units concentrated in all U.S.

Seeking: All U.S.
Seeking in Canada? Yes
Exclusive territories? Yes
Homebased option? Yes
Kiosk option? No
Employees needed to run franchise: 0
Absentee ownership? Yes

COSTS
Total cost: $10.4K-15.1K
Franchise fee: $9.5K
Royalty fee: 3-5%
Term of agreement: 5 years renewable at $500
Franchisees required to buy multiple units? No

FINANCING
In-house: Franchise fee
3rd-party: None

QUALIFICATIONS
Info not provided

TRAINING
At headquarters: 2 days

BUSINESS SUPPORT
Newsletter
Meetings
Internet
Field operations/evaluations
Purchasing cooperatives

MARKETING SUPPORT
Co-op advertising
National media campaign

RECRUIT

Current financial data not available

1701 Westwind Dr., #107
Bakersfield, CA 93301
Ph: (800)962-5550
Fax: (661)859-2888
www.mysportsfranchise.com
Athletic recruiting exposure service for high school athletes & college coaches
Began: 1996, Franchising since: 2001
Headquarters size: 7 employees
Franchise department: 1 employee

U.S. franchises: 36
Canadian franchises: 0
Other foreign franchises: 0
Company-owned: 0
Units concentrated in all U.S.

Seeking: All U.S.
Seeking in Canada? Yes
Exclusive territories? Yes
Homebased option? Yes
Kiosk option? No
Employees needed to run franchise: 0
Absentee ownership? Yes

COSTS
Total cost: $12K-45K
Franchise fee: $9.5K
Royalty fee: 0
Term of agreement: 5 years renewable at no charge
Franchisees required to buy multiple units? No

FINANCING
No financing available

QUALIFICATIONS
Net worth: $50K
Experience:
    Sports or sales background

TRAINING
At headquarters
At franchisee's location
Long-distance training

BUSINESS SUPPORT
Newsletter
Meetings
Toll-free phone line
Internet
Field operations/evaluations

MARKETING SUPPORT
Co-op advertising
Direct-mail marketing

RECREATION ▶ **TRAVEL**

ALL ABOUT HONEYMOONS

Financial rating: 0

950 S. Cherry St., #108
Denver, CO 80246
Ph: (303)757-0881
Fax: (303)753-1796
www.aahfranchise.com
Travel agency specializing in
    honeymoons
Began: 1994, Franchising since: 2003
Headquarters size: Info not provided
Franchise department: 8 employees

U.S. franchises: 11
Canadian franchises: 0
Other foreign franchises: 0
Company-owned: 0
Units concentrated in AZ, CO, FL, GA,
    LA, MA, NC, NV, OH, SC, VT

Seeking: All U.S.
Focusing on: CA, MD, MN, VA, WA
Seeking in Canada? Yes
Exclusive territories? Yes
Homebased option? Yes
Kiosk option? No

Employees needed to run franchise: 0
Absentee ownership? Yes

COSTS
Total cost: $9.1K-28.1K
Franchise fee: $9K/18K/27K
Royalty fee: 1-3%
Term of agreement: 10 years renewable
    at $500
Franchisees required to buy multiple
    units? No

FINANCING
In-house: Equipment
3rd-party: None

QUALIFICATIONS
Net worth: $0
Cash liquidity: Franchise fee
Experience:
    Industry experience
    Customer service skills

TRAINING
At headquarters: 3 days (optional)
At franchisee's location: (Optional)
30-day orientation program (optional)
Internet classes

BUSINESS SUPPORT
Newsletter
Meetings
Toll-free phone line
Grand opening
Internet
Field operations/evaluations

MARKETING SUPPORT
Co-op advertising
Ad slicks
National media campaign
Regional marketing
Direct-marketing mailers
Emails

CARLSON WAGONLIT TRAVEL

Ranked #184 in Entrepreneur Magazine's 2005 Franchise 500

Financial rating: $$$$

Carlson Pkwy., P.O. Box 59159
Minneapolis, MN 55459-8207
Ph: (866)248-3499
Fax: (734)495-1413
www.carlsontravel.com
Travel agency
Began: 1888, Franchising since: 1984
Headquarters size: 775 employees
Franchise department: 140 employees

U.S. franchises: 778
Canadian franchises: 0
Other foreign franchises: 0
Company-owned: 24
Units concentrated in all U.S.

Seeking: All U.S.
Seeking in Canada? No
Exclusive territories? No
Homebased option? No
Kiosk option? No
Employees needed to run franchise:
    Info not provided
Absentee ownership? No

COSTS
Total cost: $2.5K-10.4K
(Franchise sells conversions only.)
Franchise fee: $1.5K
Royalty fee: $950/mo.
Term of agreement: 5 years renewable
    at $1K
Franchisees required to buy multiple
    units? No

FINANCING
In-house: Franchise fee
3rd-party: None

QUALIFICATIONS
Experience:
    Industry experience
    General business experience
    Marketing skills

TRAINING
At headquarters: 3 days
At franchisee's location: Varies
Workshops: 1-2 days each

BUSINESS SUPPORT
Newsletter
Meetings
Toll-free phone line
Internet
Field operations/evaluations

MARKETING SUPPORT
Co-op advertising
Ad slicks
National media campaign
Regional marketing

CRUISEONE INC.

Ranked #188 in Entrepreneur Magazine's 2005 Franchise 500   *Financial rating: $$$*

1415 N.W. 62nd St., #205
Ft. Lauderdale, FL 33309
Ph: (800)892-3928
Fax: (954)958-3697
www.cruiseonefranchise.com
Cruise-only travel agency
Began: 1989, Franchising since: 1993
Headquarters size: 50 employees
Franchise department: 60 employees

U.S. franchises: 448
Canadian franchises: 0
Other foreign franchises: 0
Company-owned: 0
Units concentrated in all U.S.

Seeking: All U.S.
Seeking in Canada? No
Exclusive territories? No
Homebased option? Yes
Kiosk option? No
Employees needed to run franchise: 0
Absentee ownership? No

COSTS
Total cost: $9.8K-26.3K
Franchise fee: $9.8K
Royalty fee: 3%
Term of agreement: 5 years renewable
    at no charge
Franchisees required to buy multiple
    units? No

FINANCING
No financing available

QUALIFICATIONS
Cash liquidity: $20K

TRAINING
At headquarters: 8 days

BUSINESS SUPPORT
Newsletter
Meetings
Toll-free phone line
Internet

MARKETING SUPPORT
Co-op advertising
Ad slicks
Regional marketing

CRUISE PLANNERS/AMERICAN EXPRESS TRAVEL SERVICE

Ranked #118 in Entrepreneur Magazine's 2005 Franchise 500   *Financial rating: $$$$*

3300 University Dr., #602
Coral Springs, FL 33065
Ph: (888)582-2150/(954)227-2545
Fax: (954)344-0875
www.beacruiseagent.com
Cruise/tour agency
Began: 1994, Franchising since: 1999
Headquarters size: 30 employees
Franchise department: 3 employees

U.S. franchises: 474
Canadian franchises: 0
Other foreign franchises: 0
Company-owned: 0
Units concentrated in all U.S.

Seeking: All U.S.
Seeking in Canada? No
Exclusive territories? No
Homebased option? Yes
Kiosk option? Yes
Employees needed to run franchise: 1-2
Absentee ownership? Yes

COSTS
Total cost: $8.99K-19.9K
Kiosk cost: Varies
Franchise fee: $8.99K
Royalty fee: 3-0%
Term of agreement: 3 years renewable
    at no charge
Franchisees required to buy multiple
    units? No

FINANCING
No financing available

QUALIFICATIONS
Net worth: $17.1K
Cash liquidity: $8.99K

TRAINING
In Ft. Lauderdale, FL: 5 days

BUSINESS SUPPORT
Newsletter
Meetings
Toll-free phone line
Internet
Purchasing cooperatives

MARKETING SUPPORT
Co-op advertising
Ad slicks
National media campaign
Regional marketing

RESULTS TRAVEL

Ranked #66 in Entrepreneur Magazine's 2005 Franchise 500   *Financial rating: $$$$*

Carlson Pkwy., P.O. Box 59159
Minneapolis, MN 55459-8207
Ph: (888)523-2200
Fax: (763)212-2302
www.resultstravel.com
Travel services
Began: 2000, Franchising since: 2000
Headquarters size: 775 employees
Franchise department: 140 employees

U.S. franchises: 864
Canadian franchises: 0
Other foreign franchises: 0
Company-owned: 0
Units concentrated in all U.S.

Seeking: All U.S.
Seeking in Canada? No
Exclusive territories? No
Homebased option? No
Kiosk option? No
Employees needed to run franchise:
    Info not provided
Absentee ownership? No

COSTS
Total cost: $25-8.3K
(Franchise sells conversions only.)
Franchise fee: to $1.5K
Royalty fee: to $300/yr.
Term of agreement: 1 year renewable
    at $600 for main location
Franchisees required to buy multiple
    units? No

FINANCING
No financing available

QUALIFICATIONS
Experience:
    Industry experience
    General business experience
    Marketing skills
    Must own an existing travel agency

TRAINING
Orientation training: 1-2 days
National meeting: 2 days

BUSINESS SUPPORT
Meetings
Toll-free phone line

MARKETING SUPPORT
Co-op advertising
National media campaign

SEAMASTER CRUISES

Current financial data not available

701 Carlson Pkwy.
Minneapolis, MN 55305
Ph: (763)212-1359
www.seamastercruises.com
Cruises
Began: 2004, Franchising since: 2004
Headquarters size: 140 employees
Franchise department:
Info not provided

U.S. franchises: 15
Canadian franchises: 0
Other foreign franchises: 0
Company-owned: 0

Seeking: All U.S.
Seeking in Canada? No
Exclusive territories? No
Homebased option? Yes
Kiosk option? No
Employees needed to run franchise: 0
Absentee ownership? No

COSTS
Total cost: $5.5K-16.4K
Franchise fee: $9.5K
Royalty fee: 3%
Term of agreement: 5 years renewable
Franchisees required to buy multiple
    units? No

FINANCING
No financing available

QUALIFICATIONS
Net worth: $10K
Cash liquidity: $10K
Experience:
    General business experience
    Marketing skills

TRAINING
At headquarters: 5 days
On Caribbean cruise: 7 days

BUSINESS SUPPORT
Newsletter
Meetings
Toll-free phone line
Internet
Security/safety procedures
Purchasing cooperatives

MARKETING SUPPORT
Co-op advertising
Ad slicks
Regional marketing
Electronic marketing

TRAVEL NETWORK

Ranked #325 in Entrepreneur Magazine's 2005 Franchise 500

Financial rating: $$$$

560 Sylvan Ave.
Englewood Cliffs, NJ 07632
Ph: (800)669-9000/(201)567-8500
Fax: (201)567-4405
www.travelnetwork.com
Travel agency
Began: 1982, Franchising since: 1983
Headquarters size: 18 employees
Franchise department: 9 employees

U.S. franchises: 264
Canadian franchises: 3
Other foreign franchises: 61
Company-owned: 1
Units concentrated in all U.S.

Seeking: All U.S.
Seeking in Canada? Yes
Exclusive territories? Yes
Homebased option? Yes
Kiosk option? No
Employees needed to run franchise: 2
Absentee ownership? Yes

COSTS
Total cost: $34.2K-99K
*(Low-cost option available to
    conversions only.)*
Franchise fee: $3.95K-29.9K
Royalty fee: $250-750/mo.
Term of agreement: 15 years renewable
    at $500
Franchisees required to buy multiple
    units? No

FINANCING
In-house: Franchise fee
3rd-party: None

QUALIFICATIONS
Net worth: $15K
Cash liquidity: $15K-30K
Experience:
    General business experience
    Marketing skills

TRAINING
At headquarters: 3 days
At franchisee's location: 4 days per year
Quarterly at headquarters

BUSINESS SUPPORT
Newsletter
Meetings
Toll-free phone line
Grand opening
Internet
Lease negotiations
Field operations/evaluations
Purchasing cooperatives

MARKETING SUPPORT
Co-op advertising
Ad slicks
National media campaign
Regional marketing

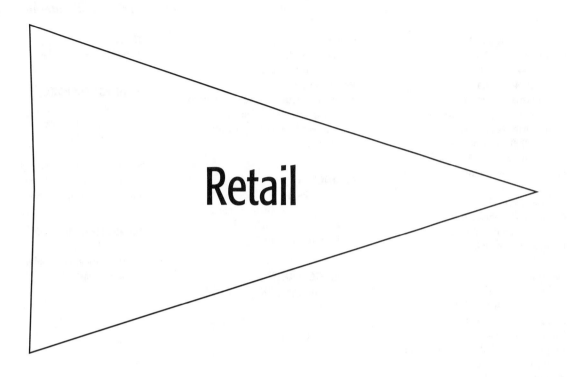

Retail

RETAIL

ELEPHANT HOUSE

Current financial data not available

1608 Pine Knoll Dr.
Austin, TX 78758
Ph: (800)276-2405/(512)833-0384
Fax: (512)833-0172
www.elephanthouse.com
Greeting cards
Began: 1991, Franchising since: 1991
Headquarters size: 5 employees
Franchise department: 1 employee

U.S. franchises: 51
Canadian franchises: 12
Other foreign franchises: 217
Company-owned: 0

Seeking: All U.S.
Seeking in Canada? No
Exclusive territories? Yes
Homebased option? Yes
Kiosk option? No
Employees needed to run franchise: 0
Absentee ownership? Info not provided

COSTS
Total cost: $28K-44.5K
Franchise fee: $10.2K
Royalty fee: 0
Term of agreement: 7 years renewable
    at no charge
Franchisees required to buy multiple
    units? No

FINANCING
No financing available

QUALIFICATIONS
Net worth: $50K-100K
Cash liquidity: $25K-50K

TRAINING
At franchisee's location: 4 days
Additional training as needed

BUSINESS SUPPORT
Newsletter
Toll-free phone line

MARKETING SUPPORT
Marketing brochures
National/regional account support

HERMAN'S WORLD OF SPORTS

Current financial data not available

1055 Stewart Ave., #4
Bethpage, NY 11714
Ph: (516)470-9000
Fax: (516)470-9004
www.hermansdirect.com
Direct sales of sporting goods, team
    uniforms & apparel
Began: 2000, Franchising since: 2003
Headquarters size: 12 employees
Franchise department: 4 employees

U.S. franchises: 12
Canadian franchises: 0
Other foreign franchises: 0
Company-owned: 0

Seeking: All U.S.
Seeking in Canada? No
Exclusive territories? Yes
Homebased option? Yes
Kiosk option? No
Employees needed to run franchise:
    Info not provided
Absentee ownership? Yes

COSTS
Total cost: $44K-116K
Franchise fee: $16.7K-50K
Royalty fee: 6%
Term of agreement: 5 years renewable
    at 25% of current fee
Franchisees required to buy multiple
    units? No

FINANCING
In-house: None
3rd-party: Accounts receivable,
    equipment, franchise fee,
    inventory, payroll, startup costs

QUALIFICATIONS
Cash liquidity: $72K
Experience:
    General business experience
    Marketing skills

TRAINING
At headquarters: 5 days

BUSINESS SUPPORT
Meetings
Toll-free phone line
Grand opening
Internet
Security/safety procedures
Field operations/evaluations
Purchasing cooperatives

MARKETING SUPPORT
Co-op advertising
National media campaign
Regional marketing

MARAD FINE ART

Financial rating: $$

992 High Ridge Rd.
Stamford, CT 06905
Ph: (203)322-7666
Fax: (203)329-9836
www.maradfineart.com
Commercial framed art reproductions
Began: 1938, Franchising since: 2000
Headquarters size: 3 employees
Franchise department:
    Info not provided

U.S. franchises: 3
Canadian franchises: 0
Other foreign franchises: 1
Company-owned: 1
Units concentrated in Northeast

Seeking: All U.S.
Seeking in Canada? Yes
Exclusive territories? Yes
Homebased option? Yes
Kiosk option? No
Employees needed to run franchise: 1-2
Absentee ownership? No

COSTS
Total cost: $42K-69K
Franchise fee: $35K-60K
Royalty fee: 4%
Term of agreement: Varies renewable
    at 50% of fee
Franchisees required to buy multiple
    units? No

FINANCING
No financing available

QUALIFICATIONS
Net worth: $200K
Cash liquidity: $75K
Experience:
    General business experience
    Marketing skills

TRAINING
At franchisee's location: 3 days

BUSINESS SUPPORT
Info not provided

MARKETING SUPPORT
Co-op advertising
Regional marketing

PURIFIED WATER TO GO

Ranked #288 in Entrepreneur Magazine's 2005 Franchise 500

Financial rating: $$$$

5160 S. Valley View Blvd., #100
Las Vegas, NV 89118-1778
Ph: (800)976-9283/(702)895-9350
Fax: (702)895-9306
www.watertogo.com
Retail water & nutrition stores
Began: 1992, Franchising since: 1995
Headquarters size: 9 employees
Franchise department: 3 employees

U.S. franchises: 71
Canadian franchises: 3
Other foreign franchises: 0
Company-owned: 0

Seeking: All U.S.
Seeking in Canada? Yes
Exclusive territories? Yes
Homebased option? No
Kiosk option? Yes
Employees needed to run franchise: 1-2
Absentee ownership? No

COSTS
Total cost: $25K-200K
Kiosk cost: $12.5K-29.5K
Franchise fee: $12.5K-29.5K
Royalty fee: 5-6%
Term of agreement: 5 years renewable
at $5K
Franchisees required to buy multiple
units? Outside U.S. only

FINANCING
In-house: None
3rd-party: Equipment, franchise fee,
inventory, startup costs

QUALIFICATIONS
Net worth: $150K
Cash liquidity: $25K-40K
Experience:
General business experience
Customer service skills

TRAINING
At headquarters: 5 days
At franchisee's location: 1-3 days
At annual convention

BUSINESS SUPPORT
Newsletter
Meetings
Toll-free phone line
Grand opening
Internet
Purchasing cooperatives

MARKETING SUPPORT
Co-op advertising
Ad slicks
National media campaign

SUPPLY MASTER USA

Current financial data not available

6C White Deer Plaza
Sparta, NJ 07871
Ph: (800)582-1947/(973)729-5006
Fax: (973)729-1975
www.supplymasterusa.com
Mobile distribution of commercial &
industrial products
Began: 1989, Franchising since: 2001
Headquarters size: 3 employees
Franchise department: 1 employee

U.S. franchises: 3
Canadian franchises: 0
Other foreign franchises: 0
Company-owned: 1

Seeking: All U.S.
Seeking in Canada? No
Exclusive territories? Yes
Homebased option? Yes
Kiosk option? No
Employees needed to run franchise: 0
Absentee ownership? Yes

COSTS
Total cost: $12.95K-22.7K
Franchise fee: $4.5K-10K
Royalty fee: $25-100/wk.
Term of agreement: 5 years renewable
at 10% of current franchise fee
Franchisees required to buy multiple
units? No

FINANCING
No financing available

QUALIFICATIONS
Net worth: $25K-35K
Cash liquidity: $15K-20K
Experience:
Industry experience
General business experience

TRAINING
At headquarters: 4 days
At franchisee's location: 2 days

BUSINESS SUPPORT
Meetings
Toll-free phone line
Field operations/evaluations

MARKETING SUPPORT
Ad slicks
Regional marketing

WIRELESS DIMENSIONS

Current financial data not available

3901 S.W. 47th Ave., #400
Davie, FL 33314
Ph: (888)809-4934/(954)791-4993
Fax: (954)791-4994
www.wireless-dimensions.com
Wireless accessories
Began: 2002, Franchising since: 2002
Headquarters size: 25 employees
Franchise department: 5 employees

U.S. franchises: 139
Canadian franchises: 0
Other foreign franchises: 0
Company-owned: 0

Seeking: All U.S.
Seeking in Canada? Yes
Exclusive territories? Yes
Homebased option? No
Kiosk option? Yes
Employees needed to run franchise: 0-4
Absentee ownership? Yes

COSTS

Total cost: $23K-34K
Kiosk cost: Same as total cost
Franchise fee: $6.9K
Royalty fee: 6%
Term of agreement: 4 years renewable
    at no charge
Franchisees required to buy multiple
    units? No

FINANCING

In-house: Franchise fee
3rd-party: None

QUALIFICATIONS

Info not provided

TRAINING

At headquarters: 1 week
At franchisee's location: 1 week

BUSINESS SUPPORT

Newsletter
Meetings
Toll-free phone line
Grand opening
Internet
Field operations/evaluations
Purchasing cooperatives

MARKETING SUPPORT

Ad slicks
Regional marketing

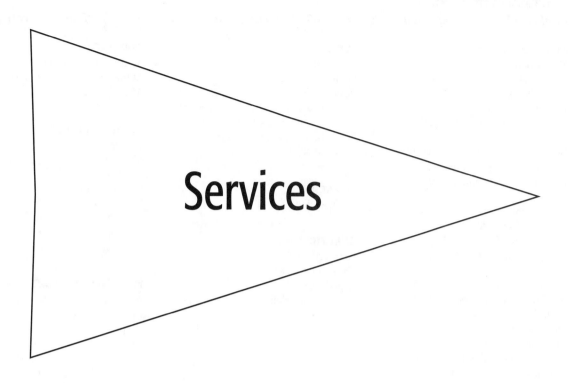

Services

DRY CLEANING TO-YOUR-DOOR
Ranked #500 in Entrepreneur Magazine's 2005 Franchise 500   *Financial rating: 0*

1121 N.W. Bayshore Dr.
Waldport, OR 97394
Ph: (800)318-1800
Fax: (541)563-6938
www.dctyd.com
Dry cleaning pickup & delivery
Began: 1994, Franchising since: 1997
Headquarters size: 5 employees
Franchise department:
    Info not provided

U.S. franchises: 96
Canadian franchises: 0
Other foreign franchises: 0
Company-owned: 0
Units concentrated in all U.S.

Seeking: All U.S.
Seeking in Canada? Yes
Exclusive territories? Yes
Homebased option? Yes
Kiosk option? No

Employees needed to run franchise:
    Info not provided
Absentee ownership? Info not provided

COSTS
Total cost: $39.99K
Franchise fee: $24.5K
Royalty fee: 4.5%
Term of agreement: 10 years renewable
    at no charge
Franchisees required to buy multiple
    units? No

FINANCING
No financing available

QUALIFICATIONS
Net worth: $75K
Cash liquidity: $24.5K

TRAINING
At franchisee's location: 1 week
Classroom training: 1 week

BUSINESS SUPPORT
Newsletter
Meetings
Toll-free phone line
Grand opening
Internet
Security/safety procedures
Field operations/evaluations
Purchasing cooperatives

MARKETING SUPPORT
Co-op advertising
Ad slicks
Regional marketing

PRESSED4TIME INC.

Ranked #284 in Entrepreneur Magazine's 2005 Franchise 500   *Financial rating: $$$*

8 Clock Tower Pl., #110
Maynard, MA 01754
Ph: (800)423-8711/(978)823-8300
Fax: (978)823-8301
www.pressed4time.com
Dry cleaning pickup/delivery; shoe
    repair
Began: 1987, Franchising since: 1990
Headquarters size: 5 employees
Franchise department: 2 employees

U.S. franchises: 172
Canadian franchises: 2
Other foreign franchises: 7
Company-owned: 0

Seeking: All U.S.
Seeking in Canada? Yes
Exclusive territories? Yes
Homebased option? Yes
Kiosk option? No
Employees needed to run franchise: 0
Absentee ownership? No

COSTS
Total cost: $24K-32.9K
Franchise fee: $21.5K
Royalty fee: 4-6%
Term of agreement: 10 years renewable
    at 10% of current franchise fee
Franchisees required to buy multiple
    units? No

FINANCING
No financing available

QUALIFICATIONS
Net worth: $50K
Cash liquidity: $30K
Experience:
    Marketing skills

TRAINING
At headquarters: 3 days
At franchisee's location: 3 days
After opening: 1 day

BUSINESS SUPPORT
Newsletter
Meetings
Toll-free phone line
Grand opening
Internet
Security/safety procedures
Field operations/evaluations
Purchasing cooperatives

MARKETING SUPPORT
Ad slicks
Marketing materials
PR program

SERVICES ▶ **GIFTS**

THE ORIGINAL BASKET BOUTIQUE

Current financial data not available

#16, 363 Sioux Rd.
Sherwood Park, AB T8A 4W7 Canada
Ph: (877)622-8008
Fax: (780)416-2531
www.originalbasketboutique.com
Custom gifts & gift baskets
Began: 1989, Franchising since: 1989
Headquarters size: 4 employees
Franchise department: 4 employees

U.S. franchises: 2
Canadian franchises: 20
Other foreign franchises: 0
Company-owned: 0

Seeking: All U.S.
Seeking in Canada? Yes
Exclusive territories? Yes
Homebased option? Yes
Kiosk option? No
Employees needed to run franchise: 1-2
Absentee ownership? Yes

COSTS
Total cost: $37.5K-47K
Franchise fee: $20K
Royalty fee: 4%
Term of agreement: 5 years renewable
    at $500
Franchisees required to buy multiple
    units? No

FINANCING
No financing available

QUALIFICATIONS
Net worth: $40K

TRAINING
At headquarters: 3-4 days

BUSINESS SUPPORT
Newsletter
Internet
Field operations/evaluations
Purchasing cooperatives

MARKETING SUPPORT
Sales leads

3D MEMORIES

Financial rating: $$$

64 Seagull Cir.
Colorado Springs, CO 80921
Ph: (719)481-5710
Fax: (719)481-0665
www.handmolds.com
Personalized keepsakes
Began: 2001, Franchising since: 2004
Headquarters size: 4 employees
Franchise department: 2 employees

U.S. franchises: 1
Canadian franchises: 0
Other foreign franchises: 0
Company-owned: 0

Seeking: All U.S.
Seeking in Canada? No
Exclusive territories? Yes
Homebased option? Yes
Kiosk option? Yes
Employees needed to run franchise: 0
Absentee ownership? No

COSTS
Total cost: $6.2K-15.4K
Franchise fee: $4.9K-9.9K
Royalty fee: 5%
Term of agreement: 5 years renewable
   at $1.5K
Franchisees required to buy multiple
   units? No

FINANCING
No financing available

QUALIFICATIONS
Cash liquidity: $5K

TRAINING
At headquarters: 1 week

BUSINESS SUPPORT
Newsletter
Meetings
Internet
Lease negotiations
Security/safety procedures

MARKETING SUPPORT
Co-op advertising

SERVICES ► **HOME INSPECTIONS**

ALLSTATE HOME INSPECTIONS & ENVIRONMENTAL TESTING

Ranked #372 in Entrepreneur Magazine's 2005 Franchise 500

Financial rating: $$$

2097 N. Randolph Rd.
Randolph Ctr., VT 05061
Ph: (800)245-9932
Fax: (802)728-5534
www.allstatehomeinspection.com
Home inspection & household
   environmental testing
Began: 1989, Franchising since: 1996
Headquarters size: 5 employees
Franchise department: 5 employees

U.S. franchises: 40
Canadian franchises: 1
Other foreign franchises: 0
Company-owned: 2

Seeking: All U.S.
Seeking in Canada? No
Exclusive territories? Yes
Homebased option? Yes
Kiosk option? No
Employees needed to run franchise: 1-3
Absentee ownership? Yes

COSTS
Total cost: $29.7K-49.2K
Franchise fee: $23.9K
Royalty fee: 7.5%
Term of agreement: 6 years renewable
   at $2K
Franchisees required to buy multiple
   units? No

FINANCING
In-house: None
3rd-party: Equipment

QUALIFICATIONS
Cash liquidity: $7.9K-24K
Experience:
   Industry experience

TRAINING
At headquarters: 10 days
Additional training as needed

BUSINESS SUPPORT
Newsletter
Meetings
Toll-free phone line
Internet
Field operations/evaluations

MARKETING SUPPORT
Ad slicks
National media campaign
Regional marketing
Telephone Outreach Project (TOP)

AMERISPEC HOME INSPECTION SERVICES
Ranked #102 in Entrepreneur Magazine's 2005 Franchise 500   *Financial rating: $$$$*

889 Ridge Lake Blvd.
Memphis, TN 38120
Ph: (800)426-2270/(901)820-8500
Fax: (901)820-8520
www.amerispecfranchise.com
Home inspection service
Began: 1987, Franchising since: 1988
Headquarters size: 45 employees
Franchise department: 4 employees

U.S. franchises: 313
Canadian franchises: 72
Other foreign franchises: 0
Company-owned: 2

Seeking: All U.S.
Seeking in Canada? Yes
Exclusive territories? Yes
Homebased option? Yes
Kiosk option? No
Employees needed to run franchise: 3
Absentee ownership? No

COSTS
Total cost: $26.4K-64.6K
Franchise fee: $19.9K/29.9K
Royalty fee: 7%
Term of agreement: 5 years renewable
    at no charge
Franchisees required to buy multiple
    units? No

FINANCING
In-house: Franchise fee
3rd-party: None

QUALIFICATIONS
Net worth: $50K
Cash liquidity: $10K-15K
Experience:
    Industry experience
    General business experience
    Marketing skills

TRAINING
At headquarters: 2 weeks
Correspondence training: 27 weeks

BUSINESS SUPPORT
Newsletter
Meetings
Toll-free phone line
Internet
Field operations/evaluations
Purchasing cooperatives

MARKETING SUPPORT
Co-op advertising
Ad slicks
National media campaign
Regional marketing

THE BRICKKICKER HOME INSPECTION
Ranked #235 in Entrepreneur Magazine's 2005 Franchise 500   *Financial rating: $$$*

849 N. Ellsworth St.
Naperville, IL 60583
Ph: (888)339-5425
Fax: (630)420-2270
www.brickkicker.com
Home/property inspection service
Began: 1989, Franchising since: 1994
Headquarters size: 19 employees
Franchise department: 6 employees

U.S. franchises: 173
Canadian franchises: 0
Other foreign franchises: 0
Company-owned: 28
Units concentrated in all U.S.

Seeking: All U.S.
Seeking in Canada? No
Exclusive territories? Yes
Homebased option? Yes
Kiosk option? No
Employees needed to run franchise: 1-2
Absentee ownership? No

COSTS
Total cost: $14.3K-53.7K
Franchise fee: $7.5K-25K
Royalty fee: 6%
Term of agreement: 7 years renewable
    at no charge
Franchisees required to buy multiple
    units? No

FINANCING
In-house: Franchise fee
3rd-party: None

QUALIFICATIONS
Net worth: $50K
Cash liquidity: $20K
Experience:
    General business experience
    Marketing skills

TRAINING
At headquarters: 5-10 days
At franchisee's location: 2-4 days
Ongoing

BUSINESS SUPPORT
Newsletter
Meetings
Toll-free phone line
Grand opening
Internet
Security/safety procedures
Field operations/evaluations
Purchasing cooperatives

MARKETING SUPPORT
Co-op advertising
Ad slicks
National media campaign
Regional marketing

THE HOMETEAM INSPECTION SERVICE
Ranked #171 in Entrepreneur Magazine's 2005 Franchise 500　　　*Financial rating: $$$$*

575 Chamber Dr.
Milford, OH 45150
Ph: (800)598-5297
Fax: (513)831-6010
www.hmteam.com
Home inspection service
Began: 1991, Franchising since: 1992
Headquarters size: 25 employees
Franchise department: 13 employees

U.S. franchises: 342
Canadian franchises: 8
Other foreign franchises: 0
Company-owned: 0

Seeking: All U.S.
Seeking in Canada? Yes
Exclusive territories? Yes
Homebased option? Yes
Kiosk option? No
Employees needed to run franchise: 1
Absentee ownership? No

COSTS
Total cost: $19.5K-46.1K
Franchise fee: $11.9K-29.9K
Royalty fee: 6%
Term of agreement: 10 years renewable
　　at no charge
Franchisees required to buy multiple
　　units? No

FINANCING
In-house: Franchise fee
3rd-party: Equipment, startup costs

QUALIFICATIONS
Cash liquidity: $7.5K
Experience:
　　Industry experience
　　General business experience
　　Marketing skills

TRAINING
At headquarters: 2 weeks
At franchisee's location: As needed
At annual meetings

BUSINESS SUPPORT
Newsletter
Meetings
Grand opening
Internet
Security/safety procedures
Field operations/evaluations

MARKETING SUPPORT
Co-op advertising
Ad slicks
National media campaign
Access to national advertising fund

HOUSEMASTER HOME INSPECTIONS
Ranked #223 in Entrepreneur Magazine's 2005 Franchise 500　　　*Financial rating: $$$$*

421 W. Union Ave.
Bound Brook, NJ 08805
Ph: (800)526-3939
Fax: (732)469-7405
www.housemaster.com
Home inspection service
Began: 1971, Franchising since: 1979
Headquarters size: 24 employees
Franchise department: 24 employees

U.S. franchises: 338
Canadian franchises: 37
Other foreign franchises: 0
Company-owned: 0
Units concentrated in all U.S.

Seeking: All U.S.
Seeking in Canada? Yes
Exclusive territories? Yes
Homebased option? Yes
Kiosk option? No
Employees needed to run franchise: 1-5
Absentee ownership? Yes

COSTS
Total cost: $25K-65K
Franchise fee: $12K-29K
Royalty fee: 5-7.5%
Term of agreement: 5 years renewable
　　at no charge
Franchisees required to buy multiple
　　units? No

FINANCING
In-house: Franchise fee
3rd-party: Franchise fee

QUALIFICATIONS
Net worth: $50K
Cash liquidity: $20K
Experience:
　　Marketing skills
　　Management skills

TRAINING
At headquarters: 1 week
Technical training

BUSINESS SUPPORT
Newsletter
Meetings
Toll-free phone line
Grand opening
Internet
Security/safety procedures
Field operations/evaluations
Purchasing cooperatives

MARKETING SUPPORT
Co-op advertising
Ad slicks
National media campaign
Regional marketing
Annual conferences
Proprietary software
Database marketing

INSPECT-IT 1ST PROPERTY INSPECTION

Ranked #403 in Entrepreneur Magazine's 2005 Franchise 500　　　*Financial rating: $$$*

8541 E. Anderson Dr., #102
Scottsdale, AZ 85255
Ph: (800)510-9100/(480)355-3250
Fax: (480)355-3255
www.inspectit1st.com
Property inspection service
Began: 1991, Franchising since: 1998
Headquarters size: 4 employees
Franchise department: 3 employees

U.S. franchises: 60
Canadian franchises: 0
Other foreign franchises: 0
Company-owned: 0
Units concentrated in all U.S.

Seeking: All U.S.
Seeking in Canada? No
Exclusive territories? Yes
Homebased option? Yes
Kiosk option? No
Employees needed to run franchise: 0
Absentee ownership? No

COSTS

Total cost: $33K-51K
Franchise fee: $24.9K-27.9K
Royalty fee: 6-7%
Term of agreement: 10 years renewable
　　at no charge
Franchisees required to buy multiple
　　units? No

FINANCING

No financing available

QUALIFICATIONS

Net worth: $75K
Cash liquidity: $30K

TRAINING

At headquarters: 2 weeks
Yearly continuing education

BUSINESS SUPPORT

Newsletter
Meetings
Toll-free phone line
Grand opening
Internet
Field operations/evaluations
Purchasing cooperatives

MARKETING SUPPORT

Co-op advertising
Ad slicks
Regional marketing

NATIONAL PROPERTY INSPECTIONS INC.

Ranked #185 in Entrepreneur Magazine's 2005 Franchise 500　　　*Financial rating: $$$$*

9375 Burt, #201
Omaha, NE 68114
Ph: (800)333-9807
Fax: (800)933-2508
www.npiweb.com
Home & commercial property
　　inspections
Began: 1987, Franchising since: 1987
Headquarters size: 15 employees
Franchise department: 7 employees

U.S. franchises: 222
Canadian franchises: 10
Other foreign franchises: 0
Company-owned: 0
Units concentrated in all U.S.

Seeking: All U.S.
Seeking in Canada? Yes
Exclusive territories? Yes
Homebased option? Yes
Kiosk option? No
Employees needed to run franchise: 1
Absentee ownership? No

COSTS

Total cost: $28.5K-31K
Franchise fee: $21.8K
Royalty fee: 8%
Term of agreement: 10 years renewable
　　at no charge
Franchisees required to buy multiple
　　units? No

FINANCING

In-house: None
3rd-party: Accounts receivable,
　　equipment, franchise fee,
　　inventory, payroll, startup costs

QUALIFICATIONS

Cash liquidity: $23K
Experience:
　　General business experience
　　Marketing skills

TRAINING

At headquarters: 2 weeks
Field training: 1 week (optional)

BUSINESS SUPPORT

Newsletter
Meetings
Toll-free phone line
Internet
Field operations/evaluations
Purchasing cooperatives

MARKETING SUPPORT

Ad slicks
Regional marketing
Corporate relocation referral program

PILLAR TO POST
Ranked #86 in Entrepreneur Magazine's 2005 Franchise 500

Financial rating: $$$$

13902 N. Dale Mabry Hwy., #300
Tampa, FL 33618
Ph: (877)963-3129
Fax: (813)963-5301
www.pillartopost.com
Home inspection service
Began: 1994, Franchising since: 1994
Headquarters size: 18 employees
Franchise department: 11 employees

U.S. franchises: 372
Canadian franchises: 85
Other foreign franchises: 0
Company-owned: 0
Units concentrated in all U.S.

Seeking: All U.S.
Seeking in Canada? Yes
Exclusive territories? Yes
Homebased option? Yes
Kiosk option? No
Employees needed to run franchise: 2
Absentee ownership? No

COSTS
Total cost: $28.7K-46.5K
Franchise fee: $18.9K-28.9K
Royalty fee: 7%
Term of agreement: 5 years renewable
  at $2.5K
Franchisees required to buy multiple
  units? No

FINANCING
In-house: Franchise fee
3rd-party: None

QUALIFICATIONS
Net worth: $100K
Cash liquidity: $50K
Experience:
    General business experience
    Marketing skills

TRAINING
At headquarters: 2 weeks

BUSINESS SUPPORT
Newsletter
Meetings
Toll-free phone line
Internet

MARKETING SUPPORT
Co-op advertising
Ad slicks
National media campaign
Regional marketing

PROSPECTION LLC

Financial rating: $$$$

7100 E. Pleasant Valley Rd., #260
Independence, OH 44131
Ph: (866)328-7720 ext. 10
Fax: (216)674-0652
www.prospectionusa.com
Property inspections
Began: 2003, Franchising since: 2003
Headquarters size: 30 employees
Franchise department: 5 employees

U.S. franchises: 2
Canadian franchises: 0
Other foreign franchises: 0
Company-owned: 0
Units concentrated in CO, FL, KS, LA,
  MS, NH, OH, TX

Seeking: All U.S.
Seeking in Canada? No
Exclusive territories? No
Homebased option? Yes
Kiosk option? No
Employees needed to run franchise: 1
Absentee ownership? Yes

COSTS
Total cost: $15.2K-38.5K
Franchise fee: $6K-12K
Royalty fee: Varies
Term of agreement: 7 years renewable
  at no charge
Franchisees required to buy multiple
  units? No

FINANCING
In-house: Franchise fee
3rd-party: None

QUALIFICATIONS
Info not provided

TRAINING
At regional training facility: 6 days
Online training: 4 hours

BUSINESS SUPPORT
Newsletter
Meetings
Internet
Purchasing cooperatives

MARKETING SUPPORT
Co-op advertising
Regional marketing
Marketing literature

WORLD INSPECTION NETWORK

Ranked #176 in Entrepreneur Magazine's 2005 Franchise 500   *Financial rating: $$$*

6500 6th Ave. N.W.
Seattle, WA 98117
Ph: (800)967-8127
Fax: (206)441-3655
www.winfranchise.com
Home inspection service
Began: 1993, Franchising since: 1994
Headquarters size: 12 employees
Franchise department: 3 employees

U.S. franchises: 204
Canadian franchises: 0
Other foreign franchises: 0
Company-owned: 0

Seeking: All U.S.
Seeking in Canada? No
Exclusive territories? Yes
Homebased option? Yes
Kiosk option? No
Employees needed to run franchise: 0
Absentee ownership? Yes

COSTS
Total cost: $41.7K-49.5K
Franchise fee: $25K
Royalty fee: 7%
Term of agreement: 5 years renewable
    at 5% of franchise fee
Franchisees required to buy multiple
    units? No

FINANCING
In-house: Franchise fee
3rd-party: None

QUALIFICATIONS
Net worth: $40K
Cash liquidity: $13K
Experience:
    Marketing skills
    Working knowledge of
    Windows-based software
    Construction/remodeling experience
    Sales skills

TRAINING
At training facility: 2 weeks

BUSINESS SUPPORT
Newsletter
Meetings
Toll-free phone line
Grand opening
Internet
Security/safety procedures
Purchasing cooperatives

MARKETING SUPPORT
Co-op advertising
Ad slicks
National media campaign
Regional marketing

SERVICES   **PHOTOGRAPHY**

A DAY TO CHERISH WEDDING VIDEOS

Current financial data not available

10174 S. Memorial Dr.
South Jordan, UT 84095
Ph: (801)253-2450
www.adaytocherish.com
Wedding & special-occasion videos
Began: 2004, Franchising since: 2004
Headquarters size: 2 employees
Franchise department: 2 employees

U.S. franchises: 1
Canadian franchises: 0
Other foreign franchises: 0
Company-owned: 1

Seeking: All U.S.
Seeking in Canada? No
Exclusive territories? Yes
Homebased option? Yes
Kiosk option? No
Employees needed to run franchise: 0
Absentee ownership? No

COSTS
Total cost: $33.4K-38.4K
Franchise fee: $17.5K
Royalty fee: 6%
Term of agreement: 10 years renewable
    at $3K
Franchisees required to buy multiple
    units? No

FINANCING
No financing available

QUALIFICATIONS
Cash liquidity: $17.5K

TRAINING
At headquarters: 6 days
At franchisee's location: 2 days

BUSINESS SUPPORT
Internet
Field operations/evaluations

MARKETING SUPPORT
Marketing training

LIL' ANGELS PHOTOGRAPHY

Ranked #348 in Entrepreneur Magazine's 2005 Franchise 500　　　　*Financial rating: $$$$*

4041 Hatcher Cir.
Memphis, TN 38118
Ph: (800)358-9101
Fax: (901)682-2018
www.lilangelsphoto.com
Preschool & day-care photography
Began: 1996, Franchising since: 1998
Headquarters size: Info not provided
Franchise department:
　　Info not provided

U.S. franchises: 98
Canadian franchises: 1
Other foreign franchises: 1
Company-owned: 4

Seeking: All U.S.
Seeking in Canada? No
Exclusive territories? Yes
Homebased option? Yes
Kiosk option? No
Employees needed to run franchise: 1
Absentee ownership? Yes

COSTS
Total cost: $30.7K-35.2K
Franchise fee: $17K
Royalty fee: 0
Term of agreement: 10 years renewable
　　at no charge
Franchisees required to buy multiple
　　units? No

FINANCING
No financing available

QUALIFICATIONS
Cash liquidity: $32K
Experience:
　　Sales experience

TRAINING
At headquarters: 6 days
At franchisee's location: 2 days
At regional & annual conventions

BUSINESS SUPPORT
Meetings

MARKETING SUPPORT
Networking for securing
　　multi-location accounts

THE SPORTS SECTION

Ranked #191 in Entrepreneur Magazine's 2005 Franchise 500　　　　*Financial rating: $$$*

2150 Boggs Rd., #200
Duluth, GA 30096
Ph: (866)877-4746
Fax: (678)740-0808
www.sports-section.com
Youth & sports photography
Began: 1983, Franchising since: 1984
Headquarters size: 130 employees
Franchise department: 35 employees

U.S. franchises: 215
Canadian franchises: 2
Other foreign franchises: 10
Company-owned: 0

Seeking: All U.S.
Seeking in Canada? Yes
Exclusive territories? Yes
Homebased option? Yes
Kiosk option? No
Employees needed to run franchise: 2-4
Absentee ownership? No

COSTS
Total cost: $24.7K-61.6K
Franchise fee: $12.9K-33.9K
Royalty fee: 0
Term of agreement: 10 years renewable
　　at $1K
Franchisees required to buy multiple
　　units? Outside U.S. only

FINANCING
In-house: Equipment
3rd-party: None

QUALIFICATIONS
Cash liquidity: $18.9K-55.2K
Experience:
　　Marketing skills
　　Sales experience

TRAINING
At headquarters: 3-1/2 days
At franchisee's location: 5 days

BUSINESS SUPPORT
Newsletter
Meetings
Toll-free phone line
Grand opening
Internet
Security/safety procedures
Field operations/evaluations

MARKETING SUPPORT
Co-op advertising
Ad slicks
Regional marketing
Relationship w/several national
　　organizations

THE VISUAL IMAGE INC.

Financial rating: 0

100 E. Bockman Way
Sparta, TN 38583
Ph: (800)344-0323
Fax: (931)836-6279
www.thevisualimageinc.com
Preschool & pet photography
Began: 1984, Franchising since: 1994
Headquarters size: 3 employees
Franchise department: 3 employees

U.S. franchises: 19
Canadian franchises: 0
Other foreign franchises: 0
Company-owned: 2

Seeking: All U.S.
Seeking in Canada? Yes
Exclusive territories? Yes
Homebased option? Yes
Kiosk option? No
Employees needed to run franchise: 1-2
Absentee ownership? Yes

COSTS
Total cost: $37.3K-37.5K
Franchise fee: $23.5K
Royalty fee: 0
Term of agreement: 3 years renewable at $2K
Franchisees required to buy multiple units? No

FINANCING
In-house: Equipment, franchise fee
3rd-party: None

QUALIFICATIONS
Net worth: $50K
Cash liquidity: $35K
Experience:
    General business experience
    People skills
    Sales skills

TRAINING
At headquarters: 2 weeks
At franchisee's location: 1 week

BUSINESS SUPPORT
Newsletter
Meetings
Toll-free phone line
Internet
Field operations/evaluations
Purchasing cooperatives

MARKETING SUPPORT
Co-op advertising
Ad slicks
Regional marketing
Website

SERVICES ▶ **REAL ESTATE**

ASSIST-2-SELL

Ranked #78 in Entrepreneur Magazine's 2005 Franchise 500

Financial rating: $$$$

1610 Meadow Wood Ln.
Reno, NV 89502
Ph: (800)528-7816/(775)688-6060
Fax: (775)823-8823
www.assist2sell.com
Discount real estate services
Began: 1987, Franchising since: 1993
Headquarters size: 20 employees
Franchise department: 20 employees

U.S. franchises: 398
Canadian franchises: 5
Other foreign franchises: 0
Company-owned: 1
Units concentrated in all U.S.

Seeking: All U.S.
Seeking in Canada? Yes
Exclusive territories? Yes
Homebased option? No
Kiosk option? No
Employees needed to run franchise: 3
Absentee ownership? No

COSTS
Total cost: $35K-62K
Franchise fee: $19.5K
Royalty fee: 5%
Term of agreement: 5 years renewable at $2.995K
Franchisees required to buy multiple units? No

FINANCING
No financing available

QUALIFICATIONS
Cash liquidity: $25K+
Experience:
    Industry experience (minimum 2 years)

TRAINING
At headquarters: 5 days

BUSINESS SUPPORT
Newsletter
Meetings
Toll-free phone line
Internet

MARKETING SUPPORT
Ad slicks

AVALAR REAL ESTATE & MORTGAGE NETWORK

Ranked #389 in Entrepreneur Magazine's 2005 Franchise 500

Financial rating: $$$$

2911 Cleveland Ave., #A
Santa Rosa, CA 95403
Ph: (800)801-4030
Fax: (707)584-7950
www.avalar.biz
Real estate & mortgage services
Began: 1999, Franchising since: 1999
Headquarters size: 14 employees
Franchise department: 6 employees

U.S. franchises: 20
Canadian franchises: 0
Other foreign franchises: 0
Company-owned: 8

Seeking: All U.S.
Seeking in Canada? Yes
Exclusive territories? Yes
Homebased option? No
Kiosk option? No
Employees needed to run franchise:
    Info not provided
Absentee ownership? Info not provided

COSTS
Total cost: $31K-315.5K
Franchise fee: $4.4K-12.5K
Royalty fee: 5%
Term of agreement: 5 years renewable
    at no charge
Franchisees required to buy multiple
    units? No

FINANCING
No financing available

QUALIFICATIONS
Net worth: $250K/500K
Cash liquidity: $50K-100K
Experience:
    Industry experience
    General business experience
    Marketing skills

TRAINING
At headquarters: 5 weeks
At franchisee's location: Varies

BUSINESS SUPPORT
Newsletter
Meetings
Grand opening
Internet
Purchasing cooperatives

MARKETING SUPPORT
Based on needs of each franchisee

BETTER HOMES REALTY INC.

Financial rating: $$$$

1777 Botelho Dr., #390
Walnut Creek, CA 94596
Ph: (800)642-4428/(925)937-9001
Fax: (925)988-2770
www.bhr.com
Real estate
Began: 1964, Franchising since: 1975
Headquarters size: 6 employees
Franchise department: 2 employees

U.S. franchises: 40
Canadian franchises: 0
Other foreign franchises: 0
Company-owned: 0
Units concentrated in CA

Seeking: West
Focusing on: CA
Seeking in Canada? No
Exclusive territories? Yes
Homebased option? No
Kiosk option? No
Employees needed to run franchise:
    Info not provided
Absentee ownership? No

COSTS
Total cost: to $61.5K
Franchise fee: $9.95K
Royalty fee: Varies
Term of agreement: 5 years renewable
    at no charge
Franchisees required to buy multiple
    units? No

FINANCING
No financing available

QUALIFICATIONS
Experience:
    Industry experience
    General business experience

TRAINING
At headquarters
At franchisee's location

BUSINESS SUPPORT
Newsletter
Meetings
Toll-free phone line
Grand opening
Internet

MARKETING SUPPORT
Co-op advertising
Ad slicks
Agent marketing program

RE/MAX INT'L. INC.

Ranked #10 in Entrepreneur Magazine's 2005 Franchise 500   *Financial rating: $$$$*

P.O. Box 3907
Englewood, CO 80155-3907
Ph: (800)525-7452/(303)770-5531
Fax: (303)796-3599
www.remax.com
Real estate
Began: 1973, Franchising since: 1975
Headquarters size: 450 employees
Franchise department: 10 employees

U.S. franchises: 3,383
Canadian franchises: 565
Other foreign franchises: 1,097
Company-owned: 28
Units concentrated in all U.S.

Seeking: All U.S.
Seeking in Canada? Yes
Exclusive territories? No
Homebased option? No
Kiosk option? No
Employees needed to run franchise: 2
Absentee ownership? Yes

COSTS
Total cost: $20K-200K
Franchise fee: $10K-25K
Royalty fee: Varies
Term of agreement: 5 years renewable
Franchisees required to buy multiple
    units? No

FINANCING
In-house: Franchise fee
3rd-party: None

QUALIFICATIONS
Experience:
    Industry experience
    General business experience
    Marketing skills

TRAINING
At headquarters: 5 days
At semi-annual convention
Conference

BUSINESS SUPPORT
Newsletter
Meetings
Toll-free phone line
Grand opening
Internet
Security/safety procedures
Field operations/evaluations
Purchasing cooperatives

MARKETING SUPPORT
Ad slicks
National media campaign
Regional marketing
Brochures, magazines & videos
Proprietary satellite TV network
Online extranet

REALTY DIRECT FRANCHISE CORP.

Financial rating: $$$

20 Pidgeon Hill Dr., #104
Sterling, VA 20165
Ph: (800)359-5220/(703)327-2428
Fax: (703)852-3508
www.realtydirect.com
Real estate
Began: 2001, Franchising since: 2003
Headquarters size: 20 employees
Franchise department: 4 employees

U.S. franchises: 7
Canadian franchises: 0
Other foreign franchises: 0
Company-owned: 4
Units concentrated in all U.S.

Seeking: All U.S.
Seeking in Canada? No
Exclusive territories? Yes
Homebased option? Yes
Kiosk option? No
Employees needed to run franchise: 5
Absentee ownership? Yes

COSTS
Total cost: $29.9K-43.9K
Franchise fee: $16.9K
Royalty fee: 2%
Term of agreement: 6 years renewable
    at $2K
Franchisees required to buy multiple
    units? No

FINANCING
No financing available

QUALIFICATIONS
Net worth: $100K
Cash liquidity: $50K
Experience:
    Industry experience
    General business experience
    Marketing skills

TRAINING
At headquarters: 4 days
At franchisee's location: 1 day

BUSINESS SUPPORT
Newsletter
Meetings
Toll-free phone line
Internet
Purchasing cooperatives

MARKETING SUPPORT
Co-op advertising
National media campaign
Templates

REALTY EXECUTIVES INT'L. INC.

Ranked #73 in Entrepreneur Magazine's 2005 Franchise 500   *Financial rating: $$$$*

2398 E. Camelback Rd., #900
Phoenix, AZ 85016
Ph: (800)252-3366/(602)957-0747
Fax: (602)224-5542
www.realtyexecutives.com
Real estate
Began: 1965, Franchising since: 1973
Headquarters size: 15 employees
Franchise department: 4 employees

U.S. franchises: 604
Canadian franchises: 28
Other foreign franchises: 31
Company-owned: 0
Units concentrated in all U.S.

Seeking: All U.S.
Seeking in Canada? Yes
Exclusive territories? Yes
Homebased option? No
Kiosk option? No
Employees needed to run franchise:
    Info not provided
Absentee ownership? Yes

COSTS
Total cost: $18.6K-88.1K
Franchise fee: $1K-26K
Royalty fee: $50/licensee
Term of agreement: 5 years renewable
    at no charge
Franchisees required to buy multiple
    units? No

FINANCING
In-house: None
3rd-party: Accounts receivable,
    equipment, franchise fee,
    inventory, payroll, startup costs

QUALIFICATIONS
Cash liquidity: $20K
Experience:
    Industry experience
    General business experience
    Marketing skills

TRAINING
At headquarters: 3 days
At annual meetings

BUSINESS SUPPORT
Newsletter
Meetings
Toll-free phone line
Grand opening
Internet
Lease negotiations
Security/safety procedures
Field operations/evaluations

MARKETING SUPPORT
Co-op advertising
Ad slicks
National media campaign
Regional marketing

WEICHERT REAL ESTATE AFFILIATES INC.

Ranked #213 in Entrepreneur Magazine's 2005 Franchise 500   *Financial rating: $$$$*

225 Littleton Rd.
Morris Plains, NJ 07950
Ph: (973)359-8377
Fax: (973)292-1428
www.weichert.com
Real estate
Began: 1969, Franchising since: 2000
Headquarters size: 1200 employees
Franchise department: 17 employees

U.S. franchises: 95
Canadian franchises: 0
Other foreign franchises: 0
Company-owned: 180

Seeking: Northeast, South, Southeast,
    Midwest
Seeking in Canada? No
Exclusive territories? Yes
Homebased option? No
Kiosk option? No
Employees needed to run franchise: 15
Absentee ownership? Yes

COSTS
Total cost: $45K-254K
Franchise fee: $25K
Royalty fee: 6%
Term of agreement: 7 years renewable
    at $1K
Franchisees required to buy multiple
    units? Outside U.S. only

FINANCING
No financing available

QUALIFICATIONS
Experience:
    Industry experience
    General business experience
    Marketing skills

TRAINING
At headquarters: 4 days
At franchisee's location: Ongoing
At annual conference

BUSINESS SUPPORT
Newsletter
Meetings
Toll-free phone line
Grand opening
Internet
Field operations/evaluations
Purchasing cooperatives

MARKETING SUPPORT
Co-op advertising
Ad slicks
National media campaign
Regional marketing
PR program
Custom marketing materials

WHY USA

Financial rating: $$

8301 Creekside Cir., #101
Bloomington, MN 55437
Ph: (952)841-7050
Fax: (952)841-7061
www.whyusa.com
Real estate
Began: 1988, Franchising since: 1989
Headquarters size: 10 employees
Franchise department: 4 employees

U.S. franchises: 61
Canadian franchises: 0
Other foreign franchises: 0
Company-owned: 2

Seeking: All U.S.
Seeking in Canada? No
Exclusive territories? Yes
Homebased option? No
Kiosk option? Yes
Employees needed to run franchise: 2
Absentee ownership? Yes

COSTS
Total cost: $17K-103.4K
Kiosk cost: $20K
Franchise fee: $19.99K/9.5K
Royalty fee: Varies
Term of agreement: 3 years renewable
 at no charge
Franchisees required to buy multiple
 units? No

FINANCING
In-house: Franchise fee
3rd-party: None

QUALIFICATIONS
Experience:
 General business experience
 Marketing skills

TRAINING
At headquarters: 3 days
At franchisee's location: 2 days
Conferences
Monthly teleconferences

BUSINESS SUPPORT
Meetings
Internet
Lease negotiations
Field operations/evaluations

MARKETING SUPPORT
Co-op advertising
Ad slicks
Campaigns

SERVICES ▶ **SECURITY**

INTERQUEST DETECTION CANINES
Ranked #346 in Entrepreneur Magazine's 2005 Franchise 500

Financial rating: $$$

21900 Tomball Pkwy.
Houston, TX 77070-1526
Ph: (281)320-1231
Fax: (281)320-2512
www.interquestfranchise.com
Canine detection services
Began: 1988, Franchising since: 1999
Headquarters size: 12 employees
Franchise department: 9 employees

U.S. franchises: 42
Canadian franchises: 0
Other foreign franchises: 0
Company-owned: 1

Seeking: All U.S.
Seeking in Canada? No
Exclusive territories? Yes
Homebased option? Yes
Kiosk option? No
Employees needed to run franchise: 2
Absentee ownership? No

COSTS
Total cost: $46.5K-85.3K
Franchise fee: $30K
Royalty fee: 6%
Term of agreement: 10 years renewable
 at $3K
Franchisees required to buy multiple
 units? No

FINANCING
In-house: Equipment
3rd-party: Franchise fee, startup costs

QUALIFICATIONS
Net worth: $250K
Cash liquidity: $50K
Experience:
 General business experience
 Marketing skills

TRAINING
At headquarters: 2 weeks
At franchisee's location: 2 days
Quarterly quality assurance training

BUSINESS SUPPORT
Newsletter
Meetings
Toll-free phone line
Internet
Field operations/evaluations

MARKETING SUPPORT
Co-op advertising
National media campaign

SHIELD SECURITY SYSTEMS

Current financial data not available

1690 Walden Ave.
Buffalo, NY 14225
Ph: (716)681-6677
Fax: (716)636-8819
www.shieldsecurity.net
Burglar/fire alarm installation & sales
Began: 1976, Franchising since: 1992
Headquarters size: 4 employees
Franchise department: 5 employees

U.S. franchises: 7
Canadian franchises: 0
Other foreign franchises: 0
Company-owned: 1

Seeking: All U.S.
Seeking in Canada? Yes
Exclusive territories? Yes
Homebased option? Yes
Kiosk option? No
Employees needed to run franchise: 2-4
Absentee ownership? Yes

COSTS
Total cost: $33.8K-60.7K
Franchise fee: $30K
Royalty fee: 5%
Term of agreement: 10 years renewable
    at $1.5K
Franchisees required to buy multiple
    units? No

FINANCING
No financing available

QUALIFICATIONS
Net worth: $250K
Cash liquidity: $50K
Experience:
    General business experience
    Marketing skills

TRAINING
At headquarters: 7 days
At franchisee's location: 7 days
Online training: 4-6 weeks

BUSINESS SUPPORT
Newsletter
Meetings
Toll-free phone line
Internet
Security/safety procedures
Field operations/evaluations
Purchasing cooperatives

MARKETING SUPPORT
Ad slicks
Corporate marketing plan

SIGNATURE ALERT SECURITY

Financial rating: 0

746 E. Winchester St., #G10
Salt Lake City, UT 84107
Ph: (800)957-1030/(801)743-0101
Fax: (801)743-0808
www.signaturealert.com
Security systems
Began: 1999, Franchising since: 2003
Headquarters size: 9 employees
Franchise department: 7 employees

U.S. franchises: 16
Canadian franchises: 0
Other foreign franchises: 0
Company-owned: 3
Units concentrated in AZ, CA, CO, IN,
    NV, SC, TX, UT, VA

Seeking: All U.S.
Seeking in Canada? No
Exclusive territories? Yes
Homebased option? Yes
Kiosk option? Yes
Employees needed to run franchise: 2
Absentee ownership? No

COSTS
Total cost: $22K-42K
Franchise fee: $10K-19K
Royalty fee: 10%
Term of agreement: 10 years renewable
    at $3K
Franchisees required to buy multiple
    units? No

FINANCING
No financing available

QUALIFICATIONS
Net worth: $100K
Cash liquidity: $25K-41K

TRAINING
At headquarters: 5 days
At franchisee's location: 2 days
Regional training: 2 days

BUSINESS SUPPORT
Newsletter
Meetings
Toll-free phone line
Grand opening
Internet
Security/safety procedures
Field operations/evaluations
Purchasing cooperatives

MARKETING SUPPORT
Co-op advertising

SERVICES ▸ **SENIOR CARE**

COMFORCARE SENIOR SERVICES INC.

Ranked #384 in Entrepreneur Magazine's 2005 Franchise 500　　　*Financial rating: $$$*

2510 Telegraph Rd., #100
Bloomfield Hills, MI 48302
Ph: (800)886-4044
Fax: (248)745-9763
www.comforcare.com/franchise
Nonmedical home-care services
Began: 1996, Franchising since: 2001
Headquarters size: 15 employees
Franchise department: 15 employees

U.S. franchises: 41
Canadian franchises: 0
Other foreign franchises: 0
Company-owned: 1
Units concentrated in all U.S.

Seeking: All U.S.
Seeking in Canada? No
Exclusive territories? Yes
Homebased option? No
Kiosk option? No
Employees needed to run franchise: 1
Absentee ownership? Yes

COSTS
Total cost: $40K-55K
Franchise fee: $15.5K
Royalty fee: 3-5%
Term of agreement: 10 years renewable
　at $2K at most
Franchisees required to buy multiple
　units? No

FINANCING
In-house: Accounts receivable
3rd-party: Franchise fee, startup costs

QUALIFICATIONS
Net worth: $60K
Cash liquidity: $30K

TRAINING
At headquarters: 1 week
At franchisee's location: Several times
　per year
Training available for key employees

BUSINESS SUPPORT
Newsletter
Meetings
Toll-free phone line
Grand opening
Internet
Lease negotiations
Security/safety procedures
Field operations/evaluations
Purchasing cooperatives

MARKETING SUPPORT
Co-op advertising
Ad slicks
Regional marketing
Online ordering
Strategic alliances
PowerPoint presentations

COMFORT KEEPERS

Ranked #116 in Entrepreneur Magazine's 2005 Franchise 500　　　*Financial rating: $$$$*

6640 Poe Ave., #200
Dayton, OH 45414
Ph: (800)387-2415
Fax: (937)264-3103
www.comfortkeepers.com
Nonmedical in-home senior care
Began: 1998, Franchising since: 1999
Headquarters size: 22 employees
Franchise department: 5 employees

U.S. franchises: 465
Canadian franchises: 6
Other foreign franchises: 0
Company-owned: 0
Units concentrated in all U.S.

Seeking: All U.S.
Seeking in Canada? No
Exclusive territories? Yes
Homebased option? Yes
Kiosk option? No
Employees needed to run franchise:
　15-20
Absentee ownership? No

COSTS
Total cost: $41K-68K
Franchise fee: $23.2K
Royalty fee: 5-3%
Term of agreement: 10 years renewable
　at no charge
Franchisees required to buy multiple
　units? No

FINANCING
In-house: None
3rd-party: Equipment, franchise fee,
　startup costs

QUALIFICATIONS
Net worth: $75K+
Cash liquidity: $40K-60K
Experience:
　General business experience
　Marketing skills
　Able to manage people

TRAINING
At headquarters: 1 week
At franchisee's location: 1-2 days
Ongoing training

BUSINESS SUPPORT
Newsletter
Meetings
Toll-free phone line
Grand opening
Internet
Security/safety procedures
Field operations/evaluations
Purchasing cooperatives

MARKETING SUPPORT
Co-op advertising
Ad slicks
Regional marketing
Franchisee websites

ELDIRECT HOMECARE

Current financial data not available

716 W. Sycamore
Fayetteville, AR 72703
Ph: (479)443-7173
Fax: (479)443-0183
www.eldirecthomecare.com
Non-medical in-home care
Began: 1996, Franchising since: 2002
Headquarters size: 6 employees
Franchise department: 6 employees

U.S. franchises: 0
Canadian franchises: 0
Other foreign franchises: 0
Company-owned: 2

Seeking: All U.S.
Seeking in Canada? No
Exclusive territories? Yes
Homebased option? No
Kiosk option? No
Employees needed to run franchise: 2
Absentee ownership? Yes

COSTS
Total cost: $21.9K-29.7K
Franchise fee: $15K
Royalty fee: 5%
Term of agreement: 10 years renewable
    at 10% of current franchise fee
Franchisees required to buy multiple
    units? No

FINANCING
No financing available

QUALIFICATIONS
Info not provided

TRAINING
At headquarters: Up to 5 days
At franchisee's location: Up to 5 days

BUSINESS SUPPORT
Newsletter
Meetings
Toll-free phone line
Grand opening
Internet
Security/safety procedures
Field operations/evaluations
Purchasing cooperatives

MARKETING SUPPORT
Co-op advertising
Ad slicks
National media campaign
Regional marketing

GRISWOLD SPECIAL CARE

Ranked #331 in Entrepreneur Magazine's 2005 Franchise 500

Financial rating: $$$$

717 Bethlehem Pike, #300
Erdenheim, PA 19073
Ph: (215)402-0200
Fax: (215)402-0202
www.griswoldspecialcare.com
Nonmedical home-care services
Began: 1982, Franchising since: 1984
Headquarters size: 70 employees
Franchise department:
    Info not provided

U.S. franchises: 77
Canadian franchises: 0
Other foreign franchises: 2
Company-owned: 8
Units concentrated in CT, DE, FL, GA,
    IL, MA, MD, MI, NJ, OH, PA, SC,
    TN, TX, VA, VT

Seeking: Northeast, South, Southeast,
    Midwest, Southwest
Focusing on: FL, GA, KY, MA, MD,
    MI, MO, NJ, OH, PA, RI, SC, TN,
    TX, VT, WV; other states evaluated
    on a case-by-case basis
Seeking in Canada? Yes
Exclusive territories? Yes

Homebased option? Yes
Kiosk option? No
Employees needed to run franchise: 1-2
Absentee ownership? No

COSTS
Total cost: $15K-39K
Franchise fee: $9K
Royalty fee: Varies
Term of agreement: 7 years renewable
    at no charge
Franchisees required to buy multiple
    units? No

FINANCING
In-house: None
3rd-party: Payroll

QUALIFICATIONS
Experience:
    Industry experience
    General business experience
    Marketing skills

TRAINING
At headquarters: 1 week
At franchisee's location: 2-4 days
Ongoing in-field training
Annual workshops

BUSINESS SUPPORT
Newsletter
Meetings
Toll-free phone line
Internet
Security/safety procedures
Field operations/evaluations
Purchasing cooperatives

MARKETING SUPPORT
Co-op advertising
Ad slicks
National media campaign
Regional marketing
Ongoing phone support
Annual workshop series
Customized software
Visits

HOME HELPERS/DIRECT LINK

Ranked #97 in Entrepreneur Magazine's 2005 Franchise 500　　　　*Financial rating: $$$$*

10700 Montgomery Rd., #300
Cincinnati, OH 45242
Ph: (800)216-4196
Fax: (513)563-2691
www.homehelpers.cc
Nonmedical care services
Began: 1997, Franchising since: 1997
Headquarters size: 15 employees
Franchise department: 15 employees

U.S. franchises: 336
Canadian franchises: 2
Other foreign franchises: 0
Company-owned: 0
Units concentrated in all U.S.

Seeking: All U.S.
Seeking in Canada? Yes
Exclusive territories? Yes
Homebased option? Yes
Kiosk option? No
Employees needed to run franchise: 2
Absentee ownership? Yes

COSTS
Total cost: $25.7K-41.4K
Franchise fee: $15.9K
Royalty fee: 6-4%
Term of agreement: 10 years renewable
　　at no charge
Franchisees required to buy multiple
　　units? No

FINANCING
In-house: Franchise fee
3rd-party: None

QUALIFICATIONS
Cash liquidity: $9.5K

TRAINING
At headquarters: 5 days
Regional & national meetings: 5 days

BUSINESS SUPPORT
Newsletter
Meetings
Toll-free phone line
Internet
Security/safety procedures
Field operations/evaluations

MARKETING SUPPORT
Ad slicks
National media campaign
Electronic ad & presentation formats

HOME INSTEAD SENIOR CARE

Ranked #87 in Entrepreneur Magazine's 2005 Franchise 500　　　　*Financial rating: $$$$*

13330 California St., #200
Omaha, NE 68154
Ph: (888)484-5759/(402)498-4466
Fax: (402)498-5757
www.homeinstead.com
Nonmedical senior-care services
Began: 1994, Franchising since: 1995
Headquarters size: 60 employees
Franchise department: 9 employees

U.S. franchises: 473
Canadian franchises: 13
Other foreign franchises: 58
Company-owned: 2
Units concentrated in all U.S.

Seeking: All U.S.
Seeking in Canada? Yes
Exclusive territories? Yes
Homebased option? No
Kiosk option? No
Employees needed to run franchise: 85
Absentee ownership? No

COSTS
Total cost: $34.1K-46.1K
Franchise fee: $23.5K
Royalty fee: 5%
Term of agreement: 10 years renewable
　　at no charge
Franchisees required to buy multiple
　　units? Outside U.S. only

FINANCING
In-house: None
3rd-party: Accounts receivable,
　　equipment, franchise fee,
　　inventory, payroll, startup costs

QUALIFICATIONS
Cash liquidity: $50K-60K

TRAINING
At headquarters: 1 week
At franchisee's location: 13 weeks
Onsite visits

BUSINESS SUPPORT
Newsletter
Meetings
Toll-free phone line
Internet
Security/safety procedures
Field operations/evaluations
Purchasing cooperatives

MARKETING SUPPORT
Ad slicks
National media campaign
National lead development services

HOMEWATCH CAREGIVERS
Ranked #340 in Entrepreneur Magazine's 2005 Franchise 500 *Financial rating: $$$*

2865 S. Colorado Blvd.
Denver, CO 80222
Ph: (800)777-9770/(303)758-7290
Fax: (303)758-1724
www.homewatch-intl.com
Home-care services
Began: 1973, Franchising since: 1986
Headquarters size: 11 employees
Franchise department: 6 employees

U.S. franchises: 67
Canadian franchises: 2
Other foreign franchises: 6
Company-owned: 0

Seeking: All U.S.
Seeking in Canada? Yes
Exclusive territories? Yes
Homebased option? No
Kiosk option? No
Employees needed to run franchise: 3-30
Absentee ownership? Yes

COSTS
Total cost: $32.5K-65.9K
Franchise fee: $15K-19.5K
Royalty fee: 3-5%
Term of agreement: 10 years renewable
    at no charge
Franchisees required to buy multiple
    units? Outside U.S. only

FINANCING
No financing available

QUALIFICATIONS
Net worth: $250K
Cash liquidity: $35K
Experience:
    Industry experience
    General business experience
    Marketing skills
    Sales skills
    Management skills
    People oriented

TRAINING
At headquarters: 6 days
At franchisee's location: 2-3 days
Ongoing

BUSINESS SUPPORT
Newsletter
Meetings
Grand opening
Internet
Security/safety procedures
Field operations/evaluations
Purchasing cooperatives

MARKETING SUPPORT
Co-op advertising
Ad slicks
Regional marketing

RIGHT AT HOME INC.
Ranked #352 in Entrepreneur Magazine's 2005 Franchise 500 *Financial rating: $$$*

11949 Q St., #S-100
Omaha, NE 68137
Ph: (402)697-7537
Fax: (402)697-0289
www.rightathome.net
Senior home care & medical staffing
Began: 1995, Franchising since: 2000
Headquarters size: 14 employees
Franchise department: 8 employees

U.S. franchises: 58
Canadian franchises: 0
Other foreign franchises: 0
Company-owned: 1
Units concentrated in all U.S.

Seeking: All U.S.
Focusing on: All U.S. except HI, ND,
    RI
Seeking in Canada? No
Exclusive territories? Yes
Homebased option? No
Kiosk option? No
Employees needed to run franchise:
    Info not provided
Absentee ownership? No

COSTS
Total cost: $29.3K-65.4K
Franchise fee: $17.8K
Royalty fee: 5%
Term of agreement: 10 years renewable
    at no charge
Franchisees required to buy multiple
    units? No

FINANCING
No financing available

QUALIFICATIONS
Experience:
    General business experience

TRAINING
At headquarters: 2 weeks
At franchisee's location: Varies

BUSINESS SUPPORT
Newsletter
Meetings
Toll-free phone line
Internet
Lease negotiations
Security/safety procedures
Field operations/evaluations

MARKETING SUPPORT
Ad slicks
Website

VISITING ANGELS

Ranked #193 in Entrepreneur Magazine's 2005 Franchise 500   *Financial rating: $$$*

28 W. Eagle Rd., #201
Havertown, PA 19083
Ph: (800)365-4189/(610)924-0630
Fax: (610)924-9690
www.livingassistance.com
Nonmedical home-care services for
    seniors
Began: 1992, Franchising since: 1998
Headquarters size: 13 employees
Franchise department: 10 employees

U.S. franchises: 225
Canadian franchises: 5
Other foreign franchises: 0
Company-owned: 1

Seeking: All U.S.
Seeking in Canada? No
Exclusive territories? Yes
Homebased option? Yes
Kiosk option? No
Employees needed to run franchise: 1
Absentee ownership? No

COSTS

Total cost: $25.99K-47.2K
Franchise fee: $25.99K-47.2K
Royalty fee: 2.95-2%
Term of agreement: 10 years renewable
    at $2.5K
Franchisees required to buy multiple
    units? No

FINANCING

No financing available

QUALIFICATIONS

Net worth: $30K-50K
Cash liquidity: $15K

TRAINING

At headquarters: 5 days
Regional meetings

BUSINESS SUPPORT

Newsletter
Meetings
Toll-free phone line
Internet
Purchasing cooperatives

MARKETING SUPPORT

Co-op advertising
National media campaign
PR support
Internet marketing

SERVICES ▸ **MISCELLANEOUS**

BALLOON CAFE INC.

Current financial data not available

P.O. Box 398
Providence, UT 84332-0398
Ph: (435)752-5729
Fax: (435)787-8654
www.ballooncafe.com
Balloon design & delivery services
Began: 1999, Franchising since: 2001
Headquarters size: 2 employees
Franchise department:
    Info not provided

U.S. franchises: 2
Canadian franchises: 0
Other foreign franchises: 0
Company-owned: 0
Units concentrated in GA, UT

Seeking: All U.S.
Seeking in Canada? No
Exclusive territories? Yes
Homebased option? Yes
Kiosk option? No
Employees needed to run franchise: 1-2
Absentee ownership? No

COSTS

Total cost: $8K-30.1K
Franchise fee: $6K-20K
Royalty fee: $60-200/mo.
Term of agreement: 5 years renewable
    at $1K
Franchisees required to buy multiple
    units? No

FINANCING

No financing available

QUALIFICATIONS

Net worth: $8K-30.1K
Cash liquidity: $8K-30.1K
Experience:
    General business experience
    Marketing skills

TRAINING

At headquarters: 4-1/2 days

BUSINESS SUPPORT

Newsletter
Grand opening
Internet
Security/safety procedures

MARKETING SUPPORT

Ad slicks

BLACK DIAMOND GOLF

Current financial data not available

10914 Wye Dr.
San Antonio, TX 78217
Ph: (210)590-2384
Fax: (210)590-2386
www.theclubpolisher.com
Golf-club cleaning system
Began: 2001, Franchising since: 2003
Headquarters size: 6 employees
Franchise department: 6 employees

U.S. franchises: 55
Canadian franchises: 0
Other foreign franchises: 0
Company-owned: 0

Seeking: All U.S.
Seeking in Canada? Yes
Exclusive territories? Yes
Homebased option? Yes
Kiosk option? No
Employees needed to run franchise:
    Info not provided
Absentee ownership? No

COSTS
Total cost: $25K-100K
Franchise fee: $3K-50K
Royalty fee: 0
Term of agreement: 12 years renewable
Franchisees required to buy multiple
    units? No

FINANCING
In-house: None
3rd-party: Equipment, franchise fee,
    startup costs

QUALIFICATIONS
Net worth: $100K-500K
Cash liquidity: $50K

TRAINING
At headquarters: 2 days

BUSINESS SUPPORT
Newsletter
Meetings
Toll-free phone line
Grand opening
Internet
Security/safety procedures
Field operations/evaluations

MARKETING SUPPORT
Co-op advertising
Ad slicks
National media campaign
Regional marketing

CASE IN POINT

Current financial data not available

P.O. Box 1286
Londonderry, NH 03053-1286
Ph: (800)370-2116
Fax: (800)397-2963
www.caseinpointfranchise.com
Investigation services
Began: 1992, Franchising since: 2002
Headquarters size: 18 employees
Franchise department: 5 employees

U.S. franchises: 2
Canadian franchises: 0
Other foreign franchises: 0
Company-owned: 4

Seeking: All U.S.
Seeking in Canada? No
Exclusive territories? Yes
Homebased option? No
Kiosk option? No
Employees needed to run franchise: 1
Absentee ownership? No

COSTS
Total cost: $40K
Franchise fee: $10K
Royalty fee: 6%
Term of agreement: 10 years renewable
Franchisees required to buy multiple
    units? No

FINANCING
No financing available

QUALIFICATIONS
Experience:
    Industry experience
    General business experience

TRAINING
At headquarters: 2 weeks
At franchisee's location: 1 week

BUSINESS SUPPORT
Toll-free phone line
Grand opening
Field operations/evaluations
Purchasing cooperatives

MARKETING SUPPORT
Ad slicks
Regional marketing

COMPLETE MUSIC

Ranked #302 in Entrepreneur Magazine's 2005 Franchise 500　　　*Financial rating: $$$$*

7877 L St.
Omaha, NE 68127
Ph: (800)843-3866/(402)339-0001
Fax: (402)898-1777
www.cmusic.com
Mobile DJ entertainment service
Began: 1974, Franchising since: 1983
Headquarters size: 10 employees
Franchise department: 6 employees

U.S. franchises: 159
Canadian franchises: 2
Other foreign franchises: 0
Company-owned: 1
Units concentrated in all U.S.

Seeking: All U.S.
Seeking in Canada? Yes
Exclusive territories? Yes
Homebased option? Yes
Kiosk option? No
Employees needed to run franchise: 3-50
Absentee ownership? No

COSTS
Total cost: $19.8K-33K
Franchise fee: $12K-20K
Royalty fee: 6.5-8%
Term of agreement: 10 years renewable
　　at no charge
Franchisees required to buy multiple
　　units? No

FINANCING
In-house: Equipment, franchise fee
3rd-party: None

QUALIFICATIONS
Net worth: $50K
Cash liquidity: $10K
Experience:
　　General business experience

TRAINING
At headquarters: 9 days
At franchisee's location: 4 days

BUSINESS SUPPORT
Newsletter
Meetings
Toll-free phone line
Internet
Security/safety procedures
Field operations/evaluations

MARKETING SUPPORT
Ad slicks
National media campaign
Regional marketing

THE DENTIST'S CHOICE

Ranked #344 in Entrepreneur Magazine's 2005 Franchise 500　　　*Financial rating: $$$*

724 Mays Blvd., #10-297
Incline Village, NV 89451
Ph: (800)757-1333
www.thedentistschoice.com
Dental handpiece repairs & products
Began: 1992, Franchising since: 1994
Headquarters size: 5 employees
Franchise department: 1 employee

U.S. franchises: 125
Canadian franchises: 3
Other foreign franchises: 0
Company-owned: 1
Units concentrated in all U.S.

Seeking: All U.S.
Seeking in Canada? Yes
Exclusive territories? Yes
Homebased option? Yes
Kiosk option? No
Employees needed to run franchise: 0
Absentee ownership? No

COSTS
Total cost: $25.9K-30.1K
Franchise fee: $17.5K
Royalty fee: 1-5%
Term of agreement: 10 years renewable
　　at $1.5K
Franchisees required to buy multiple
　　units? No

FINANCING
No financing available

QUALIFICATIONS
Net worth: $25K
Cash liquidity: $25K
Experience:
　　Marketing skills
　　Mechanical skills

TRAINING
At headquarters: 1 week
Additional training as needed

BUSINESS SUPPORT
Newsletter
Meetings
Toll-free phone line
Grand opening
Internet
Field operations/evaluations
Purchasing cooperatives

MARKETING SUPPORT
Ad slicks
Comprehensive marketing manual

DRY CLEANING STATION

Financial rating: $$

8301 Golden Valley Rd., #240
Minneapolis, MN 55427
Ph: (800)655-8134
Fax: (763)542-2246
www.drycleaningstation.com
Dry cleaning
Began: 1987, Franchising since: 1992
Headquarters size: 3 employees
Franchise department: 2 employees

U.S. franchises: 25
Canadian franchises: 0
Other foreign franchises: 0
Company-owned: 1

Seeking: All U.S.
Seeking in Canada? No
Exclusive territories? Yes
Homebased option? No
Kiosk option? No
Employees needed to run franchise: 0
Absentee ownership? No

COSTS
Total cost: $48K-485.5K
Franchise fee: $15K-25K
Royalty fee: Varies
Term of agreement: 15 years renewable
    at no charge
Franchisees required to buy multiple
    units? No

FINANCING
In-house: None
3rd-party: Equipment, franchise fee,
    inventory, startup costs

QUALIFICATIONS
Net worth: $100K-500K
Cash liquidity: $20K-200K
Experience:
    General business experience
    Marketing skills

TRAINING
At headquarters: 1-3 weeks
At franchisee's location: Up to 1 week

BUSINESS SUPPORT
Newsletter
Meetings
Toll-free phone line
Grand opening
Internet
Lease negotiations
Security/safety procedures
Field operations/evaluations

MARKETING SUPPORT
Co-op advertising
Ad slicks
Regional marketing

EIGHT AT EIGHT DINNER CLUB

Financial rating: 0

P.O. Box 250682
Atlanta, GA 30325
Ph: (404)888-0988
www.8at8.com
Dinner club for singles
Began: 1998, Franchising since: 2003
Headquarters size: 4 employees
Franchise department: 1 employee

U.S. franchises: 3
Canadian franchises: 0
Other foreign franchises: 0
Company-owned: 4

Seeking: All U.S.
Seeking in Canada? No
Exclusive territories? Yes
Homebased option? Yes
Kiosk option? No
Employees needed to run franchise: 1
Absentee ownership? No

COSTS
Total cost: $28.6K-44.6K
Franchise fee: $25.5K
Royalty fee: 10%
Term of agreement: 5 years renewable
    at $5K
Franchisees required to buy multiple
    units? No

FINANCING
No financing available

QUALIFICATIONS
Net worth: $100K
Cash liquidity: $25K
Experience:
    General business experience
    Marketing skills

TRAINING
At headquarters: 30 hours

BUSINESS SUPPORT
Meetings
Grand opening
Internet
Field operations/evaluations

MARKETING SUPPORT
Co-op advertising
Ad slicks
National media campaign
Collateral material
DVDs
Signage

HOUSEWATCH U.S.

Current financial data not available

P.O. Box 576
Greenport, NY 11944
Ph: (631)477-6066
www.housewatchus.com
House watching services for
    vacation/second homes
Began: 2004, Franchising since: 2004
Headquarters size: 6 employees
Franchise department: 2 employees

U.S. franchises: 3
Canadian franchises: 0
Other foreign franchises: 0
Company-owned: 0

Seeking: All U.S.
Seeking in Canada? No
Exclusive territories? Yes
Homebased option? Yes
Kiosk option? No
Employees needed to run franchise: 1
Absentee ownership? Yes

COSTS
Total cost: $20.1K
Franchise fee: $14.5K
Royalty fee: 0
Term of agreement: 5 years renewable
    at $500
Franchisees required to buy multiple
    units? No

FINANCING
In-house: Franchise fee
3rd-party: None

QUALIFICATIONS
Net worth: $30K
Cash liquidity: $15K
Experience:
    General business experience

TRAINING
At headquarters: 1 week
At franchisee's location: 1 week

BUSINESS SUPPORT
Newsletter
Meetings
Toll-free phone line
Grand opening
Internet
Security/safety procedures
Field operations/evaluations

MARKETING SUPPORT
Co-op advertising
Ad slicks
Regional marketing

THE LIGHTEN UP! WEIGHT LOSS PROGRAM INC.

Financial rating: $

2608 3rd Ave. N.E.
Seattle, WA 98155
Ph: (206)441-8550
Fax: (206)448-5938
www.lighten-up.com
Weight-loss program
Began: 1987, Franchising since: 2003
Headquarters size: 6 employees
Franchise department: 3 employees

U.S. franchises: 3
Canadian franchises: 0
Other foreign franchises: 0
Company-owned: 1
Units concentrated in all U.S.

Seeking: All U.S.
Seeking in Canada? Yes
Exclusive territories? No
Homebased option? No
Kiosk option? No
Employees needed to run franchise: 1
Absentee ownership? No

COSTS
Total cost: $40.5K-71K
Franchise fee: 0
Royalty fee: $395
Term of agreement: 1 year renewable
    at $1K
Franchisees required to buy multiple
    units? No

FINANCING
No financing available

QUALIFICATIONS
Net worth: $50K
Cash liquidity: $20K
Experience:
    General business experience
    Marketing skills

TRAINING
At headquarters: 4 days

BUSINESS SUPPORT
Meetings
Toll-free phone line
Internet
Lease negotiations
Field operations/evaluations

MARKETING SUPPORT
Co-op advertising
Ad slicks
Weekly sales meetings by phone

MY GIRL FRIDAY

Financial rating: $$

1776 Mentor Ave.
Cincinnati, OH 45212
Ph: (513)531-4475
Fax: (513)631-3693
www.egirlfriday.com
Personal concierge services
Began: 1999, Franchising since: 2004
Headquarters size: 20 employees
Franchise department: 3 employees

U.S. franchises: 0
Canadian franchises: 0
Other foreign franchises: 0
Company-owned: 0

Seeking: All U.S.
Seeking in Canada? No
Exclusive territories? Yes
Homebased option? Yes
Kiosk option? No
Employees needed to run franchise:
    Info not provided
Absentee ownership? Yes

COSTS
Total cost: $47K-86K
Franchise fee: $31.5K
Royalty fee: 6%
Term of agreement: 10 years renewable
    at $500
Franchisees required to buy multiple
    units? No

FINANCING
No financing available

QUALIFICATIONS
Net worth: $150K
Cash liquidity: $75K
Experience:
    General business experience
    Marketing skills
    Sales experience

TRAINING
At headquarters: 4 days
At franchisee's location: 2 days

BUSINESS SUPPORT
Newsletter
Meetings
Toll-free phone line
Grand opening
Internet
Security/safety procedures
Field operations/evaluations
Purchasing cooperatives

MARKETING SUPPORT
Co-op advertising
Ad slicks
National media campaign
Regional marketing

PROFESSIONAL HOUSE DOCTORS INC.

Current financial data not available

1406 E. 14th St.
Des Moines, IA 50316
Ph: (515)265-6667
www.radonfranchise.com
Environmental & building-science
    services
Began: 1982, Franchising since: 1991
Headquarters size: 3 employees
Franchise department: 3 employees

U.S. franchises: 7
Canadian franchises: 0
Other foreign franchises: 0
Company-owned: 1
Units concentrated in IA

Seeking: All U.S.
Seeking in Canada? No
Exclusive territories? Yes
Homebased option? Yes
Kiosk option? No
Employees needed to run franchise:
    Info not provided
Absentee ownership? No

COSTS
Total cost: $15K
Franchise fee: $9.8K
Royalty fee: 6%
Term of agreement: 5 years renewable
Franchisees required to buy multiple
    units? No

FINANCING
No financing available

QUALIFICATIONS
Net worth: $50K
Cash liquidity: $10K

TRAINING
At headquarters: 2 weeks
At franchisee's location: Varies

BUSINESS SUPPORT
Newsletter
Meetings
Toll-free phone line
Grand opening
Internet
Security/safety procedures
Field operations/evaluations
Purchasing cooperatives

MARKETING SUPPORT
Co-op advertising
Ad slicks
Regional marketing

PROTOCOL LLC

Ranked #477 in Entrepreneur Magazine's 2005 Franchise 500

Financial rating: $$$$

1370 Mendota Heights Rd.
Mendota Heights, MN 55120
Ph: (800)227-5336/(651)454-0518
Fax: (651)454-9542
www.protocolvending.com
Personal-care product vending
   machines
Began: 1987, Franchising since: 1996
Headquarters size: 60 employees
Franchise department: 10 employees

U.S. franchises: 47
Canadian franchises: 0
Other foreign franchises: 0
Company-owned: 12
Units concentrated in all U.S.

Seeking: All U.S.
Seeking in Canada? Yes
Exclusive territories? Yes
Homebased option? Yes
Kiosk option? No
Employees needed to run franchise: 0-3
Absentee ownership? Yes

COSTS
Total cost: $10.2K-22K
Franchise fee: $500
Royalty fee: 0
Term of agreement: 2 years renewable
   at no charge
Franchisees required to buy multiple
   units? No

FINANCING
In-house: None
3rd-party: Equipment

QUALIFICATIONS
Net worth: $500K
Cash liquidity: $50K
Experience:
   General business experience
   Marketing skills

TRAINING
At headquarters: 1 day
At franchisee's location: Periodically
At annual convention

BUSINESS SUPPORT
Newsletter
Meetings
Toll-free phone line
Internet
Field operations/evaluations
Purchasing cooperatives

MARKETING SUPPORT
Co-op advertising
Ad slicks
National media campaign
Trade shows

SNAPPY AUCTIONS

Financial rating: $$$

2014 Glen Echo Rd.
Nashville, TN 37215
Ph: (888)490-1820
Fax: (888)490-1820
www.snappyauctions.com
eBay consignment outlets/drop-off
   stores
Began: 2003, Franchising since: 2003
Headquarters size: 6 employees
Franchise department: 4 employees

U.S. franchises: 28
Canadian franchises: 0
Other foreign franchises: 0
Company-owned: 1

Seeking: All U.S.
Seeking in Canada? Yes
Exclusive territories? Yes
Homebased option? No
Kiosk option? No
Employees needed to run franchise: 3
Absentee ownership? Yes

COSTS
Total cost: $47.1K-57.4K
Franchise fee: $15K
Royalty fee: 2-4%
Term of agreement: Info not provided
Franchisees required to buy multiple
   units? Yes, within U.S.

FINANCING
No financing available

QUALIFICATIONS
Net worth: Varies
Cash liquidity: $75K
Experience:
   Industry experience
   General business experience
   Marketing skills

TRAINING
At headquarters: 1 week
At franchisee's location: 1 week

BUSINESS SUPPORT
Newsletter
Meetings
Toll-free phone line
Grand opening
Internet
Security/safety procedures
Field operations/evaluations

MARKETING SUPPORT
Co-op advertising
Ad slicks
PR support

SUPER CLEAN YACHT SERVICE FRANCHISING INC.

Financial rating: $$$

910 W. Coast Hwy.
Newport Beach, CA 92663
Ph: (949)646-2990
Fax: (949)646-9311
www.supercleanyachtservice.com
Pleasure boat cleaning & detailing
Began: 1984, Franchising since: 1999
Headquarters size: 12 employees
Franchise department: 3 employees

U.S. franchises: 3
Canadian franchises: 0
Other foreign franchises: 0
Company-owned: 1
Units concentrated in CA

Seeking: All U.S.
Focusing on: CA, FL, TX
Seeking in Canada? No
Exclusive territories? Yes
Homebased option? Yes
Kiosk option? No
Employees needed to run franchise: 4
Absentee ownership? Yes

COSTS
Total cost: $12.7K-50.8K
Franchise fee: $7.5K-25K
Royalty fee: $500/mo.
Term of agreement: 5 years renewable
at $1.5K
Franchisees required to buy multiple
units? No

FINANCING
In-house: Franchise fee
3rd-party: None

QUALIFICATIONS
Net worth: $15.5K+
Cash liquidity: $2.5K
Experience:
Marketing skills

TRAINING
At headquarters: 11 days
At franchisee's location: 3 days

BUSINESS SUPPORT
Newsletter
Meetings
Toll-free phone line
Grand opening
Internet
Security/safety procedures
Field operations/evaluations
Purchasing cooperatives

MARKETING SUPPORT
Co-op advertising
Ad slicks
Regional marketing

SERVICES ► OTHER FRANCHISES

HOMESAFE INSPECTION INC.
604 S. 16th St.
Oxford, MS 38655
Ph: (866)327-7233
www.homesafeinspection.com
Home inspections specializing in
infrared/acoustic technology
Financial rating: Current financial
data not available

HOMES 4SALE BY OWNER NETWORK
5151 Monroe St., #106
Toledo, OH 43623
Ph: (866)823-9983
www.homes4salebyownernetwork.com
Web-based real estate marketing
services for homeowners
Financial rating: Current financial
data not available

MUSIC BLAST
2620 Regatta Dr., #102
Las Vegas, NV 89128
Ph: (702)869-0099
www.musicblast.us
Musical performance troupe
Financial rating: Current financial
data not available

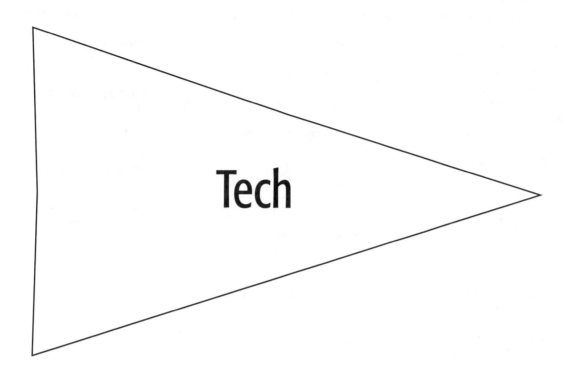

Tech

TECH **INTERNET**

INSTANTFX

Current financial data not available

12 2nd Ave. S.W.
Aberdeen, SD 57401
Ph: (605)225-4122
Fax: (605)225-5176
www.instantfx.biz
Website design & hosting services
Began: 2004, Franchising since: 2004
Headquarters size: Info not provided
Franchise department:
    Info not provided

U.S. franchises: 156
Canadian franchises: 0
Other foreign franchises: 0
Company-owned: 1
Units concentrated in all U.S.

Seeking: All U.S.
Seeking in Canada? Yes
Exclusive territories? No
Homebased option? Yes
Kiosk option? No
Employees needed to run franchise: 1-2
Absentee ownership? Info not provided

COSTS
Total cost: $4.3K-7.2K
Franchise fee: $3.5K
Royalty fee: $25/wk.
Term of agreement: 5 years renewable
    at no charge
Franchisees required to buy multiple
    units? No

FINANCING
No financing available

QUALIFICATIONS
Net worth: $15K
Cash liquidity: $7.5K
Experience:
    Marketing skills
    Sales skills

TRAINING
Via web: 3 days

BUSINESS SUPPORT
Newsletter
Meetings
Toll-free phone line
Internet

MARKETING SUPPORT
Ad slicks

WSI INTERNET

Ranked #53 in Entrepreneur Magazine's 2005 Franchise 500　　　　*Financial rating: $$$*

5915 Airport Rd., #300
Toronto, ON L4V 1T1 Canada
Ph: (905)678-7588
Fax: (416)649-3872
www.wsicorporate.com
Internet services
Began: 1995, Franchising since: 1996
Headquarters size: 100 employees
Franchise department: 25 employees

U.S. franchises: 562
Canadian franchises: 112
Other foreign franchises: 999
Company-owned: 1

Seeking: All U.S.
Seeking in Canada? Yes
Exclusive territories? No
Homebased option? Yes
Kiosk option? No
Employees needed to run franchise: 1
Absentee ownership? No

COSTS
Total cost: $40K-50K
Franchise fee: $39.7K
Royalty fee: 10%
Term of agreement: 5 years renewable
　　at no charge
Franchisees required to buy multiple
　　units? No

FINANCING
No financing available

QUALIFICATIONS
Net worth: $68K-82K
Cash liquidity: $5K
Experience:
　　General business experience

TRAINING
At headquarters: 7 days

BUSINESS SUPPORT
Newsletter
Meetings
Toll-free phone line
Internet
Purchasing cooperatives

MARKETING SUPPORT
Co-op advertising
Ad slicks
Marketing materials

TECH　　　　MISCELLANEOUS

COMPUTER MEDICS OF AMERICA INC.

Current financial data not available

10322 Chain of Rock St.
Eagle River, AK 99577
Ph: (907)694-0371
Fax: (800)878-8539
www.computermedicsofamerica.com
Mobile computer repair services
Began: 2000, Franchising since: 2003
Headquarters size: 2 employees
Franchise department: 2 employees

U.S. franchises: 24
Canadian franchises: 1
Other foreign franchises: 0
Company-owned: 1
Units concentrated in all U.S.

Seeking: All U.S.
Seeking in Canada? Yes
Exclusive territories? Yes
Homebased option? Yes
Kiosk option? No
Employees needed to run franchise: 0
Absentee ownership? No

COSTS
Total cost: $16K-18K
Franchise fee: $15K
Royalty fee: 0
Term of agreement: 5 years renewable
　　at $1K
Franchisees required to buy multiple
　　units? No

FINANCING
In-house: Franchise fee
3rd-party: None

QUALIFICATIONS
Experience:
　　Industry experience
　　General business experience

TRAINING
At headquarters: 1 week

BUSINESS SUPPORT
Meetings
Internet

MARKETING SUPPORT
Info not provided

COMPUTER TROUBLESHOOTERS

Ranked #181 in Entrepreneur Magazine's 2005 Franchise 500　　　　　*Financial rating: $$$*

3904 N. Druid Hills Rd., #323
Decatur, GA 30033
Ph: (770)454-6382
Fax: (770)234-6162
www.comptroub.com
Computer services & support
Began: 1997, Franchising since: 1997
Headquarters size: 4 employees
Franchise department: 4 employees

U.S. franchises: 179
Canadian franchises: 14
Other foreign franchises: 174
Company-owned: 1
Units concentrated in all U.S.

Seeking: All U.S.
Focusing on: All U.S. except HI, ND,
　RI, SD
Seeking in Canada? Yes
Exclusive territories? Yes
Homebased option? Yes
Kiosk option? No
Employees needed to run franchise: 1
Absentee ownership? Yes

COSTS
Total cost: $17.3K-26.5K
Franchise fee: $12K
Royalty fee: $220/mo.
Term of agreement: 10 years renewable
　at no charge
Franchisees required to buy multiple
　units? No

FINANCING
In-house: None
3rd-party: Accounts receivable,
　equipment, franchise fee,
　inventory, payroll, startup costs

QUALIFICATIONS
Net worth: $15K
Cash liquidity: $10K
Experience:
　Industry experience

TRAINING
At headquarters: 2 days
At franchisee's location: 2 days
In New York City: 2 days
In Lansing, MI: 2 days

BUSINESS SUPPORT
Newsletter
Meetings
Toll-free phone line
Internet
Field operations/evaluations

MARKETING SUPPORT
Co-op advertising
Ad slicks
National media campaign
Regional marketing

CONCERTO NETWORKS INC.

　　　　　　　　　　　　　　　　　　　　　　　　　Financial rating: $$$$

501 W. Broadway, #800
San Diego, CA 92101
Ph: (866)551-4007/(619)501-4530
Fax: (619)501-4531
www.concertonetworks.com
Computer & information technology
　services
Began: 2002, Franchising since: 2003
Headquarters size: 14 employees
Franchise department: 10 employees

U.S. franchises: 31
Canadian franchises: 0
Other foreign franchises: 2
Company-owned: 0
Units concentrated in CA, FL, MA, NJ,
　NY, OR, PA, WA

Seeking: All U.S.
Seeking in Canada? No
Exclusive territories? Yes
Homebased option? Yes
Kiosk option? No
Employees needed to run franchise: 1-2
Absentee ownership? Yes

COSTS
Total cost: $23.4K-47.9K
Franchise fee: $15.8K
Royalty fee: 14%
Term of agreement: 10 years renewable
Franchisees required to buy multiple
　units? Yes, within U.S.

FINANCING
In-house: None
3rd-party: Franchise fee, startup costs

QUALIFICATIONS
Net worth: $100K
Cash liquidity: $30K
Experience:
　Industry experience
　General business experience
　Marketing skills

TRAINING
At headquarters: 1 week

BUSINESS SUPPORT
Newsletter
Meetings
Toll-free phone line
Grand opening
Internet
Security/safety procedures
Field operations/evaluations
Purchasing cooperatives

MARKETING SUPPORT
Co-op advertising
Ad slicks
National media campaign
Regional marketing

EXPETEC

Ranked #362 in Entrepreneur Magazine's 2005 Franchise 500　　　　　*Financial rating: 0*

P.O. Box 487
Aberdeen, SD 57401
Ph: (888)209-3951
Fax: (605)225-5176
www.expetec.com
Computer, printer & telecommunications sales & services
Began: 1992, Franchising since: 1996
Headquarters size: 23 employees
Franchise department: 3 employees

U.S. franchises: 156
Canadian franchises: 0
Other foreign franchises: 1
Company-owned: 0

Seeking: All U.S.
Seeking in Canada? No
Exclusive territories? Yes
Homebased option? Yes
Kiosk option? No
Employees needed to run franchise: 1-2
Absentee ownership? Yes

COSTS
Total cost: $7.2K-9.5K
Franchise fee: $6.5K
Royalty fee: 15%
Term of agreement: 5 years renewable at no charge
Franchisees required to buy multiple units? No

FINANCING
No financing available

QUALIFICATIONS
Cash liquidity: $6.5K
Experience:
　　General business experience
　　Marketing skills

TRAINING
At headquarters: 1 week

BUSINESS SUPPORT
Newsletter
Meetings
Toll-free phone line
Internet
Lease negotiations
Field operations/evaluations

MARKETING SUPPORT
Ad slicks
Regional marketing
Direct-mail program

FRIENDLY COMPUTERS

Ranked #333 in Entrepreneur Magazine's 2005 Franchise 500　　　　　*Financial rating: $$*

3145 N. Rainbow Blvd.
Las Vegas, NV 89108
Ph: (800)656-3115/(702)458-2780
Fax: (702)869-2780
www.friendlycomputers.com
On-site computer services & sales
Began: 1992, Franchising since: 1999
Headquarters size: 36 employees
Franchise department: 14 employees

U.S. franchises: 54
Canadian franchises: 0
Other foreign franchises: 0
Company-owned: 3

Seeking: All U.S.
Seeking in Canada? Yes
Exclusive territories? Yes
Homebased option? Yes
Kiosk option? Yes
Employees needed to run franchise: 1-4
Absentee ownership? Yes

COSTS
Total cost: $19.9K-307.6K
Kiosk cost: $19.9K-31.7K
Franchise fee: $14.9K/25K
Royalty fee: 3%
Term of agreement: 10 years renewable at $2.5K
Franchisees required to buy multiple units? No

FINANCING
In-house: Franchise fee
3rd-party: Equipment

QUALIFICATIONS
Experience:
　　General business experience

TRAINING
At headquarters: 1 week
At franchisee's (retail) location: 1 week

BUSINESS SUPPORT
Newsletter
Meetings
Toll-free phone line
Grand opening
Internet
Lease negotiations
Purchasing cooperatives

MARKETING SUPPORT
Co-op advertising
Ad slicks
Regional marketing

RESCUECOM

Financial rating: 0

2560 Burnet Ave.
Syracuse, NY 13206
Ph: (800)737-2837
Fax: (315)433-5228
www.rescuecom.com
Computer consulting & repair services
Began: 1997, Franchising since: 1998
Headquarters size: 40 employees
Franchise department:
    Info not provided

U.S. franchises: 80
Canadian franchises: 0
Other foreign franchises: 0
Company-owned: 0
Units concentrated in all U.S.

Seeking: All U.S.
Seeking in Canada? Yes
Exclusive territories? Yes
Homebased option? Yes
Kiosk option? No
Employees needed to run franchise: 1-3
Absentee ownership? No

COSTS
Total cost: $14K-95K
Franchise fee: $2.5K-28.9K
Royalty fee: 9-24%
Term of agreement: 5 years renewable
    at 25% of current fee
Franchisees required to buy multiple
    units? No

FINANCING
No financing available

QUALIFICATIONS
Net worth: $50K-100K
Cash liquidity: $20K
Experience:
    Industry experience
    General business experience

TRAINING
At headquarters: 1 week
At franchisee's location: 1 week

BUSINESS SUPPORT
Newsletter
Meetings
Toll-free phone line
Grand opening
Internet
Lease negotiations
Security/safety procedures
Field operations/evaluations
Purchasing cooperatives

MARKETING SUPPORT
Co-op advertising
Ad slicks
National media campaign
Regional marketing

SOFT-TEMPS WORLDWIDE

Financial rating: 0

1280 N.E. Business Park Pl.
Jensen Beach, FL 34957
Ph: (800)221-2880
Fax: (772)225-3136
www.stfranchise.com
Computer training & consulting
Began: 1999, Franchising since: 2002
Headquarters size: 24 employees
Franchise department: 10 employees

U.S. franchises: 26
Canadian franchises: 0
Other foreign franchises: 0
Company-owned: 0
Units concentrated in all U.S.

Seeking: All U.S.
Seeking in Canada? No
Exclusive territories? No
Homebased option? Yes
Kiosk option? No
Employees needed to run franchise: 0
Absentee ownership? Yes

COSTS
Total cost: $1.99K-3.99K
Franchise fee: $995
Royalty fee: $75/mo.
Term of agreement: 7 years renewable
    at $500
Franchisees required to buy multiple
    units? No

FINANCING
No financing available

QUALIFICATIONS
Net worth: $2K
Cash liquidity: $1.99K
Experience:
    Marketing skills
    IT experience

TRAINING
At headquarters: 4 days (optional)
At franchisee's location
Online training

BUSINESS SUPPORT
Newsletter
Meetings
Internet
Field operations/evaluations
Purchasing cooperatives

MARKETING SUPPORT
Co-op advertising
Ad slicks
National media campaign
Internet
Direct mail

Top 10 Low-Cost Franchises for 2005

1. Curves	www.buycurves.com	Women's fitness & weight-loss centers
2. Jackson Hewitt Tax Service	www.jacksonhewitt.com	Tax preparation services
3. Jani-King	www.janiking.com	Commercial cleaning
4. RE/MAX Int'l. Inc.	www.remax.com	Real estate
5. ServiceMaster Clean	www.ownafranchise.com	Commercial/residential cleaning & disaster restoration
6. Liberty Tax Service	www.libertytaxfranchise.com	Income-tax preparation services
7. Kumon Math & Reading Centers	www.kumon.com	Supplemental education
8. Chem-Dry Carpet Drapery & Upholstery Cleaning	www.chemdry.com	Carpet, drapery & upholstery cleaning
9. Jan-Pro Franchising Int'l. Inc.	www.jan-pro.com	Commercial cleaning
10. Merle Norman Cosmetics	www.merlenorman.com	Cosmetics studios

Source: *Entrepreneur* Magazine's 2005 Franchise 500®

State Franchise Authorities

CALIFORNIA

California Department of Corporations
The Commissioner of Corporations
Department of Corporations
320 West 4th St., #750
Los Angeles, CA 90013
(866) 275-2677; (213) 576-7500
www.corp.ca.gov

HAWAII

Business Registration Division
Securities Compliance
Department of Commerce and
    Consumer Affairs
1010 Richards St.
Honolulu, HI 96813
(808) 587-2727
www.businessregistrations.com

ILLINOIS

Franchise Division Office of the
    Attorney General
Chief, Franchise Division
Office of the Attorney General
500 South Second St.

Springfield, IL 62706
(217) 782-4465
www.ag.state.il.us/consumers

INDIANA

Securities Commissioner
Indiana Securities Division
302 W. Washington St., Room E 111
Indianapolis, IN 46204
(317) 232-6681
www.in.gov/sos/securities

MARYLAND

Office of the Attorney General
Securities Division
200 St. Paul Pl., 20th Fl.
Baltimore, MD 21202-2020
(410) 576-6360
www.oag.state.md.us/securities

MICHIGAN

Antitrust and Franchise Unit
Department of the Attorney General
Director, Consumer Protection Division
670 Law Bldg.

Lansing, MI 48913

(517) 373-7117

www.michigan.gov/ag

MINNESOTA

The Commissioner of Commerce

Minnesota Department of Commerce

85 7thplace E., #500

St. Paul, MN 55101-2198

www.commerce.state.mn.us

NEW YORK

New York State Department of Law

Bureau of Investor Protection and Securities

120 Broadway, 23rd Fl.

New York, NY 10271

(212) 416-8200

www.state.ny.us

NORTH DAKOTA

The Commissioner of Securities

North Dakota Office of Securities Commissioner

Office of the Securities Commissioner

600 East Blvd., Fifth Fl.

Bismarck, ND 58505

(701) 328-2910

www.ndsecurities.com

RHODE ISLAND

Rhode Island Division of Securities

Director, Division of Securities

233 Richmond St., #232

Providence, RI 02903

(401) 222-3048

www.dbr.state.ri.us

SOUTH DAKOTA

South Dakota Division of Securities

Director, Division of Securities

445 East Capitol Ave.

Pierre, SD 57501

(605) 773-4823

www.state.sd.us/drr2/reg/securities

VIRGINIA

State Corporation Commission

Division of Securities and Retail Franchising

1300 East Main St., 9th Fl.

Richmond, VA 23219

(804) 371-9051

www.state.va.us/scc

WASHINGTON

Department of Financial Institutions

Securities Division

P.O. Box 9033

Olympia, WA 98507-9033

(360) 902-8760

www.dfi/wa/gov

WISCONSIN

The Commissioner of Securities

Wisconsin Securities Commission

P.O. Box 1768

Madison, WI 53701

(608) 266-3364

www.wdfi.org

Other Information Sources

FTC INFORMATION

Contact the Federal Trade Commission (FTC) for general investment information if you are interested in buying a franchise or business opportunity venture. The Web site is well worth a visit, and the FTC encourages investors to contact the agency if they discover an unlawful franchise practice.

Internet: www.ftc.gov

Phone: Consumer Response Center at (877) 382-4357

U.S. Mail: Federal Trade Commission, Attn: Consumer Response Center, Washington, DC 20580

BETTER BUSINESS BUREAU

Look for your local office of the Better Business Bureau in the phone book or on the Web.

Glossary

Arbitration. Formal dispute resolution process that is legally binding on the parties.

Business Format Franchise. See the definition of "franchise."

Business Opportunity. A package of goods and materials that enables the buyer to begin or maintain a business. The Federal Trade Commission and 25 states regulate the concept.

Copyright. The legal right protecting an original work of authorship that is fixed in a tangible form.

Earnings Claim. A statement by a franchisor regarding the financial performance of existing franchisees or a projection of how a particular investor/franchisee will perform. Earnings claims may be made by a franchisor, but if so, they must be presented in item 19 of the UFOC.

Federal Trade Commission's Franchise Rule. The 1979 trade regulation rule by which all franchisors in the United States are required to deliver a presale disclosure document.

First Personal Meeting. A disclosure trigger under the Federal Trade Commission Rule; not a casual or chance meeting but a detailed discussion about a specific franchise opportunity.

Franchise. The law defines a franchise as the presence of three factors: 1) the grant of trademark rights, 2) a prescribed marketing plan, or significant control or assistance in the operation, or a community of interest, and 3) payment of a franchise fee for the right to participate. In business terms, the franchisee receives full training in the operation, follows a detailed set of business techniques, uses the franchisor's trademark and pays a continuing royalty for participation in the program.

Franchise Agreement. The contract by which a franchisor grants franchise rights to a franchisee.

Franchisee. One who receives the rights to a franchise. The owner and operator of a franchised business.

Franchise Fee. The money a franchisee is required to pay for the right to participate in the franchise program. Under the federal rules the minimum amount of franchise fee payment allowed before disclosure is required is $500. A franchise fee includes any lump sum initial payment and ongoing royalty payments.

Franchise Investment Laws. The laws of the Federal Trade Commission and 14 states that regulate the sale of a franchise.

Franchise Relationship Laws. State franchise statutes in 19 jurisdictions that generally restrict terminations or nonrenewals of franchise agreements in the absence of "good cause." See appendix A.

Franchisor. The person or company that grants franchise rights to a franchisee.

Limited Liability Company. A relatively new form of business organization with the liability-shield advantages of a corporation and the flexibility and tax pass-through advantages of a partnership.

Mediation. Professionally assisted negotiation. Now frequently used as a first step to resolve a dispute between a franchisor and franchisee. Mediation is generally nonbinding, unless the parties agree to a resulting settlement.

Patent. An inventor's right protecting an invention, new device, or innovation.

Product Franchise. The legal definition is the same as a "franchise." In business terms, it is a system for the distribution of a particular line of products, usually manufactured and/or supplied by the franchisor.

Renewal. Most franchise agreements grant the franchisee the right to renew the initial contract term for additional time at the end of the initial term. The contract may impose conditions on the right to renew, such as providing timely written notice, signing a new form of agreement, and paying a renewal fee.

Royalty Fee. The continuing payment paid by a franchisee to the franchisor. Usually calculated as a percentage of the franchisee's gross sales.

Territory. The rights granted to a franchisee that offer a restriction on competition within a stated area.

Trademark. A word, phrase, or logo design that identifies the source or quality of a product. A service mark means the same thing, but identifies a service.

Trade Show. An exhibition of businesses offering franchises and/or business opportunity packages.

Transfer. The sale of franchise rights by a franchisee to the buyer of all or a portion of the franchisee's business.

UFOC. Uniform Franchise Offering Circular, the specialized franchise disclosure statement that franchisors must deliver to prospective franchisees at the earlier of (1) the first personal meeting for the purpose of discussing the sale or possible sale of a franchise, or (2) ten business days (14 calendar days in Illinois) before the prospect signs a franchise agreement or pays money for the right to be a franchisee.

Index

Listings Index